14-96

9/1/07

THE
SHAAR
PRESS
THE JUDAICA IMPRINT
FOR THOUGHTFUL PEOPLE

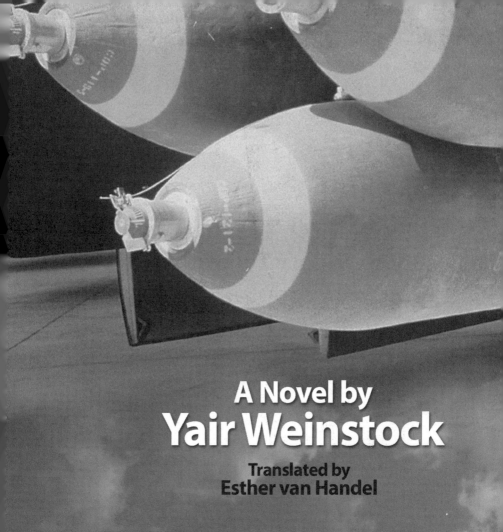

A Novel by
Yair Weinstock

Translated by
Esther van Handel

THE
SHAAR
PRESS

DUAL ALLEGIANCE

Published by **SHAAR PRESS**
Distributed by MESORAH PUBLICATIONS, LTD.
4401 Second Avenue / Brooklyn, N.Y 11232 / (718) 921-9000

Distributed in Israel by SIFRIATI / A. GITLER
6 Hayarkon Street / Bnei Brak 51127

Distributed in Europe by LEHMANNS
Unit E, Viking Business Park, Rolling Mill Road / Jarrow, Tyne and Wear, NE32 3DP/ England

Distributed in Australia and New Zealand by GOLDS WORLD OF JUDAICA
3-13 William Street / Balaclava, Melbourne 3183 / Victoria Australia

Distributed in South Africa by KOLLEL BOOKSHOP
Shop 8A Norwood Hypermarket / Norwood 2196, Johannesburg, South Africa

ISBN: 1-57819-053-3 Hard Cover
ISBN: 1-57819-054-1 Paperback

Printed in the United States of America by Noble Book Press
Custom bound by Sefercraft, Inc. / 4401 Second Avenue / Brooklyn N.Y. 11232

PROLOGUE

The great rain forest,
Amazon Valley, northern Brazil, 1975

Stubborn rays of sun tried to fight their way through the canopy of myriads of treetops. Beneath the foliage, colorful birds flew about, screeching shrilly. Monkeys swung from limbs or lay motionless for hours on end, occasionally extending a languid hand toward a nearby branch for some fresh leaves to nibble. Lower down still, ants marched in regimented lines and venemous snakes slithered silently.

The serenity in the great rain forest was deceptive. In reality, varied forms of life struggled for survival, and the relationship between predators and prey was preserved in a harmonious balance as old as the world.

The serenity in the sleepy, isolated village of Dilo de la Pedra, on the edge of the rain forest, was deceptive as well. Among the rows of old brown houses with yellow thatched roofs, nothing moved. The villagers, whose livelihood would derive from the grain harvest a month hence, did not trouble themselves to leave their homes on that hot, humid day.

Late in the afternoon, the Indian villagers sat in their yards, smoking pipes, sipping dark, sweet tea, and chatting with the neighbors in their native dialect. With half-closed eyes, they observed the burning orange-gold sphere drop lower in the sky.

In the yard of the house closest to the forest, three men with features recognizably different from the villagers' relaxed in easy chairs and spoke quietly among themselves in Hebrew.

"They should be here in half an hour," said Yosef Berning, glancing at his watch. He strained his ears, but there was no hum of a light plane's motor or the roar of a truck caravan's engines in the distance.

The giant fidgeted in the chair and scratched his balding pate as his small, evil eyes scoured the sky. Then he rubbed his huge palms nervously and sat straight up. When twenty minutes had passed, he jumped to his feet. "We shouldn't have relied on Robert Brown. He's a traitor — I told you that from the beginning."

Zev Shachar, short and skinny, with kind brown eyes that served as a window for his sharp mind, also stood up. "Leave Brown alone. He's only a courier who transmits messages."

"We'll see about that," snapped Yosef. "Don't forget what's at stake."

Yechezkel Shoshan leaned back and appeared to be dozing, but in fact he was as tense as the others. Would the truckloads of weapons change hands smoothly, according to plan? Or would something go wrong at the last minute, ruining the whole lucrative deal, as it had two years earlier? Even here, where the only law was that of the jungle and where government officials had been bribed to look the other way, there was no guarantee of success.

Yechezkel drew a walkie-talkie out of an attaché case, played around with the buttons, and barked into the mouthpiece, "Barak here. Do you hear me?"

At first, the walkie-talkie was silent. Then it buzzed with static, which ultimately gave way to intelligible sentences.

"Eagle here. I hear you, Barak. We had a delay. We'll be arriving in five minutes."

"Eagle, are you sure?"

"You're coming over garbled," mumbled the walkie-talkie, and fell silent.

Something was strange and different, but they could not put a finger on it.

Suddenly a silhouette glided out of the edge of the horizon as if it were bursting out of the setting sun. They heard the hum of a light motor as a small, low-flying plane glided down to a small clearing in the forest near Dilo de la Pedra.

Almost at the same time, they heard the roar of twenty trucks. The motors groaned and coughed with effort as the caravan climbed the road rising out of the valley. Under thick layers of tarpaulin, they carried heavy freight: millions of bullets; thousands of cannon rockets, hand grenades, illumination rounds, rifles, and submachine guns; and even one hundred fifty Strela shoulder missiles. In addition, there were several small boxes a thousand times as deadly as the conventional weapons.

From the opposite side, the purchaser's caravan of forty small, empty trucks came down the hill toward the meeting place near the clearing, where the weapons would change hands.

The villagers quietly disappeared into their houses. At such a time, it was better not to see or be seen, and they would be well rewarded for cooperating.

The three Israelis looked at one another with triumphant smiles. Their efforts had not been in vain; their work had borne fruit. Soon the multi-million dollar deal would be completed and the profits shared.

The plane landed in the clearing. Eagle was just in time to personally supervise the weapons transfer. Waving their hands, Yosef and Zev ran eagerly to greet him. Yechezkel, always cool and deliberate, set out slowly. Yosef and Zev were mildly surprised that the door of the plane had not yet opened.

When they were close to the plane, the door finally opened. They did not see Eagle. Instead, three masked men jumped out. They were holding submachine guns.

"Take cover!" screamed Zev.

But it was too late. As soon as the shooting began, Yosef's huge body dropped heavily to the earth, and Zev fell dead beside him.

The shooting was the signal for the caravan of small trucks to stop. It froze like a snake poised for attack. Dozens of armed men jumped out and began shooting at the big trucks that were making the final leg of the journey up the hill.

The bullets struck the live ammunition. The trucks began to explode noisily in a spectacular display of multicolored fireworks. Huge, crackling flames billowed up to the sky, and balls of fire shot out to the sides.

The last trucks in the caravan had not been hit. In a desperate attempt to escape the inferno, their drivers jerked back and tried to turn around in the narrow road. But there was no room to turn. The trucks went over the edge of the cliff and plunged into the ravine below.

The fire, explosives, and weapons consumed each other in a huge chain reaction until the entire caravan had turned into mangled skeletons of metal amidst tongues of fire. The darkening sky was red from the flames, the air filled with choking smoke.

Yechezkel went back into the house that had served as their headquarters and picked up the walkie-talkie.

"Kodkod, do you hear me? It's Barak."

"Kodkod to Barak, did all go well?"

"Negative. All was destroyed." He was sobbing. "Eagle didn't arrive. Someone on the inside betrayed us. They liquidated Yosef and Zev."

There was stunned silence at the other end. Then the voice said, "Barak, go over to emergency procedures. Wait for us to come get you; meanwhile, make yourself inconspicuous."

"Roger," said Yechezkel. "Kodkod, I know who betrayed us."

"Barak! Don't talk over the walkie-talkie. We'll speak face to face."

Barak did not answer.

"Barak? Barak? Barak?" asked the walkie-talkie into the empty space.

A silhouette slipped out of the house and was swallowed up in the darkness. He had achieved his objectives. No one was left who could testify — except for himself, of course.

Several days later, an epidemic of bubonic plague broke out in Dilo de la Pedra. The village was quarantined. No one set foot there except for medical teams wrapped from head to toe in special suits that provided protection against chemical and biological weapons. Over half the villagers died, and when the danger of infection had passed, the survivors were relocated. Within two months, Dilo de la Pedra has been wiped off the map.

Jerusalem, 2002

A sheet of white lightning lit up the inky sky like a flash of an arc lamp. It was followed by peals of thunder. Torrents of rain washed the sandstone exterior of a low apartment building in the quiet, affluent residential neighborhood of Rechaviah, in the center of Jerusalem.

Inside, a tired-looking man wrapped in a faded bathrobe sat at the kitchen table. His usually alert green eyes, now dull and begging for sleep, absent-mindedly skimmed the previous day's newspaper.

The aroma that wafted from a colorful mug on the table tickled his nostrils, and he gratefully accepted the invitation. The coffee revived him. He wiped the edges of his graying moustache and tried to focus on the crowded page in front of him. A small notice in a thin black border, barely discernible on the bottom of the page, caught his attention.

Suddenly, there was a frightended gasp.

The gasp had come from deep inside him. The tiny letters had somehow managed to form an image on his retina, and from there they penetrated his lethargic brain.

Never did Daniel Klein read tiny notices of this type. Yet tonight, when every cell in his body cried out for rest, this annoying notice was somehow pushed into his consciousness.

"Rabbinical Court of Tel Aviv," was the title. The notice informed the public that the court had received the following claims involving estates and wills. Anyone wishing to contest a claim was asked to do so within fifteen days. Otherwise, the court would dispose of the estates as it deemed fit.

Among eleven lines of cases listed, Daniel somehow noticed:

Case number 6574. Name of deceased: Portman, Avraham Zeidel. Date of death: 17 Tammuz 5761. Claimant: Tzadok, Yoel.

The notice was signed by Rabbi S. Bloom, Secretary of the Court.

That was all.

Daniel felt his blood racing through his arteries. Anger welled up inside him, totally dispelling his weariness. It evolved into a burst of energy that could have pushed a train up a steep hill.

Then images began to stream through his memory. He recalled his first meeting with Avraham Zeidel Portman.

☙❦❧

Daniel Klein had moved to Rechaviah as a young married man. During the first few weeks, he managed to meet only his next-door neighbor. One evening, when he returned from *kollel,* he ran into a neighbor with whom he had not yet exchanged a word. The tall, thin man with sunken cheeks, a white beard, and a threadbare suit was dragging some bulging old cloth shopping bags up the path to the building.

"May I help you?" Daniel offered politely.

The old man peered at him through the thick lenses of his glasses. "No, thank you," he said in a youthful voice that contrasted with his elderly appearance. "I'm managing just fine by myself."

It seemed the man was proud and had chosen to maintain his independence. Daniel continued on ahead, but something made him turn back and give a quick glance. The old man had set the shopping bags down on the ground and he was breathing heavily.

Daniel retraced his steps. "Perhaps I really should carry the bags for you," he said delicately. Without waiting for permission, he grabbed the worn cloth handles and walked into the building with the old man. The man stopped in front of the first door, which bore the nameplate "Portman."

"Thank you is a banal expression," breathed the old man, with a suspicious wetness glistening in his eyes. "But I am telling you thank you."

❧

That had been Daniel's first meeting with Avraham Zeidel Portman. After that came many others.

In the course of time, Daniel got to know the neighbor whom everyone affectionately called "Zeidel." The old man seemed to be alone in the world. Surprisingly, though, he lived in a huge (by Israeli standards) apartment that spread over the whole first floor, taking up the space of two apartments.

In Jerusalem, most apartments are not rented; they are bought for the price of a private home abroad. A standard apartment contains a combination living–dining room, kitchen, two or three bedrooms, and several balconies; more than that is considered a luxury. Zeidel's neighbors could not understand why a man living alone needed a seven-room apartment. And if that were not enough, the huge yard of the building and one of the storerooms were also registered under the name "Portman."

Zeidel did not seem bothered by what his neighbors thought. Good-natured and easy-going, he made friends easily with everyone, including little children. He liked to joke around and express his opinion about any topic under discussion, from the weighty problems of foreign policy and national security to the price of stocks on the exchange.

There was one subject, though, that was absolutely taboo. Zeidel never spoke a word about himself. If anyone tried to speak to him about his private life, he would immediately withdraw into utter silence that made the questioner feel uneasy. People got the message and learned not to ask.

Residents of the neighborhood held differing opinions about Zeidel. Some said he was a bachelor who had never married. Others argued vehemently that he had once had a family, but they had left him under strange circumstances. People who claimed to be in the know asserted that he was not the simple character he appeared to be; his past had been marred by a terrible, dark secret. But the friendly families who lived peacefully together in Zeidel's building did not lend an ear to the local gossips. In his own building, at least, Zeidel's image was untarnished.

Regardless of what had happened in the distant past, Zeidel became Daniel Klein's acquaintance and his daily *chesed* project.

As Zeidel, alone and thirsty for companionship, advanced in years, he weakened physically became increasingly dependent on Daniel. He apologized profusely for the trouble he caused, but he also made frequent requests. Daniel found himself ever busier dealing with light bulbs that burned out, electric wires that short-circuited, rusty water pipes that burst, and worn furniture that regularly needed fixing. The old apartment, which had not been maintained, was in dire need of repair that its elderly owner could not provide. Eventually Daniel wound up running the Portman home as if it were his own.

"Why am I doing this?" Daniel asked himself more than once, when he gave up hours intended for resting or for being with his children for Zeidel's sake. The old man had turned into a burden, but Daniel did not know how to refuse. Any time Zeidel asked for something, Daniel would drop everything and run to help him. Whenever Peninah, Daniel's wife, asked how long this would go on, he would answer with a smile that this was a rare opportunity to do a mitzvah purely for the sake of Heaven. Zeidel, after all, would never be able to pay him back even if he wanted to. Who knew better than Daniel that the old man was poverty-stricken!

Nevertheless, in the inner recesses of his heart nestled a timid hope. Zeidel must be at least somewhat grateful for everything he had done for him. Surely Zeidel would express his gratitude by mentioning Daniel in his will — if not as his heir, then at least as a partial beneficiary. Daniel's children were almost of age, and marrying them off would entail making hefty down-payments on apartments for the young couples. Zeidel's double apartment, worth at least half a million dollars, was the subject of Daniel's secret dreams.

Then, one day, an ambulance with a wailing siren took Zeidel to the hospital. Two days later, he was gone.

People began to assemble in the building's courtyard for the funeral. Daniel went down the steps to pay his last respects to the deceased. Suddenly, all his dreams evaporated.

In front of Zeidel's door, with his back toward Daniel, stood a tall, fat man with a small yarmulke perched atop curly black hair. Daniel stopped short and observed the stranger carefully. He was trying to insert a key into the keyhole, but thus far none of the keys on the huge ring he was holding fit.

"Who are you?" asked Daniel, forcing himself to stay calm.

The stranger turned to face him. His round, dark, unshaven jowls repulsed Daniel. "Pleased to meet you," he said. "My name is Yoel Tzadok." He extended a sweaty hand and added in the same breath, "And now please don't disturb me."

"Nevertheless, perhaps I might know what you are looking for in the house of the deceased?"

Yoel exhaled nervously when another key disappointed him and refused to enter the keyhole. "What happened here?" he murmured. "No key fits."

"Of course your keys won't fit," Daniel informed him coldly. "I was in charge of Zeidel's apartment, and I changed all the locks with my own hands. If you would like to enter, you will need my help — and first you will have to explain to me what business you have here."

Yoel's angry eyes followed Daniel's lips as he spoke, and he shook his head with obvious displeasure. "Let's see if you can stop me," he hissed mockingly.

He whipped out a cell phone and called a professional locksmith.

"What do you say now?" he challenged Daniel.

"That you are breaking the law," Daniel said with quiet anger. "You can't enter a private home without a court order."

The professional arrived within minutes, and Daniel tried to stop him. But he was in for a surprise. Yoel pulled a court order from his pocket. He thrust it under Daniel's nose, gloating over his downfall.

"So you're going in, but not without me," said Daniel in a menacing tone.

Yoel chuckled. "No problem. You're not disturbing me."

Daniel admitted defeat. "I never dreamed there was a court order." He stopped the professional, who was bending over his toolbox. "It's a pity to ruin the locks." He pulled out his own key ring and opened all four locks. Zeidel had had an obsessive fear of robbers. At his request, Daniel had installed lock after lock until Zeidel felt secure.

Daniel was amazed that this stranger had managed to obtain a court order. Whom did he represent? he asked aloud, and Yoel answered with infuriating simplicity. "I took care of Zeidel, and he registered his property in my name. I'm looking for the will."

Daniel's face turned blood red. "*You* took care of Zeidel?" he shouted. "I took care of him for the last twenty years as if he were my own father. I never saw you here!"

The blinds in the house were closed. Yoel pressed a few switches, and the yellow light of incandescent bulbs flooded the room.

Totally ignoring Daniel's fulmination, Yoel searched in all the vases and the old china. His fat fingers rummaged through dusty papers and leafed through paid water and electric bills. "The envelope with the will was here," he murmured straight into Daniel's ears, as he felt the shelf beneath the china closet. "He told me so twice."

"I don't believe you," said Daniel sharply.

Yoel gave up the search. He turned off the lights, left the apartment, and waited in the hall while Daniel locked up. Then he turned to Daniel calmly. "I can understand your anger," he said firmly, "but it will get you nowhere. I took care of Zeidel before you ever dreamt of living here. He loved me like an only son and registered at least half of his estate in my name. Whether you like it or not, I am his heir!"

wo of the third-floor neighbors, Mrs. Shipholtz and Mrs. Levi, came downstairs on their way to the courtyard. They heard Yoel Tzadok's words and immediately grasped the situation.

"Mr. Klein," said Mrs. Levi, her eyes riveted to the stone floor tiles. "We all know how devotedly you cared for Zeidel, but there is something I want to reveal to you."

She hesitated for a moment. "Zeidel told me several times that he was planning to leave his entire estate to the Shaar HaTalmud Yeshivah. Their rabbis undertook to study Mishnah and pray for his soul during the year of mourning."

Mrs. Shipholtz nodded in agreement. "He told me the same thing more than once," she added quietly.

The blood drained from Daniel's face. Yoel was an unknown character, but Mrs. Levi was the principal of a girls' elementary school and Mrs. Shipholtz taught in a prestigious seminary. These upright, honest, and highly respected women would not sully their mouths with falsehood. Both spoke with the firm conviction that they were delivering the final will and testament of the deceased. Farewell, double apartment. It had been a rosy dream, but now it was gone.

As Daniel walked out to the courtyard, he could almost taste the bitterness of failure. Several times during the eulogy delivered by a neighborhood rabbi, Daniel fixed accusing eyes on the *tallis*-draped body, eyes that asked silently, *What didn't I do for you, Zeidel? Where is your gratitude?*

He cast a glance at his newfound competitor. The neighbors' words had had a subduing effect on him, too. Yoel melted into the crowd, but after two or three minutes disappeared down the street. The funeral did not especially interest him.

Listlessly, Daniel followed the deceased to the end of the block, where he stood and waited until the funeral procession had disappeared from sight. He returned home and sank wearily onto the sofa. The oppressive summer heat on this fast day of the Seventeenth of Tammuz, as well as the incident with Yoel Tzadok, had left him drained. Zeidel had indeed made a mockery of him, exploiting him for twenty years and then leaving him not a penny.

He turned the matter over in his mind, examining it from all angles. Suddenly, he jumped up, ordered a taxi, and hurried to the cemetery in the hope of arriving before the burial was completed. Daniel was obligated in the honor of the deceased and had to rise above petty, selfish considerations.

Something here was not as simple as it appeared on the surface. Zeidel had hinted to him more than once that he would not deprive him after one hundred twenty. After the funeral he would check calmly whether there had been a mistake — or worse, a malicious scheme to acquire Zeidel's estate.

❦

The next day, Daniel filed a claim with the Jerusalem rabbinic court regarding Zeidel's estate. A polite clerk informed him that the matter would be looked into and a reply forthcoming.

Weeks passed, which turned into months. Daniel's intensive work as a *kashrus* supervisor in a hotel left him neither time nor energy to pursue pipe dreams nor to look into why the promised reply had not arrived after half a year.

Until tonight. Until he read the notice from the Tel Aviv court. He could not take that sitting down. Why was the Tel Aviv court taking charge of a Jerusalemite's estate? And how had Yoel Tzadok succeeded where he himself had failed? Why had they put *him* off with an excuse, but given Yoel serious consideration?

With a start, he realized that he would pay a high price for his procrastination. Had he made the effort and invested some time, the name Daniel Klein might have appeared in the court's notice instead of Yoel Tzadok. And now he might have lost Zeidel's double apartment with garden and storeroom!

Daniel leaned back weakly in his chair, and the cup of coffee trembled in his hand. Where was honesty and justice in the world? How could some stranger who had not lifted a finger for the deceased in twenty years scoop up the inheritance merely by attacking at the right moment?

This was the end of Daniel's peace of mind. He knew that from now on, he would flagellate himself nonstop for having lost this fortune to a slick swindler.

In the morning, after a night of tossing and turning, he made his decision. He would fight.

Notices about wills and marriage registrations are placed in Israeli newspapers regularly to invite appeals and clarifications, but almost no one reads these notices, much less takes any action against them. That is why the voice of Rabbi Shimon Bloom, secretary of the Tel Aviv court, registered surprise when Daniel Klein called his office and asked to appeal the case of Avraham Zeidel Portman's estate. Rabbi Bloom barely recalled what it was about, but when Daniel insisted, he asked the clerk in charge to check the files.

After a few minutes he returned to the phone. "I think you have no chance of appealing the case," he said. "Yoel Tzadok has the will of the deceased."

"What?" shouted Daniel. "That's a lie! Portman didn't leave a will!"

"Excuse me?"

Daniel explained. "Yoel and I searched all the closets and drawers in his home right before the funeral, and we found nothing. Only I have the keys to the apartment. How, then, did Yoel get hold of a will?"

"I hear." Rabbi Bloom leaned back in his upholstered office chair and fingered the curly gray telephone cord. His eyes sparkled behind his thick glasses. He was gearing up for action. "I'll look into the matter and get back to you. Give me your telephone number."

"I'm sure it's fake!" said Daniel angrily. "There is no will!" Rabbi Bloom could almost hear Daniel's heart beating. Daniel considered telling him about Zeidel's determination to bequeath his wealth to a Torah institution, but he shut his mouth at the last second. If Zeidel had indeed bequeathed his estate to the Shaar HaTalmud Yeshivah, both he and Yoel would lose in equal measure. Moreover, Daniel had not been ashamed to go to the yeshivah office and ask whether it was true that they had been awarded Mr. Portman's estate. The office manager had laughed. "Do you mean the check of two thousand shekels that the *rosh yeshivah* received from the deceased a year ago, with a request to have someone say Kaddish and study Mishnah during the year of mourning? That yes, but not a cent more." He assured Daniel with an amused smile that the moment he heard about a fat inheritance, he would let him know. Two thousand shekels … go rely on two neighbors! There was no will and there never had been!

"Don't jump to conclusions," Rabbi Bloom muttered into the receiver and crossed his legs. "The deceased may have entrusted his will to a lawyer, or some relative whose existence you don't know of. I'll call you back later."

Daniel waited tensely for a few hours. Finally, in the evening, the court secretary called him back.

"Mr. Klein, if you don't have a strong case, you can say Kaddish over this inheritance. Yoel Tzadok has a will witnessed by Yariv Stempel, attorney and notary. The deceased placed the will in his hands five years ago."

Even without seeing himself in the mirror, Daniel knew he had turned white. *Zeidel, you traitor! For twenty years I took care of you day and night. Whenever you called, I came running. How many times did I go with you to the emergency room? I spent entire nights in the hospital with you. This is your gratitude?* He breathed deeply in an effort to calm down.

"Who is this attorney Yariv Stempel, anyway?" he asked scornfully. "I've never heard of him. This story is strange any way you look at it. Five years ago, I was taking care of Zeidel Portman just like an only son takes care of his beloved father. None of the neighbors had patience for him, not to mention that stranger, Yoel Tzadok, who never showed his face there. Zeidel never even mentioned his name. Why should he suddenly leave him all his money? Half I could somehow understand, but everything?"

The secretary began to show signs of impatience. "Sir, my position does not permit me to answer questions of that nature. I am not familiar with this file. If you have evidence that the will is a forgery, very well. But if you only want to vent your frustration, please look for a different address."

The secretary took advantage of Daniel's silence to give him the benefit of professional experience. "I can tell you that this is not the first such incident. Old people display capriciousness in many areas, most especially regarding their will. I've heard thousands of stories about wills and inheritances, each one stranger than the next. It could be that Mr. Portman owed a lot of money to Mr. Tzadok and had to transfer all his assets to pay the debt."

Daniel was taken aback. He had never thought of that possibility. With a confused stammer, he hurriedly ended the conversation.

His emotions became more turbulent from moment to moment. It was clear to him that a screaming injustice had been committed. He was standing by, helplessly watching himself being robbed.

Helplessly? Not necessarily!

Daniel put on his suit jacket, wrapped a wool scarf around his neck, and went out to the street. The *daf yomi shiur* would restore his peace of mind.

❧

"That is why we cannot say *kim leh bederabbah mineh* here, even though on the surface there seems to be a similarity between the two cases." Rabbi Segel ended his *shiur* and gently closed the Gemara. Someone quickly stood up and recited the short Mishnah, "Rabbi Chananyah ben Akashyah said … ," followed by Kaddish. Then the assembled dispersed.

Daniel approached Rabbi Segel and cleared his throat.

Rabbi Yochanan Segel was a lively, dynamic man with a pleasant expression on his face. His beard, prematurely white, lent him dignity. His sunken cheeks now expanded in a smile. "Oh, my good friend Reb Daniel, I see you have a question on what we learned in the *shiur*."

"Not exactly."

Never had Rabbi Segel seen Daniel so agitated. He studied Daniel for a minute as if seeing him for the first time. What he saw was a man with brown hair, a pug nose, lips taut with tension, and a short beard that had begun to turn gray. Worry and anger clouded his green eyes, and the wrinkles beside them made him look older than his years.

Rabbi Segel placed a soothing hand on Daniel's shoulder. "Come, let's sit down for a minute and you can tell me what happened."

"Do you have time for me?" asked Daniel, relieved. Rabbi Segel was usually in a hurry after the *shiur* to get to a *shiur* that he gave in a different synagogue.

"For a good friend like you, I have time. Besides, my next *shiur* has been delayed by half an hour because of a *simcha*."

Daniel presented his problem in brief. Rabbi Segel gave a clear, sharp answer.

(A) Present an appeal to the court. (B) If the will is handwritten, or even if the deceased only signed it, request a graphological examination of the handwriting and comparison with other handwriting samples of the deceased. The will might be a forgery.

he taxi that Daniel had called passed apartment buildings covered with the traditional Jerusalem stone and modern office buildings with facades of green glass. Daniel surveyed the scenery with weary eyes and wondered whether modern offices like these fell prey to robbery in broad daylight, as he had.

The driver grew impatient with Daniel's extended silence. "You look sad," he said, trying to draw his passenger into a conversation.

Any other day, Daniel would have told the driver not to stick his nose into his passengers' personal affairs, but now the warm, human note touched his heart. He smiled weakly. "Sometimes a tired person looks sad."

"No," said the driver confidently. "I have years of experience. I can tell the difference between exhaustion and despair."

Daniel fell silent. The driver indeed looked like a sympathetic, caring person. But in five more minutes their paths would part. Why should Daniel confide in a stranger? At last he said, "The world is full of injustices." This noncommittal sentence reflected his mood of the past few days.

The taxi went down a curved road and pulled up in front of the house of Shammai Shaulov, graphologist. Daniel paid the driver and counted the change. The driver took another long glance at him. "You know," he said thoughtfully, "the day began with a thick cover of clouds. You wouldn't have expected to see a drop of sun all day. Yet now the clouds have parted and the sun is shining through them. Do you know why? Because today is Wednesday. I once heard that ever since the first Wednesday of Creation, when the sun was set in its place in the sky, there hasn't been a Wednesday when the sun doesn't come out. Despite the heaviest snow or the blackest clouds, the sun will suddenly shine, even if just for a moment, to remind us that it exists."

Daniel smiled and thrust one foot out of the taxi. The driver was not yet finished. "Why am I telling you this? So that you'll know that even when things look difficult and depressing, the sun will always peek through a crack. Remember that."

"I'll remember," promised Daniel, managing at last to exit the taxi.

Shammai Shaulov was a tall, balding man nearing sixty with intelligent brown eyes and a lithe, slim build. His high forehead ridged with horizontal furrows and his narrow face conveyed serenity and deep understanding. These qualities helped him deal with troubled clients, for whom a graphologist often serves as psychologist and spiritual counselor.

Daniel set a photocopied paper down on the desk.

"Is this the will?" Shaulov asked calmly.

"Yes." Daniel blinked nervously. Fortunately, part of the will was handwritten.

Shaulov read the paper intently through thick reading glasses. Certain words and letters piqued his professional interest, and he marked them with a green highlighter. "If I had the original," he said casually, "I could check how much pressure the writer exerted on the paper. That would tell me a great deal."

Daniel gnashed his teeth. "It was hard enough for me to get this page. The court secretary did me a favor letting me take it for a graphological examination."

For a second, the graphologist raised his eyes from the document and glanced at Daniel. It would have been instructive to check the handwriting of the man sitting before him. He clasped his hands, leaned back comfortably in his chair, and turned on a small Dictaphone. Then he began to speak slowly and carefully, choosing his words. "My professional opinion concerning the document known as the will of Avraham Zeidel Portman is that the handwriting is authentic."

"Just a minute!" cried Daniel as he drew an envelope from his jacket pocket. "How could I forget? I brought along a few notes written by the deceased so that you could compare the handwriting."

The graphologist's eyes lit up. "Now we've moved to a different ballpark."

For a few moments, he checked and compared the various documents, turned over the notes, and felt them lightly with his fingers to detect the amount of pressure exerted by the writer. Then he gave his opinion.

"The handwriting specimens that you gave me confirm my previous opinion. The will was definitely written by the author of the notes. The handwriting is the same; it is definitely not a fake or an imitation. It's the same personality, with identical components, and the man knew very well what he was doing. True, while he wrote he was in a state of psychological stress and suffered from inner disquiet, the source of which is not clear to me. Nevertheless it does not contradict the authenticity of the document itself.

"Would you like to hear a general graphological opinion about the man?" he asked pleasantly.

Daniel felt as if he had been socked in the chin. "No, thank you," he managed to say. "I knew him well." He fumbled in his wallet, paid the graphologist's fee, pulled himself out of the chair, and made his way to the door.

✃

That night, Daniel waited anxiously for the children and Peninah to go to sleep. Then, to be on the safe side, he waited an extra half hour. Only when he was convinced that no one would know of his movements did he go quietly out the door.

He did not turn on the light in the stairwell. He knew that at this late hour there was almost no chance of running into anyone. Still, the time-honored principle that, "Whatever can go wrong, will go wrong," operates also at night.

Usually the dim light of the streetlamp filtered into the stairwell through the tall windows. Tonight, the streetlamp had inexplicably gone out. He went down in total blackness, grasping the curved railing although he knew every step by heart.

The sixteen steps that separated his apartment from Zeidel's seemed to him to have turned into a minefield. Sixteen mines. He stopped after each step, extended his foot, and cautiously felt for the step underneath.

At last, he reached Zeidel's door. He heaved a sigh of relief. Once he got inside, he would feel at home. But before that, he would have to pass a serious hurdle. More accurately, four hurdles — the four locks. Opening each lock would send an explosion of noise like a bomb blast into the dead silence of the night.

With grotesque effort, he covered the locks with one hand while turning the key with the other, hoping desperately that the soft flesh of his palm would muffle the sound. But the noise was horrific, at least to his own ears. He hoped fervently that the angel of dreams was doing his job well that night.

At last the door graciously creaked open on its hinges, loudly enough to awaken anyone who was still asleep after the turning of the keys. Any minute, all the neighbors would come running to investigate who was prowling the deserted apartment. Truth be told, there was no need to ask. Everyone knew that the keys were still in the hands of Daniel Klein.

He went in, closed the door behind him, and locked it. For five minutes he leaned against the wall of the pitch-black apartment, breathing deeply in an effort to regain his composure. He did not dare turn on any lights.

Tensely he waited to hear the expected knocks on the door.

No knocks came. Apparently the neighbors were sleeping more deeply than he had thought. The apartment was absolutely silent, as was the rest of the building.

It was time to act.

His trembling hand made its way to the switch. A yellowish light suddenly flooded the room, sending some spiders scurrying in panic.

He looked around. The apartment, neglected even during its owner's lifetime except for Daniel's attempts to restore it from time to time, had not changed in the half year since Portman's death. No man had been here; no man had touched it. Only the spiders had had a field day, weaving their webs in the corners of the ceiling and between the legs of the old chairs. A heavy layer of dust had settled over the apartment, and the air was musty.

Of course no one had broken in. Zeidel had had a deathly fear of robbers, which Daniel figured was normal for old people. To calm him, Daniel had installed three additional locks on the door, bars on the windows, and a telephone with caller identification.

Daniel surveyed the apartment. To his right was the large living room, with a still functional, heavy black dial phone from forty years ago. To the left was a long corridor that led to two bedrooms. One of them had indeed been used for sleeping. There Zeidel had slept in a spartan iron bed, and there Daniel had installed the up-to-date phone. The second bedroom was piled high with big cartons filled with old documents. In the past, its neglected appearance had repulsed him, and he had kept his distance. Now the time had come to examine it. The two other large rooms were nearly bare. He had nothing to look for there, nor in the kitchen. He knew its cabinets well; he himself had put all the dishes in place after Pesach. The service porch contained only an old washing machine and two kerosene stoves, which, for reasons of nostalgia, Zeidel had liked to use the week before Pesach, after the regular stove was *kashered*.

Daniel hesitated. He knew the apartment inside out — except for the room with the cartons and the living room cabinets, which he had never touched. He had always respected Zeidel's privacy and had never dreamed of trespassing in his private world. So what was he doing here now?

Now it was different. He had to know what was going on. He had to find the hidden will, if it existed at all.

With trepidation, he approached the carton room. He took a deep breath and entered the darkness.

For two minutes, he stood there breathing the musty air. Then he turned on the light and closed his eyes for two minutes more, giving the insects a chance to run into their holes. As he stood there with his eyes closed, he felt that someone was watching him.

Daniel laughed at himself. His imagination was running wild, that was all. Who could get into a locked house? But his breathing had become rapid and shallow, and his heart beat like ten drums. The feeling that someone was watching him at that moment was palpable.

He opened his eyes.

He saw no one, only dozens of large cartons stacked on a rusty iron bed, just as they had stood for many years. Hesitantly, he opened the carton nearest to him.

Inside was a mass of papers. If that was what filled each carton, it would take weeks to go through them all. What had Zeidel been doing before he retired? Had he worked in the national archives?

With a feeling of revulsion, he began leafing through the files. The top layer of papers consisted of water and electric bills from forty years ago, stamped to indicate they had been paid. But in the second layer, he made a shocking discovery.

A ten year old thank-you letter from a yeshivah in the Negev began: "To our distinguished friend, the honored philanthropist." This was followed by three lines of honorific titles leading to the name "Rabbi Avraham Zeidel Portman." The yeshivah thanked him for his magnanimous donation of 72,000 shekels.

Could this be the same Zeidel who would haggle with the grocer over every penny and always figure how to cut costs? From where did this pauper amass such a fortune to donate? And what was his connection with the yeshivah in the Negev?

That was only the beginning. As Daniel continued his search, he found dozens of other receipts for more standard amounts donated to various yeshivahs and *kollels* throughout the land. But after burrowing to the bottom of the carton, he came up with a receipt for 36,000 shekels that had been donated by "our dear friend who pursues charity and kindness, the noble Rabbi Avraham Zeidel Portman, *shlita,* may he soon merit to greet the Messiah."

Daniel was dumbfounded. Tonight he had discovered a new facet of the personality of Zeidel Portman. This pauper, who had skimped on the very bread that he ate, had been a generous philanthropist who secretly supported yeshivahs, *cheders, kollels*, orphanages, soup kitchens, and synagogues. From where did he get the money? How had he managed to hide beneath the guise of a pauper? And finally, where were the certificates of appreciation that were customarily awarded in such cases?

Suddenly, the silence of the night was shattered by a jarring noise. Both telephones were ringing at once.

Where should he run to stop that frightening noise? The living room, with the old phone, was closer, but the phone with caller identification was in the bedroom.

Daniel bounded to the bedroom and looked at the numbers that appeared on the screen. The local number that ended with two zeroes indicated a public phone nearby. He picked up the receiver. "Hello."

At first there was a long silence and the sound of panting. Afterwards a voice, made artificially deep, said, "I am following your activities, and asking myself how a respectable person like you rummages through someone else's house at night like a thief."

Daniel was dumbstruck. When he recovered somewhat, he opened his mouth but no sound came out.

On the third try, his voice returned, but it trembled. "Who are you?" he asked.

"Someone concerned about your welfare," said the deep voice. "If you want to stay out of trouble, leave Portman's house immediately and don't touch anything."

There was noise as if the receiver had been thrown down and was swinging in the air, banging against the side of the phone booth from time to time, and the sound of feet running. It seemed to Daniel that from the silent street, he also heard the identical sound of running feet. If he was right, this conversation had taken place from the public phone beside Rose's Flower Shop.

Trembling slightly, Daniel put down the receiver. Despite the fierce cold in the unheated apartment, his body was covered with sweat.

Who was the anonymous caller?

If it was Yoel Tzadok or his agent, how did he know exactly when Daniel would decide to enter Portman's apartment? If it was a neighbor awakened by the noise, why would he use such silly subterfuge techniques?

Gradually, the fear ebbed away. No, he was not afraid. If anyone in the world had a right to enter this apartment, it was he, Daniel Klein! Thanks to him, the water, electricity, and phone lines had not been cut off. He would continue to manage the apartment until it became clear, once and for all, to whom Zeidel's property belonged.

The feeling that someone was watching him had been justified. Someone was indeed trailing him, someone who was worried about Daniel's search and who wanted desperately to stop him from making an important discovery.

Daniel was not about to give in to the threat. He would overcome his fear and continue searching until he found the document that he sought.

❧❦❧

Of all the mailboxes in the building, only Avraham Zeidel Portman's had always been full. The other neighbors received an average of one or two letters a day, but Zeidel's big wooden mailbox had overflowed with requests for help from yeshivahs, families in distress, various charity organizations, and Torah institutions from all across the country. The neighbors had laughed at the thought of the miserable pauper receiving such mail.

We should have known better, Daniel told himself. *Institutions don't waste stamps. If everyone sent letters to Zeidel, he surely donated something. There had to be a good reason why this modest old man had been targeted by fund-raisers.*

Determined to find out information, Daniel burrowed through the third carton, asking himself again and again, *How could we have been so wrong? How is it that we didn't know the real Zeidel?*

The old man had managed to fool everyone.

In the depths of the cartons, Daniel found more and more receipts for a "generous donation." The smallest amount was seventy-two shekels (or lirahs as the case might be), and this increased in multiples of ten, twenty, a hundred, or a thousand. Zeidel seemed to have cherished the number seventy-two, perhaps because it is the *gematriya* of the word *chesed*, as well as four times *chai*. He had donated hundreds of thousands of shekels to charity in his last years. From where did an old man living on a modest monthly stipend get such enormous sums? Had he sold the apartment and used the money from the sale? Evidently not, for he would have had to move.

The further Daniel dug into the cartons, the more complex the riddle of Zeidel became. Out of a large, dusty envelope came an ornately framed picture of Zeidel as he had looked years earlier. Dressed in a dignified suit and hat, he was shaking hands with a famous *rosh yeshivah* and accepting a plaque as patron of the yeshivah. Deeper still, on the very bottom of the worn carton, lay three more pictures that recorded similar handshaking scenes with other renowned *roshei yeshivah*, with the plaques resting beside them.

At least one riddle had been solved. The yeshivahs had not failed to show gratitude for the generous contributions they had received. Zeidel had hidden every sign of recognition as if it were incriminating evidence. What extreme humility!

Perhaps all my effort is only to discover that Zeidel was a hidden tzaddik, thought Daniel. *Money I won't get out of it, only the knowledge that I served a great* tzaddik *unawares.*

From the street, he heard the milk truck arrive at the grocery. It was three-thirty already. He had only one hour until the first of the early risers began stirring Rabbi Tzvi Shipholtz the *masmid* would leave for his usual pre-dawn *chavrusah* in the synagogue.

I need to be quick, he thought, yawning out loud. His eyelids felt very heavy. He opened the window in the hope that the fresh, chilly air filtering in through the *tris* would wake him up. But it did not. He dozed while sitting on a hard chair.

Suddenly he woke up with a start. A strong smell assaulted his nostrils, and he jumped up in panic. "Fire, fire!" he shouted hysterically, but then slapped his hand over his mouth lest he give himself away. He ran from room to room; there was no sign of fire anywhere. He returned to the carton room and sniffed. Here the smell was strong, and it intensified as he drew closer to the open window. With supreme effort, he pulled up the half-broken *tris* and peered out.

Red flames were billowing up in the courtyard beneath the window. Someone had piled newspapers there and set them on fire. Had it been summer, when the weather in Jerusalem is dry, the entire courtyard would have gone up in flames. But now the bushes, moist from rain, refused to cooperate with the flames; instead, they merely spread choking smoke. Only the newspapers burned.

Daniel ran to the bathroom to look for a pail, but found only an old tin bowl. He filled it with water and ran to the front door. At the entrance he stopped short. The door had a handle only from the inside; the moment you stepped outside and the door closed behind you, it locked automatically. He did an about-face and raced to the window, spilling almost all the water on the way. He rushed back to the faucet, re-filled the bowl, ran to the window, and tossed the water out.

He missed. The water splashed against the stone wall, and the small fire continued to blaze. Twice more he ran and filled the bowl. Finally he managed to aim the water onto the fire burning under the window and he hit its core. With a fierce hiss, the fire went out, sending clouds of white smoke undulting through the courtyard.

Worriedly, Daniel watched the neighbors' windows. If the smoke stubbornly clung to the wall, one of the neighbors was sure to wake up in a panic and call the fire department.

Then, right before Daniel's eyes, the miracle he needed took place. A light breeze carried the smoke in the opposite direction. After a few minutes, the smoke dissipated altogether.

Trembling and exhausted, Daniel sank down onto the chair beside the cartons, wiped his burning forehead, and took stock of the situation. Fortunately, no one had yet woken up, and the fire had been effectively extinguished. But the message was clear: Someone knew about his nocturnal visit to Zeidel's apartment, and that someone would use every possible means to chase him out of there — evidently with good reason. And precisely on account of that, Daniel was determined to stay.

Four-fifteen. In a quarter of an hour, Rabbi Tzvi Shipholtz would come down the stairs, and at five the first of the newspapers would be delivered. Daniel would lose his privacy. Tomorrow night he would return. He would keep coming back night after night and dig his way through Zeidel's papers until he found the real will.

Absently, he extended his hand to a carton with a picture of a small oven on the side, of the type that had been used in Israel before modernization set in. He recognized the picture; the oven itself was buried inside one of Zeidel's kitchen cabinets. It probably had not been used in fifty years, but Zeidel harbored warm memories of it. Evidently it reminded him of magic moments in his mother's kitchen. He opened the carton and dove in, knowing Zeidel's tendency to hide the important things deep down.

Underneath a stack of *dati* newspapers from the sixties, he discovered a heavy package wrapped in paper and held together by a crumbling blue rubber band. He tore the rubber band, unrolled the paper, and abruptly, dozens of yellowed pages fell to the floor.

He gathered them up. They were letters, or copies of letters, in Zeidel's handwriting. Daniel decided that he would read one or two and then slip away through the stairwell and return home. Peninah would surely wake up when he came in, but she would ask no questions. She knew that whenever her husband was worried he had trouble sleeping, and that he was best left alone until the mood passed.

With half-closed eyes he began reading the first letter. From line to line, his sleepiness evaporated. He read letter after letter with mounting interest. *Poor Zeidel. I really never knew you. Please forgive me for all the negative thoughts I had about you. How much one person could hide?*

At four-thirty, with the precision of a Swiss watch, the light was turned on in the stairwell. Tzvi Shipholtz opened his door and went downstairs. Just to be safe, Daniel waited a few more minutes after the light went out and Shipholtz had put some distance between himself and the building.

As he went upstairs, Daniel recalled a war story. During World War II, the Nazis plundered Europe's cultural treasures. As the German forces approached Paris, the French removed many of the great paintings from the Louvre Museum and hid them. They also tried to camouflage the best ones by having artists quickly paint new pictures over the rare paintings. After the war, the artists were asked to remove the camouflage from the pictures. One day — so goes Parisian legend — one of the artists sent a telegram to the treasurer of the museum: "I peeled off a cheap picture of swans on a lake, under which I found Vincent van Gogh's sunflowers. I peeled them as well, and again came to a cheap painting of lions in Africa. Should I continue peeling?"

This past night, Daniel had peeled away one of Zeidel's layers, revealing a wealthy philanthropist camouflaged beneath the facade of a pauper. With the letters, Daniel had peeled away an additional layer, revealing a picture even more surprising than the previous one. Should he continue peeling?

5

Moshiko (Moshe) Sharabi's steps were meant to be quiet, but they echoed throughout the street. He knew that he was violating the first rule that Asaf had taught him: "Never stand out." This morning when he dressed, he had neglected to put away the dress shoes he had worn to the party last night and take his rubber-soled sport shoes instead. It would cost him heavily. At the very least, a comment would be jotted down in his file in red ink.

He crossed a quiet street, almost an alley. There it was. At the end of Rue Blaise Pascal was a small, curving lane that led into the Charles Aznavour Park. In the afternoon, senior citizens whiled away the time sitting on its picturesque wooden benches, and children frolicked among the big oak trees under the supervision of doting mothers. But in the morning, the park was almost empty. A few homeless people who had spent the night on the benches might linger there, but their senses were too dulled to notice even an approaching tank. A peaceful chat between two men on a bench would not attract so much as a casual glance.

It was not Moshiko who had chosen the park. His superiors had researched the geography of Paris for two weeks straight before deciding that this small park in Montmartre would be the ideal site for a meeting with the purchaser's agent.

Everything had been agreed upon, down to the smallest detail. Moshiko wore a brown jacket over his blue tricot shirt and held a folded copy of *Le Monde* in his hand. The purchaser's agent would find him sitting on the right side of a bench beneath an oak tree on the bark of which "Michelle" had been carved with a knife. Moshiko would delve into the editorial with his sunglasses nestled in his black hair. He was expecting to see a tall, thin man with a long, narrow face and nervous black eyes incapable of focusing on a single point for more than five seconds. The man would have a narrow nose, lower lip slightly extended, and a sharp chin. He would be wearing a tweed jacket over a purple silk shirt and Reebok running shoes, and he would be holding a stylish leather attaché case. He would sit down on the left side of the bench and read the weekly magazine *L'Express*.

The success of such a meeting depends on the initial click — the first moment that the purchaser's and seller's agents size each other up and check whether all the details match. Any deviation, such as blue jeans instead of suit pants or mauve suspenders in place of a yellow tie, could indicate a trap.

As Moshiko approached the end of the quiet street, his tension mounted. The chirping of birds and the pastoral tranquility, he knew, concealed gun barrels and nervous trigger fingers.

He was about to cross the street when suddenly he felt a light tap on his shoulder. He nearly fainted from fear. "Tell me, what got into you?" someone whispered to him in Hebrew. "Change your shoes immediately!"

The short, fat redhead who whispered these words seemed to have materialized out of nowhere. He handed Moshiko a plastic bag containing his sport shoes; waited to receive the bag back, this time with dress shoes inside; and disappeared down the street as stealthily as an escaping lizard. Moshiko watched the red mane get smaller and smaller. He had seen the fellow somewhere before, not here in Paris, but perhaps in the home office. He did not know his name and surely would not learn it anytime in the near future. That was the norm in Nati's corporation. Moshiko knew only Asaf, Amit, and one or two more.

Besides not knowing the names of the rest of the staff, he did not know their *modus operandi* either. The bag of shoes was a typical example. They knew he was liable to forget something — people are only human. And imbibing a large quantity of alcohol at night increases the chances of being less than 100% meticulous, not to mention ruining a multimillion-dollar deal because of a small mistake.

Precisely for this reason, the staff was trailing him day and night and watching his every move. He was on his way toward a deal that had been in preparation for the past half year. Countless coded phone conversations and telegrams had been exchanged on account of it. Now Moshiko, the seller's agent, was about to meet "Charlie," the purchaser's agent. *His name is Charlie as much as mine is Charles de Gaulle*, thought Moshiko.

When he crossed the street, he understood how timely the changing of shoes had been. The cobbled stones echoed noisily with each step. Walking there with dress shoes would have been as quiet as a fighter plane flying at low altitude. With such backing from the staff, you felt more confident. It was nice to know that someone behind you worried about you and corrected your small mistakes.

The park was entirely empty. A small sign at the entrance stated in French that the Charles Aznavour Park, named for the famous French singer, had been built with a donation from his family. *Please preserve the quiet and cleanliness of the place,* it urged, *and do not smoke.*

Whoever had chosen this park had made an excellent choice. There could be no better place for a meeting between two people interested in maximum privacy.

Without much effort, Moshiko found the bench under the oak tree that bore the inscription "Michelle," sat down on the right side of the bench, and opened *Le Monde.*

Charlie was ten minutes late — a bad sign. Perhaps the purchaser had changed his mind at the last minute. Moshiko tried to read, but did not manage to piece the letters together. He could sense too much hidden activity lurking beneath the park's peaceful exterior.

Cautiously, he raised his eyes and tossed a casual glance at the row of trees in front of him. Between the trees he saw nothing, but a distance behind them, at the rear of the quiet park, he caught sight of a tall apartment building. He cast a second glance. His trained eye discerned two prone silhouettes in attack position at its seventh-story windows. He could not see their weapons from here, but the position left no room for doubt. Asaf was taking no chances. He had sharpshooters covering the area from afar. A tiny microphone hidden in Moshiko's brown jacket and a miniature earphone stuck into his ear provided a hot line to them in case anything went wrong.

Moshiko shoved his head back into the pages of the newspaper. With great effort he managed to concentrate on the first page of the article, when a powerful instinct forced him to look up toward his left, to the roof of a tall office building facing the park. His blood nearly froze in his veins. Three sharpshooters, no less, had the area covered from that side. He smiled bitterly. *Mutual suspicion is a splendid basis for cooperation. Two sharpshooters on one side, three on the other, and I'm in the middle like a sitting duck.*

Actually, he could understand Charlie and his gang. Ultimately, despite the current cooperation, purchasers are scared of sellers. It was always possible that behind this arms deal was an intelligence agency of some foreign nation, out to catch the straw man and his senders. These would be interrogated and tortured into revealing information about the world's terror organizations. He could also understand his boss, Nati, who was the corporation's CEO, and his right-hand man, Asaf. The multimillion-dollar deal was liable to be a bloody trap set by a terrorist organization bent on toppling senior Israeli officials. Both sides had sent sharpshooters with nervous trigger fingers in preparation for any slight deviation from the plan. No insurance agency with knowledge Moshiko's real profession would have agreed to insure his life. It wasn't worth a penny.

Suddenly, he heard dry leaves crunching underfoot. Moshiko lifted his head cautiously and observed a tall, thin man holding a wine-colored leather attaché case in his left hand.

Until this point, everything had taken place exactly according to plan. But now the newcomer stopped, took a prolonged look at the roof of the office building on which the three sharpshooters were stationed, and gave a hand signal that Moshiko interpreted as, "All is in order."

This was a deviation from the scenario both sides had agreed upon. Moshiko knew that the slightest deviation was absolutely forbidden. The two sharpshooters that Asaf had stationed on the seventh floor of the apartment building behind the park knew it, too. Perhaps one of them even interpreted the signal as, "Open fire." In his eagerness to protect Moshiko, he aimed the first bullet toward the three sharpshooters on the roof of the office building.

The scenario in the park was canceled. Moshiko and Charlie did not sit and read on either side of the bench. Instead, they scrambled for cover as the sharpshooters began to exchange fire with silenced guns. Thus far there were no wounded on either side.

"What got into you?" Charlie barked into his sleeve. "I signal 'Everything under control' and you send bullets in every direction? What are you shooting for?" He listened a moment to a voice emanating from a tiny earphone in his right ear and said, "You mean they attacked, and you're defending yourselves?"

Charlie crawled toward Moshiko. "Why are your friends firing on my men? Tell them to stop!"

Moshiko felt for his handgun. In his world, the first rule was, "Be suspicious." He had not yet made sure that the man facing him was the one whom they had agreed on. "What did you signal to your friends up there?"

The man continued crawling through the grass toward him. Moshiko became even tenser. "You heard me. I signaled 'Everything under control,' and then your friends started shooting. You Israelis are nervous people. You have loose trigger fingers."

"Tell me, what's the signal?"

The man whipped the *L'Expresse* out of his pocket, waved it in front of Moshiko, and hollered, "Okay, okay, so I didn't go exactly according to all these idiotic signals. Anyway I don't read French!"

Moshiko liked him. This fellow had class. He, like Moshiko, scorned formalities. "Cease fire, friends!" Moshiko hollered into the mouthpiece in his jacket. "Cease fire!"

There was a brief silence. Then a voice whispered into his ear, "Are you sure?"

"Two hundred percent."

"Fine, as long as you take responsibility. If anything happens, *you'll* have to make the arrangements for removing your corpse from the park."

Judging from his black humor, that was Amit, one of the top-notch operatives Moshiko knew. The exact opposite of tough, purposeful Asaf, Amit possessed a very high degree of humaneness; they said he had the soul of a poet. Ironically, he had wound up in the thorny field of arms deals, and was so good at it that the boss would not exchange him for his right hand.

"If the police noticed the shooting," Moshiko retorted angrily, "the deal is over and I'll be the scapegoat. Asaf will blame me, and the boss believes only Asaf."

Amit was calm and confident. "Don't worry about a thing. In this hole, you won't find even the tire of a patrol car. From this moment, we're returning to readiness."

The fracas ended without casualties. This fact contributed favorably to the continuation of the deal that had almost died before it was hatched. The two agents sat down again on the bench, skipped the reading of newspapers, and got down to business.

"So what do you want?" began Moshiko.

Charlie sounded as if he did not believe his ears. "After all our talks, you ask what we want?"

"First of all, we have never negotiated with each other. We are here representing some party or parties. Second, you are undisciplined, but I must conform to protocol. You can't get out of it. Start from the beginning."

Moshiko's words were calculated and deliberate. In another minute, when the purchaser's agent began speaking, his every word would be recorded. Those were the rules of the cruel game. You conduct negotiations with a purchaser, you earn millions, and you are ready to do him in a second before he does you in.

"Fine." The purchaser's agent acquiesced. He also knew the rules of the game. He was fully aware that any extra word he said was liable to incriminate him one day, but he, and whoever stood behind him, had already taken this into account.

"My name for this purpose is Charlie. I represent the AVC, under the leadership of Carlos Fernandez. Our headquarters, as you know, are in the Turbo harbor, in northwest Colombia, but I came here from our branch in the port city of Dar-es-Salaam on the shores of the Indian Ocean. What else would you like to hear? In what country Dar-es-Salaam is located?"

Moshiko had already changed his opinion about Charlie three times. At first he had thought Charlie was an Arab, then he figured he was of Latin origin, judging by his hot temperament. Now his accent sounded British.

"Geography didn't interest me even in elementary school," retorted Moshiko, and leaned back casually. "I know that Dar-es-Salaam was the former capital of Tanzania, before the city of Dodoma replaced it. I want to know who the people behind you are — but the whole list, without any omissions or shortcuts, and exactly what you want. Give me a complete purchase order."

"I represent the AVC, under the leadership of Carlos Fernandez," he repeated like a broken record.

Moshiko lit a cigarette, exhaled the smoke into Charlie's face, and regarded him with a disinterested look. "On other occasions, didn't you speak about the Irish underground?"

"I represent the AVC, under the leadership of Carlos Fernandez," Charlie repeated for the third time. "You can verify the truth with Carlos Fernandez himself. I know that you know everything about me, and I don't understand why you have to degrade me with irrelevant interrogations."

But Moshiko had his orders. There were fixed procedures to prevent one from falling into any trap that the enemy might set. Moshiko had to go through the series of annoying questions in order to arrive at the next question, which would verify the purchaser's identity once and for all.

"Give me the name of the most important cell in your militia, and its motto."

Charlie heaved a sigh of relief. The torturous session was about to come to an end. He recited like a robot, "The most important cell is Cecil Rhodes, named for the founder of Rhodesia (Zimbabwe, today), whom our leader Carlos Fernandez greatly admires. The fixed password is his eternal words, 'When they dictate shameful, pitiful peace conditions to you, go out to war.' Did I pass the test? Will you give me a shot of whiskey?"

But the Israeli agent did not let up his pressure even for a moment. He was maddeningly purposeful. "What do you want?"

Charlie leaned forward and looked with deep animosity into the frightened eyes of his conversation partner. "Why? Why do you have to get me angry?"

The tiny microphone in Moshiko's ear chirped lightly. "Tell him that if he doesn't list what he wants right now, he will get nothing!"

Moshiko repeated Asaf's order word for word. Charlie capitulated.

"Fine. We are engaged in a difficult war with the leftist guerilla organization RARC. Until now, we resisted them with our bare hands, saws, and machetes. We need real weapons. We spoke about 2,500 M-16s, 5.56-millimeter bullets, with Mox V iron sights."

"The main weapon of the armies of the Western world," recited Moshiko as if reading from a paper. "Yes, that is the attack rifle preferred by all because of its long range."

Charlie ignored the comment and continued. "1,500 XM-177 E2 guns."

"In other words, the short version of the M-16," Moshiko cut into his words. "It excels in lightness and ratio of firepower to gun size. You have a big appetite, my friend. Do you want to hear the answer?"

"I haven't finished yet," Charlie protested. "We want to receive 300 Rocket-Propelled Grenade launchers."

Moshiko smiled. "The Soviet soldiers used to say that the only difference between a live Soviet unit and a dead one is an RPG. What else?"

"Enough!" Asaf hollered into his ear. "We've finished for today. Tell him he'll get everything they requested. It isn't necessary to wait eight hours to hear the whole list. Agree with him on the most important part, the price: Everything in cash, in new, large-portrait American $100 bills that must be brought to the next meeting in a special attaché case. End the discussion now!"

Asaf was pleased, and the boss would be, too. The talk between the two sides had been recorded in its entirety, to the last word. The two enemy militias in South America were a first-rate cover. Whoever the purchaser actually was, Asaf's company had a solid alibi.

Moshiko thought that, at most, the shoe incident would end with some red ink in his file. Asaf, however, had no intention of letting the matter go by quietly.

"What's the matter with you?" Asaf thundered when Moshiko entered the apartment they shared in a drab, run-down Parisian apartment building. "I recommended you as the perfect man for the meeting, and you came wearing a pair of jungle drums! I felt like shooting you on the spot. You're lucky that your tom-toms didn't alert the gendarmes."

With a display of nonchalance, Moshiko took off his sunglasses and smoothed his thick hair. Then, still ignoring Asaf, he calmly removed his brown jacket and hung it over the back of a chair.

That was his second mistake of the day.

Even in his late fifties, Asaf was a strong giant of a man. His huge, steel fingers grasped Moshiko's shoulder in a very painful grip and turned him until the two were face to face.

"What's the meaning of this?" Moshiko demanded. He was seething with anger and insult.

Slowly Asaf relaxed his grip. "You will look at me when I speak to you," he hissed.

"Yes, Father. Fine, Father. Anything else, Father?" Moshiko shot back mockingly.

A punch in the stomach sent Moshiko reeling. He collapsed on the sofa.

"We've finished for today," said Asaf, referring to the lesson about elementary precautions to which agents of arms dealers must adhere. He glanced at his watch and strode toward the door.

Suddenly he spun around to face Moshiko. "There's a price for forgetting. I wasn't needed to observe the sale today; I came only to enjoy my protogé's success. But instead of pride, you brought me shame with your repeated failures. Yesterday you disappeared on us and drank a lot at a party; this morning you frightened all of Paris with your racket-making shoes. Your movements conveyed fear and aroused suspicion. You have to memorize the rules and improve performance.

"You are therefore being punished. This evening you will not leave this apartment. I'm locking you in from the outside until tomorrow morning. Don't worry, you won't starve. There are containers of milk and cans of beer in the refrigerator, and Amit was kind enough to send in a supply of vegetables and snacks in case you get hungry."

Moshiko's serene front cracked. He jumped off the sofa and bounded toward Asaf. "You can't do this to me," he pleaded. "I have plans for tonight."

Asaf smiled cynically and taunted Moshiko with obvious relish. "The only thing you will do tonight is read *Le Monde.* You will sit here and eat crackers. What will you spread on them? Umm, I would offer you peanut butter from the shelf above the kitchen sink. No! Tuna spread, with thinly sliced tomatoes, would be better. Try adding chilled fresh celery stalks in a small dish, dipped in Greek salad dressing. Now that's a delicacy!" he added with a dreamy expression, as if savoring the taste.

Beside the door, he paused a moment and added seriously, "Don't be angry with me; those are the regulations. According to the boss's code, a sales agent who messes up must be taught a lesson."

Without waiting to hear Moshiko's reaction, Asaf left, locking the door behind him.

"They treat their men like little children," Moshiko muttered to himself as he collapsed wearily on the sofa.

A minute later, though, he pulled himself together and got up. From the window, he watched Asaf cross the street toward the apartment building directly opposite. Moshiko's angry frown gave way to a smile, and a mischievous gleam sparkled in his eyes. He was not about to spend the evening nibbling chilled celery stalks.

He strode purposefully to his bedroom. There, hidden within the case of his personal computer, his private kingdom was located — the kingdom of Moshiko, the eavesdropper.

Electronic equipment and transistors had always been Moshiko's favorite playthings. As a child, while his friends were assembling and disassembling Lego, Moshiko was taking apart broken transistor radios. Instinct guided him in unraveling the secrets of electronic circuits. After that he repaired radios that even technicians despaired of. Then he became familiar with microwave transceivers. But he did not stop there. He honed his skills continuously.

As a teenager, Moshiko began to read the professional literature, and in all his free hours he worked at electronics. He developed a keen interest in microelectronics a few years before they entered the consumer market, and he focused on microscopic listening devices, or "buttons." His secret hobby was planting buttons everywhere. He laughed quietly. If Asaf knew what lay beneath the smart card of his cell phone, he would faint. Even when the phone was off, the implanted ear continued to listen.

❧

In the dingy apartment building across the street from Moshiko, Asaf took the elevator up to the fourth floor, rang one of the doorbells, and waited for the guard to identify him on the closed-circuit camera. When he heard the short buzz, he pushed the door and entered.

Inside, four men were waiting for him. Seated at the head of the table was obviously the oldest by far. His hair, dyed brown, was meant to cut his apparent age to forty-five, but the deep creases in his cheeks, the hanging skin of his double chin, and the white hair roots revealed that he was over seventy. Yet the gleam in his eyes and his boundless energy, robust health, and sharp mind still kept Nati, the boss, on par with the younger members of the management team.

At the end of the table sat Amit Mizrachi, and on either side, Dubik Cooperman and Malkiel Yahalom, in their mid-thirties. They were waiting impatiently for Asaf.

"What did you do with Moshiko?" The boss poured a cup of espresso from an appliance within arm's reach and offered it to Asaf. "Have a drink. You must be parched from waiting in the building behind the park."

"Parched? I almost got a bullet in my head!" Asaf wiped gleaming beads of sweat from his glistening forehead. "Nowadays, every kid becomes a sharpshooter and shoots freely. As for Moshiko, I left him locked in the apartment in accordance with regulations, to do some soul-searching and to learn a lesson."

"Now, to the main point. What did they make up there?" The boss leaned back in his chair, and his light blue eyes rested lazily on the face of Asaf, his right-hand man. Nati trusted him completely; Asaf had been unquestionably faithful to him for decades.

"Do you want numbers and quantities?"

"No." The boss suppressed a bored yawn. "Just the general idea. We all know the refrain by heart. Afterwards we'll go over the exact list together."

"Fine. They want thousands of M-16 rifles and XM-177s, and of course, bullets in the millions. Also rocket-propelled grenade launchers."

"I understand." The boss stroked his chin pensively. "By the way, you said, 'They want.' Do you have any idea who this mysterious 'they' is?"

A sudden fit of coughing attacked Asaf, and he nearly choked on his espresso. Nati must be getting old if the identity of buyers suddenly began to interest him.

"The middleman, Charlie, presented himself as an agent of the AVC Freedom Fighters under the leadership of Carlos Fernandez."

For protocol's sake, the boss had to react. "We've heard of it."

Here Dubik broke in. "You've covered yourself, Nati," he said with suppressed anger. "But I have reason to assume that behind your anonymous Charlie is the Lebanese arms and diamonds dealer, Aziz Jibril, who has been acquiring arms for Al-Qaeda since 1998. Their purchase order includes sophisticated explosives for preparing powerful bombs. But the cherry on top is several dozen Stinger anti-aircraft missiles, which are highly accurate and dangerous because of their advanced target-locking capabilities.

"Nati, admit it. Asaf didn't let Charlie read the list till the end so that the Stingers wouldn't be mentioned. That's why you don't let Asaf talk about them, either."

"So?" asked the boss, looking as innocent as a one-year-old.

Dubik tipped over the empty chair beside him and let it fall noisily to the floor. "As Israelis, aren't we crossing a dangerous line, Nati? What will all these weapons be aimed at? Honestly, won't the Stingers bring down El Al planes around the world?"

Several sphinx-like faces looked at Dubik coldly as he asked his rhetorical question. No one uttered a syllable.

Nati looked hurt. "Gentlemen, how could you suspect a loyal Zionist like me of such a thing? Amit, please record in the protocol: In light of Mr. Dubik Cooperman's piercing questions, the request for a purchase by Charlie, who represents the AVC, has been denied because of a suspicion that he is actually buying for Al-Qaeda. And now on to the next question: What about the request of the IDA?"

"Approved," replied Asaf tersely.

"I would like to make a suggestion," said the boss's slick voice, straight into the ears of Moshiko, who was listening from across the street. "We'll supply them with the AK 74s that we got from the Nicaraguan police force in exchange for mini-Uzi submachine guns and Jericho pistols."

"The IDA will be very angry," objected Malkiel, "when instead of advanced Western weapons, they get backward Soviet ones that went out of circulation several years ago."

"We don't owe them anything beyond that."

Here Nati's voice became faint. A long series of beeps and static disturbances irritated Moshiko's ears before everything ended in absolute silence.

Moshiko slapped his forehead in frustration. Why did the instrument have to stop broadcasting just at the crucial moment?

He ran to the refrigerator and guzzled two cans of beer. His hobby allowed him to hear many things in various places, but never had he heard such sensitive information. Nati's arms company received camouflaged purchase orders from Israel's worst enemies, and Moshiko himself, a veteran of one of Israel's crack combat units, had been sent to negotiate this dirty deal!

True, the request had been turned down precisely because of this suspicion. Yet something did not smell right, though he could not put his finger on it.

For a long time he sat by the window, his forehead creased in thought, gazing at the lights of Paris.

He himself had been involved in obtaining the mini-Uzi submachine guns and Jericho pistols. With his own hand he had signed a request form and attached the end-user certificate.

An end-user certificate, the document testifying whom the weapons were meant to reach, had to be supplied by the buyers. Israeli companies wishing to sell Israeli arms had to present the certificate to SIBAT, an office of the Ministry of Defense that checked its authenticity. Nati's corporation had presented the request with an end-user certificate signed by the representative of the Mexican National Guard. How had the weapons gotten to Nicaragua?

This was not a hard question, Moshiko knew. A government official who had no interest in the weapons might sign the certificate in return for a contribution to his personal retirement fund. Thus a certificate could acquire the necessary signatures and confirmations and the weapons could still get into dubious hands.

Moshiko did not expect the boss and his colleagues to be listed in the *Who's Who of Saints.* Nevertheless, here something smelled really rotten.

He went to bed, shut the light, and tried to fall asleep. But doubt tormented him as he tried in vain to make order out of the whirlwind of his thoughts. If the IDA asked to buy weapons, why did the boss have to fool them by supplying them with outdated Soviet arms? And wouldn't the IDA see what they were getting? What was really going on there?

It was nearly dawn when Moshiko fall into a light, fitful sleep.

⊛

Midnight. An El Al plane took off from Charles de Gaulle airport. Moshiko sat next to the window and stared at the lights of Paris capering beneath him. Suddenly, a strong light flashed beside the right wing, and the entire plane shook. "We're dropping," called the pilot over the loudspeaker. "Al Qaeda terrorists have shot a Stinger missile at us. Buckle up tight!"

The plane dropped with dizzying speed, and Moshiko knew his fate had been sealed. *What a fool I was that I didn't foil the sale. I could have saved myself!*

He tried to fasten the buckle of his safety belt, but his hands were heavy as lead, and his fingers disobeyed him.

He wanted to scream, but his throat did not cooperate. Again he opened his mouth. This time he tried with all his might, determined to overcome the block. Success! He felt the scream flowing out of his lungs: "Help! Help!"

Amit shook his shoulders forcibly. "What are you dreaming about?" he demanded. "Why are you screaming for help at four-thirty in the morning? You woke me up and you'll wake up the rest of the neighborhood, too!"

Moshiko sat bolt upright in bed. He was bathed in sweat. His eyes were out of focus, his thoughts confused. At first he could not remember where he was. The dream had been so tangible, he was sure he had been on a plane about to crash onto the streets of Paris.

Amit regarded him with concern. "You took what happened today in the Charles Aznavour Park too much to heart. You must have dreamed that the sharpshooters were shooting at you."

Moshiko put his bare feet on the cold floor. Caught up entirely in the paralyzing fear, he was still breathing quickly. He looked at Amit. "You can't imagine how close you are," he said quietly.

Amit relaxed when he saw Moshiko returning to himself. "Drink a cup of cold water and don't get carried away with fears. My friend, that's how it is in the world today. If you want to earn big bucks on our fading planet, you've got to be tough and disregard everything they taught you in school."

Moshiko went barefoot to the refrigerator, poured himself a glass of cold water, and downed it in a single gulp. After three glasses, his breathing stabilized and he became calm. Amit had already fallen asleep, judging by his rhythmic breathing. But Moshiko still trembled slightly. In his imagination, the plane had not stopped dropping. He went out to the small, open balcony and watched the lights of Paris.

He was not the type to become frightened by dreams. But now, after a short sleep and under the influence of the clear night air, Moshiko soberly analyzed the conversation he had overheard. Something in that meeting of the corporate management had troubled him even before he fell asleep. Now he finally figured out what: the speed with which Nati had given in to Dubik! Although Dubik had no proof, Nati had retreated with the speed of light from a multimillion dollar deal! Suspicious, indeed.

Moshiko took stock of the situation. Only the two of them were staying in the apartment that night, and Amit was fast asleep in the other bedroom. He returned to the kitchen, shut the door quietly, and turned on the light. Amit must not wake up! He dialed a long string of digits. There were four rings, and then a sleepy voice.

"Hello."

"Yaniv, are you awake? It's Moshiko," he whispered into the receiver.

"Who?"

"Your brother, Moshiko. Wake up." The whisper was too loud.

"Well, well, Moshiko. What made you suddenly decide to call at such an hour?"

"I had no choice. It's a matter of saving many lives."

Yaniv Sharabi let out a yawn that was heard from Tel Aviv to Paris. "What are you talking about?"

Moshiko tried to be brief and to the point. This was difficult, considering that his younger brother had been sleeping very soundly after a twelve-hour stint guarding Tel Aviv's Central Bus Station from suicide terrorists. Moshiko spoke forcefully, tersely, and clearly. Yaniv's sleepiness dissipated, and his initial surprise changed to firm determination.

"Okay, I'll do it," he promised.

"Remember. I'm depending on you," Moshiko warned him.

"No problem."

Neither of the brothers could sleep anymore that night. They were busy planning a course of action.

As Moshiko left his house, his cellular phone vibrated in his blazer pocket. "Hello," he answered.

"Good morning, Moshiko. Can we talk?"

"Where are you, Yaniv?"

"On my way to work."

"I thought you were on your way to me," said Moshiko, disappointed. "Why did you change your mind?"

"Sorry to let you down, but do you really expect me to take a week off from work just because of your gut feeling?"

"It's not just a feeling," said Moshiko decisively. "I have solid proof. But I can't speak now. Call me at nine tonight my — that is Paris — time; I'll be alone at home."

❧

That evening, Moshiko waited anxiously for the small phone in the palm of his hand to ring. At 9:01 the instrument buzzed.

"If no terrorist blew himself up in the Central Bus Station today," said Yaniv, "it wasn't thanks to me. I couldn't concentrate on my work. All day long I thought about what you told me, and I decided there is no compelling reason for flying to Paris."

Moshiko got angry. "Yaniv, there *is* a compelling reason, but it can't be discussed on the phone. Come here and you'll be convinced."

Yaniv capitulated. "Are you sure, Moshiko?"

"A million percent. By the way, the vacation and the tickets are on me, of course."

"Okay. I'll be there the day after tomorrow."

⸙

Two days later, at eight in the morning, a curly-haired young man with penetrating black eyes and a round face landed at the Charles de Gaulle Airport. He lost no time phoning Moshiko.

"I'm here," he called cheerily.

"Wonderful, Yaniv. I knew I could count on you. How are you?"

"Just fine. But how do I get to you?"

"Simple. Take Line 2 on the Metro to Barbes Rochechouart in the 18th Arrondissement. You'll notice a lot of different ethnic groups. I'm here precisely because it's a low-class neighborhood. Get off the Metro at Barbes Boulevard. Continue to Rue Myrha, and from there to Rue de la Goutte d'Or. It's a very unpleasant street where decent citizens are afraid to walk at night alone. Go about thirty meters, count till building number 5, and go up to the third floor."

An hour and a quarter later, the brothers embraced warmly.

⸙

"So what's all the fuss about?" asked Yaniv after he had showered and drunk a glass of passion-fruit juice. "Ever since Abba died, you've been like a father to me. Whatever you tell me, I do. But just between us, didn't you make a mistake inviting me here?"

Moshiko wrapped his palm around the gold edges of his glass and took a sip of juice. In honor of his visitor, he had taken out the only two matching glasses he owned. "Look, Yaniv, I might be making a mountain out of a molehill — or, even worse, unfairly suspecting people who are paying me a fat salary. On the other hand, I might be right."

"On what basis did you decide that Nati is willing to sell arms to Al-Qaeda? That's a very serious accusation. He will have to account not only to the Israeli government, but also to the whole world, first and foremost the United States."

"On the basis of this." Moshiko set a small tape recorder on the table and pressed PLAY.

They heard Dubik's voice. "You've covered yourself, Nati. But I have reason to assume that behind your anonymous Charlie is the Lebanese arms and diamond dealer, Aziz Jibril, who's been acquiring arms for Al-Qaeda since 1998. Their purchase order includes sophisticated explosives for preparing powerful bombs. But the cherry on top is several dozen Stinger anti-aircraft missiles, which are highly accurate and dangerous because of their advanced target-locking capabilities."

"You understand?" asked Moshiko. "Now listen to the continuation, after the noise that sounds like a chair falling."

Dubik sounded angry. "As Israelis, aren't we crossing a dangerous line, Nati? What will all these weapons be aimed at? Honestly, won't the Stingers bring down El Al planes around the world?"

There was a long silence, then Nati's voice, sounding hurt. "Gentlemen, how could you suspect a loyal Zionist like me of such a thing? Amit, please record in the protocol: In light of Mr. Dubik Cooperman's piercing questions, the request for a purchase by Charlie, who represents the AVC, has been denied because of a suspicion that he is actually buying for Al-Qaeda. And now on to the next question: What about the request of the IDA?"

"Approved."

"That's Asaf, my instructor and mentor," said Moshiko grimly.

Next they heard Nati's plan to cheat the IDA by supplying them with outdated Soviet weapons instead of the modern Western ones ordered. After that the battery died.

Yaniv was furious. "Moshiko, you made me come all the way to Paris for that? Dubik merely expressed an unfounded suspicion. Nati immediately gave in and canceled the deal!"

"You didn't understand," retorted Moshiko. "That's what they wanted me to hear."

"What?"

"Yes indeed," nodded Moshiko. "Nati is a bulldozer. They give in to him; he never gives in to anyone. He doesn't abandon sure deals merely because weapons might fall into the hands of our enemies. His motto in life is: If we can make a few more pennies, why not?"

"What's wrong with that?" laughed Yaniv. "Everyone follows that motto. Don't you and I try to earn the maximum?"

"But only Nati cheats the whole world all the time for the sake of money. In every deal he makes, he finds an excuse to pull some trick. But it wasn't just that. I had the opportunity to hear a few other executive meetings."

Yaniv laughed loudly. "How many instruments did you plant there? Have you tapped every cell phone in the area?"

Moshiko was not smiling. "It happens that someone forgets his cell phone in the car, and then what? I planted a button in the barrel of an ancient gun that decorates the wall behind Nati's chair. That way I'm always connected, on-line, to executive meetings."

"And what did you hear?" asked Yaniv, his curiosity piqued.

"Not much," admitted Moshiko. "The discussions are pretty boring. They analyze the details of the lists and how to fill the order. The discussion that I played for you was unusual — which is why I think it was staged specially for me. Nati and Asaf may have their suspicions of me on account of my expertise in microelectronics.

"Nevertheless, I assume Charlie is an agent for a straw organization covering for Al Qaeda, and I wouldn't be surprised if Nati is prepared to sell arms even to Osama bin Laden. To assuage his guilty conscience, he'll make sure that half the guns are outdated models from the former Soviet Union."

"Isn't Nati afraid of the wrath of his cheated customers?" wondered Yaniv.

Moshiko emptied the glass and wiped the droplets from the edges of his lips. "No. He knows they will need him in the future also. He gains the edge over his competitors through his low prices and the tips he provides with every sale."

Yaniv stood up and went over to the window. Outside, a fray was developing among a few dark-skinned youths. "Nice street you have here," he observed wryly.

"As I told you, that's exactly why we live here. The police are afraid to come, the black market flourishes, and everyone does as he pleases. Nati chooses his areas of operation carefully."

Yaniv paced the room as he thought. After a long silence, he stopped in front of Moshiko, who was soldering ultrafine copper wires on a small transistor board. "In my opinion, you're wrong. Your Nati has probably learned to walk the tightrope between the legal and the illegal. You have no case against him."

Moshiko unplugged the soldering iron from the electric current and left his project. From the gleam in his brother's eyes, Yaniv could tell that a bold idea was hatching in his mind.

"I will have a case," he announced dramatically.

"What are you talking about?" asked Yaniv.

Moshiko said simply, "You will rent an apartment in the area. I noticed a small one, two blocks away. You will present yourself as Jafar Hashemi — an excellent name; it sounds like a cross between an Iranian and a Sudanese. You will represent the Organization of Oppressed Freedom Fighters of Spain, which any intelligent person understands is a cover name. You will meet Nati's agent — that is, me — and present a long purchase order that begins with short-range missiles, anti-aircraft cannons, and shells. The list will end with a used, fully equipped missile ship from the Israeli Navy. You will let Nati's agent understand that the final destination of the dozens of tons of weapons might definitely be the Hezbullah in Lebanon, the men of Sheikh Hassan Nasrallah. America has been pressuring Iran to stop supplying arms to the Hezbullah, and Nasrallah is looking for an alternative to Iran. I'm burning with curiosity to hear how Nati and Asaf will answer you. Those two snakes are about to fall into a deep pit."

"Moshiko, are you tired of living? If you're right and Nati really is a dangerous gangster, he'll mow us both down. You're playing with fire!"

Moshiko examined a wire so thin it was almost transparent. He spoke quietly, as if to himself. "You don't have a chance unless you take a risk."

"A risk?" jumped Yaniv excitedly. "You're talking about certain death." He approached the window and pointed to the passersby. "See, Moshiko. People come and go, speak and argue."

"Punch and hit," Moshiko added drily.

"That happens, too." Yaniv smiled. "But see what vitality. They want to live. What about you? Are you fed up with life?"

Moshiko sat down again and plugged in the small soldering iron. A faint smell of burning and a thin column of white smoke rose from where the hot iron had unintentionally touched a wire's plastic cover. His fingers trembled slightly. "I've decided to take action. I must remove the mask from Nati's face and find out whether he's a criminal. But if my suspicion is right, he must be stopped before it's too late. If he agrees to cooperate with you when you pose as a Hezbullah agent, I'll bring the Mossad into the picture and make sure he stands trial in criminal court."

Yaniv succumbed to his older brother's iron will. "But they'll notice that we look alike," he said weakly. "Picture it. The seller's agent sits across from the buyer's agent in some forsaken park, and suddenly Asaf sees through his binoculars that the two agents are brothers! Won't he shoot us both dead?"

"Do you think makeup is only for aging politicians to use in press studios?" said Moshiko firmly. "Smear up your whole face, put on thick glasses, and stick on a moustache and a little beard so that even Ima wouldn't recognize you!"

An amused smile lit up Yaniv's worried eyes. "Speaking of Ima, you can thank her for having insisted on speaking Arabic at home. That way I'll be able present myself as Jafar Hashemi."

⁂

A new figure appeared in the black market of the Barbes Rochechouart Quarter of Paris and gave out small cards with a fax number. Arabic-speaking Jafar Hashemi presented himself as an agent of the Oppressed Freedom Fighters of Spain, while dropping hints about the Hezbullah and frequently mentioning the name Hassan Nasrallah. He let it be known that he was backed by a party with an unlimited budget and a keen interest in purchasing a large quantity of weapons.

It took only two days to sow the seeds. The second evening, when Yaniv entered the one-room apartment Moshiko had rented for him, the fax sprang to life and began to spew out papers. Yaniv leafed quickly through them, looking for names and numbers that matched his brother's list.

He found it.

A page on the bottom of the pile bore the signature "Asaf." Yaniv read it eagerly.

"If you are interested in a good deal, our company will be happy to help you. We provide broad variety, high quality, and proven effectiveness — all at the world's lowest prices. In addition, we offer tips and advice that will help you in the future, and our agents will be at your service whenever you wish."

Yaniv phoned Moshiko. "It worked," he said excitedly. "They took the bait."

Moshiko sounded skeptical and gloomy. "The question in this case is who is trapping whom. I have a request, Yaniv."

"Yes?"

"Let's not talk about it on the phone. We'll meet in some neutral place. Bring along the paper. I want to see whether it's a trap."

They arranged to meet in the small supermarket on Rue des Poissonniers, halfway between them and a five-minute walk for each. Yaniv folded the paper, put it into his trouser pocket, and set out at the same time that Moshiko did.

Two hours later, Moshiko was beside himself with worry. Yaniv never arrived at the supermarket, his cell phone was not on, and no one answered his phone at home.

8

Every evening, between the hours of eight and ten, people, mostly uninvited visitors, would climb the worn and partly broken outdoor stairs of an old, two-story, red-shingle-roofed house in Jerusalem's Beis Yisrael section. They did not have to knock on the clean white door with the small ceramic nameplate that was inscribed "Mindelman Family" before entering. These hours were Elitzafan Mindelman's time for advising and helping the public, and anyone who wanted could walk right into his study — or, if need be, sit in the living room to await his turn.

First-time visitors were surprised to see that the simple, modest, three-bedroom apartment looked almost the same as it had fifty years earlier. It displayed few signs of modernity, not even a computer or microwave oven. The most modern, up-to-date item was a clothes dryer. There were few decorations; most noticeable was the earthenware flowerpot on the windowsill in which green mint herbs grew.

Elitzafan welcomed each visitor with a smile. He lent a sympathetic ear; soothed, encouraged, and recommended doctors for those with rare medical problems; arranged loans for the needy; found schools for students who had difficulty in being accepted; and made peace between two sides in a dispute. People would enter the modest apartment in Beis Yisrael sad or angry and depart smiling.

Elitzafan's family had accustomed themselves to a home that was open to the public every evening. Devorah and her four daughters either stayed out of the house or occupied themselves in the bedrooms and kitchen. Chedvi, the eldest, read books of Jewish thought that challenged the mind and satisfied the soul. Tirtzah, younger than Chedvi by fifteen months, could sit for hours solving crossword puzzles. Twenty-two year old Leah'le spent most evenings in the homes of weak students, whom she tutored for a very modest fee. Kreindy, the youngest, volunteered for a *chesed* organization.

After the four girls came three boys. Menashe and Yehoshua studied in out-of-town yeshivahs and came home only once a month. Nachum'ke, who came home from *mesivta* at nine-thirty, enjoyed watching the visitors.

That evening, after the last visitor left, the apartment became strangely silent. Now the sounds of the street intruded. A car door slammed, children who did not want to go to sleep played ball, cats cried in garbage dumpsters, some American yeshivah students held a loud discussion in the middle of the street, and the deteriorating transformer of the nearby streetlamp buzzed monotonously.

Elitzafan went to the refrigerator and removed a small container of yogurt. The phone rang, and he answered. Someone who did not have to identify himself spoke excitedly, and Elitzafan's sad eyes lit up with hope.

Two minutes later, the phone rang again. Chedvi picked it up and immediately brought the receiver to her father. "Abba, it's for you."

"Who is it?" he asked automatically.

Chedvi shrugged her shoulders, covered the mouthpiece, and whispered, "He didn't want to say."

Elitzafan took the receiver. "Hello," he said pleasantly.

"Am I speaking with Elitzafan Mindelman?"

The anonymous speaker innocently asked a few questions. He did not intend to cause Elitzafan any unpleasantness. Nevertheless, the air left Elitzafan's lungs and the color drained from his cheeks.

Devorah was pressing a pile of shirts. Out of the corner of her eye, she observed her husband's white face. As he replaced the receiver, he looked like a deflated tire, crushed and thin. She set the hot iron down and ran to him. "What happened?" she asked fearfully. "What did they tell you?"

"Nothing special," he muttered weakly, tried to make light of the matter. His arms shook suddenly and fell to his sides. Devorah had not seen him under such stress in years.

"And who was the previous caller?" she asked, automatically straightening her *tichel*.

The smile returned to his face. "It was Emanuel, with a new suggestion for Chedvi."

∎c

Emanuel Klopstein was a successful, well-known *shadchan* of unknown age. His blazing red hair, his freckled, wrinkle-free face, and huge blue eyes made him look forty, but the fact that his friends from school were marrying off grandchildren suggested he was closer to sixty-five. This bundle of energy could not sit still for a minute. His ears were sensitive antennas, his eyes cameras that took continuous pictures of anyone who was not yet paired up with a life partner. His brain worked feverishly every possible minute calculating the various aspects of *shidduchim*: who to match up with whom, is it suitable or not, should he or should he not suggest it. He worked with all his heart and soul to bring about engagements.

Emanuel took care of the elite of the *charedi* public, as well as those of the most difficult, problematic suggestions. Elitzafan's daughters had entered Emanuel's lists as the elite, and a few years later were transferred to the problematic department.

It had started six years earlier, when Chedvi was nineteen. Emanuel, like everyone else, had heard of Elitzafan, who so devotedly helped the public. Chedvi was a Heaven-fearing, intelligent, pretty girl with wonderful character traits, a pleasant personality, and a steady job, whose aspiration in life was to support her husband so that he could study Torah day and night. Emanuel was sure that within two weeks, Elitzafan would have a diligent, bright young scholar as a son-in-law; in fact, he had the perfect name in his briefcase when he called at Elitzafan's home.

The girl's side inquired about the boy and his family, and gave a positive answer. The boy's side, surprisingly, did not hasten to reply. Emanuel pressured them, but succeeded in eliciting only vague excuses.

It happens, they say, in the best of families.

Emanuel suggested a second boy, a good friend of the first. His family, too, did not agree to the match. Something was going awry in the inquiry stage.

Emanuel went on to a third excellent suggestion. This *shidduch*, too, died with the inquiries.

After the same happened with another four top fellows, Emanuel realized there was a problem. During the inquiries, someone was speaking ill of the Mindelmans and chasing away potential suitors.

Emanuel was astounded. Who would ruin things for such a kind person as Elitzafan, who devoted his evenings to helping the public free of charge? Did Elitzafan have hidden enemies, perhaps a jealous neighbor? Emanuel decided to look into the matter himself. Disguising his voice and hiding under a false identity, he called friends and neighbors of the Mindelmans and made "inquiries for the purpose of a *shidduch*."

He received very positive information. He heard only good things about the kind communal worker and his devoted wife. Chedvi was praised highly as a clever, talented girl with a sterling character.

So where is the problem? Emanuel asked himself.

"Such a wonderful girl, with every desirable quality!" people said sympathetically as the years passed. "How did she get in a bind?"

It wasn't just Chedvi. None of the younger sisters would think of starting *shidduchim* until the one ahead of her was engaged. All four of Elitzafan's daughters were of marriageable age, and all four were "stuck."

Emanuel invested herculean efforts trying to uncover the identity of the mysterious *shidduch* saboteur, but to no avail. He was not the only volunteer detective. Other *shadchanim* as well as community leaders who wanted to bring gladness into Elitzafan's home tried as well. One after another, they gave up. The *shadchanim* stopped calling Elitzafan's house.

Only Emanuel did not forget Chedvi. Occasionally he would call and suggest an outstanding boy. But after a few days, silence would set in once again.

Elitzafan continued to welcome each visitor with a smile. Only in Elitzafan's family were there few smiles, other than a forced one here and there.

This evening, Emanuel again suggested an excellent boy for Chedvi. Why, you ask, was Matti Langer still around at the advanced age of twenty-seven? When his friends from yeshivah were marrying and starting families, Matti wasn't even interested in *shidduchim*. He was waiting for his older brother, Chanoch. At a certain stage the rabbis had said he need not wait anymore, but Matti was afraid of hurting Chanoch's feelings. Anyway, Matti was so deeply immersed in his studies that waiting had not been too difficult. A few months ago, Chanoch had finally gone to the *chupah,* leaving the field open to Matti, and Emanuel lost no time suggesting him for Chedvi.

This time, Emanuel would try a new tactic. He would hint to the boy that in the course of the inquiries, someone would try to whisper bad things about the family. Forewarned is forearmed!

❦

Devorah Mindelman put on her Shabbos suit and hurried to the house of a childhood friend who was celebrating her daughter's engagement.

Together, the happy mothers of the *chasan* and *kallah* held the plate and threw it on the floor with perfect synchronization, before a flashing camera. Devorah, standing on the side, wiped away a tear that slid from her eye. *Ribbono shel olam, when will Devorah celebrate the engagement of her own daughter?* thought one of her friends as she watched her.

But the friend had misinterpreted the tear. At that moment, Devorah was not thinking of herself. She was participating with all her heart in her friend's happiness.

Devorah did not play the role of *tzaddekes.* She really and truly rejoiced in the good fortune of others.

She also had where to escape, a place where the pain in her heart was released and her inner serenity and joy were restored.

A permanent fixture in one of Jerusalem's largest girls' elementary schools was the school secretary, Devorah Mindelman sitting at the computer beneath an oversized picture of the Chofetz Chaim. She would be carrying on conversations over two phones simultaneously while her fingers danced across the keyboard. Capable, efficient, and down-to-earth, Devorah was responsible for hundreds of girls and thousands of details. It was hard to imagine the school functioning without Devorah's dynamic presence. Her work output was formidable; it would take five people to replace her. The principal's worst fear was that one day Devorah might resign. That day, the principal was certain, the school would collapse like a tower of cards.

At home, Devorah was an energetic housewife, devoted mother, excellent cook, and, of course, helpmate of her husband. Without Devorah at his side, Elitzafan would not have been able to serve the public as he did.

In the school office or at home, no one ever saw Devorah become upset or raise her voice; she was always calm and matter-of-fact. Some even thought she was an iceberg to whom words like "emotion" or "feeling" were theoretical concepts. No one could imagine her writing poems by candlelight at the wee hours of the morning, or composing a rhyme in honor of some occasion. Devorah was known to be an energetic, practical, realistic doer.

☙❧

Flora Simchoni–Freilich was the diametric opposite of Devorah Mindelman. Even her delicate, fragile appearance placed her in the world of dreams and fantasy. Her head was covered with a burgundy scarf embroidered with the signs of the Zodiac. Her suits were adorned with delicate metal accessories in which she saw attachment to a spiritual reality. Her *modus operandi* combined the sacred and the mundane as well as realism and fantasy. Whenever she set out to any destination, she began by putting her right foot first. Despite the difficulty involved, she was careful to have all the buttons in her family's wardrobe positioned so that the right side of the garment came out on top. "Making the right prevail over the left" was a concept frequently on her lips, in addition to "the descent of abundance from the upper worlds." She spoke about the flow of positive and negative energy so much that you felt she actually saw the energy moving. The body's meridian lines were an integral part of her daily speech.

She solved problems at their root, that is, she claimed she could solve almost any problem in the world by treating its root; Her varied methods of treatment were based on "reading" various things. Her successful career had begun with reading coffee grounds. Although she did not invent the art of reading the murky dregs of coffee, she did improve it to unimaginable dimensions. For the purpose of reading herbs, she equipped the women who sought her help with mint roots, which they planted in earthenware flowerpots and grew in their homes for exactly seven weeks. At the end of this period, the herbs were brought to Flora, who examined them and then told the planter what had befallen her during the growth period, what problems she had suffered, and how to remedy them.

Reading wicks was similar in principle but different in practice. The women brought her the burnt wicks of the candles they had lit for Shabbos, taking care to preserve the shape of the charcoal at the tip. She examined the wick, especially its blackened edge, in the light of a powerful spotlight, closed her eyes in concentration, and then determined what the problem was and how it could be solved. In certain instances, Flora would pour a bit of olive oil into a glass vial and rekindle the wick in a dark room.

Her ability to diagnose both physical and emotional problems through the blackened tips of wicks was astounding — at least according to the devoted followers who saw the Divine presence in Flora's every word. A demonstration of the burning wicks in a dark room convinced even her vehement opponents of her magical abilities. With her face illuminated by an orange-blue light (she added a little kerosene to the olive oil), Flora looked like an ancient sorcerer with formidable powers.

Women who lit wax Shabbos candles could bring the remnants of the candles, but then Flora's prophetic ability was dramatically decreased because "although all a person's deeds and essence are engraved in the Shabbos candles, nevertheless the root of a person's soul is immersed in olive oil, which hints to wisdom, as is known. Therefore I see best in wicks that were used with olive oil."

The presence at her side of mystical powers, to which she was permanently connected, was undisputable. "I use only the conduit of abundance that is holy," she would say with a modest smile. "I myself am zero, absolutely nothing."

Her many admirers saw in these words the deep humility of Rebbetzin Flora Simchoni–Freilich. How, they wondered, could one woman combine spiritual powers and a desire to help others together with the humility of the *tzaddikim* of old?

Flora received clients every other day of the week at odd hours, in the basement of an apartment house whose number was not divisible by two. She accepted payment (only for covering necessary expenses; all profits were transferred directly to a fund for poor brides over which she presided) only in multiples of five or nine, but never of two.

The waiting room in Flora's basement was crowded with women from all circles and backgrounds. Anyone who suffered physical or emotional pain could come there for treatment, although she was most helpful to women with low foreheads.

The presence of a rational, cold, intelligent woman like Devorah Mindelman in Flora's basement was like the presence of a giraffe at the North Pole. Devorah's friends would have fainted had anyone told them that Devorah was there every Thursday. The soulful conversations filled Devorah's heart with comfort and Flora's pocketbook with money.

The Thursday visits had begun after the first few *shidduchim* offered to Chedvi were torpedoed. Devorah had been sure that such a special girl would be snatched up quickly. To her surprise, it turned out that the world outside of mimeographed papers was much more cruel and harsh than she had imagined. True, she knew that there was a skeleton in the family closet and that anyone with a long memory might dig it up, but she never dreamt that the past would have such horrific ramifications on the present. A secret enemy did not miss a chance to inform the boy's side whenever a *shidduch* was suggested. *Father in Heaven,* she wondered, *why are Chedvi and her sisters to blame for what happened before they were born?*

For a long time, Devorah had wrestled with the storm raging inside her. When she could take it no longer, she began searching desperately for support and solace. A good friend told her about Rebbetzin Flora Simchoni–Freilich, who healed broken hearts.

Flora was the right person at the right time. She did not promise to solve the problem overnight. On the contrary, she announced in advance that the process would be long, because it was "something very deep that comes from destructive energies powerful enough to destroy a city."

"That bad?" Devorah was horrified.

"Yes." Flora raised her eyes from the sediment of Turkish coffee that had collected at the bottom of the cup. "I see a broken halo at the rim of the cup, which tells me that you are deeply wounded. You are simply crushed."

"That's true," Devorah confirmed. Finally there was someone who understood her pain.

The reader focused her gaze on the wet brown grounds. "I see here an abnormal flow of negative energy, like a bomb. Do you see it, too?" She pointed to the sediment, which was higher on one side than on the other.

"Do I see it?" stuttered Devorah. She tried unsuccessfully to see the flow of negative energy, but who was a simple woman like her to argue with an authorized reader who conducted ongoing dialogues with the heavenly hosts?

Flora turned the cup over and let the muddy sediment drip slowly onto the saucer. What an industrious housewife hurried to wash down the drain turned out to be a gold mine of information.

Flora's eyes flashed in horror as they examined the drops dripping onto the white porcelain saucer. She let out a choked cry.

"What do you see?" asked Devorah, terrified.

Here Flora proved that her powers were real. "I see a black stain on your family history. You have an enemy who knows about the episode and uses every opportunity to ruin things for you."

"You're right," said Devorah. "That's exactly what happens!" She burst into tears, thereby disproving the iceberg theories regarding her. There are people who have learned to suppress their feelings and people whose reason is more active than their emotions, but no human being is without feelings altogether.

Flora stared at the brown coffee grounds. For a second, Devorah thought she looked like a gypsy fixing her eyes on a crystal ball.

Devorah brushed the heretical thought away instantly. Heaven forbid! Flora was no trickster, or even worse, someone using the forces of impurity. She was a proper Rebbetzin who used a variety of methods to help people in distress.

Suddenly Flora laughed. "Do you know why I'm laughing?" she asked Devorah rhetorically. Without waiting for an answer, she said, "I'm happy for you, because in the end you will be happy. All this is only a temporary obstruction. I see all the negative flow stopping. Look!" The brown drops had ceased flowing from the upside-down cup. "You will yet be happy. You will bring all your children to the *chupah*. Go find a good photographer for the wedding of your eldest daughter."

"Amen," said Devorah. How she yearned for it! Flora knew how to put her finger on her weak point and release the ache in her heart. The dam broke, and all the stored-up pain was washed away in a flood of tears.

A fleeting thought crossed her mind. *I would have paid a psychiatrist a fortune, too. So what if I give the money instead to a distinguished Rebbetzin?*

From then on, Devorah visited Flora's basement every Thursday. True, Chedvi still had not become engaged, and from time to time another dream got smashed against the rocks of harsh reality. But Devorah's pain was eased. No longer was she alone in the battle. Flora was her Wailing Wall, her personal psychiatrist who always lent an attentive ear and words of comfort in time of distress. After examining the wicks left from Shabbos evening and the mint herbs that grew in an earthenware flowerpot on her windowsill, Flora soothed Devorah and assured her that the negative flow was weakening. The enemy was losing its power, and good news was on its way.

Occasionally Devorah would ask herself whether she had fallen prey to a charlatan's enticement. But she was no longer able to break away, and not only because of the moments of comfort and encouragement that Flora so generously granted her. Devorah was a closed type who ate herself up inside, beneath a calm exterior. If not for Flora, the pain would have collected inside Devorah's heart until it burst or she developed a stress-related illness. Thanks to the wick reader, she was able to remain serene and calm in the face of her four unmarried daughters who were growing older by the day. And after a year of weekly visits, Flora even gave Devorah a special reduced fee.

In all the years of her marriage, visiting Flora's basement was the only thing that Devorah, devoted wife that she was, had ever done without her husband's full knowledge and consent. He knew only that she went to a Rebbetzin for emotional support and made donations to the Rebbetzin's charity fund. A vague inner feeling warned Devorah that if Elitzafan had the full picture, he would disapprove, so she was compelled to conceal the truth from him. She was that desperate.

⊱⊰

It was late at night when Elitzafan knocked at the door of Rabbi Yekusiel Cohen, one of Jerusalem's greatest scholars. Rabbi Cohen was expecting him; his assistant had scheduled the visit.

In the past, Elitzafan had been a regular visitor here. After he himself began serving the public, time constraints made his visits less frequent. Now, though, he felt the same desperation that had driven Devorah to Flora's basement. If the present suggestion were to fall through, he was sure his heart would collapse under the strain.

The outdated furniture, the old *sefarim,* and the serene atmosphere were all familiar to him. Yet each time he came, the simplicity of the apartment amazed Elitzafan anew.

Rabbi Cohen had been poring over some heavy volumes on his table. At the sight of Elitzafan, his face lit up. He extended a warm hand and shook his guest's hand heartily. "How are you, my dear student?" he inquired.

Elitzafan answered: "Blessed is Hashem each and every day."

"And what brings you to me?" asked Rabbi Cohen.

The chair creaked as Elitzafan sat down on it. "I am in great distress," he said with uncharacteristic openness. "I have four daughters of marriageable age. The oldest, Chedvi, is twenty-five."

"What is their problem?"

"Me," said Elitzafan, shocking the old rabbi. "Some unknown party knows about my past and uses that knowledge to ruin every *shidduch* suggested before it takes off. For six years *shidduchim* have been suggested for Chedvi, and not once did the other side get back to us. I'm about to collapse. I can't take it anymore."

Rabbi Cohen patted his visitor's hand affectionately. "Elitzafan, do not worry. Salvation is near." He leaned his high forehead on his fist and thought a while. When he broke his silence, his voice was clear and alert. "That party may be seeking revenge for some reason. But that is irrelevant. Your daughter's time has simply not yet come. When it does, no power in the world will be able to ruin the *shidduch*. They can ask the whole neighborhood, the whole city, even the whole country — but they will skip that party. It will be as if he does not exist."

Elitzafan returned home with a soothed heart. After Rabbi Cohen's few words, he fully believed that salvation was near.

The image of peeling layers stayed with Daniel all night. Underneath the lonely old man of little means whom Daniel had known, he had recently discovered a wealthy philanthropist who modestly hid all traces of his donations in the bottom of old cartons. But all of this was dwarfed by the new layer that Daniel uncovered in the yellowing pages ripped out of a children's notebook. As Daniel read page after page, he felt as if his heart were about to break.

Elul 5736

To my precious only son, whom I cherish with all my heart,

The High Holy Days are approaching, and this year I feel that they are really days of awe. I don't believe this is happening to me. I still can't grasp that I fell from the greatest heights to the lowest depths.

I could overcome everything, if only I knew that my family were with me, standing at my side in this difficult hour. But to my sorrow, my only son has no faith in his father. I am trying to accept the will of Heaven.

Tell Ima that I send her regards and wish her a kesivah vechasimah tovah.

Abba

Daniel turned to the next letter.

Isru Chag Sukkos 5737

My dearest Elitzafan,

I write with tears, not with ink.

Spending the joyous festival of Succos in prison was extremely painful. I ask myself a hundred times a day what sin I committed to deserve such terrible punishment.

I know you are ashamed of me. You don't believe my claim that I am innocent. I can absorb every blow except for that.

Elitzafan, where is your gratitude? I'm sorry to have to remind you, but as the Mesillas Yesharim writes, some things are so obvious that there is no need to speak about them — yet precisely because of this, they are forgotten.

Do you remember being the most coddled child in the neighborhood? You wore the finest clothes and played with toys that children in Rechaviah could only dream of. Your bar mitzvah reception in the Kings' Hotel was the most splendid affair of 5726. It was attended by all the big shots of Israel, of whom your father was one.

I lost my status not because of any crime I committed, but because a single person, assisted by a corrupt system, framed me.

I promise you that I am innocent! It is bad enough that your mother lost faith in me and left me, but my heart aches a hundred times more because you, my only child, followed her.

You can take your living father out of Gehinnom without the trouble of eleven months of Kaddish. Just write me three words: "I believe you" — and you will give me the strength to deal with all my suffering.

Just three words. For you it's nothing; for me, it's everything.

Your father, who loves you despite everything,

Avraham Zeidel Portman

After reading the two letters in Zeidel's apartment, Daniel quietly went home to bed and drew the quilt up over his eyes so that dawn's first rays would not disturb his sleep. The thoughts spun around in his head.

Tonight, another mask had fallen from Zeidel's face. How many more masks were there?

Zeidel had not been alone in the world after all. Those who had always said he had a family were right; he had an ex-wife and an only son, Elitzafan.

Zeidel had been a member in good standing of the top echelons forty years earlier. Something happened that had taken him down in one shot. What was it?

The thoughts whirled through Daniel's head, making him pleasantly dizzy until his eyes closed and he fell asleep.

When Daniel woke up that morning, the apartment was bathed in silence. He was alone. Peninah had quietly dressed and fed the children and had sent them off to school. Evidently she understood that he had been up all night.

As he washed his hands, the name "Elitzafan Portman" suddenly appeared before him as if on a giant poster.

There was such a person. If in 5726 he had been thirteen, now he was in his late fifties. Interesting who the man was, Zeidel's only son. His heir. *Here I am fighting with Yoel Tzadok over Zeidel's will, when Zeidel has a legal heir to whom his entire estate will be transferred.*

Daniel dressed hastily.

If Zeidel had a son, how did Yoel Tzadok enter into the picture?

By mistake Daniel put salt instead of sugar into his coffee. He dumped it all into the sink and went about making a new cupful.

When he left home, it was too late to *daven* locally. He took a taxi to the bustling *shtiblach* of Zichron Moshe, where one can always catch a *minyan*. He mustered supreme effort to concentrate on the prayers, but the perpetual tumult of the big synagogue, with hundreds of men shoving in, did not help the storm raging in his head.

As he left the synagogue an hour later, he passed a man with a graying beard, refined face, and alert eyes. For a second, Daniel's eyes met his.

Of course Daniel recognized him immediately. Who didn't know the brilliant Elitzafan Mindelman? Twice Daniel had needed his sage advice.

An unanswered riddle had always bothered Daniel whenever he saw Mr. Mindelman's face. It somehow looked familiar to him. Now he knew why. It bore a decided resemblance to Zeidel.

The eyes were the same, and so was the shape of the unusually long, narrow face. Only the lips and the nose were different. Could Mr. Mindelman be Zeidel's only son, Elitzafan? The name Elitzafan was certainly rare. But if it was the same Elitzafan, why wasn't his last name Portman?

When Daniel finally arrived at Rabbi Segel's *daf yomi shiur,* the words of the Gemara swam in front of his eyes. But when he began his daily work as a *mashgiach* in the kitchen of the Munbaz Hotel, his mind instantly became focused.

As soon as Daniel entered his kingdom, he forgot about the outside world; nothing existed for him except for his work. He focused exclusively on what was going on behind the two swinging doors with the round windows that denied the kitchen privacy and dampened any desire to mix a nonkosher ingredient into the food. He separated *terumos uma'asros,* sifted flour, helped check large quantities of rice, and kept a careful eye on anything placed in the huge pots.

If someone were to eat nonkosher food, Heaven forbid, the guilt would weigh heavily on Daniel's conscience for the rest of his life. He, and his faithful assistant were directly responsible for the *kashrus* of the kitchen, with its staff of chefs and their helpers. The chefs knew that he was liable to be anywhere at any given moment. They did not appreciate his strict standards, but they respected him sincerely for his unswerving loyalty to Halachah.

Five minutes after Daniel left the Munbaz Hotel, though, the questions returned to haunt him. He had to find out once and for all whether Elitzafan Portman, Zeidel's son, was actually Elitzafan Mindelman.

That evening, Daniel leafed through the phone book and dialed. He had to know the truth. The answer was worth half a million dollars at the very least.

A girl's voice answered. "Is this Mr. Mindelman's house?" he asked hesitantly.

"Yes."

"May I speak to him for a minute?"

"Who wants him?"

"A Jew." He would gladly have identified himself, but in case it were a mistake, it would be better for him to remain anonymous.

The girl did not persist. "Abba, it's for you."

"Hello," said a pleasant voice.

Daniel almost hung up. Why was he doing such a foolish thing? He overcame his embarrassment and asked, "Am I speaking with Mr. Elitzafan Mindelman?"

"Yes, how can I help you?"

For a few seconds Daniel was silent. Then he said, "Umm, I had a neighbor by the name of Avraham Zeidel Portman, and I wanted to ask…."

"What?" Elitzafan was shocked.

"That is, did you know him?" he heard himself ask.

Elitzafan had not yet recovered. Confusion was evident in his voice. "I didn't understand you."

"I only asked if you knew him."

The initial shock passed. "Who are you?" demanded Elitzafan angrily.

"It doesn't matter," Daniel answered hastily. "I'm sorry if I've offended you. I would like to come explain myself in person."

"Don't bother," Elitzafan said coldly.

Daniel hung up, shaken. He had made a fine mess of things. Yet it was not for nothing. Judging by Elitzafan's strong reaction, his guess had been right on target.

11

After Shabbos, when dirty dishes and pots rested on the kitchen counters waiting to be washed, and the dining room chairs perched upside down on the table so that the stone floor could be washed, the doorbell rang in the Langer home. The door was opened, and the redheaded *shadchan* Emanuel Klopstein strode right into the dining room. "*Gute voch!*" he boomed cheerfully. "Nothing to be embarrassed about, Mrs. Langer. The mess in my house is worse."

He examined the pictures on the wall through the legs of the chairs. "Oh, what a nice painting of Rav Schach," he exclaimed with feigned enthusiasm. "And the picture of this distinguished rabbi — who is it?"

"That's my father," answered Mr. Langer. "That's not a painting. It's a photograph taken at my wedding."

"At your wedding?" Emanuel's enthusiasm increased. "Weddings are what's brought me here." His voice dropped to a hoarse whisper. Glancing at the son, he looked around cautiously and asked, "Is it possible to speak?"

Matti Langer straightened out his yarmulka and went with his parents into the girls' room, the only room that was in order at that hour. Emanuel smoothed the red tie on his round stomach, loosened the knot slightly, and announced dramatically, "I have a fantastic *shidduch* for you. Something totally out of the ordinary. You haven't heard a suggestion like this from any *shadchan*."

Matti mustered his self-control to keep from laughing. Mr. Langer smiled patiently and said, "Who is it, if I may ask?"

"Have you heard of Elitzafan Mindelman?"

"Of course," said Mr. Langer. "Who hasn't?"

"He has a daughter, Chedvi. Her sterling lineage and upbringing shine in her. A wonderful girl, age twenty-three" — every *shadchan* takes two years off a girl's age — "with all the qualities anyone could possibly want, and not a single fault. Make your inquiries, and get back to me within a few days. I have no doubt that your answer will be positive. There's no one like her in the world!"

Matti could no longer restrain herself. "In the whole world? Are you sure?"

Emanuel surveyed him with wily eyes. "I like you, Matti. You have a good sense of humor."

Taking advantage of the newly created rapport, Emanuel dragged Matti into the topsy-turvy dining room and whispered a warning into his ears. "Someone is going to try to ruin the *shidduch*. Don't get upset if you hear strange things."

The boy had a sharp mind. "Why, do they have enemies?" he said calmly. "Well, who doesn't? Especially a public figure like Mr. Mindelman!"

Emanuel heaved a sigh of relief. Here was a fine fellow, with his head screwed on straight. Perhaps this time the *shidduch* would move forward. "Yes, you're right on target. Apparently he has one or two enemies. People tend to be influenced by *lashon hara,* especially in such a delicate, sensitive area as *shidduchim.*"

❦

Evening *seder* session in the *mesivta* would end in ten minutes, and many of the boys had already left their seats. They quickly returned the large volumes to their places in the bookshelves, which appeared to sink under the load. Fourteen-year-old Gadi Alishvili began looking toward the clock. Abba and Ima were surely waiting at home eager to hear how the day had gone for their oldest son, who had begun *mesivta* just a few months earlier. It was Thursday, Ima's baking day. Would there be chocolate-chip cookies or vanilla? Yeast cakes filled with jelly, or spice cake? Saliva filled his mouth at the very thought.

"Patience, Gadi," said his *chavrusah* and private tutor, Matti Langer. "Let's just finish reading this part of the *Ritva* together. When you see the explanation inside the Gemara, you'll understand the *shiur* much better."

Gadi made the effort, concentrated, and understood. A smile of satisfaction spread across his face. The pleasure of homemade cookies shrank to insignificance beside the pleasure of new understanding of the text.

After leaving the *beis midrash*, Matti crossed the street and headed for the public telephone on the far corner. He was curious about what was happening with the *shidduch*.

"What's doing, Ima?" Matti's voice resounded with joy of life.

"Everything is fine, *baruch Hashem*," she answered warmly.

"Did you manage to find out anything?"

"Plenty! You won't believe what terrific reports we received about the Mindelman family, and especially about the girl herself. It looks good to us."

"Wonderful!" he exclaimed happily. "Have you given the *shadchan* an answer?"

"I was just talking it over with Abba. We were discussing whether to give the go-ahead or continue inquiring."

In the background, Matti could hear his father's measured tones. "I think that we have sufficient information for the meantime. If things progress and become serious, we'll conduct a broader investigation."

Five minutes after Matti hung up, Mrs. Langer called Emanuel's cell phone and told them they were ready to proceed."

The *shadchan's* head spun. He almost opened a bottle of Chivas Regal in honor of the good news. Unbelievable! This was the first time someone was giving a positive answer to the Mindelmans!

Hands trembling, he dialed the number. Devorah picked up the receiver.

"I have good news today!" proclaimed Emanuel triumphantly. "The boy's side is ready to proceed."

"What?" Devorah almost fell off her chair.

"Just what you heard," Emanuel hooted with unrestrained joy. "I would like to get the *shidduch* off the ground as quickly as possible — of course, according to all the normal procedures. You'll be hearing from me very soon."

Tears flooded Devorah's cheeks. This was a historic event. For the first time in six years they had passed the inquiry stage safely. Why, just a few days ago Rebbetzin Simchoni–Freilich had promised that good news was on the way, and already her promise had been fulfilled. Devorah would call to give her the news, as she always did. But husbands come first.

Elitzafan had successfully reconciled two neighbors who, just an hour before, had been at each other's throats, when the phone rang in his study. Usually Elitzafan did not answer phone calls while he was meeting with people, but this time he glanced at the call-identification screen and recognized Devorah's cell number.

"Where are you?" he asked.

"I'm in the kitchen, but I couldn't wait another minute. Elitzafan, the Langers are ready to proceed," she whispered. "Do you believe it? They made inquiries, and their answer is positive."

"Praise Hashem, for He is good," Elitzafan replied with a trembling voice. Goose bumps covered his back. Only two days earlier, he had visited the old rabbi, and already his blessing had been fulfilled!

Elitzafan's joy was contagious; the two neighbors left smiling and pleased. Then he went to the kitchen. While eating a light supper, he asked what exactly Emanuel had said. He had not heard so pleasant a background melody in a long time.

An atmosphere of delicate euphoria permeated the Mindelman home. Their hearts fluttered between hope and fear. *Let it not be ruined! Let everything go well!*

On Friday, Emanuel called the Langers and hesitantly asked what was next. Mr. Langer said he would like to meet the Mindelmans and discuss the financial arrangements.

Emanuel hurried to bring the answer to the modest apartment in Beis Yisrael. Inside, a feeling of imminent salvation swept the entire Mindelman family. Happy, healthy peals of laughter echoed through the house for the first time in years. When Menashe and Yehoshua called from yeshivah to wish their parents a good Shabbos, Devorah told them excitedly that soon there would be good news from Chedvi, but it was to be kept quiet, for "blessing lies only in what is hidden from the eye."

Yehoshua almost broke into a dance. How difficult it was to keep his sweet secret! But Menashe was more reserved and viewed everything in the light of reason. He thought about what he had heard and decided it was too early to rejoice. Six years filled with disappointments do not end instantly as though with a magic wand. Someone would surely try to sabotage this *shidduch*, too. On Shabbos afternoon he said the entire Book of *Tehillim* for his sister.

Little did he know how close he was to the truth.

◦◦◦◦◦◦

Mr. Langer and Matti were eating *melaveh malkah* together when the phone rang. Matti picked it up.

"Matti Langer?" asked an unknown voice.

"Correct."

"You don't know me, but you can call me Tuvyah. Was a girl named Chedvi Mindelman suggested to you?"

Matti wanted to slam the receiver down. He surmised the continuation of the phone call. But the caller surprised him by saying, "It's a wonderful suggestion. Rav Mindelman is a renowned individual, and his daughter Chedvi is full of virtues."

The caller spoke as warmly as a *shadchan*. Then, without warning, his voice turned cold and venomous. "I wanted to add one more point: There is a dark secret tied to this family. Please take it into consideration, and don't say I didn't warn you."

The conversation ended.

Matti turned white. The words "dark secret" are a powerful weapon that no mortal can withstand. They stimulate the imagination to conjure up anything from a hereditary mental illness of the *chasan's* mother to the baptism of the *kallah's* family a century ago. They are certainly enough to close down any *shidduch* office.

"What did they tell you?" asked Mr. Langer, putting down his fork as Matti slowly replaced the phone receiver. The color of Matti's face frightened him.

Matti repeated the conversation.

"We'll have to make a thorough investigation," said Mr. Langer. "Actually, I had been wondering why such a special girl isn't married yet."

"Let's put things in perspective," said Matti. "It's nothing but an anonymous phone call. Why should it carry weight?"

"Nevertheless," said Langer, "we'd better investigate further."

A wearying round of phone calls led him to several other families for whom the *shidduch* had been suggested. All of them repeated the same sentence. "We heard there's a stain on the family."

At midnight, Mr. Langer concluded sadly, "We must inform the *shadchan* that we are not continuing."

Matti protested. "Emanuel warned me from the beginning that someone would make trouble."

"Matti," said Mr. Langer, "you're innocent and inexperienced. Your father has seen more of the world than you have. Apparently there is something to all the talk; where there's smoke, there's fire. That wily Emanuel knew that you would hear negative information, and he warned you in advance in order to neutralize the influence. Take my advice, and don't stick a healthy head into a sickbed."

Matti gave in. The combination of "a healthy head in a sickbed" with "dark secret" was fatal. The Mindelmans might as well have been demons with tails and horns.

Sunday evening, Emanuel called to find out when the Langers wanted to meet the Mindelmans to discuss financial arrangements. Mr. Langer stammered that on Monday evening he had a wedding, on Tuesday he attended a *shiur* that he could not possibly miss, on Wednesday his neighbor was making a bar mitzvah, and on Thursday he always helped his wife prepare for Shabbos.

In his long career as a *shadchan*, Emanuel had heard enough evasive answers to fill a book. Had he wished, he could have supplied the stammering Mr. Langer with a long list of more elegant and clever excuses, from the classic, "It's not suitable" to, "Something new came up," which is more refined, and even to, "Our kabbalist/rabbi/rebbe/grandfather/neighbor advised against."

It's good that he didn't continue; he might have said that next Motza'ei Shabbos he would have to attend a funeral, thought Emanuel gloomily as he put down the phone. So that was that. Even this spark of hope had been extinguished. How would he break the news to the Mindelmans?

He decided to do nothing. He would not call; in fact, he would even disconnect his phone. He was not capable of shoving the bitter pill down the Mindelmans' throats. They would understand themselves what had happened. Disappointment had been their companion for six years now. They were used to silent phones.

⌘

That was a serious mistake. A veteran *shadchan* should know how to face a problem head-on and not hide when one side backs off. Emanuel's inability to look the Mindelmans straight in the eyes and tell them the truth made matters even worse. At first they naively thought there was a technical delay, but when Emanuel's cell phone was never on and his family never knew when he would return, a red light went on in Elitzafan's head.

"I think they've ruined it again," he said to Devorah grimly. "I don't like Emanuel's silence."

Just then Nachum'ke came home from *mesivta.* He hung up his jacket on a hanger and said casually, "Abba, I met Emanuel in the street just now. When he saw me, he turned his eyes away. He suddenly remembered an important call and took out his wallet instead of his cell phone. You should have seen him speaking into his wallet. 'Where are you?' he said. 'You're waiting for me right now? I'll be over immediately.' And he ran off as if he had seen a monster."

Nachum'ke's colorful story filled in the missing pieces of the puzzle. Elitzafan's fears had not been groundless. The *shadchan* really had cut off contact, and the reason was obvious.

From her room, Tirtzah heard the conversation. Chedvi didn't hear it. She was babysitting for the children of her old classmate Blumi. The moments of laughter and games with the little ones made Chedvi forget her own troubles.

Chedvi answered the phone with a content, gurgling baby in her arms. "Shalom, Tirtzah. What's new?" Even over the phone you could heard the giant smile that came from a happy heart.

A strange silence hung over the other side of the line. And then, "Chedvi, I have to tell you."

"Tell me what?" Chedvi wiped some pureed squash off the baby's plump cheeks.

Tirtzah said quickly, "It seems that this new suggestion, too, has — has gone the way of all the others."

"No!" The baby fastened his eyes on his babysitter's face, from which the smile had vanished. He sensed a change in the atmosphere and stopped gurgling.

"I'm serious, Chedvi," said Tirtzah, brokenhearted. "What will be? Why are people so evil?"

"I don't believe it, Tirtzah," said Chedvi, trying to stay calm. "I'm sure everything will be all right."

But her heart felt as if it was squeezed by a vise. She put the baby down in the crib and sank weakly into a chair.

Her glance swept the children's room: the crib, Blumi's three little children sleeping peacefully on pull-out beds that converted into a sofa every morning, the fluorescent light, the toy shelves, the colorful pictures on the walls. Everything here was bright; only inside her heart, the world was dark gray. All her hidden hopes, aspirations, rosy dreams, the moments of happiness for which she had waited days and nights, the glowing future that was so close she could feel it — all had vanished like quicksilver because of a bad heart and a wagging tongue. Suddenly a picture of herself as she would look fifty years from now flashed through her mind: a lonely, childless old maid with white hair, walking slowly down the street, leaning on a walker.

One big, round teardrop made its way out of the corner of her eye and flowed down her face, and after that another and another. Chedvi put her head down to hide her weakness from the contented baby, but her shaking shoulders gave her away.

Elitzafan, returning from *Shacharis,* ran up the stairs just as Chedvi came racing down on her way to work. "Good morning, Chedvi," he said warmly, trying to sweeten the bitterness of the previous evening. "Did you eat breakfast?"

"No," she answered frankly. Her eyes were a bit red, either from lack of sleep or from crying. Tirtzah's call had dashed her hopes. Six years had passed since her parents first decided that she was ready to build a Jewish home. During the first two years, she had been relieved whenever a suggested *shidduch* fell through. She felt unprepared for the responsibility of marriage, but did not dare oppose her parents.

Even then, a vague worry had gnawed at her. The consistent pattern of *shidduchim* dying in the inquiry stage was alarming. She hoped that when she was ready for marriage, the mysterious matter would somehow be set right.

Nothing had ever been set right. For the past four years, every time a *shidduch* was suggested, she waited fearfully, hoping that the anonymous slanderer would not strike.

But he always did.

❧

Felix Goldmark was not only Elitzafan's downstairs neighbor but also his good friend. The religious scientist from Scandinavia had fallen in love with Jerusalem and settled there despite the long daily commute to his job in Ashdod. Beneath Felix's dark blue beret, a tall, broad forehead gave him the appearance of a serious intellectual. His wise blue eyes and silver beard lent him dignity, and his permanent smile marked him as a warm, friendly person, although he tended to be quiet. At the same time, he had a remarkable ability to remain cool and calm under the most trying circumstances.

Felix was rarely home, and when he was, he spent most of the time facing a computer screen covered with complicated diagrams and unintelligible computations, as classical music streamed through his earphones.

Felix was a conversationalist with perfect European manners. He would hear the next person out to the end without interrupting. Only after the other had not one word left would Felix open his own mouth — and then insightful comments would emerge, the fruits of a deep thinker's analytical abilities and clear perception.

Elitzafan had befriended Felix a decade earlier, a short time after the Goldmarks moved in. During the month that the Goldmarks were waiting for their phone line to be installed, they often used the phone of their obliging neighbors on the second floor.

Elitzafan had made the acquaintance of the busy scientist the first time he had come to use the Mindelmans' phone. Felix had finished his phone conversation and was arguing with Devorah that the accepted payment was two shekels per conversation, rather than one shekel as she claimed. In the end, he acceded to her, placed one shekel on the table, and went to the door. Just then the last visitor seeking Elitzafan's help left, and Elitzafan came out of his study.

"Are you our new neighbor?" Elitzafan asked him.

"I am indeed," the man with the blue beret answered with a quiet, shy smile and a slight accent. Elitzafan extended his hand in welcome and engaged him in a polite conversation that unexpectedly took off and lasted late into the night, while the shekel that Devorah had refused danced between Felix's bony fingers.

Over the years, a deep emotional bond developed between the two neighbors. Elitzafan tested Felix's discretion by revealing some unimportant personal information that he knew would get back to him if Felix babbled.

Felix was found to be an unparalleled guardian of secrets. His lips were sealed. Elitzafan tested him a few more times and decided conclusively that his neighbor could be trusted.

From then on, many personal confessions flowed into the scientist's ears. Felix would listen in silence. Only after being convinced that Elitzafan had nothing more to add would he cautiously offer Elitzafan sagacious advice.

Today, Felix was up-to-date in Chedvi's *shidduchim* matters. Elitzafan could see how much it pained him by the slight contortion of distress on Felix's face upon hearing how another intriguing suggestion had fallen through.

❧

After breakfast, Elitzafan was on his way out when he passed the Goldmarks' door. Surprisingly, it was wide open, revealing keys, money, and cards strewn over the dining room table. Felix had shaken out the contents of his wallet, and now he bent over the table, carefully searching through the mess.

"Good morning, Felix," Elitzafan called out, nodding his head as he passed. "Is something wrong?"

"I lost my personal magnetic card," said Felix. "It unlocks the door of my office. Until I find it, there's no point in going to Ashdod. Guess I'm on vacation until they make me a new card. Come in and sit down."

Elitzafan found himself seated in the Goldmarks' kitchen, sipping grapefruit juice and unburdening his aching heart. The latest *shidduch* fiasco warranted a detailed analysis. Then came an account of the upsetting phone call from some prying person two weeks earlier, who had uncovered his connection with Avraham Zeidel Portman.

Felix had good control over his facial muscles, but his frequent blinking revealed that the speaker's troubles touched his heart. Elitzafan finished and waited to hear some wise, comforting words.

Felix disappointed him by saying, "I think you're being foolish."

No one else would have dared say such a thing to Elitzafan — which was precisely why he needed Felix.

"Why?" asked Elitzafan.

"By showing that it frightened you, you've played into his hands. By the way, he might be the *shidduch* saboteur. Do you have his phone number?"

"No. He blocked it."

Felix took a small piece of paper and wrote a few lines in neat handwriting. Elitzafan read from the side:

"I would like to be involved in the next *shidduch* suggestion. Perhaps I can help find the saboteur.

"If that man calls again, don't get angry. Be nice to him."

"Do you understand?" Felix asked, handing the note to Elitzafan. "When you tell the person not to bother coming, you ruin your chance of finding out who is torpedoing your *shidduchim*. I'm sure he will call again. When he does, invite him graciously for a visit."

Elitzafan gnashed his teeth. "How can I be nice to such a person?"

Felix gave him a penetrating glance. "If you're concerned about your daughters' future, you *must* be nice to him."

❧

Felix must have been blessed with telepathic powers.

Ever since his unfortunate phone conversation with Elitzafan, Daniel Klein could not rest. He felt he had done a terrible injustice by upsetting him merely to satisfy his own curiosity. After two weeks of deliberating, he mustered his courage and called back, this time without blocking his own phone number.

He tried hard to sound pleasant. "Is this the Mindelman family?"

"Yes," answered a youthful voice.

"May I speak to your father?" Even to his own ears, he sounded nauseatingly saccharine.

Elitzafan took the receiver. "Yes?"

"I spoke to you two weeks ago," stammered Daniel, "regarding my neighbor Avraham Zeidel Portman."

"Correct." Suspicion and tension filled the receiver. Elitzafan peered at the call identification screen. The number appeared!

"I think I didn't explain myself. I would like to come over and speak to you directly."

Remembering Felix's advice, Elitzafan forced himself to say in a friendly tone, "When would you like to come?"

"Is now a good time?"

Elitzafan was tired, but he was determined to draw his prey into the trap. "How much time will it take you to get here?"

"I'm taking a taxi. I'll be at your house in twenty minutes."

❧

Peninah was watching as Daniel unexpectedly donned his hat and jacket. "Where are you going?" she asked.

"I have an appointment with Elitzafan Mindelman," he said hurriedly and opened the door.

"Are you going to suggest a *shidduch* to him?"

"What are you talking about?"

Peninah accompanied Daniel out to the street. While he waited for the taxi, she told him that the Mindelmans had a twenty-five-year old daughter who was still single despite the father's excellent reputation and the girl's own wonderful qualities. And as if that were not enough of a problem, she had three sisters stuck in line behind her.

The taxi arrived. As he rode, he thought about what Peninah had said. Suddenly an idea flashed through his head. Shmuli, the twenty-eight-year-old son of his neighbors the Patankins, was a yeshivah student of rare quality who had very high standards for a *shidduch*. Surely Elitzafan's daughter met those standards. As a gesture of appeasement, Daniel would suggest Shmuli to Elitzafan. Perhaps Heaven had chosen him to be a good messenger.

The taxi let Daniel off in a narrow alley in Beis Yisrael. Upstairs, Elitzafan was waiting for him. The *posek* was sitting at the dining room table, ostensibly looking over some important faxes. Actually, he was grappling with the strong feelings of curiosity, bitterness, and suspicion that welled up inside him. At the same time, a cool, level-headed part of him asked, "On what basis did I decide that he is the *shidduch* saboteur? First let's hear what he has to say."

The tense lines of his face revealed Daniel's trepidation as he entered the Mindelmans' living room. His teeth gnawed mercilessly on his lower lip, and his knees trembled slightly.

Elitzafan, rising to greet him, forced himself to extend a welcoming hand rather than administer a stinging slap. "Sit down, please. What can I offer you?"

"Nothing, thank you. I ate before I came."

"Perhaps a cup of coffee?"

"No, please don't go to any trouble. All I want is a few minutes to explain myself."

Elitzafan pushed aside the pile of faxes and gave Daniel a piercing look. "Yes, I'm listening."

Daniel cringed before the anger in Elitzafan's eyes. It seemed altogether out of proportion with the few words he had said during that unfortunate phone call. He coughed and cleared his throat to buy time. Meanwhile an idea entered his head. First he would win his way into Elitzafan's good graces by suggesting the *shidduch*.

"I would like to suggest an excellent match for your eldest daughter Chedvah," Daniel announced.

"In order to suggest *shidduchim*," said Elitzafan in a hostile tone, "you must know the family background and not burst in like a bull in a china shop. There are enough *shadchanim* who make suggestions. You came about a different matter. Let's proceed to that." But even as he spoke, Elitzafan regretted the anger that he felt. *Who decided that this guest is really your enemy? Give him the benefit of the doubt!*

Daniel was defeated even before he began. *What bitterness! What torment!* Six years of anguish burned in Elitzafan's eyes, confirming what Peninah had said half an hour ago. Daniel rated the pain as ten on the scale of Job.

Daniel chose to become his own character witness. If Elitzafan was indeed Zeidel's son, he would surely be happy to hear what Daniel had to say: "During the past twenty years, I had the privilege of assisting my dear elderly neighbor Avraham Zeidel Portman. I took care of all his needs. Somehow it occurred to me that there might be a connection between you. His son was also called Elitzafan, a rare enough name. And your face resembles Zeidel's."

Elitzafan looked as if he had received an electric shock. His shoulders fell and he slumped over like a rag doll. His anger gave way to abject misery. His lips trembled. All his self-control could not hold back the tears, which began to flow down onto his gray beard.

"I beg you," he said, reaching out and grabbing the lapels of Daniel's jacket, "get out of my life! Have you come to destroy me? I'm going through Gehinnom in this world even without your help."

An astonished Daniel scrambled to his feet. He wanted to weep together with this anguished man, but realized that the best thing to do was to leave the house posthaste. He bolted down the steps, stumbling over his own feet.

What was the secret of this man, who had been revealed to him in a light that surely no stranger had ever seen?

There was only one way Daniel could think of to solve the mystery: to return to Zeidel's apartment and read some more documents.

⁂

Elitzafan was still in a stormy mood later that evening when he went to report to Felix. The scientist asked him to describe exactly what had happened. After Elitzafan finished, Felix gave his opinion.

"You are doing one foolish thing after another. A: You didn't even ask him his name. B: You exposed your weakness. C: You let him go without milking him for information about the *shidduch* he wants to suggest for Chedvi.

"Let him suggest the *shidduch*, and let's see, under laboratory conditions, how and at what stage the poisonous slander creeps in."

Elitzafan stared in astonishment at Felix, who continued to speak with level-headed coolness. "Call him back. Apologize for your behavior, and invite him back for another visit. This time I want to be present so that I can scrutinize him from close up. You have a rare opportunity to catch the criminal in the act. To give it up is simply irresponsible."

13

With a satisfied smile, Yaniv shoved the fax into his pocket. Asaf and his armaments gang were marching into the trap like blind horses. Now all he had to do was go to the supermarket on Rue de Poissonniers and show Moshiko the fax. Moshiko would get the business rolling, and within a few more days the two brothers Sharabi, one representing the seller, the other the buyer, would meet in a deserted park in an outlying suburb of Paris and negotiate an arms deal. If all went well, Asaf himself would come to the second meeting, and perhaps even the legendary boss himself. Some other unexpected agents would also come to this meeting — a few of Europe's best Mossad agents.

Easy as pie. Yet Yaniv suddenly thought of the man holding a raw egg, imagining how a chick would hatch from it, mature, and lay eggs — and while he was thinking, the egg fell from his hand and broke, shattering his dreams.

After this, strange feelings washed over Yaniv. He wondered why he felt so unsettled. Taking a five-minute walk to the supermarket is quite different from driving a tank into Gaza.

The long-forgotten image of his sixth-grade teacher suddenly floated to the surface of his mind. The only religious teacher in his public school had boldly tried to impart values drawn from Jewish tradition. His classroom wall had sported a poster that proclaimed, "With help from Above, you can cross the ocean; without it, you can't cross the street."

The poster was right! Only now did Yaniv see how true it was. Success seemed within easy reach, yet he had a premonition that he would not reach the supermarket.

He was almost ready to give up the idea of meeting Moshiko. But was the danger at home or outside? To go or not to go? He stood beside the door and tossed a coin. The lot fell on "To go." The danger, then, was lurking for him at home!

His heart pounded fiercely. The feeling of danger grew stronger from moment to moment until it was almost palpable. Yaniv had not experienced such fear since the time he had stopped a terrorist who was about to blow himself up.

For a moment, he held his breath. Then he surveyed his surroundings.

His gaze wandered over the faded pink draperies that the last tenant had left; the old sofa that served him as a bed; the wall, bare except for an impressionist landscape. Nothing had changed. *Mere fantasies,* he rebuked himself.

What he failed to check, though, was the fire escape.

When he tried to open the door, the key danced in his hands, as if it had an independent life. *Someone will think I'm drunk, or worse yet, drugged.* After a stubborn struggle, the door opened.

A shiver ran down his spine as he stepped into the dimly lit stairwell. He walked carefully, his back to the wall. Suddenly something fell on his head and showered his eyes with white particles. He looked up in fright.

The paint on the ceiling was peeling, that was all. Who would have imagined that Paris, the City of Lights, contained a section as run-down and neglected as Barbes!

Yaniv continued down the stairs. Then with quiet, agile steps, he flitted like a shadow through the corridor. It looked empty, but he had a feeling that an ambush had been prepared for him. He made a 180-degree turn while taking a high jump off the ground.

His sharp eyes noticed nothing unusual, yet the nervousness and fear did not leave him. He hid the fax behind a wastebasket and returned to the apartment to take his electric stun-gun and small pistol.

As soon as he opened the door, his blood froze in his veins. He wanted to escape, but it was too late.

Yaniv had visitors.

Two slim youths had broken into his apartment, entering through the window near the metal fire escape in the back of the building. The third, middle-aged and fat as a barrel, was still climbing up. All three looked typically Arab, though their moustaches were shaved. He fell into their hands like a ripe fruit.

A strong, muscular security guard like Yaniv did not submit easily. He resisted valiantly, delivering karate chops with his hands and kicks with his legs. But he was outnumbered. After a short battle, he lay sprawled on the floor with the fat Arab sitting on his stomach, while the other two pinned down his arms and legs.

The Arab sitting on him was apparently the head of the gang. He bent over Yaniv's face and scanned him with small black eyes. Yaniv noticed that the whites were covered with spidery red capillaries, and he detected the smell of alcohol beneath the strong mouthwash.

"Who are you?" asked the fat Arab in English. "For whom do you work?"

The pressure on Yaniv's chest and stomach made breathing difficult. "I won't say a word until you get off me," he said in perfect Arabic. "I'm not a chair."

"Who are you?" barked the fat man again, this time in Arabic.

"If you want an answer, get off me."

The attacker gave in and stood up. Yaniv breathed freely. "I am Jafar Hashemi, a purchasing agent for the Hezbullah."

"Liar!" hissed the fat one. "We work for the Hezbullah, and we haven't heard of you."

Yaniv looked at him with scorn. "Don't speak to me that way. What's your name? Who's in charge of you? My rank is undoubtedly higher than yours. I don't take my orders from either Hassan Nasrallah or Aziz Jibril."

The fat man's eyes narrowed as he stared at him. The grasp on Yaniv's hands and legs eased slightly and hurt less. "Then from whom do you take orders?"

Yaniv was prepared for this moment. "Tell me who you are!" he retorted. The victim's tough manner of speech conveyed authority that impressed his assailants.

"I am Abdul Ruzak, Abu Samir to you."

Yaniv's keen senses detected a slight difference in his tone of voice, which signified a changeover from victory to surrender. At that moment he knew his life had been saved. "Take my wallet out of my pocket," he told Abu Samir.

Abu Samir was cautious. "El Hindi," he ordered the fellow who had pinned Yaniv's hands to the floor, "take out his wallet."

They believe me, thought Yaniv.

El Hindi released his hands. Yaniv resisted the temptation to take advantage of the opportunity. The next battle would be fought not with physical strength but with cleverness.

The wallet was withdrawn. Three cheers for Moshiko, who had had the foresight to equip him with essential documents: an Iranian passport under the name of Jafar Hashemi; an airline ticket showing that he had arrived from Teheran last month and would fly back in ten days; and, most important of all, a letter from the Iranian Ministry of Defense authorizing Mr. Jafar Hashemi to purchase arms for the Hezbullah. The paper was signed by Dr. Ali Reza Bakhtiari, director of the purchasing department for the Iranian Ministry of Defense and a senior aide of Iranian President Mohammad Khatami.

Abu Samir read the letter carefully. He neither whistled in amazement nor expressed regret. He tried to reach one of his superiors by phone to confirm Jafar Hashemi's story, but reception was poor and each time he tried, the conversation was quickly cut off. After a number of unsuccessful attempts, he allowed Yaniv to sit on a chair.

Yaniv stretched his limbs. All his muscles ached as if he had been run over by a steamroller. He never knew that sitting in a chair could be so pleasant.

Abu Samir continued to play tough, but Yaniv saw through him. The Arab was afraid of him. "For the moment, we'll give you the benefit of the doubt. If it turns out that you really were sent here from Teheran, I will have to apologize. But if you are lying—" His cheeks stretched in a threatening grimace.

"We will check your story," he said suddenly. "Jamil, go down to the photo shop at the corner and make us copies of these documents."

Jamil, who had pinned down Yaniv's legs, dispatched his errand with alacrity and returned with three copies of each document. Abu Samir was pleased with the quality.

"Jamil and I are leaving," he said. "El Hindi will stay to watch you until we finish checking your papers. If all is in order, you will be released — but you will not be rid of us. You will not recognize us, but we will always be in back of you, watching you and listening to every word.

"And the main thing is: you are drafted for our holy cause. You know why we are here, and from today, you will work together with us."

He returned the original documents to Yaniv and left with Jamil. El Hindi stayed to guard Yaniv.

๛

Moshiko was worried. Two hours had passed since the brothers were to have met in the supermarket, and Yaniv had not yet arrived nor could he be reached by phone. There was only one thing to do.

As soon as Yaniv heard the key turn in his door, he coughed loudly to signal the visitor, "I'm not alone." Moshiko understood that something was amiss and immediately switched to emergency procedures.

"*Salaam*, Jafar!" he called as he walked in.

On the sofa, beneath the impressionist picture, Yaniv lay pale and shivering. One foot rested on the floor; the other made a small wastebasket dance so that the plastic wrappers inside rustled rhythmically.

"What happened to you, Jafar?" Moshiko asked in Arabic. He had never seen his younger brother in such bad shape.

Yaniv was as fearless as he was brave and strong. But the prolonged acting had sapped his energy, and the threat of being tailed from now on did not aid his recovery.

"What's wrong with resting? Why hurry? Speed is from the devil," said Yaniv, citing the Arab outlook on life. He winked at Moshiko, then glanced at a corner of the room, where El Hindi was sitting and watching them.

Moshiko noticed the bulge of a pistol at the Arab's waist. It was all too clear: Yaniv was a captive. Only Moshiko could release him, and that would take shrewdness and tact.

He extended a hand to the guard. "Pleased to meet you," he said. "The name is Monir Abu Marwan. I work together with Jafar. Are you his guest?"

"Not exactly," replied El Hindi frankly. "I'm guarding him until we check his identity."

"I don't know whether Jafar had the brains to tell you the whole story. Did he tell you about the large missile factory that we work for? Shihav 3 is our project."

Moshiko, who was well prepared, spewed forth detail after detail without giving El Hindi a second to stop and think. As he spoke, he kept his face turned toward the window to prevent El Hindi from noticing the family resemblance.

El Hindi's astonished eyes darted between Moshiko and Yaniv. What he heard definitely impressed him. He phoned Abu Samir and spoke to him enthusiastically.

Abu Samir was convinced. He finally managed to make contact with someone who promised to run a check on the name Jafar Hashemi. For Abu Samir, the weak promise was the ladder he needed to climb down the tall tree. He directed El Hindi to leave Yaniv's apartment, after warning Yaniv again that he would be under continuous surveillance.

When the two brothers were left alone, Yaniv laughed in relief and embraced Moshiko. "You saved me," he whispered.

"I? What did I do?" asked Moshiko. "The miracle was that El Hindi believed me. Imagine what would have happened otherwise!"

Yaniv updated Moshiko and concluded, "I have two choices. The easy way out is to return to Israel. Believe me, guarding Tel Aviv's Central Bus Station from suicide terrorists scares me less than being tailed by the Hezbullah here in Paris. In a few hours, they will discover that there is no such person as Jafar Hashemi, and I will have to dig myself a grave."

"There *is* a person named Jafar Hashemi," said Moshiko with an amused smile. "You even have some superficial resemblance to him. I didn't choose the name by chance."

Yaniv turned red. "I should have figured that out myself. Forgive me for not trusting you."

"What is your other choice?"

"To stay here. I'll do whatever you say."

"Stay here and play a double game," said Moshiko firmly. "Continue to walk around as if nothing happened. Keep dropping hints that you are looking for weapons for the Spanish Freedom Fighters while the Hezbullah shines dimly in the background. That way Asaf will not feel he has you in his pocket.

"I was wrong about Asaf. He's no fool. I'm afraid that he, too, is suspicious of you. The fax that you got from him may be bait at the end of a dangerous hook."

"You already said that," Yaniv reminded him.

"Yes," said Moshiko with a sour expression. "I debate with myself over it all the time. One moment I think they sell arms eagerly and blindly to all who want to buy; the next moment I think the boss is a cold, calculating man bent on tripping up his opponents."

"Then what do we do?" asked Yaniv.

Moshiko stood up proudly, eyes flashing. "There's no choice. We return to the original plan. You will meet Asaf's agent, that is, me, and present a request for weapons."

"Do you know what Abu Samir wants?" Yaniv shot back. "He spoke about negotiating a deal for 140 Stinger missiles. Standard weapons are child's play compared to what they're planning. He also mentioned long-range missiles, which the Hezbullah is planning to station at Israel's northern border — missiles that can cover the entire Land of Israel and threaten every citizen."

"What are you upset about?" retorted Moshiko. "That's what you're here for, to buy missiles or at least negotiate over them. This way we'll kill two birds with one stone. The Hezbullah agents will meet with Asaf's men, and we'll have the Mossad show up at the meeting. What could be better?"

Yaniv changed the subject. "Shouldn't I move to a different apartment?" he asked worriedly. "You see how easily those thugs got in. I'm in constant danger day and night. Aren't you worried about the fate of your younger brother?"

The corners of Moshiko's eyes wrinkled in a tiny smile. "Remember our faithful guard on the doorpost, which the previous tenant left behind? Surreptitiously, kiss the mezuzah whenever you come in or go out, and pray that Hashem will watch over you. If a nice fellow like you asks, He will surely listen."

14

Maison Pierre is not listed in the tour guides of the French capital. The store bears a close resemblance to its owner, Pierre Almozig: aging, dusty, and lacking vision. The storefront and unattractive display windows seem designed to keep customers away. Once in half an hour, a middle-aged customer might wander in to hunt for a bargain.

Pierre was not concerned by the light traffic in his store. Long ago he had despaired of raking in big profits from the sale of clothes. Instead, he invested every free minute in his hobby. Most of the workday, Pierre stood at his easel in a room with a northern exposure that served as a studio. Using pictures as models, he painted landscapes and portraits in watercolor or oil. Pierre's paintings won enthusiastic reviews in the papers and were displayed in popular galleries.

Pierre did not need to wait on customers. For that he had hired a lithe Italian named Leonardo Pantoloni, as practical and down-to-earth as Pierre was artistic and up in the clouds. Leonardo was a good salesman who treated every customer well. But since the shop was empty most of the time, Leonardo had plenty of free time on his hands.

Leonardo put this time to good use. In the cabinet beneath the cash register he had an advanced communications system linked to a satellite dish stationed on the roof of the building, ten flights up, and swallowed up among a forest of similar dishes. It looked like them, but the information that streamed through it was of a different nature. These were not ordinary media broadcasts, but sensitive, classified information.

The Italian salesman in the sleepy shop was in fact an active Mossad agent who had been given the unusual name Sheket, which means "Quiet," when he was born in Tel Aviv in the middle of the Yom Kippur War. His parents, Adinah and Samuel Lapid, chose the name "to express our deep longing for tranquility and quiet." Their wish was not fulfilled either in their country or in the personality of their son. Sheket was a tornado of an individual. When he received his draft notice, he volunteered for combat and was assigned to an elite commando unit. There he satisfied his thirst for action and met Moshiko Sharabi. When they finished their tour of duty, they went their separate ways but remained firm friends. Moshiko found work in an Israeli company that sold weapons, and Sheket enlisted in the Mossad. Eventually Sheket was put in charge of all agents in France and Belgium. They communicated with him in various ways, mainly through the computer in Maison Pierre.

Sheket was helping a woman who wanted a fake-fur coat when he caught sight of Moshiko near the cash register. "Wait patiently," he called in Italian as he climbed down the ladder with four coats.

Moshiko waited for Sheket to finish helping his customer. Sheket never failed to amaze him. The native Israeli spoke perfect French and Italian without a trace of a foreign accent. He also ran a secret communication station in the shop with such discretion that no intelligence activity was discernible. Even Moshiko, who knew about it, could not guess where the equipment was hidden.

Only after the customer had gotten into a taxi did Sheket turn to Moshiko. "What's up?" he said in Hebrew. "Are there any problems?"

"Big ones," said Moshiko. He glanced at a few figures who peered in from the outside for a minute, shook their heads, and continued walking. "Is it safe to speak here?"

"You can speak without fear until the next customer comes," laughed Sheket. "Pierre is busy making a charcoal sketch of his grandson. At this very moment, he is totally focused on the baby's dimples. Let's hear your story."

Moshiko, too, made a sketch, but with words. He described his growing suspicion about the weapons deal shaping up between Asaf's company and the Hezbullah, represented by Yaniv/Jafar. Sheket listened carefully without interjecting a single word of his own.

"If Asaf is willing to sell guns to enemies of his country," he said after Moshiko had finished, "what stops him from selling much more dangerous weapons? The principle is the same: treachery."

"What are you going to do about it?"

Sheket stared pensively at the cobwebs in a corner of the ceiling. Then he began to insert all the details in code into his Palm Pilot. Moshiko understood nothing of the unintelligible numbers and half words on the small screen. When Sheket finished, he thrust the Palm Pilot into his pocket, gave Moshiko a penetrating look, and quietly answered his question. "I'm going to transfer the information to my superiors. That's all I can do."

❧❦❧

The meeting between the seller's and purchaser's agents was conducted according to all details of the protocol. This time Moshiko remembered to change his shoes, and his steps were as quiet as those of a cat stealing into the aromatic kitchen of an alert housekeeper. This time, no red-ink comment would be recorded in his file. Not only did he not stand out; in his gray wool blazer, he almost blended in with the walls of the buildings on the way to Charles Aznavour Park.

Nevertheless, Moshiko was uneasy. He had gone too far with this meeting. *Ever since Abba passed away,* he reflected, *I've been the guardian of my younger brother. If anything happens to Yaniv, how will I look Ima in the face?*

Once again he crossed the quiet street and entered a small, curved lane. As usual, it was a pre-noon hour, and this time the park was totally empty. Even the homeless vagabonds did not seem to have slept here overnight. Moshiko shivered, not only from cold. This game was liable to cost him dearly. Each of the picturesque wooden benches tempted him to sit down and not continue to the meeting point.

He found the oak tree with "Michelle" carved on it. Now it bore a new etching: a peace dove with spread wings.

He settled himself on the left side of the bench, spread the newspaper *Figaro* over his knees, and cast a few furtive glances at his surroundings.

Gazing at the seventh-story windows of the tall apartment building behind the park, his sharp eye distinguished four silhouettes in attack position, evidently Asaf's sharpshooters. Moshiko could visualize their fingers on the triggers and their eyes in the telescopic sights. Each one of them could shoot a bird in flight from a distance of a hundred meters; they could even count your teeth if you smiled. With their sophisticated listening devices, they also heard every word you said. His jacket button, with its microtransmitter, was their ear. Next he glanced at the roof of the tall building on the left side of the park. As he expected, a ring of sharpshooters was stationed there as well, probably from Abu Samir, who had threatened to tail Yaniv.

He turned his attention to the etching of the dove on the tree trunk. It was a work of art, stunningly beautiful. When you examined the dove from close up, you could even see its eye gleam.

Gleam?

He studied the dove's eye. Bingo. Someone had cleverly carved the dove here in order to plant a listening device, perhaps even a miniature camera, in its eye.

A light breeze caressed his sweating face. The feeling of being a sitting duck intensified tenfold. Three parties would be eavesdropping on every word said here.

He heard the crunching of dry leaves. Yaniv was arriving. This time Moshiko would not have to study his fellow conspirator's face. No matter how well made up Yaniv would be, Moshiko would recognize him.

From this moment, Moshiko told himself, *I am no longer his brother. I know him only from our joint meetings in our work for the Iranian Ministry of Defense — but only Abu Samir knows about that. How does one play a three-way game, with Asaf, the Mossad, and the Hezbullah separately? Every word can turn into a mine that will explode in my face.*

Yaniv arrived. The fellow certainly had class. With his expensive European suit and elegant black attaché case, Yaniv looked every inch the Arab businessman trying to seem like a person of Western culture. Who had made him up so perfectly, flattening his narrow nose, filling out his sunken cheeks, and erasing the protrusion of his chin? The elegant glasses erased any remaining lines of resemblance.

He paused for a moment, as if trying to decide where to sit. The decision fell on the bench on which Moshiko was sitting and reading the back page of *Figaro*. Yaniv quickly became absorbed in *L'Expresse*. The act was perfect. A passerby would have noticed nothing out of the ordinary.

Two whole minutes passed as they read their newspapers. Moshiko coughed first. "Hmm… is there anything interesting to read in *L'Expresse*?"

"Would you like to exchange papers?" Yaniv pitched his voice very low. He was wise to do so; their voices were similar. They exchanged newspapers and frittered away five additional minutes.

"Why are you dreaming? Get down to business!" whispered Moshiko's tiny earphone. Asaf, on the seventh floor, had lost patience. "These foolish games are getting on my nerves. We all know what the two of you are there for. There is not a single gendarme anywhere in the area and certainly not from the DST.[1] Get going!"

Moshiko turned to Yaniv. "Who are you?" His English was finely honed, with a British accent.

"I am Jafar Hashemi," answered Yaniv with a heavy Arabic accent. "And who are you?"

"I go by the code Blue Panther. Whom do you work for, Mr. Hashemi?"

"For the Spanish Freedom Fighters."

"What do you want to buy?"

Yaniv bent forward in order to contrast with Moshiko, who was leaning back in a relaxed pose.

"We're talking about 200 M-15A4 tactical carbines with Picatinny rails."

"An excellent instrument. Clever choice," said Moshiko approvingly. "The M-15A4 is a good choice for sharpshooting in close quarters. What else?"

"Fifty Browning FN double-action only pistols."

"The pistol famous for its quality and reliability. Tell me, do you by any chance work for the boy scouts?"

"Why?"

"Pistols and guns are for boy scouts, not for serious fighting."

---

1. Direction de la Surveillance du Territoire, the French intelligence agency.

"We'll get to the heavy equipment soon. But I have a detailed list and I prefer to go in order. Do you also sell Heckler & Koch?"

Blue Panther acted indignant. "Apparently you didn't make a market survey before you came to us. We work with all the world's large weapon manufacturers: America's Smith & Wesson, Beretta, American Derringer, and Springfield Armory, as well as Austria's Glock, Steyr Mannlicher, and even Czechoslovakia's CZ. But all of those are children's toys. What about heavier things — guided missiles, radar equipment, drones?"

That was the signal for transferring to stage two of the sale, in which the Spanish mask falls, revealing the face of the Hezbullah. Moshiko now communicated with Yaniv through prearranged signals. He crossed his legs to convey, "I want to tell you something," then closed his fist for, "Let's argue a little."

"If you don't like small purchases, I can find other dealers, with lower prices," barked Yaniv. "You don't have a monopoly on the market."

"You're a bunch of babies," Moshiko shot back. "Ten-year-olds playing bow and arrow." His fist clenched more tightly, a code for, "Add to the fire."

"Very well, I have nothing to look for here." Yaniv picked up his attaché case and jumped to his feet. "You're not serious." He began to move away.

"It's a pity," said Moshiko.

"What's a pity?" asked Yaniv curiously, stopping.

"I have a few items for you at reduced prices. But if you've found someone else...."

"Now you're talking." Yaniv retraced his steps.

"Offer him Stinger missiles," Asaf whispered into the earphone. "But only if he doesn't say explicitly that he's working for the Hezbullah."

Heavy clouds hung overhead, and a cold wind blew, but Moshiko's forehead was covered with beads of sweat. Asaf was a wily fox. Until now there had been no clue that Moshiko's corporation was prepared to sell arms to a terrorist organization hostile to Israel. Asaf's latest instruction was just what he needed, but the Mossad would not be able to intercept it even by satellite. Yes, he could incriminate Asaf by whispering into the mouthpiece, "Okay, Asaf, I'll offer him a hundred Stinger missiles on condition that the name Hezbullah won't appear in the contract," but those would probably be his last words.

How could he draw Asaf into the trap? How could he make the Mossad believe that he had not told wild stories to Sheket?

"Okay, Asaf," he whispered. He was walking a tightrope. Asaf could get angry at him for mistakenly revealing his name, but Moshiko had not crossed the red line.

"Are you crazy?" the earphone barked. "If you mention the name Asaf once more, the park will no longer be named for Charles Aznavour but for Moshiko Sharabi."

"Have you heard about Stinger missiles?" Moshiko asked. His left thumb was folded over, to say, "Don't mention the Hezbullah."

"I have," said Yaniv coldly.

"I can offer you a dream package. A hundred almost-new Stinger missiles at closeout prices. As a result, Spanish politicians will be afraid to board airplanes. The government of Spain will give you whatever you want."

"Excellent, but we were never so violent." Yaniv thought quickly. Asaf had cleverly evaded the trap by forbidding any mention of the Hezbullah. Now the Mossad would not believe Sheket's story, and Asaf would be free to do as he pleased. On the other hand, Abu Samir's men were also listening to every word. If he didn't mention that he was conducting the purchase on their behalf, they would liquidate him on the way back. He decided to take action, come what may.

His face lit up with a mysterious smile. "You know what? We in Spain don't need the Stinger. But we have some good friends in the Hezbullah who would welcome the suggestion."

"Fine," said Moshiko, admiring Yaniv's solution. Yaniv had eaten his pie and left it whole. "But I think I will have to ask some of my superiors for their opinion."

"Tell him no way," Asaf whispered into the earphone. "We don't sell weapons to the Hezbullah. Period."

Yaniv's face turned yellow when he received a negative answer. As for Moshiko, he was very worried. One of them had gone too far. It would be a miracle if they arrived home alive.

❦

Late one night, Daniel Klein was patting his pocket to see whether the keys to Zeidel's apartment was in it. Tonight he would go in again and search for documents that might shed light on the strange behavior of the distinguished communal worker Elitzafan Mindelman.

Just then the phone rang and Daniel picked it up. "Hello," said a familiar voice. "This is Elitzafan Mindelman. May I speak to Mr. Klein?"

"This is Daniel Klein."

"I wanted to apologize for my behavior when you came over last week. I was on edge — perhaps sometime I will tell you why. Meanwhile I hope you will give me the benefit of the doubt. In any case, you wanted to suggest a *shidduch* for my eldest daughter, and I rashly put you off. I've changed my mind and would be most interested in hearing the details."

"The young man is my neighbor's son," Daniel said reluctantly, with a mixture of anger and curiosity. *Why should I help him after he chased me out of his house like a street dog?*

"Perhaps this would be better discussed in person." Embarrassment poured out of the receiver. "That is, if you don't mind honoring me with a second visit."

Curiosity won out over the anger. "When would a visit be convenient?" asked Daniel.

"Whenever it is convenient for you. Perhaps tomorrow night at ten?"

"Fine."

"Tomorrow night at ten in my house," concluded Elitzafan and hung up. His eyes met Felix's and both men smiled in satisfaction. The fish had swallowed the bait. Tomorrow night, the picture would become clear. Tomorrow night, perhaps they would find out who the *shidduch* saboteur was.

15

Moshiko was scanning the headlines of the Israeli newspapers in a kiosk when his cell phone rang. He put the phone to his ear. A voice with a rolling Italian accent said, "This is Leonardo Pantoloni. With whom am I speaking?"

"Anzio Piranezzi to you," chuckled Moshiko.

"Moshi — excuse me, Anzio — we must meet urgently."

"When are you free?"

"In two hours."

"I'll see you then at the Bonaparte."

Bonaparte is a quiet book store where customers can combine the pleasures of browsing through books, dining, and listening to soothing music. It caters to intellectuals and deep-thinkers.

Moshiko picked out a light novel, ordered a glass of mineral water, and tried to read — but the letters danced in front of his eyes. What happened to Yaniv? After the meeting in Charles Aznavour Park, they had parted ways. Six hours had passed, and still he had not heard from Yaniv. Had Abu Samir's men, or perhaps the Mossad, kidnapped him?

A thin waiter with dyed blue and yellow hair bent over him. "May I offer you something?" he asked pleasantly. A person did not come to a store–restaurant on a cold evening to sip mineral water. "This evening we have slices of breaded veal and a side dish of potatoes with olives and rosemary. Oh, I know, you're vegetarian. I have an amazing delicacy for you! Artichoke hearts in whipped walnut cream. Second course, creamed mushroom soup with spicy croutons and sliced onions. Whoever has eaten the soup even once comes back to us always. Would you like to order?"

"I'm waiting for a friend who will join me in a few minutes," said Moshiko, looking toward the door. "It wouldn't be polite to begin without him."

"You're right," said the waiter, backing off with a polite, phony smile to continue circulating among the tables with an order pad and a ready pen.

Sheket appeared at Moshiko's side suddenly, as appropriate for a seasoned agent. "So what shall we have this evening?" he asked Moshiko in French. "Cold mineral soup with the flavor of plastic?"

"I'm not in the mood for jokes this evening, Sheket." Moshiko's sorrowful gaze was fixed on a furry, fat white cat curled up under the next table. "My brother Yaniv didn't return from the meeting. This is the second time he's disappeared on me in two days."

"I don't have good news for you either," said Sheket, getting directly to the point. "I passed the information on to the higher-ups, and their reaction was disappointing. So was your meeting today, as the Mossad sees it."

"The dove's eye?" Moshiko tried.

"I don't know what you mean," said Sheket, a touch too quickly.

Sheket ignored Moshiko's wink and continued. "From the Mossad's point of view, Asaf is as clean and pure as a bar of soap. Not a word of what you or Jafar Hashemi said proves anything underhanded is going on. Asaf is allowed to sell rifles to the Spanish underground; at most, it's the business of the Spanish government.

"But there's more to it. They were indignant that anyone would try to impugn Asaf and Nati, two of the greatest patriots in the State of Israel. My boss spoke about Nati in glowing terms. The feats of bravery in which Nati was involved in Palmach days are still classified. Nati and Asaf can be relied upon blindly, and their allegiance to Israel is —"

"Dual," Moshiko cut in.

"What did you say?"

"I said their allegiance is dual," Moshiko said hotly. "Yes, they are big patriots — they celebrate Independence Day religiously. But their foremost allegiance is to themselves; that is, to their bank accounts. I guarantee you that at this very moment they're negotiating a rotten deal that will bring them many millions."

❧

Moshiko was on target. This meeting, in contrast to Moshiko's, was held in an anonymous apartment in the heart of Paris, in the absence of cameras and microphones. Asaf arrived together with Nati's faithful men who had been with him many years: Amit Mizrachi, Dubik Cooperman, and Malkiel Yahalom. Nati himself would join them for the signing.

Across the table from Asaf, flanked by two strong young henchmen, sat a fat, middle-aged man. All three had Arab features. The table was laden with crackers, dips, smoked fish, cheeses, pitchers of juice, and bottles of soda — out of respect for the customs of their guests, who abstained from alcohol.

"Let me introduce you. Dubik, Malkiel, Amit, meet a very serious client, Mr. Abdul Ruzak, a.k.a. Abu Samir."

Abu Samir nodded and smiled politely. His eyes darted around the table. Those Israelis did not know how to take a hint. He had said "no alcoholic beverages" only so that they would put out as many bottles of whiskey as possible. Not only hadn't they put out some expensive, sharp Johnny Walker Black Label — there wasn't even any Johnny Walker Red Label in sight. How do you conduct serious negotiations without a stiff drink?

"To the right of Abdul Ruzak is his assistant, Basm Al Zarzur, and to his left, Ramz El Hindi. These gentlemen have come to conduct negotiations for a party that need not be mentioned explicitly."

"Why, are you afraid of eavesdroppers?" laughed Dubik Cooperman.

Asaf enjoyed the question. "No. I changed my cell phone, the one in which Moshiko had planted a button. The whole apartment was also 'cleaned' yesterday. Our master technician, Moshiko, would give his soul to hear this conversation. But this time he is out."

Asaf poured himself a tall glass of orange juice and threw in a few ice cubes from a gleaming silver bucket. "Actually, he is always out — except when I want him to hear. I know he suspects us, so I keep him dancing like a marionette on a string. You should have seen him at the meeting this morning, when I told him to offer Jafar Hashemi the Stinger missiles only if he didn't say explicitly that he worked for the Hezbullah. Moshiko's entire forehead was covered with sweat, as if he were in a sauna."

"Who is this Jafar Hashemi?" asked Abu Samir. "Is that his real name or not? We interrogated him in his apartment, and he gave us impressive documents. I called Iran, and they told me there really is such a person, someone appointed directly by Dr. Ali Reza Bakhtiari, head of the purchasing department of the Iranian Ministry of Defense, one of the senior aides of Iranian President Mohammad Khatami."

"I don't know who the man is, and it doesn't interest me," Asaf took a long sip. "I like a serious buyer with meat on his bones, not a boy scout who wants pistols and guns. I almost told Moshiko to offer him whistles."

Malkiel started fidgeting. "What's the purpose of this meeting?"

"What's the hurry?" asked Asaf, who had finished the juice and was noisily munching crackers and lox.

"Why waste time?"

"We'll get to the point soon. But I have the impression that our friend Abu Samir would like to drink something that is truly wet. Dubik just went out to buy a few bottles of Glenfiddich Scotch and one of Johnny Walker Blue Label, which is well worth the few hundred dollars that it costs. Such a distinguished buyer should be treated right!"

❧✺❧

Moshiko was driving his Renault home when the phone rang. One look at the screen sent his heart racing. It was Yaniv!

"What's up, Yaniv? Where did you disappear to?"

"I was followed — by Abu Samir's friends. I had trouble shaking them." Yaniv sounded very tired.

"Take some lessons in dry cleaning from Sheket," said Moshiko with a smile. "The Mossad teaches its agents sophisticated techniques."

Yaniv ignored the interruption. "I was desperate. I considered stealing a pocketbook from an old lady so that the police would arrest me. But I was afraid of trouble with the passport."

"So what did you do?"

"I went into a hospital and complained of sharp pains on my right side. The doctors suspected appendicitis. You should have seen Basm's eyes when they wheeled me, in a hospital gown, into the x-ray room. He knew I was laughing at him and the emergency room staff both."

"Yaniv, I think it's time to pack your suitcase and go home. The business here is getting messy, and I don't want you mixed up in it."

"Did something happen?"

Moshiko parked his car near the house, shut the lights, and silenced the motor. "Yes, I think so. Asaf and the rest disappeared suddenly. Something big is cooking, and I want to smell the pot. The problem is that for a few days, now, my electronic ears haven't picked up anything."

"I'm in this with you, Moshiko."

"You go home and take care of Ima."

"No!"

"Yes! Yaniv, I'm your big brother. Besides, now that you're under suspicion, there's nothing left for you to do here."

Yaniv acquiesced. With a heavy heart, he arranged his return flight for that evening.

⊗≁❦⊚

The note on the door said that the public would be received that evening until 9:30. Even so, it dragged out. Two arguing neighbors who had come for mediation were requested to return another day.

At a quarter to ten, the house quieted down. Elitzafan gathered together the papers that had accumulated on his desk. Under the pile he carefully hid a small tape recorder, upon the advice of Felix, who was unable to attend. Felix would listen to the recording later that night.

At ten after ten, Daniel knocked at the door. Elitzafan welcomed him with a broad smile, shook his hand, and led him into the study.

"Here we can speak comfortably about private matters." Elitzafan tried to speak normally, but his voice suddenly became a deep bass. Perhaps emotion had taken charge of his vocal cords.

"Certainly," said Daniel.

Just then Devorah entered carrying a tray. She set down two cups of hot coffee, a plate of chocolate-chip cookies, and an ashtray, in case the guest wanted to smoke. Then she quietly left.

"Have some cookies," said Elitzafan. "They are homemade."

Daniel recited the blessing and took a bite. "Let me get to the point," he said, twirling his gray *peyos*. "I've known Shmuli Patankin since he was an infant; he's the son of the neighbors in the next entrance. His parents are solid gold. The father runs a free-loan fund that helps many people in need. And the boy himself — " Daniel became very excited. "Such a boy you don't find. He's a rare diamond mined from the Ural Mountains, with a certification of quality from the American Institute of Standards. Not only is he a brilliant scholar, refined, and handsome, but he has a special soul, woven from threads of pure silk." Daniel pushed his glasses back up over the bridge of his nose. "Shmuli Patankin is one in a million."

Elitzafan cupped the ends of his beard in his hands. Ignoring the compliments that the *shadchan* had heaped on the head of his victim, he probed with the cool purposefulness of a surgeon's scalpel, "Do you have their answer yet?"

"Whose answer?" Daniel took another sip of coffee. The cookies were really special. If a good relationship developed, maybe he would get the recipe for Peninah.

"The Patankins'. Have you suggested the *shidduch* to them yet?"

"No," replied Daniel. "First I wanted to hear what you have to say."

Elitzafan put his own cup down noisily on the saucer. "If so, we haven't done anything. I thought the boy's side had already given you an answer.

"Go to the Patankins. Suggest it to them. They will start looking into it. They will hear wonderful things about Chedvi and the family. And then—" his face contorted with pain "—and then someone will call them and warn them that there is some dark secret linked to the Mindelman family."

Elitzafan searched Daniel's face for suspicious signs — dilation of pupils, sudden raising of eyelids, rapid breathing, or cessation of breathing — as per Felix's instructions. There were none. Daniel was horrified by Elitzafan's emotional suffering but not surprised. He had seen it during his first visit, two weeks ago.

"Why do you speak that way?" asked Daniel. "Is there a Heavenly decree that someone must ruin things for you?"

"It certainly seems that way." Elitzafan groaned and drummed the table nervously. "Go suggest the *shidduch* to the Patankins, and we'll watch the balloon burst."

Perhaps the time is ripe to reveal the secret, thought Daniel. "Perhaps I can help you." His voice betrayed him, suddenly becoming high and jarring. "Why are they making trouble for you?"

Elitzafan put his head down, then picked it up. He repeated this several times, as if he were doing exercises. Should he confide in Daniel or shouldn't he? A feeling in his heart told him that Felix had made a mistake; Daniel was innocent of all guilt. But the bitter experiences of the last six years had made him so suspicious that he trusted almost no one. At last he answered, "At this stage I cannot reveal anything to you. Perhaps the day will come, though, when I will."

As he escorted Daniel to the door, he searched for the right words. "Suggest the *shidduch* to your neighbors. If a miracle happens," he said, with trembling lips, "and it goes well, you will hear surprising things from me."

16

The Renault drove slowly down the road. Moshiko was not focused enough to drive quickly, pass other cars, or make sharp turns. His thoughts were racing around Yaniv, who was touring Paris briefly before boarding a flight home. *Was I right to send him away?* he wondered. *Undoubtedly Yaniv will be much safer in Israel, protecting Tel Aviv's Central Bus Station from suicide terrorists, than here in Paris, being tailed by Abu Samir and his gang. What will they say in the streets of Paris, that the star buyer of the Spanish Freedom Fighters and the Hezbullah failed at the start and ran away from France like a scared rabbit? Let them talk!*

One thing did bother Moshiko, though. The special bond between the two brothers had always been based on total sincerity and honesty. Now, for the first time ever, Moshiko had lied to Yaniv. He had told him he could no longer eavesdrop on Asaf and his friends. That was an outright lie.

❧❦❧

Curly-haired, flat-nosed Dubik Cooperman was a poor boy from a *moshav* who, with vision and initiative, had opened new vistas for marketing weapons. For seven years he had climbed the hierarchy of the arms company until he reached the top, a position he shared with Nati and Asaf. A few successful deals, for which he took a hefty middleman's fee, had turned him into a millionaire.

"Nouveau riche," his friends would comment with a smile when Dubik showed up with some new status symbol. He wore custom-made suits — woe to whoever soiled them even slightly, albeit by accident! He traveled through Europe in prestigious sports cars: Lamborghinis, Porsches, and Ferraris. While his personal chauffeur drove, Dubik could sprawl in the comfortable passenger seat and place long-distance phone calls or make entries in his palm computer — which was always the latest model, although keeping up with the changes was so confusing that files were erased, the diary was riddled with errors, and phone numbers were often wrong.

Dubik's greatest weakness was for watches, especially sport watches. It had started when he was fourteen, with inexpensive models; his collection included fifteen Citizens, twenty-two Seikos, and seven Breitlings. But for Dubik, that was not enough. Recently, a little bird had whispered in his ear that the really rich people, who were featured on the front pages of exclusive financial magazines such as *The Marker* and *Fortune,* bought custom-designed watches. Dubik immediately ordered a gold watch from Rolex, waited a year for them to design a model especially for him — the only such watch in the world — and laid down twenty thousand dollars for the privilege.

From then on, this watch almost never left his left hand. Dubik danced, swam, and even dived with the expensive watch. The only time Dubik took off his precious timepiece was when he went to bed. The watch exerted a bit of pressure on his wrist. To fall asleep, he needed to feel absolutely unencumbered.

In the middle of the Jafar Hashemi affair, a burst pipe had forced Moshiko and Amit out of their apartment. Dubik graciously invited them to spend two nights in his luxurious mansion in the heart of Paris, not far from the Champs Elysées. The pair took him up on his offer. Amit enjoyed every moment in the guest bedroom, which was elegant enough to belong to Prince Charles. Moshiko barely slept. When everyone else was fast asleep, he treated himself to a tour of the mansion.

The door of Dubik's bedroom was unlocked. Dubik was sleeping on his back, mouth open, snoring loudly. If time had permitted, Moshiko would have enjoyed the sights: the original oil paintings, purchased in renowned art galleries; the dim pink and purple lights radiating from recessed spots in the ceiling; the bed, which could be shifted to different positions at the touch of a button; the magnificently carved, solid wood headboard; the custom-made sheet, with an enlargement of a photograph Dubik had taken of dolphins swimming in the ocean; the fully stocked mini-bar; and racks of weights and various exercise equipment within easy reach of the bed. The sight that Moshiko took note of was the night table, on which lay Dubik's pride and joy — his gold Rolex.

Moshiko quietly picked up the watch and took it to his room. With a fine pocketknife and jeweler's screwdriver, he skillfully removed the cover and looked for dead space. He found it between the wall of the watch and the mechanism. Moshiko took a picture of the inside of the watch, put the cover back on, and returned the watch to the night table in Dubik's bedroom.

The next morning, Moshiko brought the photograph to Sheket. That same afternoon, Sheket furnished him with one of the world's most sophisticated listening devices, a product of the Mossad laboratories. That night, Moshiko planted the button in Dubik's Rolex.

From then on, Moshiko could hear all of Dubik's conversations — and Dubik sat beside Asaf at every important meeting, including the one with the purchasing agents of the Hezbullah.

❧❦☙

The splash of a drink being poured into a glass. Noisy sips, and lusty smacking of the lips. "This is delicious! It's been a long time since I've tasted anything like this."

"Have another one, Abu Samir." It was Asaf's cold voice, no mistake about it. "Have you ever tasted a velvety flame flowing down your throat? That's Johnny Walker Blue Label. Expensive, but worth every franc. To your health, Abu Samir!"

"To your health!" said a guttural voice. Glass clinked. "To a most successful deal!"

"And without that Blue Panther Moshiko." The burst of mocking laughter was cruel and sharp as a lion's bite. "Shall we get down to business?"

"Yes, in the name of the merciful Allah and with the permission of our esteemed leader, Sheikh Hassan Nasrallah," came the guttural voice.

The cat was out of the bag. Abu Samir spoke explicitly about buying 150 Stinger missiles, RPG launchers, anti-tank grenades, rockets, and high-quality plastic explosives, "not the type produced in Gaza that explode in our heroes' hands."

Moshiko listened with growing horror and disgust at the revelation of the treachery of these Israeli businessmen. How faithfully they celebrated Israel's Independence Day! They made barbecues, hit passersby with plastic hammers, sang songs of the homeland with chassidic fervor, and hung the blue and white flag on their balconies. Now they were negotiating in the friendliest manner with Israel's sworn enemies, the Hezbullah terrorists, over weapons that would be used against Israel.

Time was running out. If Moshiko didn't hurry, Yaniv would miss his plane.

Moshiko managed to hear something regarding "pitchblende 2," which needed to be transported from one place to another. Then Abu Samir switched to code words taken from the Greek alphabet.

Moshiko did not rely on the recording; he quickly wrote everything down. Then he drove Yaniv to the airport.

When Moshiko returned, he listened to the recording. To his dismay, the sound was blurred, the content unclear. The button planted in Dubik's watch had provided him with excellent real-time hearing, but the recorded evidence was worthless. He had only the notes. And even those only took the meeting to the point where the atmosphere began to heat up and they had switched over to code.

The conclusion was clear, though. Something very big was cooking, and Moshiko was determined to find out what it was. He would alert the Mossad, through Sheket. Tomorrow morning he would visit Maison Pierre and speak with the friendly Italian salesman, Leonardo Pantoloni.

❧

Thirty little girls ran, jumped, sang, and danced around their teacher Chedvi as she wiped the remnants of clay off the red formica tabletop. Suddenly a freckle-faced child tugged at her sleeve and said, "We have a guest."

Chedvi raised her eyes, dropped the rag, and hurried toward the guest. "Shalom, Ima! What brings you here in the middle of the day?"

Ignoring the question, Devorah asked, "Do you have an assistant who can cover for you?"

Chedvi nodded in the direction of a young woman. "My assistant Ricki can stay with the girls during lunch. But Ima, if you left school in the middle of the day, something must have happened. Is everything all right?"

"Everything is fine," said Devorah. "Come quickly."

Chedvi gave Ricki some instructions, slung her pocketbook over her shoulder, and walked out, trying to keep up with her mother's rapid pace. Devorah Mindelman never strolled; she always hurried.

"Rebbetzin Flora agreed to see me in the middle of the day, just this once, as a special favor," said Devorah, mildly excited. "You know that Reb Daniel Klein came to suggest a *shidduch* with his neighbors' son Shmuli Patankin. We inquired and heard that the boy is exceptional in every way. So I decided to mention you for the good before Rebbetzin Flora."

Chedvi stopped short. "Ima!" There was a note of pleading in her voice. Invariably rational, and very clever, she had no use for Flora.

Devorah looked at Chedvi in surprise. "I'm doing it for you, and you turn up your nose? I turned the world over to get us an appointment outside the usual reception hours. In three hours, Rebbetzin Flora will be on a plane to France, where hundreds of admirers await her. Here, I have the wicks from last Shabbos. A pity you didn't light a candle as I asked you to."

Chedvi shrugged her shoulders and lifted her eyes heavenward in despair. She saw eye to eye with her mother on all but one subject — Flora Simchoni–Freilich.

"But Ima, what can you see in oily pieces of rolled cotton that are slightly charred at the ends?"

"That's what our physical eyes see," said Devorah, quickening her pace even more. "Flora looks at the wicks in a spiritual dimension. Do you know that all our past and future is impressed on the wicks of Shabbos?"

"For those who believe it."

They reached the building, went down to the shelter, and waited beside the door. Everything seemed ordinary in the daytime, without the colorful groups of Flora's followers.

Flora was waiting for them impatiently. She had not yet packed her suitcases. She always left everything for the last minute, improvised, and lived from hand to mouth. Now she opened the door even before they could ring the intercom.

"Did you bring them?" she asked immediately.

Suddenly she noticed Chedvi. "Oh, are you the one for whom hundreds of women say *Tehillim* every day? Your mother is a great woman. If not for her, I don't even want to think what would happen to you!"

Chedvi's cheeks flushed a deep red. Flora knew that Chedvi did not trust her, and she was paying her back with interest. At least no one else was present.

"Did you perhaps also light a candle on *Erev Shabbos*?" Flora asked in honeyed tones. "It would have made life much easier for me."

"Maybe next Shabbos," Chedvi muttered, wiping her brow to cover her eyes and evade Flora's direct gaze.

Devorah pulled a plastic container out of her bag. It had been relegated to a special category when it was chosen to store the holy wicks.

"Ah, the holy, pure wicks." As Devorah watched in reverent silence, Flora fished the oily wicks out with a tweezer and placed them in small, clean glasses. Then she pulled down the *tris,* shut the light, and lit the wicks.

Nine tiny blue-and-orange flames capered in the darkness, casting giant shadows on the walls. Flora looked alternatively at the huge shadows and the small flames. She covered the *tichel* on her head with a transparent silk kerchief, covered her eyes with the fine silk for a few seconds, and again opened them.

An aura of mysticism enveloped the room. The electrified atmosphere sent titillating tension through the spectators from head to toe.

Devorah was mesmerized by the burning wicks. Chedvi tried to block their influence. "There is nothing real in this," she whispered, but nine glowing lights burned in her pupils.

"Did you see?" whispered Flora.

"See what?"

"The evil is finished." The whisper grew louder. "Your troubles are about to end."

Suddenly she stood up, raised the *tris,* and turned on the light. Then she pressed Devorah's hand emotionally and announced, "*Mazal tov!* Chedvi is going to get engaged soon."

"Are you sure?" asked Devorah in surprise.

"If I'm wrong, may my plane fall into the sea," cried Flora. "How did you not see the *chasan* in the light of the candles? A terrific learner who is righteous, handsome, considerate, serious, and refined is approaching your house with giant strides. Happiness is right around the corner. *Mazal tov!*"

Devorah breathed heavily. With her hypnotic powers, Flora had infused Devorah's imagination with the image of a wonderful boy approaching her house, which was festively lit up and filled with elated guests in honor of Chedvi's engagement.

Chedvi could not maintain her indifference. Flora had played on the most delicate strings in her soul. She wiped away a tear.

"I don't make up nonsense, Devorah," whispered Flora in a trembling voice. "Only Hashem knows how much I want your happiness. Only He knows how longingly I await that happy day when you will shout over the phone, 'Flora, I get a *Mazal tov!* My Chedvi is engaged!'"

For a minute there was frozen silence. Then Devorah covered her face with her hands and began to sob quietly. Chedvi struggled desperately against the dam of tears that threatened to burst. Suddenly, she found herself hugging her mother and weeping together with her.

Flora watched what her few words had done. Soon the great pain that erupted in a flood of tears swept her, too. Forgotten was the suitcase that needed to be packed; forgotten was the plane waiting on the runway. Flora fell on the necks of Devorah and Chedvi and wept together with them. The barriers fell. The three women turned into one weeping mass, trying to break through the gates of mercy with their tears.

❦

Daniel read the small nameplate: "Welcome to the Patankins." For a moment he stood there reminiscing.

As a child, Shmuli had been clever, energetic, full of life, and, truth be told, wild. The major mischief maker had matured into a Heaven-fearing young Torah scholar of noble character. His proud neighbors were forced to admit that the child had finally matured.

Daniel knew Shmuli well and had a warm rapport with him, but his father was a different story. Daniel had hardly ever exchanged more than a polite "*Shalom*, how are you?" with him.

Daniel mustered his courage and rang the bell.

The door was opened by a tall man with a gray beard that was turning white, a broad forehead, thick, arched eyebrows, and jet-black eyes sparkling from behind old-fashioned plastic framed glasses that gave him a stern look. He was still holding the monthly ledger of the free-loan fund, which he had just been reviewing.

"May I come in?"

"What a question!" Mendel replied. "Come in!"

Mendel's serious expression gave no clue of the warm hospitality he was about to extend to his visitor. Daniel was seated at the dining room table, and despite his protests that he was a neighbor from the next entrance and had just eaten at home, Mendel was not satisfied until the table was laden with pretzels, cakes, cookies, chocolates, and sodas. "And now," he said at last, "let's hear what brings you."

"The world was created to be inhabited," said Daniel by way of introduction, and he quoted a verse to prove the point.

"Quite true," said Mendel warmly. "And how does that apply to us this evening?"

"I have come to suggest a *shidduch* for your son Shmuli."

"With whom?"

"With the wonderful daughter of the distinguished scholar Mr. Elitzafan Mindelman."

"Mr. Mindelman?" exclaimed Mendel in surprise. His bushy eyebrows became even more arched, but his voice became cooler. "Indeed, he is a very distinguished person. I have heard much about him. But…."

"**B**ut what?" asked Daniel Klein. Although he was prepared for something to go wrong, it was still hard to take.

Mendel sat up straight in his chair, and it seemed to Daniel that he was also straightening his way of thinking. "I'll tell you. On the one hand, it would suit me very well to make a *shidduch* with a devoted Jew like R' Mindelman. But the girl herself — something bothers me."

"What could bother you about such a wonderful girl?" laughed Daniel. "When King Solomon said that a good woman is one in a thousand, he was referring to Chedvi Mindelman! First of all, she has a profession — she is a certified kindergarten teacher. Besides that, she's a crown of roses: Heaven-fearing, full of good character traits, and beautiful outside and in. I doubt whether you would find ten more like her in all of Jerusalem."

Mendel leaned back in his chair. "If she really is as wonderful as you say, why is she still single at the age of twenty-five?"

Daniel pretended to study the floor. Time had ravaged the stone tiles. Almost each one was cracked, if not broken. They urgently needed to be changed. But the master of the house did not seem to care. He was more interested in helping the needy through the free-loan fund that he administered than in renovating his house. "How old is your Shmuli?" asked Daniel, aware that he was stepping on sore toes.

"Twenty-eight."

"And what has been holding *him* up all this time?"

Mendel's eyes shone with fatherly pride. "Everyone knows that Shmuli is very picky."

"So is Chedvi. She will not take anything less than the best! I tell you that she and Shmuli are a couple made in Heaven. They are as perfectly matched as… as… as a pot and its cover."

Mendel was in unusually good spirits. A few minutes before Daniel came, a donor had brought him a check of $10,000 for the free-loan fund. Every now and then, Mendel hummed a happy tune under his breath. Daniel noticed Mendel's high spirits and decided to exploit the momentum to the hilt. "I understand that you are interested in this suggestion," he stated as a fact.

"What?"

"You inquire about Chedvi Mindelman, and we will speak again a few days," Daniel concluded.

Mendel placed his hand on his forehead. Despite his joy, he remained levelheaded. "I will consult my wife when she comes home and give you an answer soon."

He rose to escort Daniel to the door. Daniel followed the time-worn path of *shadchanim*. "I'm sure your answer will be positive."

"Remember," said Mendel, "that my side is only 50% of the story. There's a second side as well."

"Actually," said Daniel, "the only one who is really in charge of the *shidduch* is Hashem. He has the whole 100%!"

❧❦❧

"Abba, you're not listening."

"What is it?" said Daniel, shaking himself out of his reverie. "What did you say?"

"I've been speaking to you for five minutes, and you don't hear a word!"

Ten-year-old Dassi, sitting across from her father, had been trying unsuccessfully to capture his attention ever since he returned from the Patankins.

"You're right."

Daniel was weighing the chances for the *shidduch* to succeed, and his emotions rose and fell like a seesaw. One minute he was sure that the Patankins would agree. Hadn't Mendel said that a *mechutan* such as Elitzafan was suitable for him? The next minute, pessimism gained the upper hand. Mendel had asked penetrating questions. Besides, an anonymous caller was liable to frighten them.

During his visit, he had thought of warning Mendel in advance that someone would try to slander the Mindelmans. Perhaps this warning could neutralize the poison, like a vaccination. But when Daniel was about to speak, something stopped him. Imagine saying, "Listen, I'm suggesting a fantastic *shidduch*, but there is some dark secret in the family history." That's all you need. Mendel would have shown him the door.

Now Daniel regretted his silence. The blow would surely arrive just as it always did. Mendel would get cold feet and flee. Daniel was foolish not to have taken the sting out in advance!

Perhaps it was not too late. If only he could find a magic formula that would not frighten Shmuli's parents, but would allow them to understand that the *kallah's* father had an enemy who slandered him.

How does one manage to walk the fine line? The situation was so delicate. One word was enough — actually, even the inflection was sufficient — to destroy a *shidduch* in its sensitive initial stages. Like a raw egg, any tap would crack its delicate shell. "*Ribbono shel olam,*" he whispered, "give me the right words!"

"Are you *davening,* Abba?" asked Dassi.

"What?" asked Daniel.

"You mentioned the *Ribbono shel olam,* so I thought you were *davening.* Would you like a cup of tea, Abba?"

"Thank you anyway, Dassi, but I'm too tired. Can I take you up on your kind offer tomorrow?"

"Yes, and with jelly cookies, too, Abba."

Daniel's head ached from the heavy burden of thoughts. He took an aspirin and went to bed.

At two o'clock in the morning he woke up feeling fresh and clear. His headache was gone, and the adrenaline was flowing through his veins. He grabbed his clothing from a nearby chair and dressed in the dark. Hoping he didn't look like a clown, he slipped out.

The four locks on Zeidel's door made noise as always when he turned the keys, but Daniel was no longer afraid. At most, people would think he had to check something in the empty apartment. Everyone knew he had the keys, and he had a legitimate excuse to enter.

He turned on the light and made a quick survey of the apartment before going over to the cartons. Better safe than sorry.

But it was not so safe.

The kitchen faucet was dripping. Evidently, the washer had worn away. Still not a reason to worry. The two drawers in the living room were not closed completely. *Did I close them properly?* he asked himself. Usually he didn't leave clues behind. The door to the bathroom was slightly ajar. Most important of all, the cartons themselves seemed to have been moved around. The large carton with the picture of the electric train from America, evidently the toy of little Elitzafan, no longer stood out among the other cartons.

Someone had been here.

He recalled that the first time he had stolen into the apartment, he had felt a pair of eyes observing him. Then he had laughed at himself and chalked it up to imagination. Now he had that same feeling once again. If someone had entered Zeidel's abandoned apartment and touched everything, why shouldn't he have planted a hidden camera here?

Daniel spent the next half hour searching for a hidden camera or lens. He turned on the lights in all the rooms, combed every corner, and touched every suspicious protrusion.

He found nothing. Everything was in order. Now Daniel began to doubt his suspicions. Perhaps he himself had moved the electric train carton. He had dozed on a chair, run to extinguish the small fire in the courtyard, and left the apartment before dawn. Under such circumstances, even the fussiest housewife would not have left the apartment in tip-top shape.

Feeling calmer, he approached the carton that had once housed an electric train from America — a big, expensive toy that only the wealthy could acquire forty years ago. He lowered the carton to the floor and opened it.

Daniel rubbed his eyes in astonishment. The carton was still being used for its original purpose! The electric train, with all its parts, was lying inside. The child who had played with it had taken good care and put it back into its box.

When you are an only child, without pesky brothers and sisters to ruin your toys, you can take good care of everything. Had Elitzafan Mindelman once played with this train?

Daniel was overcome by a childish urge to play with the train. As a child of eight or nine, such a toy had been his heart's desire. How he had begged his parents to buy him an electric train! But who had an extra penny for such luxuries? They had bought him a small train made of blue metal that ran on a spring and broke in a week. A high-quality, expensive toy like this was the stuff of which dreams were made.

He examined the high-quality engine and cars. The battery compartment rattled. An inner part must have come loose. Daniel took a small screwdriver from the kitchen drawer and opened the cover of the battery compartment.

Instead of the four fat, heavy batteries he expected, he found a flat, shiny brown metal box with golden letters in English — an expensive cigar box, a luxury that only the rich could allow themselves.

With trembling hands, he opened the box.

The original American blend, Virginia cigars were no longer there. Instead, there was a thin, long, yellow key with an unusual head: round, with a beautifully crafted relief of a lion's head. Had little Elitzafan hidden the key inside the engine, or was an adult responsible? What door would this unusual key open?

Daniel gently put the cover back on. Then, with renewed vigor, he attacked the cartons of documents. There were a few carbon copies of letters that astounded him. If he had not recognized Zeidel's handwriting, he would have sworn that he had not written them. The Zeidel he had known held firm rightist opinions on politics and security, but the Zeidel of the early 1960s seemed to have been a radical leftist.

On the bottom of the pile was an empty envelope addressed to Mr. Avraham Zeidel Portman, 4 Peki'in Street, Tiberias.

⌘

At night, Felix went up to Elitzafan's apartment and listened to the recorded message in the study. Daniel Klein's voice rose from the small tape recorder.

"I've known Shmuli Patankin since he was an infant; he's the son of the neighbors in the next entrance. His parents are solid gold. The father runs a free-loan fund that helps many people in need. And the boy himself—such a boy you don't find. He's a rare diamond mined from the Ural Mountains, with a certification of quality from the American Institute of Standards. Not only is he a brilliant scholar, refined, and handsome, but he has a special soul, woven from threads of pure silk. Shmuli Patankin is one in a million."

He continued to listen. "Why do you speak that way? Is there a Heavenly decree that someone must ruin things for you?" And then, "Perhaps I can help you. Why are they making trouble for you?"

Felix shut the recorder. Elitzafan looked at him with eager expectation. He valued Felix's opinion in matters requiring scientific or psychological analysis.

As always, Felix spoke calmly and deliberately. "If you wish, I'll run a scientific analysis of the tape with professional equipment. But in my opinion, it's unnecessary. You can erase him from the list of suspects; he's a good, wholesome man who wouldn't hurt a fly. Your enemy is elsewhere."

❧❧❧

Maison Pierre was again empty of customers. For Pierre Almozig, who was painting a frog leaping into the water, the world had ceased to exist. Sheket was sure that in the next hour Monsieur Almozig would not leave his easel unless the building collapsed. Sheket locked the store, turned on his computer, and began to quickly type in the information Moshiko had given him. The term "pitchblende" tickled some gray cells at the back of his brain, but the crowning glory was the Stinger missiles that the Hezbullah wanted to acquire.

Sheket had been trained to relay information without personal opinions or conclusions. At Mossad headquarters they would put the details together and draw the necessary conclusions.

Only yesterday, Sheket had been informed that Al-Qaeda cells throughout the world were preparing for a new type of terror: using missiles to shoot down passenger planes. There were clues linking Al-Qaeda to the Hezbullah, an organization that had an interest in shooting down Israel-bound planes.

Had Moshiko provided Sheket with the original tape of the meeting between Asaf and Abu Samir, the story would have been a great deal simpler. Go convince people that this is the verbatim text of the conversation, not the lies of a frustrated employee settling a score with his boss.

Sheket e-mailed his report to Mossad offices in Paris and Tel Aviv. After that, there was nothing to do but sit back and wait for a response.

❧

At the word "pitchblende," the recipient of Sheket's e-mail jumped to his feet and gasped. *Has Sheket gone out of his mind?*

Someone was trying to pin a blood libel on his employer! His first inclination was to press "Delete" and dispose of the message. On second thought, he e-mailed a coded message to Amnon, Sheket's immediate superior in Paris.

The coded message caused Amnon to raise an eyebrow. It couldn't be! First of all, Nati and Asaf were above suspicion. Second, there were better addresses for getting "pitchblende." And yet, a purchase order had been made!

An hour after Sheket sent the information, he received a reply from Amnon: Put a tail on Nati, Asaf, Dubik Cooperman, Malkiel Yahalom, Amit Mizrachi, and … Moshiko Sharabi!

Sheket did not even smile. Tailing both accuser and accused was not a new innovation. There was always room for surprises. Perhaps even Moshiko wasn't on the side of the good guys.

18

Moshiko did excellent work — under laboratory conditions. In Dubik's mansion, Moshiko's hands shook with fear as he screwed the bottom plate of the gold Rolex watch back on.

Two nights later, Dubik sleepily took off his precious watch and put it down just a bit too close to the edge of the night table. His eyes closed even before the watch fell down and landed without a sound on the thick Persian carpet.

When Dubik woke up the following morning, the first thing he did was to grope with closed eyes for the watch, but all he felt was smooth wood. His heart skipped a beat. He jumped out of bed and began to search for the watch.

He soon found it lying beside the bed — but in two pieces. The bottom had come off.

Dubik's blood rushed to his head. Twenty thousand dollars for a piece of junk that comes apart from one fall — and onto a rug at that! Mentally he began writing a letter of complaint to the managers of Rolex. He would tell the whole world how they had cheated him! He should have bought a more prestigious brand, but he was just beginning his career as a millionaire. Meanwhile he could only look jealously at Asaf's wrist, adorned with an $80,000 diamond-studded watch — not to mention Nati himself, who indulged in one that cost half a million. Nati wore a mansion on his wrist.

Dubik got into his red Porsche, drove as fast as he dared to the nearest watch store, and asked them to check whether the mechanism had been damaged.

The white-haired watchmaker examined the watch carefully and put it back together. "Nothing happened," he said with fatherly warmth as he returned it to Dubik. He was used to people who worship their watches. "But this piece," he said, holding a tiny button in his open palm, "does not belong to it. Someone opened the watch and put this in."

Dubik looked at the button in horror, and his mind started racing. *Moshiko played with my watch! It couldn't be anyone else! Two weeks ago, Asaf showed me a few miniature listening devices that Moshiko had planted in the cell phones of some our staff members. This one is even smaller.*

But how? The watch never leaves my wrist, except…. Ah, yes, Moshiko was an exemplary guest.

"Anything else, monsieur?" the watchmaker asked politely.

"No!" said Dubik. He picked up the watch from the counter and stormed out of the store. Moshiko had exceeded all bounds!

Twenty minutes later, Dubik pulled up in front of Asaf's house. "Look at this, Asaf," he said, almost shoving the button in his face.

Asaf wiped his bald pate with his hand. "Come a minute," he said.

They went into a second room. Out of range of the device. Asaf's green eyes gleamed with guile. "Where did you find it?"

"In my watch. Moshiko planted it there when he stayed in my house."

"Wonderful," said Asaf.

"What's wonderful about it?" demanded Dubik angrily. "Why don't you get rid of him? He's a double agent!"

Asaf put a finger to his lips. "Get rid of Moshiko? He's worth his weight in gold. If he weren't around, we would have to invent him."

Dubik scratched behind his ear, a gesture left from childhood whenever he didn't understand something and felt left behind. "What are you talking about?"

Asaf bent over the table and scribbled hurriedly on a piece of paper, "Come outside with me."

In the small garden in front of the house, as they strolled among rose bushes covered in black plastic bags for protection from the cold, Asaf explained to Dubik a few things he didn't know. "I am familiar with this button. It's not something that Moshiko is capable of. This is a modern development of the Mossad; I've seen a few like it. It means that the Mossad, or someone in the Mossad, is monitoring us through Moshiko and his listening devices. We will turn Moshiko into a double agent without his knowing it. Moshiko has no idea that we discovered this device. You will sit beside me in every important meeting, and from now on we will conduct part of our meetings directly for the ears of the Mossad and its agents. These meetings will of course be pure and white as snow. At most, we will throw them a small bone so they will not understand that we're making fun of them. But basically, we will obtain the approval of the Mossad. Get it?"

Dubik smiled with satisfaction. Say what you want, but Asaf was and has remained a wily fox with no competitors. Not for nothing had he managed to survive so many years in weapons deals, a real jungle in which only the strong and wily survive.

They went inside. Dubik put on the watch. Asaf surveyed him with a mischievous look. "We're going to sit with the new buyers."

Dubik played along. "Who are they now?"

"Good boys from Somalia, nothing serious. They want a few helicopters for civilian use. Sikorsky 76 S. Capacity 600 pounds. Something utterly innocent. Ideal for robberies, but that's not my business. We'll leave that to Interpol."

They had difficulty holding back their laughter. If Moshiko were listening now — and he listened almost twenty-four hours a day, otherwise what else was he doing alone in the apartment all day long — he would be surprised to discover that "pitchblende" and other deals had oozed from his hands like quicksilver. They were gaining precious time, time that would enable them to complete the deal of the centruy. Many things would happen after that, but they would already be far away and covered with piles of gold until the end of their lives, somewhere in the Caribbean islands, between yachts, splendid palaces, and a life of endless pleasures.

⚬❧⚬

"Pleasure breeds corruption!" thundered Mendel. "Do you understand, Ruchamah? In principle you're right. We could demand a whole apartment for a brilliant scholar like our Shmuli. But that's a recipe for an irresponsible lifestyle.

"Besides, do you want your son to build his new home on his father-in-law's corpse? If Mr. Mindelman had extra money, I wouldn't object. But he is as much of a pauper as I am. So we'll go fifty–fifty on a two-bedroom apartment in an out-of-town community for young couples, and we'll close the deal."

"Close the deal?" said Ruchamah. A special education teacher, she worked hard for every shekel of her salary. "We haven't even begun anything yet, and you're already buying an apartment. Aren't you putting the cart before the horse?"

"Why, you yourself told me that the girl is a rare pearl, correct? You heard wonderful things about her from all her friends."

Ruchamah smiled at the sweet memory of Chedvi's praises. She had personally made intensive inquiries, cross-examining every teacher and friend. Chedvi was definitely out of the ordinary, head and shoulders above the rest. The amateur *shadchan* Daniel Klein had not exaggerated. The Patankins were ready to go on to the next stage, and Daniel Klein had hinted that the girl's side had also completed their inquiries and it looked promising.

"Where will we get the money from?" asked Ruchamah.

"Where everyone gets it," laughed Mendel. The subject of money did not trouble him for a second, although he certainly did not have the necessary $50,000 in the bank. "You know the joke: The *chasan's* side undertakes to give 50%; the *kallah's* side, 50%; and *klal Yisrael,* 100%. I say it is the *Ribbono shel olam* Who undertakes to give 100%, because it is He Who gives us everything."

Suddenly he realized that it was Daniel Klein who had taught him to speak that way. Well, one could think Daniel had invented the wheel. The fundamental principles of faith are written in every siddur.

The *shidduch* got under way.

Daniel Klein was astounded. This was the first time in six years that no one had ruined a *shidduch* for Chedvi Mindelman. No anonymous nighttime caller had mentioned the dark secret that hovered like a cloud over the family.

Felix Goldmark had been right. Suspecting that the Mindelman phone might be tapped, he had instructed the Mindelmans to conduct the *shidduch* as *shidduchim* had been conducted a century ago: without a phone! The results had justified his approach.

The *shidduch* progressed stage after stage. After the inquiries came the financial arrangements and the meetings between the parents. Elitzafan and Devorah Mindelman visited the Patankins' apartment; Mendel and Ruchamah Patankin sat in the Mindelmans' living room.

For the two Jerusalem families, every knock on the door foreshadowed the approaching *Mazal tov*. Daniel Klein often had to leave his work in the Munbaz hotel to his assistant in order to go back and forth between the two families. Once he spoke with Mendel Patankin, once with Devorah Mindelman; once with Shmuli, once with Chedvi. He heard all the doubts, hesitations, and fears; he advised and transmitted messages, soothed and mediated. He learned to speak like a professional *shadchan*, to minimize every shortcoming — if not turn it into a virtue — and to blow up every virtue to giant proportions. The two families drew closer, got to know one another, and began to think in terms of being *mechutanim*.

Daniel felt euphoric. He could already see the engagement notice in the paper and smell the aroma of fresh cakes at the *vort*. He could hear the rabbi read the *tena'im*. He could see the *chasan* and *kallah*, blushing and embarrassed, shyly nodding their heads and smiling. He could touch the *shadchanus* money in his pocket.

I, Daniel Klein, succeeded where even the master shadchan himself, Emanuel Klopstein, gave up in defeat.

❧✦☙

Daniel's euphoria was miniscule in comparison to the feeling of *Mashiach's* coming that swept the quiet apartment in Beis Yisrael. The entire Mindelman family, from Elitzafan to Nachum'ke, knew that this was it. The *shidduch* had passed the point of no return. All that remained was to dress and break a plate. Devorah bought new outfits for herself and all the girls. It was quite an expense, but she had been praying many years for this moment. Chedvi laughed a lot, cracked jokes, had difficulty concentrating, and was enveloped in a rosy cloud. "May you be this happy all your life," Devorah whispered in her heart whenever she saw the radiant smile of the *kallah*-to-be. "May no one ruin your happiness."

If only Rebbetzin Flora had been in town! Devorah wished she could tell her that her prophecy was about to be fulfilled, that the righteous, handsome *chasan* was approaching the house with giant strides. Devorah would have requested Flora's amulet against the forces of evil to prevent them from ruining Chedvi's happiness. But Flora was visiting her hundreds of fans in France, and her cell phone was not on.

Menashe sent a message from yeshivah to say that he had finished preparing a *derashah* for Chedvi's *vort*. Nachum'ke bought a multi-volume set of *Chazon Ish* out of his own savings as a gift for the *chasan* — who would surely turn into a good friend in appreciation — and kept it hidden in *mesivta*.

Elitzafan inquired at the book store about a good *Shas* for the *chasan*. "Not leather bound," he told Devorah. "That's too expensive. You don't become a *talmid chacham* from a leather-bound *Shas*."

That was when Devorah knew that the die was cast. "*Mazal tov* to you, Mrs. Mindelman," she whispered to herself, turning her face aside so her husband would not see the tears in her eyes. "*Mazal tov*, Chedvi is engaged." Then she thought better of it. *No, I will not get carried away. Let's not exaggerate. Chedvi is about to get engaged. This, too, is a mighty accomplishment. Six years!*

༺✦༻

A festive air pervaded the Patankin home as well. Shmuli returned from each meeting visibly pleased. Communication flowed smoothly, and all the objectives he had marked for himself in the long days of bachelorhood were achieved one by one. It had been worthwhile to wait!

"She's a wonderful daughter of an outstanding father," he told his own father with satisfaction.

Mendel glowed with pleasure. "I never doubted it," he said, and cast a fearful glance at his old hat. It would put him to shame at the *vort*. He had to quickly buy a new hat that would befit the *mechutan* of Elitzafan Mindelman. And his suit needed to be dry-cleaned immediately.

"You know," he told his smiling son, "all the inquiries we made did not turn up a single flaw. This is a such a *mehudar esrog* that even with a microscope you won't find a single blemish."

Now he revealed a secret. "There were other suggestions that would have gotten you a complete apartment, and more. But believe me, a *mechutan* like Elitzafan Mindelman is worth everything."

⁓

The intercity bus rolled out of cold, wintry Jerusalem into the terraced, tree-studded Judean hills. It passed the barren gold and white Judean desert, the palm trees of Jericho, and a Bedouin encampment with big black tents and grazing goats. After stopping at the Tziporah Cafeteria, it continued past army bases and through the lush, warm Jordan Valley. Remarkably, the drastic changes in scenery and climate took place in only a few hours.

Daniel Klein stretched in his seat and wondered what he was doing on a bus to Tiberias. Why had he given up a day's work to make this long trip? Why did it have to be today, when the Patankin–Mindelman *shidduch* was a hairsbreadth away from conclusion? Why was some inexplicable urge impelling him to investigate the mystery of the apartment at 4 Peki'in Street?

This whole trip could well be for nothing. Perhaps he was chasing the wind. But the connection between the letter bearing the Tiberias address and the key with the lion's-head relief seemed more than coincidental. Avraham Zeidel Portman, the man of riddles, had deliberately hidden the envelope and the key for his own reasons.

At the Tiberias Central Bus Station, Daniel scooped up his winter coat, which he had needed in Jerusalem, and his attaché case, and got off the bus. A friendly taxi driver with a sweeping mustache and bermuda shorts drove him to a small street at the edge of the old part of Tiberias. "Number four is over here," he said, pointing to a two-story, well tended building covered with ivy. He collected fifteen shekels for the seven-minute ride and continued on his way.

Daniel surveyed the building. Suddenly he was gripped by paralyzing fear. Had someone maneuvered him here like a marionette on a string? Was he walking into a trap?

He thought of knocking first at the neighbor's door to ask whether anyone was living in the Portman apartment. But no, if he wanted to attract attention, he might as well stand in the courtyard and play a saxophone.

He wet his parched throat with a few sips from the bottle of mineral water in his attaché case. Then he quietly entered the building.

There were four mailboxes. Three of them were new and bore the names Azulai, Harari, Chatab. The fourth was old and broken. With great effort, he made out the faded remnants of two letters of "Portman."

He found the apartment on the first floor. His heart beat furiously as he took out the yellow lion's-head key. Would the key open the door? And if it did, what was waiting for him on the other side?

Aften-year-old boy wearing a large black velvet yarmulke stared with big eyes at the bowl of hot potato soup. He moved the silver spoon to his mouth, but time after time, instead of putting the aromatic golden liquid into his mouth, he let it drip back down into the bowl. Occasionally, big, oily drops splashed onto the festive white Pesach tablecloth, penetrated a second cloth underneath, and were absorbed in the thick weave of the bottom tablecloth.

"Stop, Shaul! You're staining the tablecloth," said Sima Poliakov as she brought more matzah to the table.

Shaul made a face and began eating. From time to time, he let the soup spill "accidentally" onto the polished wooden floor. When these small provocations were ignored, he left the table and walked over to the window.

He pulled the damask drapes aside a crack and looked into the empty street. Heavy rain poured onto the slippery oval stones and mud that lined the road. Yesterday, Shabbos afternoon, a Christian mob had gathered in the street and thrown rocks into the windows of a few houses. The frightened Jewish residents had closed their shutters. Then, as if in response to a hidden order, the angry, screaming mob suddenly disappeared, leaving the street quiet.

Heavy gray clouds hung over the city, reinforcing the feeling of impending disaster. The Jews of Kishinev knew they were sitting on a volcano that threatened to erupt at any moment, but as long as streams of boiling lava didn't burn them, they tried to conduct life as usual.

"How is it possible not to eat such delicious soup?" asked Sima. She turned to her daughter, who was fanning the coal fire in a corner. "Kreindel, did you put too much salt in the soup?"

"No, Mamma," said Kreindel, insulted. "I put in a tablespoon, exactly as you taught me."

"I meant in Shaul's bowl," said Sima, winking at Kreindel. Shaul occasionally evoked the ire of his older siblings and incited them to take revenge against him.

"I don't know what you're talking about," said fourteen-year-old Elitzafan. He swallowed another piece of potato and bit into a round matzah. "This is the delicious Pesach soup that I look forward to all year long."

Kreindel looked at Elitzafan with an expression of gratitude. Only Mamma knew how hard she worked to make the soup succeed. Sima was an excellent cook, and her oldest daughter tried to follow suit. Kreindel took young Shaul's refusal to eat as a personal insult. At least Elitzafan appreciated her efforts and even said so.

A heavy cough came from a corner of the room, where ninety-year-old Chedvah Freidel lay in a big metal bed. A white *tichel* framed her wrinkled face, and her clear, focused eyes radiated sharp understanding and warm love.

Avraham Poliakov hurried to his mother's side. "Would you like a cup of tea?"

"If it is not difficult for you, I would be very happy. Bless your firstborn, Menashe, who troubled himself to feed me the soup spoonful by spoonful." The old woman pointed to a young man with a brown beard who was quietly taking away an empty bowl.

"*Baruch Hashem* that we have the privilege of honoring you," said Avraham with satisfaction.

"The children learn from their father's example," murmured Chedvah Freidel. She followed Avraham with her eyes as he hurried to the samovar, simmering with a quiet whisper over its coals. He pushed the ornate copper spigot back and let the stream of boiling water run into a gilt-edged china cup. After the cup was full, he put it on a matching saucer, poured in tea essence from a small brass teapot, and broke off a piece of sugar to put in. Finally he set the cup down on a low stool beside the bed.

"Here, the tea is ready."

Chedvah Freidel smiled with pleasure. "After your father died, I thought I would die too, but my son has been tending to me devotedly for seventeen years."

"Please don't praise me," Avraham protested weakly. "I'm doing nothing more than fulfilling Hashem's will." He helped his mother sit up in bed so she could drink her tea comfortably. Only then did he return to his place at the head of the table.

Suddenly Shaul ran back to the table. His face was white. "Poppa," he cried, "the street isn't empty anymore! A mob of Christians is out there, walking behind the priest Tomislav. They're waving a huge wooden cross."

"Don't worry," said Avraham, stroking Shaul's head. He could feel the child's body quivering with fear. "Today is the eve of their Easter festival. They always behave like this on the eve of their festivals. And now let's finish eating our *chol ha'moed* meal quickly. Remember, it's *Erev Yom Tov.*"

The words were soothing, but Avraham Poliakov himself did not believe them. He was not naive. He knew, as did all the Jews of Kishinev, that the Christian street was fraught with combustive vapors of anti-Semitism, carefully nurtured by long years of venomous incitement. All that was missing was a spark to ignite them.

Shortly before *Yom Tov*, Avraham Poliakov took Elitzafan and Shaul to the house of his sister in a neighboring town. He returned home to spend *Yom Tov* with Chedvah Freidel, Sima, Menashe, and Kreindel.

That evening, rumors spread that the corpse of a slain Christian boy had been found in the nearby town of Dubossary. Later on, a few people ran through the streets screaming, "The body was not found in Dubossary, but in Kishinev. A Christian child was killed in Kishinev!"

Within five minutes, eyewitnesses reported the identity of the Christian boy who had been slain. The old myth about Jews adding Christian blood to their Pesach matzos now received government approval. Riders on swift horses brought a proclamation from Czar Nicolas II: Since the body of a Christian boy had been found, the Czar permitted a pogrom against the Jews.

As the police stood by idly, the frenzied Christian populace rampaged through the Jewish streets. In the middle of the seventh night of Pesach, fourteen hours after the Poliakov family ate their *chol ha'moed* meal together, a mob bombarded the door of their house. With a wild roar, dozens of rioters burst in, wielding axes and metal bars.

They broke the table and chairs, shattered the glass doors of the carved china closet, cut the colorful carpets, tore the drapes from the windows, and smashed the huge mirror that hung over the piano. Even this musical instrument, symbolic of the finest Cyrillic culture, was kicked over, its strings exposed. Then they attacked the family members, savagely slaying three generations together.

The Kishinev pogrom continued for three days. After it ended, the Jewish rescue crews that went from house to house found the Poliakov home, once a warm family nest, looking like Sodom after it was overturned. Elitzafan and Shaul tried to go in, but responsible neighbors forcibly kept them out to spare their feelings. As it was, the sight of the two young orphans weeping hysterically broke the neighbors' hearts.

The Jewish community assessed its losses: forty-seven dead; six hundred wounded, of whom many died in the coming days; fifteen hundred houses destroyed and looted; many businesses burned.

The Kishinev pogrom was a turning point for Russian Jews. Previously they had waited for the waves of anti-Semitism to subside; now they began to flee in panic. Many immigrated to the United States and Palestine.

In addition, local self-defense groups sprang up spontaneously among the youth. Although they had few weapons, in many instances they managed to frighten away inflamed rabble heading toward Jewish streets.

One of the self-defense groups, consisting of twenty orphans, was organized by Elitzafan. He was driven by a single thought: *If only we had been organized that night, we could have driven off the rioters. Then Poppa and Momma, Bubby Chedvah Freidel, Menashe, and Kreindel would all still be alive!*

Anger and frustration wreaked havoc on Elitzafan's delicate young soul. His eyes, burning with hatred, followed every Christian youth of slight build. When no one was around, he would find a pretext to start a fight. "Your father killed my parents," he would shout into the ears of a weak youth in a dark alley as he beat him with his fists. "Take that for Bubby Chedvah Freidel," he would say, delivering a blow in the eye. "What did she do to you?" A kick in the abdomen was "revenge for my brother Menashe and my sister Kreindel, whom you slaughtered."

The fire of revenge that burned in Elitzafan's innards transformed the refined, sensitive lad into a ferocious beast. Unfounded rumors spread that he had even killed some helpless old gentiles with his bare hands.

One evening, Kishinev's mayor summoned the secretary of the city's Jewish community to a secret meeting. "I want you to get the Jewish troublemaker out of here," the mayor said in a threatening tone. "He has become a public menace; rumor has it that he has already killed a few people."

"That's a lie," said the secretary hotly.

"Get him out of here," repeated the mayor. "If you don't, our men will take care of him." He made a sign of slaughter on his own neck.

That same week, Elitzafan and Shaul Poliakov were offered the opportunity to join a group of youngsters going to Palestine. The brothers agreed enthusiastically, especially since Elitzafan found out that a group of Christian thugs were planning to do him in. "We have nothing left in Kishinev anyway," Elitzafan told Shaul.

The poverty in Jerusalem was luxury for the orphans who had lost everything in Kishinev. Elitzafan became a student in a yeshivah of the Old City, and at the age of twenty-three married Tirtzah Levine, the daughter of a Jerusalem scholar. Shaul, who had no one to guide him through adolescence, did not follow in his brother's footsteps. Little by little, he drew away from his family heritage. At the age of seventeen, he left Jerusalem for the orchards of Rechovot, where he picked oranges. From there, he went on to joined the founders of Deganiah, the first kibbutz in the Land of Israel.

Elitzafan blamed himself for failing to take sufficient care of his younger brother. "He and I are the last remnants of our family," he wept in his heart. He found comfort in his only son, born thirteen years after his wedding. Elitzafan wanted to perpetuate the name of his martyred father Avraham. He added the name Zeidel as a blessing for longevity and called the baby Avraham Zeidel.

The yellow key with the lion's-head relief slipped into the lock of the door on 4 Peki'in Street and turned smoothly. The door opened, letting Daniel into a dark hallway.

He groped for the electric switch and pushed it with a loud click, but the place remained dark. The electricity had long since been disconnected.

Daniel was prepared for such a possibility. He took a small flashlight out of his attaché case. Rays of orange light ran through the hall and encountered a closed door.

Surprisingly, the air was not as stuffy as you would expect in an apartment that had been closed up for a long time. Someone had been in here recently and had opened the windows. Perhaps he had resealed everything on purpose, and now he was lying in wait for Daniel in the dark.

Think constructively, Daniel rebuked himself. *If you act like a frightened rabbit, you won't get anywhere.*

Flashlight in hand, he moved forward, toward the inside door. He felt goose bumps on his skin. What was he waiting for? A bullet, or perhaps a blow on the skull, that would transport him into another world?

Calm down, Daniel, he told himself. *No one is interested in liquidating you. On the contrary, someone very much wants you to visit. Someone bigger and stronger than you is maneuvering you like a pawn in a chess game.*

He went over to the window and pulled the *tris* open slightly. Afternoon sunshine flooded the room.

Zeidel Portman had certainly treasured simplicity and modesty. This was the typical Israeli living room of forty years earlier: an old, sunken sofa with wooden armrests, blackened from the touch of hands; patterned red and blue upholstery that housewives preferred because it didn't show dirt; two matching armchairs, also with deep depressions; bookshelves with *sefarim,* history books, and old encyclopedias.

Daniel's suit began to pick up dust from the thick layer that covered everything: the books, the shelves, the pictures on the walls, the floor. In fact, his footsteps were recorded as if he had plodded through snow.

His were not the only footprints.

Looking carefully, he was surprised to see that there were other footprints as well — two sets. The footprints led him back to the dark hallway, and from there to an inner room, also dark. He went in and opened the *tris*, attracting the attention of some curious neighbors.

This room looked like an old-fashioned government office. Its walls were covered with shelves filled with big blue looseleafs. There were a few chairs that had been knocked over, along with a small formica table that was covered with fingerprints. Clearly two people had been involved in a scuffle.

His thoughts began to run wild; his breathing became fast and shallow. The paralyzing fear gripped him again, drying his saliva. What had happened here? Had someone been kidnapped?

He went into the small kitchen in search of clues. On the old stove, he found a rolled-up piece of notebook paper. Under other circumstances he would have tossed it into the wastebasket, but now every piece of paper might be an important clue.

His heart skipped a beat as he read the hastily scribbled lines:

To Daniel Klein:

I urgently want to meet you regarding the inheritance over which both of us are fighting. I have important information to share with you. Let's meet as soon as possible. Please call my cell phone.

Yoel Tzadok

Yoel Tzadok — the heavy man he had encountered in front of Zeidel's door before the funeral! The man was supposedly his enemy. What was he looking for here? How did he know Daniel would come here? With whom had he fought before leaving him the note? Had he been kidnapped?

The questions rattled around unanswered in his head.

Perhaps the cell phone number written on the note would get him some answers. Without thinking twice, he dialed. After four rings, he heard the recorded message, "The customer cannot receive your call right now. Please call later. Thank you."

Have I come to a dead end? Daniel wondered as he returned to the inner room. *Perhaps the dusty looseleaf notebooks will teach me something new.*

When he opened the first and second notebooks and looked at the documents, he knew that the trip had been worthwhile — so worthwhile that he regretted it from the depths of his heart. Regret seared him like a third-degree burn.

20

Why did I undertake this trip? thought Daniel miserably as the bus made its way back to Jerusalem. The more he knew, the more he suffered. If only he had not been curious about the dusty apartment in Tiberias!

Before this, each new layer had revealed another sparkling aspect of Zeidel's multi-faceted personality. But the looseleafs in Tiberias had revealed a dark, ugly side. *If only I hadn't touched them!*

He recalled a legend.

Once upon a time, white elephants lived in India. So rare were they that they sold for many times the price of ordinary gray ones.

A merchant bought a white elephant at a bargain price. In order to smuggle it out of the country, he painted it gray from the tip of its trunk to its little tail. After the elephant had passed safely through customs, the merchant hosed it down until it became all white again. But to his astonishment, the white layer came off as well, exposing gray elephant skin.

Oh, Zeidel, Zeidel! Beneath your gray layer, you painted yourself white. But the paint that came off today in Tiberias left you black as tar.

So the whispers about a dark secret had been right. Zeidel had a box of worms behind his back. Box? Why, a state treasury! All the documents were there, proving Zeidel's blackness in great detail. How could Zeidel have sunk so low? How could a believing Jew betray his country and his brethren for money?

Now Daniel understood why Elitzafan had cringed at the mention of his father and why he had changed his name from Portman to Mindelman. No one would want to be identified with such a person. Even the Patriarch Jacob did not want his name mentioned together with Korach's!

Most of the passengers dozed as the bus wended its way through the dark Jordan Valley road that night. Daniel was wide awake, pursued by nightmarish thoughts. Yoel Tzadok seemed to have been kidnapped from the apartment in Tiberias after a skirmish. At this very moment, he might be struggling for his life. Should Daniel file a complaint with the police? On the other hand, perhaps it had all been staged for Daniel's benefit.

Daniel dialed Yoel's number again. All he got was the same recording.

And what should he do about the *shidduch*? It, too, was almost a matter of life and death. Why make an innocent Jewish girl suffer? On the other hand, Shmuli's blood was no less red than Chedvi's. How could Daniel send him into a family with such a dark past?

Daniel opted for the default choice: When in doubt, do nothing.

❧✦❧

Jerusalem gave Daniel a cold, stormy greeting. When he left the bus, a fierce wind blew at him, making his body shiver. The streetlamps shone with a yellow-orange light that lit up raindrops dancing in puddles. He huddled in his coat, stuck his hands deep into the pockets, and went to *daven Ma'ariv*. Perhaps when he prayed for good counsel — in *v'saknenu b'etzah tovah milfanecha* — a brilliant solution would pop into his head.

From the synagogue, he took a taxi straight home. His head nearly split from pain and oppressive thoughts. If only Peninah would say, "No one called for you"!

"Daniel, the whole world is looking for you," said Peninah when he walked in the door.

Warm air hit his face and covered his glasses with a milky vapor. "Who exactly?"

"Who isn't? You name it." She laughed and hurried to prepare a hot tea for him. Her voice reached him from the kitchen while he took off his coat and jacket and hung them on a hanger. "The hotel needed you; you picked the wrong day to leave. Asher called from yeshivah; he needs you urgently. Your *chavrusah* called to ask where you were. Rav Yochanan Segel was wondering why you didn't come to the *shiur*."

At least she hadn't mentioned Patankin or Mindelman! He heaved a sigh of relief.

Her voice continued to pursue him while he took off his wet socks. "Many others called as well. But there's one thing I can't understand. How can you bring a *shidduch* so far and then disappear exactly at the time that it needs to be tied up? Mr. Patankin and Mr. Mindelman called today about every ten minutes. Both said the same thing: They want to arrange a final meeting. Mr. Mindelman complained that each time he calls, he has to run to the public phone booth. They wanted to do it between themselves, but they thought it was improper to leave the *shadchan* out."

Daniel turned white as plaster. "If only they *would* leave me out," he said finally, his voice trembling. He hugged the hot cup in his cold hands.

Peninah looked at him as if he were out of his mind. "After all the work you put into this *shidduch*?"

His eyes darted back and forth like frightened rabbit's. Should he tell her?

He decided not to. He sighed deeply, and closed his tortured eyes. Sensing that he did not want to answer, Peninah stopped questioning him and was silent.

But the phone was not.

He barely managed to take two sips to soothe his aching throat when the phone rang. Listlessly he picked up the receiver. He recognized the number. He would recognize it even in his sleep. Mendel Patankin.

"*Shalom aleichem*, Reb Daniel. I understand that you were busy all day. But you left us dangling between heaven and earth. We have to finish the *shidduch*!"

Every word smashed at Daniel's skull like a hammer. This beautiful *shidduch* in which he had so delighted had turned into a painful wound in his heart. "Flee, Mendel, flee!" he wanted to scream with all his might. "It's not for you!"

Instead of a mighty roar, out came a miserable stutter. "Y-y-yes, you are right, Reb Mendel. Of course we must do something. Let me think how to do it."

"What is there to think about?" laughed Mendel. "It's true that you lack experience as a *shadchan* so you are a bit excited. Simply make up with Elitzafan and his wife a time and a place to meet. We will sit down together and conclude things. There is no room for surprises. We already made up that each side would pay for half the expenses — apartment, wedding, furniture, and electrical appliances — everything in the most minimal way, of course, as appropriate for two Rothschilds like us. Then we'll invite the happy couple to join us and drink a *l'chayim*."

"Yes, yes, yes," said Daniel. *What a pickle I've gotten you into, good, innocent Mendel.* Actually, Mendel himself had just handed Daniel a way out on a silver platter. Money! He would break up the *shidduch* over money!

"That's the whole problem," Daniel said fearfully. "I haven't yet made up with the other side about money. It seems to me they want to change the agreement."

Mendel was offended. So it was no accident that the *shadchan* had been unreachable. The other side had delayed him with an attempt at last-minute extortion. "What do you mean 'change the agreement'? We agreed to go fifty-fifty, no?"

Mendel was silent for a moment. Then he said, "If we start negotiating from the beginning, I want a whole apartment for my Shmuli."

"You're right, Reb Mendel," said Daniel. Then, to add fuel to the fire, he added, "Really a boy like Shmuli is worth at least an apartment, and not in the outlying areas. He's worth a whole house in Jerusalem. Don't compromise!"

"You're mocking me," suggested Mendel.

"Heaven forbid," protested Daniel strongly. He wasn't joking. He was desperately trying to get out of this *shidduch*, the sooner the better.

"Enough jokes," said Mendel lightly. "Now I expect deeds, not words. Please get the train back on track. Tell Reb Elitzafan that a distinguished person like himself does not go back on an agreement. We will return to the midpoint and break a plate tomorrow evening, *im yirtzeh Hashem*."

Daniel looked in despair toward the ceiling. *To my sorrow, it was a toy train that derailed the shidduch train.*

DUAL ALLEGIANCE □ 143

"I think the *shidduch* will be finalized either this evening, or tomorrow evening at the latest," Leah'le Mindelman told her best friend, Malki Fried, as she beat the eggs in a plastic bowl. "How many cups of sugar does the recipe call for?" She pulled the long phone cord over so she could glance at the index card on the counter beside the packages of cocoa and sugar. "I'm so excited that I'm forgetting everything."

"Who's the *chasan*?" asked Malki curiously.

"Shmuel Patankin. Everyone calls him Shmuli. He's one of the best *bachurim* in Kol HaTalmud. Actually, his *rosh yeshivah* says they never had a *bachur* like him before."

Leah'le mixed the flour and sugar in the bowl and poured in cocoa and spices. Home alone this afternoon, she had decided to indulge in a chat while baking a cake for the *vort*.

Between the chat and the cake, Leah'le didn't hear the door open. She didn't see her mother come in with eyes wide as saucers. She didn't see the horror on her face. But suddenly she did hear something: a loud, piercing scream.

"Leah'le, what have you done!"

The scream knocked Leah'le off balance. The phone cord pulled on the plastic bowl and overturned it, while dragging the open carton of eggs over the edge of the counter. The contents of the bowl spilled onto the floor, forming a thick brown puddle at Leah'le's feet that mingled with the puddle of yolks and eggshells.

Devorah, totally hysterical, slapped herself on the cheek. "What have you done, Leah'le! What have you done!"

What happened? wondered Leah'le. *What will Malki think of Ima?* Slowly the power of speech returned to her. She whispered, "Bye, Malki" into the receiver and hung up.

Devorah pointed an accusing finger at the phone. "We agreed that Chedvi's *shidduch* would not be discussed over the phone! First of all, blessing rests only on whatever is hidden from the eye. You don't reveal anything about a *shidduch* before it is announced. Why did you have to tell? And if you couldn't hold it in, then why by phone — directly into the ears of our enemies?"

Tears filled Leah'le's eyes. The picture of wounded pride, she went for a mop and pail. The members of this family had developed paranoia. How could an innocent phone call ruin a *shidduch*?

Devorah ran into her bedroom, pulled her beloved *Tehillim* out of her pocketbook, and burst into uncontrollable sobs. Until now the Patankin–Mindelman *shidduch* had not been mentioned in any phone conversation, and everything had progressed with dreamlike smoothness. But now, who knew?

Elitzafan came home five minutes later to find Leah'le weeping as she washed the kitchen floor. From the bedroom came Devorah's heartrending cry, "My G-d, my G-d, why have You forsaken me?"

He ran to the bedroom. "Devorah, what happened?"

Devorah pointed toward the phone and mumbled weakly, "Leah'le spoke about the *shidduch* on the phone. Everything is over, everything."

He couldn't believe his ears. "One phone conversation, that's all?"

Devorah returned to her *Tehillim*.

"Listen," said Elitzafan serenely, "the days of Stalin are gone. Felix's advice not to speak about the *shidduch* over the phone was a recommendation, nothing more. Even if someone does tap our phone, I doubt whether he listens continuously twenty-four hours a day."

Devorah sighed deeply. A bad premonition clutched at her heart like a crab's pincers. "I hope you're right and I'm wrong. Chedvi will be crushed if this *shidduch* falls through."

Elitzafan invoked cool reason. "Aren't you getting carried away? I spoke with Mrs. Klein several times today. I understood from her that Mendel is just as anxious to close the *shidduch* as I am. If Daniel hadn't left town today without leaving a phone number where he could be reached, we would be drinking *l'chayim* right now. So what are you upset about?"

He went outside and called Daniel Klein from a public phone. "What's happening?" he asked amicably. "Are we finalizing the *shidduch*?"

Daniel writhed like a worm on a hook. "O-of c-course the *shidduch* must be completed, without a doubt." The question was only in which direction.

At a loss as to how to continue, he simply hung up.

Elitzafan naively thought they had accidentally been disconnected. He called again. Daniel recognized the number and sat there staring at the screen.

"Why don't you pick it up?" asked Peninah. "Shall I?"

"No, don't!" he cried. "I have nothing to say to him. Heaven have mercy on us all!"

❦

After the unsuccessful attempt to reach Daniel, Elitzafan went back into the house. Leah'le, mop in hand, was still weeping and struggling to clean up the kitchen. The sound of the sobs coming from the bedroom filled her with horror.

Elitzafan gave her a gentle, apologetic smile and tried to comfort her as he helped clean up the remnants of the spill.

Under normal circumstances, Leah'le would never have let her father mop up puddles of eggs and squeeze the rag out into the pail. But at that moment she was too angry and frustrated to know what she was doing.

ভর্জ

A jarring ring broke the late-night silence. Mendel was sitting before the ledger of his free-loan fund. He had been approached for a large loan, and he had to check to see whether the funds were available.

He glanced at his watch. 1:15 a.m. Who calls at such an hour? Something terrible has happened!

"Mr. Patankin?" asked an unknown voice.

"Yes."

"I wanted to discuss an important matter with you."

"At such an hour?"

"Yes, it is something urgent that cannot be delayed." The voice was deep, confident, and persuasive.

As Mendel listened, his face gradually lost its color. When he finally put down the receiver, he put his head down on the table and groaned.

The die was cast. His Shmuli would not get engaged to the daughter of Elitzafan Mindelman. It was a miracle that Daniel had slowed the pace. As long as they had not broken a plate, no harm was done.

So that was why a wonderful girl like Chedvi was still single. True, she was innocent, and her father had done no wrong. But a grandfather who had done such abominable things was not the right *yichus* for the Patankin family.

What would he say, though, to a righteous Jew like Elitzafan Mindelman?

He had a solution. True, it was an unconventional step, but truth is the best lie!

All parties to the *shidduch* spent a sleepless night. Elitzafan tried to calm his worried wife, but in the end he himself succumbed to her fear. Misfortune had pursued him since his youth. In the wee hours of the night, when he thought Devorah had fallen asleep, he wept silently. *It's all my fault. Hashem is punishing me for my sins. I should never have abandoned my father, no matter what the court, the media, and the neighbors said about him. Even if I erred as a teenager, I should have returned to him as an adult. I should have taken my family to visit him and bring him joy. Now he's gone, and there's no way to make amends!*

Mendel did not sleep a wink. The whole night he pondered what he would tell Elitzafan in the morning.

When he finally went to the phone, his hands shook as if he had Parkinson's.

Elitzafan picked up.

"Hello, Reb Elitzafan. I'm terribly sorry, but I have something unpleasant to tell you. I thought I should tell you directly instead of through the *shadchan*."

Elitzafan quickly sat down. That was it. Devorah had been right. A thousand-pound hammer was about to come down on his head. But he had to play the game.

"Let me guess. You want to ask for more for your Shmuli."

"Not at all. If only that were the case! Listen, Reb Elitzafan, you have a wonderful daughter. The *shidduch* is beautiful. We so badly wanted to celebrate the engagement. But the problem is, I heard something about your family."

Mendel broke down and wept. "Reb Elitzafan, judge me favorably and forgive me," he managed to say before he hung up.

Devorah found her husband sitting beside the phone, staring glassy-eyed into space and muttering unclear syllables.

"The *shidduch* is off, isn't it?" she said.

21

The basement restaurant of the King David Hotel was empty of diners when the Etzel "milkmen" entered, swiftly overpowered the restaurant's fifteen Arab chefs and waiters, and trussed them like chickens. Seven innocent-looking milk containers, each containing fifty kilograms of explosives and detonators, were brought into the restaurant and placed beside the supporting pillars. So far, everything was going according to plan.

Unexpectedly, two British soldiers appeared and tried to stop the "milkmen." In the exchange of fire, one of the soldiers was killed and the other seriously wounded. Etzel met no other resistance.

The King David Hotel was the seat of British rule in Palestine. Its spacious southern wing housed Sir John Shaw's offices, General Evelyn Barker's headquarters, and the department of special investigations, which were protected by machine-gun nests, soldiers, policemen, and detectives.

A blow to the King David Hotel would be a blow to the morale of the foreign rulers.

Etzel had other considerations as well. There had to be a fitting reprisal for the British takeover of the Jewish Agency building, the symbol of longed-for Zionist rule. Finally, files of incriminating material and documents against the Haganah and Etzel had to be disposed of.

The action was not meant to take lives.

After hiding the explosives, the Jews released the Arab workers with a warning to flee for their lives. They did.

Immediately afterward a small explosion erupted, producing a cloud of smoke and a loud noise that sent passersby running in the street and covered the Etzel men's escape.

Half an hour before the big explosion, Etzel warned the King David Hotel, *The Palestine Post*, and the French consulate next door that explosives had been placed in the hotel, and the place should therefore be evacuated at once.

The hotel was not evacuated. Sir John reportedly said, "I am not here to take orders from Jews. *I give them orders!*"

At 12:37, a mighty explosion shook all of Jerusalem. The sealed basement magnified the power of the blast by several factors. The southern wing of the hotel was destroyed, killing ninety-two people, wounding forty-five, and severely damaging British prestige. A handful of Etzel men had thrust a sword into the heart of the British lion.

Under cover of the smoke and dust that covered Jerusalem for hours, the Etzel men escaped to apartments prepared in advance and changed their clothes. Some disguised themselves in the dress of the Old Yishuv: a gray *Yerushalmi chalat* with a wide sash and a low, broad-brimmed felt hat.

A young man with curly *peyos* walked down Baharan Street in Meah Shearim. His glowing eyes darted alertly to all sides. *We showed them!* his thoughts sang. Soot and the smell of smoke clung to his body. He felt his *chalat* and breathed in deeply. No, the garment would not give him away.

For Etzel fighter Avraham Zeidel Portman, the *Yerushalmi* garb was not a borrowed cover-up. It was his usual dress.

☙❧

Mendel Patankin's phone call plunged the Mindelman family into mourning.

Chedvi displayed unbelievable fortitude. "If this is Hashem's will," she said, "we must accept it with love." She slung her pocketbook over her shoulder and went to work as if nothing had happened. A teacher does not abandon the thirty little girls who are waiting for her just because she is not getting engaged.

Devorah followed Chedvi with a worried look as she walked down the street. "I pray for her mental health," she whispered to Elitzafan. "I hope she'll be okay."

"May He Who answered our father Avraham on Mount Moriah answer us," he smiled sadly. A questioning look was evident on Devorah's face, so he quickly explained. "When Avraham was about to offer his son Yitzchak as a sacrifice, all seemed lost. Then, in an instant, everything changed.

"I believe with perfect faith that Hashem's salvation will come to us, too, in a twinkling. We must strengthen our faith and trust in Him. It's easy to have faith when all goes well. The trick is to absorb a painful blow, know it is His will, and accept it with love."

That night, Felix came home to find Elitzafan waiting for him. One glance at the red eyes rimmed by black circles told the Scandinavian scientist that something terrible had occurred.

Elitzafan poured out his troubles while the deep, wise eyes regarded him sympathetically. "Was it Daniel Klein who sabotaged the *shidduch*? If so, why did he suggest it in the first place? If not, why did he stammer and hang up on me?"

Felix removed his blue beret and put on a big black velvet yarmulka. This was the first time Elitzafan had seen him without his beret. Felix hummed a Beethoven sonata quietly while weighing all the facts in his brilliant, analytical mind.

"Okay, my good friend Elitzafan," he began after a few minutes of silence. "First of all, have you had anything to eat or drink today?"

"Barely," Elitzafan confessed. He recited the blessing over a glass of grapefruit juice with deep feeling. The humane gesture touched his heart.

"Don't ask what a day we had," he said. "The boys called from yeshivah to ask when they should come to the *vort* and were shocked to hear what happened. The two girls, except for Chedvi of course, blamed Leah'le for chatting on the phone about the upcoming engagement."

"What?" Felix almost fell out of his chair. "Do you mean to tell me the *shidduch* was mentioned over the phone?"

"Yes," Elitzafan admitted shamefacedly. "Leah'le mentioned it to her friend yesterday afternoon, an hour later Daniel Klein stammered to me on the phone, and this morning Mendel Patankin called to say the *shidduch* was off."

Felix spread his hands in an expression of helplessness. The next moment he looked as if he wanted to stalk angrily out of the room. He went over to the window and stared at the dark sky and at the white lights sparkling light-years away. Finally he shouted triumphantly, "Excellent!"

"What is excellent?" asked Elitzafan.

"Excellent, everything is as clear as daylight," said Felix, pleased. "We tried a laboratory experiment, and it worked.

"I always had a feeling that Daniel was innocent, but I had no scientific basis for it. Now we have isolated the causes and gotten to the heart of the matter. Until Leah'le spoke on the phone, all went well. From the moment Leah'le spoke on the phone, everything went wrong. It is almost certain that someone is tapping your phone lines — and we will topple him with this. We will send him disinformation through the phone, and we will conduct the real *shidduch* using the old methods."

"You're really sure that Daniel Klein is innocent?" Elitzafan was clearly disappointed, like the man who consulted a reliable authority but accepted only what he wanted to hear. Elitzafan had been sure that Felix would blame Daniel. Other than the fickle *shadchan*, he had no other suspects.

For a minute Felix empathized with Elitzafan's feelings. "You are right that something here doesn't smell right." Felix let him savor the thought that he held the same opinion, but only for a second. "But nevertheless, I stick to my position. Daniel is a fine, upright person who is incapable of committing such a crime. Why, it's almost murder! People have jumped off the roof because of such things. I take my hat off to your Chedvi for holding her head up high today."

"She is a strong personality," said Elitzafan.

"Besides," said Felix, continuing his previous line of thought, "Daniel Klein would have to be a total lunatic to work so hard to bring the *shidduch* to a climax, and then sabotage it."

"That's what I told you before," Elitzafan reminded him. "That's why the question arises: What got into him? Why did he suddenly stammer and hang up on me?"

"I don't know," said Felix with uncharacteristic excitement. His hands drew circles in the air. "It is clear, though, that something definitely happened. There is only one thing to do. I will go and ask him directly."

"What, you are going to speak to him?" Elitzafan tugged at the scientist's sleeve as if he had announced a meeting with the devil.

"Absolutely." Felix pulled out his palm computer and began to type something. "Where did you say he works?"

❦

The gently lit Ivory Hall, on the mezzanine floor of the Munbaz Hotel, was half full. Groups of guests sat at round tables covered with red tablecloths and empty plates. Most of the guests were calm and restrained, although clear signs of impatience were apparent. But one heavyset, middle-aged man stood up and shouted loud enough for Felix to hear.

"What kind of hotel is this? I ordered baked salmon. Where is it?" He accosted a passing Arab waiter. "Does an order have to take forty minutes?"

The waiter's quiet answer enraged the guest even more. "Where is that *mashgiach*?" he thundered. "Call him. I want to see him with my own eyes. Never in my life have I heard such a thing!"

A few guests cringed at his coarseness, but others agreed with him and added loud complaints of their own. Felix followed the goings-on with a thin, ironic smile. He enjoyed observing human behavior as well as studying it theoretically. Besides, it was to his advantage. "I won't have to search for Daniel," he chuckled with satisfaction. "He will come to me."

A tall man with a trimmed gray beard and a white jacket walked quickly into the hall. "I was not mistaken," thought Felix. "Those are the eyes of an honest man."

"I'm the *mashgiach* of the hotel," he said pleasantly. "Did you want to ask me a question?"

"I don't want to ask," hollered the heavyset man. "I want to eat!" He wiped his sweaty face with the linen napkin. "The waiter said you declared all the food today unfit!"

"Correct," Daniel confirmed, absently straightening the *peyos* behind his ears. "My instructions must be adhered to without deviation to insure the *kashrus* of this establishment. Someone baked the meat and fish together in the oven. We had to throw out dozens of kilos of expensive food instead of serving it to the guests."

The heavyset man banged the glass goblet down on the table. "I've heard that meat and milk may not be mixed," he fumed, "but meat and fish?"

"The Code of Jewish Law forbids it because of health reasons," said Daniel pleasantly.

The complainer opened his mouth in astonishment. Daniel continued, "But let me offer you an alternative: rib steak broiled over a flame. It will be ready in a few minutes."

That restored the calm. Greatly relieved, Daniel walked toward the entrance of the hall, only to be ambushed by Felix.

An expression of distress covered Daniel's face when Felix introduced himself as a friend of Elitzafan Mindelman. Daniel gave some evasive explanation as to why the *shidduch* was off.

Felix escorted him through the corridor toward the elevators. "The fate of the *shidduch* does not interest me at this moment," said Felix. "I only want to know why you did an about-face. Did someone call you in the middle of the night and speak about a dark secret in the family history?"

"No," answered Daniel laconically and pressed the elevator button. "It's something else."

The elevator arrived. Daniel went inside, hoping to get away, but the scientist followed him in.

"Perhaps you will let me in on the secret? It's for a good cause."

The captivating smile that lit up Felix's deep brown eyes melted Daniel's defenses. He sighed deeply. "Three days ago I was in an apartment in Tiberias, where new, hair-raising facts came to light about a Jew whom I knew and liked very much, but about whom I was sorely mistaken.

"This apartment belonged to Elitzafan Mindelman's father. How sad it is for such a beloved and highly regarded individual to be the son of a despicable evildoer. I knew the father for many years, but now I see that I really didn't know him. I thought he was a nice person; actually he was an ugly monster. I regret all the deeds of kindness I ever did for him. I only pray that Heaven does not condemn me for having helped such a criminal!"

Felix looked at him sideways. "You are hurling sweeping accusations. You seem to have gotten carried away with your attack on the man. Probably it isn't as bad as you think."

"I wish you were right," said Daniel grimly. "You're invited to visit his apartment in Tiberias, at 4 Peki'in Street, and read about his crimes. They are recorded in great detail in dozens of looseleaf notebooks."

"Did you whisper something of this into Mendel's ears? Did you let him in on your thoughts about the shady dealings of Chedvi's grandfather?" The wise eyes studied Daniel carefully. With a fast, almost imperceptible motion, Felix brushed his hand against Daniel's chest to check whether his heart was beating faster.

"Heaven forbid!" Daniel was stung to the quick. "I've told no one but you. But I cannot continue to encourage this *shidduch* knowing what I know. I feel I've done a grave injustice to the boy as well as to his father. I don't think Shmuli Patankin deserves to marry the granddaughter of a man who—"

"Who what?"

Daniel searched his pockets, pulled out the yellow key with the lion's-head relief, and placed it in Felix's palm. "Go yourself to Zeidel's apartment and find out who he was."

Daniel turned around and went into the kitchen, where rows of steaks were being removed from the fire to the tables. Felix examined the yellow key thoughtfully. Perhaps it was time to take the skeleton out of the closet and examine it. What was Zeidel's secret?

F elix approached the apartment on Peki'in Street just as Daniel had
four days earlier. Like Daniel, Felix got out of the taxi and went from
the street into the courtyard. But Daniel had approached nervously,
his eyes focusing on every neighbor who glanced into the courtyard.
Felix could not have cared less whether someone would call the police and
complain of suspicious movement around an abandoned apartment.

What interested Felix was something else. His analysis had led him to
hypothesize that the apartment was under continuous surveillance. Was
his hypothesis correct?

Instead of entering immediately as Daniel had done, Felix stopped and
examined the outside of 4 Peki'in. The fifty-year-old apartment building had
recently undergone a face-lift. A well-tended garden surrounded the clean
white stucco facade, punctuated with shiny black bars on all the windows
and balconies. Nothing of interest there. Felix continued to look around.

Next door, in 6 Peki'in, an old-fashioned rain gutter had been installed
on the third floor. Under the window, attached to the pipe of the rain

gutter, was a plain, innocent-looking tin box with a small round hole in the middle, apparently an integral part of the rain gutter. Felix, who worked with systems that were a thousand times more sophisticated, would have bet that this was a camera surveying the approach to 4 Peki'in. But only through binoculars could he have seen the light rays break on the small round hole.

After quickly calculating the angles involved in taking the picture, Felix calmly entered the courtyard. Just before the area covered by the assumed lens, he lowered his beret to cover his face and quickened his pace. Felix was not about to make life easy for the photographer, whoever he was. When he entered the camera's dead space, he pushed his beret back into place.

As he stood facing the old door, Felix realized that other parties surely had copies of the lion's-head relief key. The renovation could not have been done without access to the apartment.

After two turns of the key, the door gave way. Felix knew what to expect. Daniel Klein had described a dark, dusty, quiet, one-bedroom apartment. He would enter a dark hallway. To the left would be a living room with an old sofa, nothing of interest. To the right would be the room with the incriminating looseleafs.

He slipped into the hall. Suddenly, he stopped short. Several people were talking together in the living room, to his left. He could hear one of them distinctly. A guttural voice with an unmistakable Arab accent asked in English, "Who is this man?"

Felix was not the type to be afraid. Now, for the first time in his life, his blood froze in his veins. So it was all a carefully orchestrated plot, and he had walked straight into the trap. His heart nearly stopped beating. He closed his eyes, waiting for the worst to happen.

Two minutes passed, and nothing happened. Felix dared to open his eyes.

Through the open door, he could see into the living room, dimly lit with a flashlight. Judging by the voices, there were at least five men in the room, but he saw only a single figure seated on the sofa.

Felix's back was bathed in sweat. Either the man had seen him approaching the apartment, or he had been informed, perhaps by the camera, but it was clear he knew Felix had arrived. The man's big black eyes were open wide, like a snake patiently watching its helpless victim. They were riveted on Felix, who was still standing in the hall.

For a few seconds, there was tense silence. The two men studied each other without moving a limb. Then a flash of recognition passed between the two pairs of eyes simultaneously, and they cried out together:

"Felix!"

"Yoel!"

"Felix Goldmark, what are you doing here?"

"And what are you doing here, Yoel Tzadok?"

"I asked first," laughed Yoel Tzadok, jumping up. His hand landed on the scientist's shoulder with a friendly slap. "How did you get here? You're the last person I expected to see here."

The corners of Felix's eyes wrinkled as he smiled in relief, "Who were you expecting — Daniel Klein perhaps?"

Yoel was startled. "What?! Do you know him?"

"Yes," answered Felix laconically. He pointed to a tape recorder on the sofa. "What are all those voices?"

"Since you have a high security clearance, I'll let you in on it." Yoel rewound the tape and turned it on. They sat down in the old-fashioned living room amidst clouds of dust and listened silently.

"This time we're talking about something big," said an old, hoarse voice. Felix could hear the speaker suck a cigar and blow out the smoke. "There hasn't been such a profitable deal since the big one of '98."

"Nati, don't forget that the danger this time is a hundredfold," came a much younger voice. "We're being followed, and you know as well as I do what's in store for us — thanks to Moshiko. If I were in your place, I would take care of him."

"Don't worry, Dubik," answered the hoarse voice. "Moshiko's day will come. His life isn't worth a penny. As for being followed, I'm not at all worried. I managed to shake off the American CIA, the British MI6, and the Chinese Te-Wu when we smuggled the weapons ship to India. You don't think I'll be able to shake off some Israelis?"

"What will they do with the pitchblende?" asked another young voice, more hesitant than Dubik's.

"Oh, our Malkiel is worried. Mr. Guilty Conscience, Malkiel Yahalom." More cigar smoke was blown out. "Do I know? They'll use it as chemical fertilizer in the fields. What do you care what they do with it?"

"I care," Malkiel persisted stubbornly. "Nati, this time we're crossing the last red line. Can you really say you don't care about the consequences? Don't you want to have a homeland left?"

"You sound like a worried grandmother." The coarse voice sounded as if it belonged to a big thug.

"I wasn't speaking to you, Asaf. With all due respect, I was speaking to Nati."

"Friends, the argument is totally unnecessary," said the cigar smoker. "We haven't done anything yet. We've been asked to transport a certain amount of the substance from one place to another, that's all. Beyond that, nothing interests me. Twenty million dollars is an incredible sum for one deal, and I have no intention of giving up the money."

"Twenty million dollars to destroy Israel."

A guttural English with a deep Arabic accent intervened. "Pitchblende, that's good snuff."

"Snuff for horses with colds. Your government is prepared to spend twenty million dollars to transport snuff?"

"If you don't like it, Malkiel," thundered the coarse voice, "no one is forcing you to participate. You can get up and leave right now."

"So that you can institute your evil dictatorship? Not on your life! Nati, I beg you, twenty million is quite a sum, but it breaks all conventions. Never have we done such a thing!"

There was a slight pause, then again Malkiel's voice. "I would like to inform the writer of the threatening note I just received that if anything happens to me, heads will roll. I've placed interesting material about Nati, Asaf, and Morgan Consolidated, Ltd. in the hands of several scoop-seeking journalists who are just waiting for the opportunity to use it."

"Someone here is looking for a laugh, and you, silly cat, are making a big deal out of it," came a fatherly rebuke from Nati.

At this point the recording became unclear. Yoel shut the recorder and pocketed the tape.

"Where did you get that from?" asked Felix.

"First tell me something," said Yoel. "Do you recognize these voices?"

"One is familiar," said Felix pensively. "Malkiel Yahalom was in Elta about ten years ago. Who are the others?"

"Allow me to introduce Nati Morgan, Asaf Niv, and Dubik Cooperman — arms dealers, among the biggest in the market. The hoarse one is Nati, owner and primary stockholder of Morgan Consolidated, Ltd. He's my boss. The coarse voice belongs to Asaf, Nati's assistant and right-hand man, who will take over after Nati retires."

Felix suddenly recalled his initial fright. "Who's the Arab with the guttural voice?"

"Some new buyer. Nati sells weapons to the Arabs, did you know that? He claims they're from non-hostile countries. And what about you, Felix? Are you still working for Elta in Ashdod?"

"Correct," Felix nodded. "Do you remember those days?"

"What a question!" laughed Yoel. "Twelve years can't erase the memory of Elta — or of Felix Goldmark. Let's test my memory. You come every day from Jerusalem to Ashdod by public transportation, get off in the industrial zone, and travel by internal transportation to the plant in Section 3 of Ashdod. The plant is completely surrounded by a high wall painted white, two yards high, with barbed wire on top and signs saying "Do not photograph." You ignore the giant parking lots in which I used to park; you don't own a car. You walk toward the gate and are swept inside, together with a few thousand other workers, to the world of Elta, daughter company of Israel Aircraft Industries."

"Excuse me, I am not swept inside," chuckled Felix. "I come in alone through a back door. Apart from that, everything is correct."

"And what do you do there today?" asked Yoel curiously. "At that time you were working in missiles and space systems."

"There I was, and there I am," said Felix. "I participated, as you remember, in the development of the Ofek 5 and Amos satellites. Then I was promoted to research for Arrow, the missile against tactical ballistic missiles, the only one of its type in the world."

"Sounds exciting."

"That's how it sounds. In fact, my work has actually become quite boring. All day I sit at the computer analyzing tables of numbers."

"I would gladly trade places with you instead of being one of Nati Morgan's poodles. We'll enjoy the results of your boring drawings when Arrow missiles shoot down Scud and Shihav missiles on their way to Israel."

Felix ignored the compliment. "How did you get the recording?"

"From a friend of mine who works for Nati Morgan in Paris. His name is Moshiko Sharabi."

"It sounded as if they are about to eliminate him," Felix pointed out. "He should flee — today, before it's too late!"

"If you know that, doesn't he? He heard the whole broadcast live. Moshiko is a genius in the area of micro listening devices. Most recently he planted a button in Dubik Cooperman's fancy watch. The button was discovered, and they're sure that was the last one. But they don't know Moshiko. He's the type to work with a dentist to plant a button in a patient's filling. He's planted buttons in the buckle of Nati's belt, in Dubik's left pocket, in Nati's portable computer, which he takes everywhere, in Malkiel Yahalom's expensive pen, and who knows where else. The recording you heard is from one of Moshiko's buttons.

"Now tell me, what brings you here?" asked Yoel suddenly.

Felix showed him the lion's-head key. "Daniel Klein sent me here to learn about the past of Avraham Zeidel Portman. I understand there are dozens, perhaps hundreds, of looseleaf notebooks filled with documents about his doings."

Yoel grabbed Felix's hand. "Don't ask anyone but me about Zeidel. No one knew him better than I did."

"May I ask how?" asked Felix, shaking off the painful grip. He knew from Daniel that Yoel was claiming Zeidel's inheritance. Daniel had seen Yoel as a bitter enemy ever since the meeting at the entrance to Zeidel's Rechaviah apartment on the day of the funeral.

Yoel stretched his neck like a proud peacock. "I was Zeidel's right-hand man. I know every comma and period in his life."

Perhaps Yoel was the anonymous caller who ruined all of Chedvi's *shidduchim*! Felix lost his usual composure and began to breathe quickly in excitement. "Was he a positive or negative figure?"

Yoel looked at Felix with flashing dark eyes. "There was no greater *tzaddik* than Zeidel. I'm familiar with every notebook here in the apartment and with every strange episode linked to his name. I can explain the whole business to you, and in the end you will see that he was pure and clean as a newborn babe. He had nothing to do with the corruption."

"I don't know what it's all about yet." Felix threw out a few provocative sentences to draw Yoel out. But Yoel did not take the bait.

"At this moment," said Yoel, "I don't have time to deal with the issues of Zeidel. My number one priority is the recording you just heard." He pulled the *tris* up, and the room was flooded with daylight. "Do you know what pitchblende is?"

Felix nodded.

"It's serious, right?"

"Extremely."

"Then we must do something," said Yoel.

"Certainly," said Felix. "Let me just ask you one question. Daniel found your note on the stove inviting him to call you, but your cell phone was not on. Since there were signs of a skirmish in the apartment, Daniel thought you had been kidnapped and perhaps even liquidated. What's the story?"

Yoel shrugged. "One of the neighbors, a fellow called Chatab, has set his eyes on this apartment. He has a key, and he's waiting for an opportune moment to order a garbage truck, clear out the contents, and bring in a renovation team. While I was here listening to some recordings, Chatab came in and took me by surprise. I almost died of fright. I asked him to leave the apartment, but he refused, arguing that it was his as much as mine. I had no choice but to convince him with my hands."

"I understand," said Felix. Yoel's strong hands were no laughing matter. Daniel was lucky that his own encounter with Yoel had ended in a mere exchange of words.

"I understand that you're convinced of Zeidel's innocence."

"One hundred percent," Yoel confirmed.

"Will you allow me to take a look at the looseleafs? That is why I came to Tiberias," Felix reminded him.

"Go right ahead."

Felix went into the other room and opened the *tris*. For a long time he pored over notebooks. When he finally said goodbye to Yoel, he was thoroughly confused about the complex character named Avraham Zeidel Portman. The entire matter demanded a thorough investigation. On the one hand, the incriminating documents spoke for themselves and left no room for doubt. On the other hand, Yoel Tzadok assured him that at an opportune occasion, he would tell him about Morgan Consolidated, Ltd. and the rise and fall of Avraham Zeidel Portman. He would also tell him how the two were connected to each other and about what was going on right now in Paris.

23

Felix boarded the bus to Jerusalem and chose a seat in the back, where he would be able to think undisturbed.

He knew that Iran was stepping up its efforts to acquire a nuclear warhead in the very near future. At the same time, Iranian leaders spoke openly about their desire to wipe Israel off the map; some even boasted that before long, they would be able to destroy Israel within a few minutes. Satellite pictures showed intensive activity in the $800 million nuclear reactor in the city of Bushehr and construction of an underground plant to enrich uranium in Natanz. After strong pressure by the International Atomic Energy Agency, supervisors went into Natanz, where they found 160 centrifuges showing thousands of hours of use as well as parts for another thousand.

No one believed Iran's protests of innocence. Experts assessed that after the completion of the reactor in Natanz, Iran would be able to produce enough material for an atom bomb within a year, and eventually they could produce up to five bombs a year.

While the United States was trying to stop Iran through diplomatic means, Iran was rushing to the finishing line. It had learned from North Korea's tactic: After denying for years that it was on the way to the bomb, North Korea announced that it was inside the atomic club — and thereby acquired immunity.

Felix immediately understood the meaning of the term "pitchblende" mentioned on the tape he had just heard in Tiberias. Pitchblende is an ore in which uranium occurs. Uranium must be enriched before it can undergo the chain reaction that releases atomic energy. Iran had its own plants for enriching uranium, but was in a hurry and needed more of the finished product. To mislead others, its agents spoke of pitchblende, but Felix was sure they meant enriched uranium.

Throughout the trip, Felix turned the matter over in his mind. He decided to enter the lion's den — someone had to save the people of Israel from Nati and Asaf! Felix formulated a detailed plan of action. Nothing was committed to writing; the plan was stored in his own phenomenal memory.

As soon as he returned to Jerusalem, he would begin the first stage.

❧

Daniel Klein was not pleased with letting Felix into Zeidel's Rechaviah apartment. It bothered him that strangers felt they could do as they pleased there, as if he, Daniel, were not the rightful heir.

"If you want to get to the bottom of the mystery and find out who Zeidel really was," Felix explained pleasantly as he stood outside Daniel's front door, "I think you would benefit from letting me go in and investigate the apartment methodically." True to his characteristic modesty, he didn't say "scientifically."

Felix looked like the type of person on which one could rely, and there was something persuasive about his wise, penetrating eyes. Daniel could not refuse him. "Okay," he said with a frown. He left Felix waiting outside while he went to get the key ring.

Daniel accompanied Felix into the deserted apartment. A wave of cool, dusty air hit them in the face. "Is this where Avraham Zeidel Portman lived?" asked Felix quietly.

"Yes, this is where Elitzafan Mindelman lived as a child," Daniel answered.

Felix looked at him in surprise. "What made you decide that Elitzafan Mindelman is Zeidel Portman's son?"

"I've done some research on Zeidel's family. Zeidel was divorced from his wife when Elitzafan was a youth, and she then married Shimon Mindelman. To disconnect himself from the tarnished reputation of his real father, young Elitzafan took his stepfather's surname. He and his stepfather, who passed away a few years ago, were very close."

Felix detected a note of criticism of how Elitzafan had treated his real father. He rallied to Elitzafan's defense. "And what do you know about Elitzafan's mother?" asked Felix.

"Nothing," Daniel admitted.

"Mrs. Shoshana Mindelman is in an old-age home. Elitzafan visits her there every day and waits on her hand and foot."

Without comment, Daniel led Felix into the room full of cartons and turned on the light. Felix surveyed the room with a sphinx-like face. Not a muscle moved.

At random he approached one of the cartons and opened it. Two stacks of old notebooks filled the carton from bottom to top. Felix leafed through one. The first page said, "*Shiurim* on *Bava Basra*, heard from Rabbi Alexander Frankel *shlita*. Elitzafan Portman. Winter, 5727." The other notebooks were similar. Young Elitzafan Portman had been a diligent student.

"Where did you find the key to the Tiberias apartment?" Felix asked suddenly.

Daniel showed him the carton that contained the electric train. Felix removed the cover of the battery compartment and looked carefully at the box in which the key had been found. His brow furrowed in thought.

"He was rich enough to buy expensive cigarettes," Daniel noted.

"No," the scientist corrected him. "This is a cigar box. True, a small box, but a box of cigars." He turned the box over and showed Daniel the seals in Spanish and English: "Made in Havana, Cuba," "*Hecho a mano,*" "*Cohiba Exquisitos.*"

"What are those?" wondered Daniel.

Felix chuckled. "Indications that he had good taste. *Cohiba Exquisitos* are very expensive Cuban cigars. *Hecho a mano* means that they were finished by hand."

Suddenly Felix tapped his forehead. A brilliant idea had just flashed through his mind. Now he knew what to do. Before taking action, though, he would check with Elitzafan to make his sure his guess was right. If it was, he would do some research, take a short vacation from work, and book a flight.

"You don't know how much you've helped me," he told Daniel, shaking his hand warmly.

"I didn't do a thing," said Daniel, surprised by the quiet scientist's enthusiastic outburst. Why get excited about a simple cigar box? Felix was certainly eccentric!

❧❀☙

Harrods department store in London has a special cigar department, managed by an expert, but avid cigar smokers prefer the St. James area near Piccadilly Square, where an impressive array of choice tobacco shops is concentrated. Felix entered Davidoff, a store dedicated exclusively to cigars and smoking accessories.

Felix told the young salesman who greeted him that he would like to speak to the store's owner, Edward Shakian.

Two minutes later, a polite, smiling, Armenian came over. He was wearing a gold tie, a blue shirt with mobe pearl cufflinks, and a dark, shiny jacket. Felix looked worriedly at his own plain, brown striped jacket.

"How can I help you?" asked Shakian.

"I'm looking for quality cigars," said Felix.

"All our cigars are hand rolled, and all are the finest: Montecristo, Double Corona, Panetela, Churchill, or Pyramid."

"I'm looking for more, too," said Felix.

Shakian looked at him with understanding. "I know, that's why you've come to us. We have the best smoking accessories: cigar cutters, storage boxes, humidors to keep the cigars moist and fresh, and high-quality lighters. You can purchase a simple plastic cutter here for a mere 4.5 pounds Sterling, but if you want something prestigious, I can offer you the beautiful silver-plated Davidoff lighter for 195 pounds Sterling."

"No, no!" Felix brushed the idea away with his hand.

"I understand. You want something better." Shakian smiled. "I have something really special for you: a Dupont double-flame lighter with gold finish for 280 pounds. If you have extremely refined taste, you will prefer a gold-plated lighter with Chinese lacquer of the Maduro series, also of Dupont. But it's expensive: 495 pounds."

"I greatly appreciate your profusion of exclusive items," said Felix, slightly embarrassed, "but that was not my intention. I want to buy a selection of quality cigars, and together with them I would like a few professional tips. To tell you the truth, I would like to get friendly with an avid cigar smoker. It's very important for me to make a good first impression on him."

"Very well," said Shakian with a smile, "I can give you tips that you won't hear from anyone else. I'll teach you how to cut the end of the cigar, with what to cut it, and how quickly; how to light and from what angle; how a real cigar smoker holds his cigar; and how to inhale the smoke. But come, let's see the merchandise itself."

Shakian gave him a tour of the store. "We'll begin in the Havana room. After that, how can I not show you the world-renowned Davidoff cigars? If there are good Dominican cigars anywhere in the world, they will always be Davidoff. I would recommend the Grand Cru series, with a rich flavor, and also Davidoff Special R. Smoke it, and you will feel in the clouds, sir, and if you want to get directly to Paradise, try Robusto with a dark leaf cover. But first, the Havana room."

Felix felt foolish following Shakian into a room lined with shelves filled with wide, flat cigar boxes in a variety of models and styles, displaying an enormous selection of long, thin brown cigars, each decorated with a gold and red ribbon with its special label. Felix simply wanted to impress someone. He had not realized that cigars were a whole world.

"I recommend Cohiba Panetelas and Montecristo, especially Montecristo Tubo. Hoyo de Monterrey Double Corona is not bad at all, but you should also consider Gonzalez Tres Petit Lonsdales, which is popular with experienced smokers."

The detailed explanations continued for a quite some time. At the end of the shopping spree, Felix left the store with an empty wallet; a load of boxes of the world's most expensive, choice cigars; and, most important of all, with professional tips that would guarantee him a place of honor in London's Havana Club. Of all the items he had bought, the only familiar things were the extra-large matches his wife used to light Shabbos candles.

❧

Mossad agent Sheket, alias Leonardo Pantoloni, was about to leave Maison Pierre. One hour earlier the owner, Pierre Almozig, had gone home. No customers had come in that winter afternoon. Night had fallen, and Sheket was sure that in the cold and the dark, no dowager would come to shop. He glanced a last time at the computer hidden in the cabinet under the cash register and checked his secure and encrypted e-mail. A single message awaited him. Sheket gasped. He rubbed his eyes and looked again at the screen. "No, it can't be!" he screamed silently.

But it was.

The Mossad ordered Sheket to do a Triple Zero on Moshiko, that is, to liquidate him in an innocent-looking traffic accident. And as soon as possible.

When Sheket came home, he sent a coded message inquiring as to whether there was a mistake. "I've known Moshiko since we served together in an elite commando unit," he wrote. "He has always been a super patriot. Why eliminate him?"

The response was a heavy blow. "He is selling state secrets to the enemy. He is a danger to the State of Israel."

"I wouldn't have believed you could do such a thing," Sheket whispered as he shaved. "You, Moshiko?"

That night, Sheket did not go to sleep. He sat in his bathrobe and warm slippers and a plan of action crystallized. It was the hardest thing he had ever done in his life. But there was no choice.

When Sheket first applied for a job in the Mossad, he had been asked what he would do if he discovered that his best friend was a traitor whose existence threatened the country. Sheket had replied that he would not hesitate to liquidate him.

Easier said than done. Go betray your best friend!

But it was Moshiko who was the traitor!

Shortly before dawn Sheket went to sleep, hoping that in the morning he would discover that it had all been a bad dream. Moshiko had always been and still was a loyal friend and an upright citizen.

Sheket's sleep was short and filled with nightmares. This, the hardest day of his life, caused him to regret the profession he had chosen. It was not to fight such enemies that he had joined the Mossad.

24

Chedvi valiantly tried to convey a "life-must-go-on, business-as-usual" attitude — until Shabbos evening. When Elitzafan took the Kiddush cup in his hand, tears suddenly flowed from his eyes and his voice caught in his throat. His children exchanged confused, embarrassed looks. Chedvi bent her head and almost stopped breathing. She bit her lips and grasped the back of her chair with white fingers.

Devorah rallied to the rescue. "*Nu,* Shabbos," she proclaimed loudly, and the storm subsided.

That night, Leah'le tossed in bed, flagellating herself for having ruined Chedvi's *shidduch*. If only she had controlled her desire to chat, her sister would have been a radiant, bejeweled, photographed *kallah*. But she, Leah'le Mindelman, had ruined it all. Now there were no flowers, no *chasan*, no happy laughter, no albums, no jewelry....

Instead, there was something else: weeping. The quiet sobs at three in the morning were barely audible because Chedvi's head was buried in the pillow. But Leah'le heard them.

Chedvi will never want to see my face again, thought Leah'le. But the next day, Chedvi smiled at her as usual, without a trace of blame in her eyes. Chedvi even initiated a conversation during the Shabbos meal.

In the afternoon, Chedvi took Leah'le out to the small balcony, where the succah had stood in the fall. A blast of winter wind whipped their hot cheeks. Chedvi looked at Leah'le for a long time, and then asked her softly, "Do you think I'm angry at you?"

"You certainly have good reason to be," said Leah'le.

Chedvi smiled. "Not at all. You didn't do anything. If the *shidduch* fell through, it wasn't for me. When the true *shidduch* comes — and it will come soon, with Hashem's help — no one will be able to ruin it."

Leah'le was astounded at Chedvi's invincible faith.

Chedvi looked up at the heavens, filled with heavy dark rain clouds. "It's a miracle from Heaven," she went on enthusiastically, "that you spoke on the phone and the *shidduch* ended when it did. Imagine if that shady character had slandered us after the *vort* and the Patankins had broken the engagement! That would have been a thousand times worse."

"How do you know," asked Leah'le, "that when you become engaged to your real *bashert,* no one will run to your *chasan's* house and blacken our name? You will always live in fear!"

Chedvi merely smiled and gestured heavenward.

⟡

As the arithmetic notebook filled with problems, the pencil became blunt, making thicker lines from digit to digit. "Now write: 17–8=…."

"Oh, how I hate these problems," complained Frumi, chewing the end of her yellow pencil.

Leah'le smiled. "What problems should I give you? Four plus three? Two plus five?"

"At least those would be easy," said Frumi.

"Yes," said Leah'le, "but you have to learn to go beyond ten. You'll never get ahead in arithmetic if you don't solve the problems. Now write: 17–8=…."

Frumi fastened a pair of big, innocent eyes on her tutor, who treated weak students with such remarkable patience that they dared to speak to her as to an equal.

"Tell me, Leah'le," said Frumi, "why are your eyes swollen? Have you been crying?"

Leah'le flushed. "Me? Of course not. Have you written the problem?"

"Then why are your eyes red?" Frumi scored another direct hit. "When I cry a lot, my eyes are swollen the way yours are now. Did your mother punish you? I thought big girls didn't get punished!"

Leah'le burst into laughter. Frumi had a charming personality, and at least she didn't whisper behind her back. How could Leah'le tell Frumi that she was absolutely right? A week had passed since Chedvi's *shidduch* had been called off, and Leah'le was still crying herself to sleep every night. She felt sorry for Chedvi; for Tirtzah, next in line after Chedvi and stuck waiting for her to get married first; and, truth to say, also for herself. She was stuck waiting for both of them.

Now Frumi had said aloud what others were thinking: that Leah'le could not cry endlessly without it showing. All Leah'le's friends and acquaintances were probably clucking their tongues in sympathy.

At least Chedvi was not angry at her. But Leah'le was not satisfied. She wanted to do something to restore her sister's happiness. When she finished tutoring Frumi, she would take action.

But how does one go about finding a *chasan* for one's sister?

Rebbetzin Simchoni–Freilich would know. The number was in Ima's cell phone....

❦

The bearded man wearing a beret drew several glances when he entered London's Havana Club. "Are you new here?" asked a man with rimless glasses who was leafing through *Cigar Aficionado.*

"Yes," he answered and sat down. He casually set a box of Hoyo de Monterrey Double Corona down on a table, disregarding admiring glances from all sides.

The prestigious palladium S. T. Dupont cigar cutter with China black finish that gleamed in Felix's hands prompted a smoker in cowboy boots to point out that professional smokers like him belonged upstairs.

Felix took the tip, but he felt uncomfortable and out of place in the enormous, glittering, softly lit hall with the arched ceiling and parquet flour. Irises in crystal vases, narrow glass goblets filled with apple juice and ice cubes, marble ashtrays, and smokers' magazines covered small oval tables situated with dark blue armchairs on either side.

Near the southern wall, he spotted a huge armchair. As if at random, he sat in the armchair nearest to it, put a sealed wooden box down on the table, ordered a glass of beer, and waited patiently.

According to information Felix had gathered before the trip, in a few minutes cigar enthusiast Nati Morgan would occupy "his" armchair. The owner of Morgan Consolidated, Ltd. made weekly trips from Paris to London to replenish his cigar supply, and on such occasions, he always visited the Havana Club.

A few minutes after Felix sat down, a man whose posture bespoke wealth, authority, and comfort sauntered over. His expression was tough but not threatening, and the lively sparkle in his pupils indicated an energetic personality despite his age, which was betrayed by the white roots of his dyed hair. He settled comfortably into his armchair and studied the new face across from him.

Ignoring Nati's searching looks, Felix slowly pulled a cigar out of the box. With measured movements he took out the cutter and snipped off the tip of the cigar just as Shakian had taught him: a fast, clean cut while the cigar was in a horizontal position so that no damage was done to the wrapping leaf. Still holding the cigar horizontally in his hand, he held the flame of the big match to the cigar, while rolling the cigar between his fingers so that the exposed end would burn evenly. He puffed delicately at the burnt end, which began to glow. "This ensures that the cigar will burn smoothly," Shakian had explained.

Nati's lower lip extended up over his upper lip in amazement as he watched Felix's expert movements. Felix seemed not to notice. The lighting completed, he would have to inhale and exhale slowly. He placed the cigar between his lips, as horizontally as possible, and slowly inhaled while turning the cigar between his fingers. The smell was unexpectedly sharp and repulsive, and his mouth and throat burned. He had to muster all his self-control to refrain from throwing the cigar away.

Nati went through the same steps himself, yet he was deeply impressed by the expertise displayed by the bearded guest in the blue beret. For a while, his natural curiosity struggled with his arrogance. Finally curiosity won.

"Are you from here?" he asked coolly in English.

"I'm from Israel," Felix replied in English.

"What brings you here?"

"Business." Felix allowed a large amount of ash to accumulate at the end of the cigar before shaking it into the ashtray. Shakian had warned him not to bang the cigar frequently to remove the ashes. "That will ruin your whole image and give you away in a minute," Shakian had warned him.

"I see you're a veteran smoker," Nati said approvingly. He stubbornly persisted in speaking English despite a heavy Israeli accent.

A casual conversation ensued. Nati told Felix about American comedian George Burns, a heavy cigar smoker who lived to be a hundred. A journalist had once asked what his doctor thought of his habit. Burns, cigar in mouth, had answered, "I don't know; my doctor died."

Felix remarked that when the 1961 Soviet missile crisis led to an American trade embargo on Cuba, President John F. Kennedy signed the act only after press secretary Pierre Salinger informed him that he had procured 1,200 Petit Upmann cigars.

"Petit Upmann is an excellent cigar," said Nati with a pensive expression. "I myself prefer Cohiba Esplendidos. They have a rich aroma and smooth taste.

"Did you know," continued Nati, "that once they used to wear a special jacket for smoking? What we call a tuxedo used to be known as a smoking jacket."

The atmosphere became increasingly genial. Nati volunteered that he lived in Paris, "but I come here regularly to replenish my cigar supply. London, and especially the Havana Club, is a cigar-smoker's paradise."

A few young people brought over bar stools and gathered around Nati. Gradually they drifted into speaking Hebrew. One of them related that Field Marshall Montgomery reportedly said, "I don't drink, I don't smoke, I sleep a great deal. That is why I am 100% on form!" Churchill retorted, "I drink a great deal, I sleep little, and I smoke cigar after cigar. That is why I am 200% on form!"

"Churchill was sharp," said Nati. "He also said, 'Who's afraid of Cuba? I keep Cuba in my mouth!'"

In the middle of the conversation, Felix suddenly looked at his watch, mumbled something about being late, and stood up.

"Who is that man?" asked Nati as Felix walked away.

Malkiel Yahalom watched Felix move toward the staircase. "I know him well. He didn't recognize me, but that's because more than ten years have passed since we were in Elta together." He fell silent for a minute and sucked on the shortening cigar. His voice filled with hostility. "I'll tell you who that man is. A man without character and without a conscience. He would sell his own mother."

Nati regarded Malkiel coolly. "I gather you're not particularly fond of him. What's his name?"

"Felix Goldmark. I must admit he's one of Elta's top scientists, and if the rumors are true, he is deeply involved in the Arrow missile project."

Nati mopped his brow with a handkerchief. "Felix Goldmark? I haven't heard of him. Very interesting."

Felix went out into the cold street and heaved a sigh of relief. He had succeeded in impressing Nati, and judging by the spark of recognition in Malkiel Yahalom's eyes, he knew they would meet again soon.

⚜

The Sharabi brothers had a highly developed sixth sense. But whereas Yaniv rarely had flashes of insight, Moshiko was always on-line. Intuition frequently served as his bodyguard. When he obeyed it, he was almost always right.

Moshiko was curious about his sixth sense. To understand the phenomenon better, he had consulted a famous psychologist.

The psychologist cited a documented case from April 19, 1995. A student of the University of Pennsylvania woke up from a deep sleep at 6:30 a.m. with a strange, powerful thought: "Many people are about to die in Oklahoma City." He disregarded it and went back to sleep. At 10:04 that morning, a bomb exploded in the Murrah Federal Building of Oklahoma City, destroying the building, killing 168 people, and wounding many more.

A woman who lost her mother, her two young children, and her leg in the explosion tearfully told CNN that a few minutes before the explosion, she had felt an inexplicable urge to grab her loved ones and run out of the building, but had dismissed it as mere foolishness.

"Those two people ignored the opportunity to use their sixth sense for beneficial purposes," said the psychologist. "You, too, have been blessed with this gift. Use it well, and don't worry about what people say."

After the conversation with the psychologist, Moshiko was more at ease about obeying his inner instincts.

Tonight, Moshiko's sixth sense went wild. He could almost see a sword dangling over his head.

25

The stack of notebooks that Felix had discovered in Zeidel's Rechaviah apartment piqued Daniel's curiosity. Perhaps here he would find a clue that would solve the mystery of Zeidel once and for all. Now he took a morning off, brought the carton of notebooks home, and sat down to inspect them.

The elementary school notebooks of young Elitzafan Portman were adorned with doodles; not so his notebooks from yeshivah. He seemed to have crossed from childhood to adulthood in a single jump.

A cursory glance revealed that he had been sensitive and disciplined. The *shiurim* he had heard were recorded in neat handwriting, fluent style, and fine language.

Nevertheless, he had a sense of humor, to judge from his Adar notebooks. The very first page sent Daniel roaring with laughter. Young Elitzafan had been a lively, clever, witty boy, so different from the saddened, nervous man that he was today.

Suddenly pangs of conscience jabbed at Daniel like needles. Why had he allowed Zeidel's looseleafs in Tiberias to frighten him so much? So what if Zeidel hadn't been lily white! Why did the son have to suffer for the father's sins, especially after dozens of years had passed? Why had he, Daniel Klein, evaded Mendel and Elitzafan when they had wanted to conclude the *shidduch*?

Actually, Mendel had told him about the anonymous phone call regarding the black stain on the family history. But even if Daniel was not the one who had ruined the *shidduch,* his obvious lack of enthusiasm did not help.

"Abba, what are these notebooks?"

Daniel turned around in surprise. He had not heard his son come in.

"Asher, what are you doing here in the middle of the day?"

"I went to pick up the results of my blood test," said Asher, refreshing Daniel's memory. "Since I was nearby, I decided to come home and get something to drink. Abba, may I take a peek? Those old notebooks look interesting." Before Daniel could say no, Asher had starting reading. Within a minute he was rolling with laughter. "This is great! Who wrote it?"

Asher's charm and youthful liveliness precluded any possibility of Daniel getting angry at him. "How does it look to you, Asher?"

"Outstanding!" Asher leafed through some more, and from time to time burst into laughter.

Daniel did some quick thinking. Should he take Asher into his confidence? The youth was intelligent and mature, and his skill in analyzing complex Gemara topics carried over to other areas as well. His sharp mind, clear thinking, and healthy logic made Asher just the person to help solve the mystery of Zeidel....

"Would you believe that today the author is one of Jerusalem's most esteemed scholars?" said Daniel.

"Really!" exclaimed Asher. "Who is he?"

"Elitzafan Mindelman." Daniel looked closely at his son's face to see his reaction.

Asher's eyes opened wide with amazement. "Unbelievable. Mr. Mindelman was so lively in his youth? It doesn't seem like him at all!"

He looked at the first page. "But the name on the notebook is Elitzafan Portman."

Daniel shook his head. "It's him."

Asher was thunderstruck. "Don't tell me Mr. Mindelman is the son of Zeidel, the neighbor who passed away half a year ago!"

"I am saying just that," said Daniel, like a magician drawing a rabbit out of a hat. "If you go to the *shtiblach* in Beis Yisrael, you'll see him *davening* for the *amud* each day. He's in the year of mourning for his father. But Shimon Mindelman, who was thought to be his father, passed away five years ago. When he is questioned, he gives an evasive answer about praying for the soul of some relative. He also looks a lot like Zeidel, and he reacted very strongly when I mentioned Zeidel Portman to him."

"And I thought Zeidel was all alone in the world." Asher slapped his knee. "I never saw Mr. Mindelman visiting him."

"Zeidel's family abandoned him thirty years ago. His wife demanded a divorce, and his only son Elitzafan cut off all ties — apparently for good reason. They didn't want to be identified with Zeidel because of some disgrace linked to him, which today is ruining *shidduchim* for Elitzafan's daughters. If I can find out the truth about Zeidel, perhaps his granddaughters will finally be able to get married."

Asher leaped lightly out of the chair to his full six feet, and his blue eyes smiled merrily at Daniel. "Abba, if you want my help, I will give it gladly. You can call me in yeshivah."

He put on his winter coat and his black hat. Then, with a warm "*Shalom*" and a wave, he was off.

⊙↜↝⊙

Moshiko woke up in the morning bathed in sweat after a night filled with terrifying dreams. As he poured milk into a bowl of cornflakes, he was gripped by a feeling of imminent danger.

Absently he shoveled a spoonful of cereal into his mouth. Evidently Nati and Asaf had decided to liquidate him. A hired killer was now planning how to execute the order. There are many ways of getting rid of a *persona non grata*.

It was hardly a surprise. Ever since the button he had planted in Dubik Cooperman's watch was discovered, he had been kept out of important company offers. He was not upset about the discovery of the button; he had planted five other listening instruments in the garments of the corporation's management.

Something big was in the works now, but Nati, Asaf, and the rest were speaking in undecipherable codes. Moshiko lay in ambush like a lion in the savanna and waited for a slip of the tongue. As soon as he had any solid evidence, he and his good friend Sheket would take action together. If the Mossad was sure that Nati Morgan was above suspicion despite proofs to the contrary, he and Sheket would find nonbiased parties who would listen. *If I live long enough,* thought Moshiko.

Don't torture yourself, an inner voice whispered. *Take effective action.*

The phone rang. It was Sheket.

"What's doing, Leonardo?" Moshiko asked happily. Here was one person he could trust.

"Hello, Moshiko." Sheket sounded strained. "What's new?"

"For the past two weeks they haven't let me take part in any activity. They've found me out. I'm almost under house arrest."

"Are you forbidden to go out?" asked Sheket.

"No, I'm *afraid* to go out. They're planning to eliminate me, I'm sure."

"So come with me, and we'll air you out a little," suggested Sheket. "Have you gone for a trip since you came to Paris six months ago?"

"I haven't even been to the Eiffel Tower," Moshiko confessed.

"Would you like to go there with me?" asked Sheket.

Moshiko shuddered. "No!" High places were ideal for liquidation. One light push, and then they'll say that you committed suicide. Three hundred eighty people had already jumped from the Eiffel Tower, of which only one had survived.

Sheket forced himself to sound merry. "Do you know what I suggest? Come with me to the hill."

"Which hill?"

"You've been in Paris for a half year," Sheket chided, "and you still don't know that Parisians call Montmartre 'the hill'? It's a quiet village with small, pleasant streets and few people. You'll enjoy every moment. My car is in repair, so I'll come to you soon by Metro, and we'll drive there in your Renault."

"Excellent!" Moshiko sounded pleased. Anything to get out of this oppressive vise.

"I'll be over in an hour," said Sheket and hung up. For a few minutes, he could not move a muscle. *What got into you, Sheket — to deceive your best friend! You promise him a trip to Montmartre. Its famous cemetery containing the graves of musicians, writers, poets, and artists is an ironic hint of what will come next. Together you head back to the city on the express road, where you leave him under some pretext and let someone else carry out an "innocent" traffic accident. Sheket, how will you ever look at yourself again in the mirror, even if the Mossad does think he's a traitor?*

Meanwhile Moshiko, whistling gaily to himself, quickly tidied the apartment. Then he relaxed on the couch and waited eagerly for Sheket. He could not help but glance frequently at his watch. After two weeks at home, even a brief outing with a friend promised to be a delightful experience.

26

From the staircase, Devorah heard the phone ringing inside her apartment. She quickened her pace and arrived, breathless, at the locked door. As Murphy's Law would have it, the key ring was buried deep inside her pocketbook, and by the time she unearthed it the ringing had stopped.

No matter, thought Devorah. *Whoever needs me will call again.* She put her pocketbook away and began preparing dinner before the ringing resumed. A gush of rapid, effusive words inundated her when she picked up the receiver.

"Devorah, how are you? How do you feel? Why don't I hear from you? Why have you stopped calling me?"

Devorah's eyes lit up. "Rebbetzin Flora, what a surprise!" Out of respect, Devorah set the vegetable peeler aside.

"*Nu,* what's happening? Do you know how I've been thinking about you here in France? I'm surrounded here by many righteous women, each of them a precious jewel, but I think of you and Chedvi nonstop. I have a not-so-good feeling about Chedvi. Something is not going well, right?"

How did she know everything?

"You're right, Rebbetzin Flora!" Devorah sighed deeply and looked at her reflection in the hall mirror. What wrinkles! What pallor! She had aged ten years in the last few weeks. "Chedvi was about to get engaged. The *chasan* was exactly as you had described him before your trip: a terrific learner who is righteous, handsome, considerate, serious, and refined. But at the last moment, Leah'le chatted with a friend. Apparently someone really is tapping our phone. He called the *chasan*'s side, and that was the end of the *shidduch*."

"Oh, no!" cried Flora in sympathy. "A heart feels a heart. When my hostess took me for a stroll along the River Seine, I looked into the water and thought of you. I felt that you were sad."

Devorah looked at the mirror again. True, her expression was dark. No wonder people had kept their distance lately.

"Listen, if Heaven has designated this *shidduch* for Chedvi, it will return," Flora comforted her. "But I have a different idea. Let me be Chedvi's *shadchan*!"

"What!" cried Devorah. Flora never made *shidduchim;* she only gave advice.

"I know it surprises you. It's true that I don't make *shidduchim*," said Flora, apparently reading Devorah's thoughts. "But your case is exceptional. Devorah, you and your Chedvi are always on my mind. Even here in Paris I have no rest because of you."

Devorah was speechless. Having been brought up not to show her emotions, she held them in to the choking point. "Germs wouldn't survive in your bloodstream," someone had once remarked. "It's too cold there." Yet she melted like wax in Flora's presence. Flora's emotional rapport now, in these difficult times, left Devorah overwhelmed and embarrassed like the shy little girl who came to her office for a stapler.

"I was impressed by my hosts' neighbors, the Feldmans," Flora continued. "I think they are suited to you like a stamp to an envelope. The father is a Litvish *talmid chacham*, the mother a teacher in a *charedi* girls' school. The son, Yom Tov, learns in the yeshivah of Aix-les-Bains. He's a very special boy; I'm sure he'll bring you much happiness."

Under other circumcisions, Devorah would have said no immediately — but to Flora, she spoke with respect and submission.

"Rebbetzin Flora, I'm very grateful for your goodwill," she stammered. "The fact that you think about us even in France takes a stone off my heart; I know that I am not alone. But the differences in mind-set between an Israeli girl and a French boy are too great to bridge."

"No, no!" Flora protested vehemently. "If the souls are compatible, mind-set is no problem. We've seen plenty of international *shidduchim*, with the *chasan* from India and the *kallah* from Ethiopia, or the *kallah* from Honduras and the *chasan* from Morocco. Souls are matched in Heaven, where there are no different countries. Afterwards the souls are thrown into this world, and twenty years later they begin searching for their other half." Flora spoke rapidly, as usual. "Listen to me. As soon as we finish speaking, call the Quick Flight travel agency and order two open tickets. Everything is at my expense; you and Chedvi just have to get on the plane."

Devorah squirmed. How could she refuse such a generous offer? "It's not a question of money. We don't have even minimal information about the boy. And are *they* interested?"

Flora laughed. "In an hour, I'll get back to you with twenty phone numbers so you can make inquiries. They've already agreed to the *shidduch*."

The painful question needed to be asked. "Haven't we been slandered yet?"

"They trust me blindly," said Flora. "Even if the prime minister himself were to warn them to beware of the Mindelmans, they would go ahead with the *shidduch* if I told them to."

After a few more questions and some more words of persuasion, the remnants of Devorah's resistance were crushed. Devorah's closing words, "So we'll meet in Paris in another two days. By the way, how is the weather there?" reached the ears of Leah'le, who came home from school, quietly took off her coat, and listened with a smile.

The previous night Leah'le had secretly called Flora's cell phone from Malki Fried's house. Flora was surprised and disappointed to hear that the Patankin–Mindelman *shidduch* had fallen through. Her prophecy by the light of the wicks regarding the *chasan* who "is approaching your house with giant strides" had turned out to be false. But after a few seconds of silence, Flora recovered her wits. She thanked Leah'le warmly for sharing the sad news with her, assuaged her guilty feelings for having spoken about the *shidduch* over the phone, and told her she had a brilliant idea for Chedvi. Here it was!

Devorah was excited and confused. After a few unsuccessful attempts to cut the raw potatoes with the dull side of the knife, she left the kitchen. She put her winter coat back on while giving Leah'le instructions about making dinner and then left. Leah'le figured she was on her way to Chedvi's kindergarten to share the news from France with her.

ᏋᏇᏒ

Sheket Lapid had promised Moshiko he would come soon, but that "soon" was dragging out. Sheket had said he would travel by Metro, since his car was in the repair shop. Evidently he had forgotten how long a simple subway ride could take when you aren't well versed in the timetables.

After waiting nearly an hour, Moshiko lost patience. If Sheket could not keep his word, he should not get angry if he found an empty apartment.

Moshiko went downstairs and walked aimlessly back and forth on the sidewalk while keeping an eye out for Sheket. Suddenly he spotted a notice in Hebrew prominently displayed on the bulletin board. He went over to read it.

The notice, posted by "admirers of Rebbetzin Flora Simchoni–Freilich of Jerusalem," announced that the Rebbetzin would deliver a lecture about "The Sixth Sense — Real or Imaginary" in the Patriarch Abraham Synagogue on Rue Alexander Dumas at 10:30 a.m. that very day. There would be separate seating for men and women.

Moshiko glanced at the clock. It was 10:40 — not too late. He had always been curious about the sixth sense. He hurried to Rue Alexander Dumas.

The front of the modern, new synagogue sported two giant stained glass windows with colorful symbols of the twelve tribes. Moshiko went inside to a large hall lined with red upholstered chairs on either side of a decorative wood *mechitzah*. Hundreds of men and women in the hall were hanging on to Flora's every word.

"This leads us to the question: What is the sixth sense? Is it just a vague intuition, a gut feeling? And where does it come from?"

Flora told about a man who had lost a pouch containing his passport and airplane tickets for an international flight. A mysterious feeling drew Gail Ferguson, a stranger, to an unknown place, where she found the pouch. She returned it to the owner an hour before takeoff.

Flora ridiculed Gail Ferguson for trying to reconcile the contradiction between her atheistic world view and her sixth sense. "The inexplicable sixth sense is a gift from Heaven that a rare few merit. But whoever has it," Flora cried enthusiastically into the microphone, "feels clearly that it goes far beyond intuition."

To Moshiko it seemed as if she were looking straight at him. Suddenly he became hot and uncomfortable. He got up and hurried out into the cool street.

He sauntered along the boulevard, idly watching the changing streetlights and the raindrops beginning to fall. Sheket was surely waiting for him, impatient and angry, outside his door. The lecture had taken much longer than anticipated. An hour and a half had passed since Moshiko had left the apartment.

As he approached the building, he looked around carefully. Sheket was nowhere to be seen. What he did see was that the blue paint had been rubbed off the curb stones, and there were signs of grinding brakes on the street. Evidently a vehicle had gone wild on the street.

Upon closer examination, he saw traces of blue paint on the tires of the parked Renault. The vehicle that had gone wild on the street had been his own! Who could have done such a thing? His car was locked, and no one but he had the keys.

Moshiko decided to test drive his car to check whether it had been damaged. At the same time, he would look around for Sheket. He turned on the motor and started slowly down the street.

❧❧❧

For two men who entered the Havana Club that evening, this time cigar smoking was merely a pretext.

Nati arrived first in an immaculate, freshly pressed smoking jacket with three points of a white handkerchief peeking out of the front pocket. The half-million dollar watch on his wrist — a Girard Perregaux Turbillon Opera 2 — placed him firmly in the ranks of high society. He came alone, without the bootlickers who had accompanied him two days ago, and leaned back comfortably in his blue armchair.

Felix arrived five minutes later, looking like a penguin in a fancy black tuxedo that he had rented.

Each one in turn took out his cigar and tried to impress the other. Nati chose a Bolivar Petit Corona. Felix slowly lit a Partagas, a heavy cigar out of the range of ordinary smokers.

The conversation again centered on their common hobby. Felix had done his homework before coming to the club. Nati was well versed in the secrets of the world of cigars, and Felix could not afford to be ignorant.

The waiter passed between them and set down glasses filled with port, as well as special ashtrays ordered by Nati: crystal, with a real tobacco leaf sealed between two layers on the bottom.

"I heard that the root of the word *cigar* is apparently *siker* in Mayan," Felix began, while lighting his cigar. "That is also the root of the Spanish word *cigarro,* which means a smoke."

Nati looked at him with mild amusement. "When did the term *cigar* first appear in the English dictionary?" asked Nati. He appeared to be half speaking to himself, trying to remember, as he put Felix to a sophisticated challenge.

"In 1735," Felix shot back without delay. "And the term *nicotine* was introduced by Jean Nico, the French ambassador to Portugal."

Nati contributed his part to the ping-pong game. "He's also the man who supplied tobacco powder to France's Queen Catherine da Medici to relieve her migraine headaches. At that time, tobacco was known in France as 'the queen's healing herb.' It really is a healing herb. For centuries, the tobacco plant was used to heal wounds."

"On the other hand," Felix pointed out, "Shah Abbas the First of Persia sentenced tobacco users to death, and in 1645, Czar Alexis of Russia ordered smokers exiled to Siberia!"

"Let's not forget England," said Nati. "In 1604, King James the First of England publicized 'The Accusation Against Tobacco' in which he called smoking a primitive pagan custom."

Felix quoted the text of the document from memory: "This is a branch of the sin of insobriety, which is the root of all sins… a habit despicable to the eye, repulsive to the nose, harmful to the brain, and dangerous to the lungs… The black, foul-smelling smoke of tobacco resembles more than anything else the terrible smoke of the pit."

The two smokers laughed together at the British king who never dreamt that four centuries later, his capital would boast special smoking clubs.

There was an atmosphere of pleasant camaraderie. The time had come to broach the subject of the purpose of their meeting. They looked each other in the eye. Nati cleared his throat a few times. He wanted to say something, but fell silent as he searched for the right words. Felix knew precisely what they were.

ati sucked the end of his cigar forcefully, blew out a puff of smoke, and asked casually, "How long will you be in London?"

"A few days," Felix replied indifferently. "I wanted to get away briefly and replenish my stock of cigars."

Nati hesitated. Was it possible to begin?

Felix gave him a shrewd glance and added a significant comment. "I have pressure at work, and I must return soon. They're waiting for me."

This allowed Nati to ask the all-important question, "What work do you do?"

Felix's usual answer to that frequently-asked question was, "I'm a programmer at Digital Electronics; I program the new generation of silicon nanochips for computers." At that point, questioners usually nodded wisely without asking any further questions. Among computer people, Felix did not mind displaying a little knowledge about the manufacture of nanochips. But this case was different. "I'm an employee, and am considering opening my own start-up company."

"Where do you work, if I may ask?"

Felix was silent, as if debating with himself. "I work in a large company in Ashdod."

Nati's lips opened around the cigar like a snake swallowing its prey. He drew on the cigar tensely, and tiny beads of sweat suddenly gleamed on his forehead. "A company in Ashdod," he scoffed. "I understand that you don't work in the harbor."

Felix looked around to make sure no one else was listening. Then he bent forward. "I work for Elta, if the name means anything to you."

A light smile flitted across Nati's face as quickly as an eagle's shadow. He studied Felix's serious face with an amused look and smiled again. His lips trembled, and out came a light laugh that intensified until it turned into rolling laughter. "If the name means anything to you," he repeated Felix's words again and again, fueling his laughter every time it subsided.

"You have a good sense of humor, you know?" He chuckled and coughed.

Felix remained deadpan. He leaned back in the armchair and occasionally exhaled a cloud of reeking smoke. "Perhaps you could tell me what amuses you so much."

Nati gave Felix a cunning look. "How many years are you working at Elta?"

"More than twenty."

Nati took a sip of the wine.

For a fraction of a second, Felix's face involuntarily contorted with disgust. *How can a Jew sully himself with wine that his forefathers jumped into the fire to avoid drinking?* He hoped Nati didn't notice his reaction. That could ruin the plan from the start.

Nati put the sparkling glass back down on the table and licked the drop that was beginning to descend on his chin. *A real hedonist,* thought Felix.

"I know Elta from the days when its mother company, the Israeli Aircraft Industry, was still in its infancy. And you ask if the name Elta means anything to me! What department do you work in, strategic planning or missile-and-space systems?"

So Malkiel Yahalom had blabbed. Nati knew the answer to his own question but wanted to appear innocent.

"I'm in missile-and-space systems."

For a second, a gleam appeared in Nati's eyes. Malkiel had been right. A real patriot would not have been so quick to reveal these details. Evidently Felix really did want to sell his country's secrets, and the only question was his price. But one must not jump to hasty conclusions.

"What do you do there?" asked Nati. If Felix replied that he was in accounting or fuel, Nati could close his cigar box and return to Paris.

Felix shook a roll of ashes from the cigar with a professional tap of the finger, looked Nati straight in the eye, and without a single blink said, "I work in research and development of the Arrow."

Nati was stunned by the directness of Felix's reply. Malkiel was evidently right when he said that Felix would sell his own mother.

Nati put his cigar down on the edge of the ashtray. The beads of sweat on his forehead doubled in diameter. He glanced around. There were only three other smokers in sight. Two were engrossed in a chess game. The third, with an open copy of *Cigar Aficionado* on his knees, was chatting on his cell phone. The bartender was busily arranging bottles and glasses on the counter. From time to time he filled orders from the first floor.

"The Arrow missile," said Nati. "Israel's anti-missile missile."

"Quite correct."

Nati took one giant step forward. "What field do you work in? Ballistics, launching, fuel?"

Felix did not squirm or beat around the bush. "Programming. Four of us on the staff programmed the Arrow from A to Z."

A feeling of satisfaction filled Nati's heart. It was a pleasure to work with a man who was unhampered by moral compunctions, like the degenerate philosopher who said, "My conscience is utterly clean; I have never used it."

"I understand that the Arrow missile provides a perfect solution to missile attacks on Israel," said Nati.

"Definitely." A combination of fatherly and professional pride could be heard in Felix's voice. "Together with the Amos and Ofek satellites, which will provide timely warnings, one can assume that any missile shot in Israel's direction will be destroyed by an Arrow between 200 and 400 kilometers from Israeli territory. Nice, no?"

"Four hundred kilometers?" said Nati admiringly. "That eliminates any possibility of a hit."

"We're working constantly on improving the Arrow's performance," said Felix, "and each time we achieve better results."

"Very interesting." Nati's cunning eyes sparkled again. He could proceed to the point. "How does the whole thing work?"

"Do you understand ballistics, arcs and degrees, angles of climbing and flight, azimuth, the whole kit and caboodle?" Felix played the ivy tower scientist, who knows nothing outside his own desk and the complicated mathematical equations flying around in his head like homeless birds.

"I don't need to be personally familiar with missiles," said Nati through a cloud of smoke. "I consult experts! Perhaps you could give me a demonstration, possibly a little sketch?"

Under other circumstances, the sickly sweet flattery in Nati's voice would have repelled Felix. Now it suited his purpose. Saying, "I have my portable computer here," he picked up the brown case at his feet and took out a small, state-of-the-art computer.

Nati's eyes became saucer-like. Felix drew a shiny yellow minidisk out of a flat box and inserted it into the computer's small disk drive. A hum announced the rapid turning of the disk inside. Seconds later, three-dimensional letters began to appear on the quartz screen: "Project Arrow, complete guide. Presentation and demonstration."

Nati leaned toward the computer, his tongue hanging out like a dog's on a hot day. Saying "Let me see this," he pushed Felix aside and bent even closer to the screen.

"Be my guest," said Felix. The CD that he had brought along was a fat worm quivering on the hook, and the fish was begging to swallow the bait. Nati watched spellbound as the nine-minute video showed two successful experiments with the Arrow missile and then briefly explained how the system operates. The screen displayed a few more sketches of the missile and then was empty.

For a few minutes Nati was silent, thinking about the pictures he had just seen. When he spoke again, it was with undisguised enthusiasm. "That's some project, the Arrow. It's as precise as a surgeon's scalpel."

"A scalpel is effective only in the hands of a skilled surgeon. And our staff is truly excellent." Felix's usual modesty had disappeared.

"May I have this CD, just for a day?"

Felix burst into spontaneous laughter. "First of all, this CD is for demonstration only, and is meant to give an indication of the Arrow's power." Nati did not need to know that this CD was no longer classified, and a few copies of it had already been sent out of Israel. "Second, the complete Arrow programs have been copied to a series of CDs — ten, to be precise. Third, these CDs are top secret, and there is no chance of them reaching strange hands."

Nati looked around again. The two chess players had finished their game and left, and the only smoker had extinguished his cigar and was dozing in the armchair.

Nati said only, "How much?"

This was the big moment. It was precisely for this that Felix had flown from Jerusalem to London. But first he had to play the patriotic scientist.

"Totally out of the question. Forget it."

Nati leaned forward with burning eyes. He looked like a drunkard whose bottle was in the hands of a gorilla. "How much?"

Felix smiled coldly. "You will never manage to lay hands on this set. If these CDs fall into the hands of Iran, for instance, Israel will be defenseless against the missiles with nuclear warheads that will threaten her in three or four years, if not sooner."

The enthusiasm in Nati's voice had not dampened when he asked a third time, "How much?"

Felix's adamant refusal began to soften. "I see that you're very determined. Look, I can't just take these CDs out of Elta. They're not kept in a drawer, you know. They're locked up in burglarproof safes."

"Don't tell me that the scientist who built and programmed the Arrow has no copies of the CDs," Nati retorted.

Felix put his hand over his mouth and stroked his moustache and beard. This was it. It was now or never.

"So what did you ask before?" he said casually.

Nati said very slowly, "How much?"

Felix leaned forward. His eyes narrowed to two slits, and a nervous tick set his right eyelid twitching. "It's a set of ten CDs, each of which is worth a million dollars. Plus there's an added cost for danger. If I'm caught they'll hang me in Rabin Square. All in all, fifteen million."

Nati smiled. "Someone once said that money is no guarantee of happiness, but it helps us bear its absence. I, too, believe in it. But don't be ridiculous. I'm not about to pay you such a sum."

"Do you expect me to take the risk for less?"

"Seven million is a respectable sum."

Another man in Felix's shoes would have boiled with anger. But Felix was a cool, deliberate type whose low voice and calm spirit could drive opponents wild. "The two of us are not Arab merchants haggling in the market. You started with seven when I began with fifteen in order to bring me down to ten million. But it shall not be. Either fifteen, or we part company."

"And you began high so that we could meet in the middle, right?"

"Wrong."

"Fine, no one gets everything he wants." For a second, a smile thawed Nati's frozen face. "I had indeed planned to close on ten, but in your honor I'll depart from my old principles. Eleven, and not one cent more."

Felix knew when to stop. "Fine," he said, throwing up his hands in surrender. "Let's shake hands over the deal."

"Shake hands? We'll drink!" Nati was suddenly filled with new life, and joy suffused his face with rosy color. "Steve," he called out to the bartender, "quickly, two drinks. A dry martini for me, and what will you have?"

"Nothing, thank you," said Felix, shrugging. "On second thought, a Heinekin beer."

"A large glass of Heinekin," said Nati, rubbing his hands in glee. "A double glass." He winked at the the bartender, who waved the glass toward Nati to show he had understood. It was a small barrel that held the contents of at least three bottles.

The tension subsided. The game had ended win-win.

They drank and chatted. Nati imbibed a great deal of alcohol, which loosened his tongue. He spoke about various deals and told many jokes. Felix brought the glass to his lips from time to time but drank only tiny sips. He stayed alert, listening carefully to each word, and waited patiently for a breakthrough.

After his fifth glass, Nati uttered a long, confused sentence that ended, "and then we began to enter the market of missile ships."

"And that was already after Zeidel Portman's time," Felix put in offhandedly.

Nati let out a juicy curse. "Of course it was after that idiot Zeidel," he said scornfully. "He never dreamt we would get so big. His concepts didn't go beyond helicopters at most."

Suddenly all the alcohol seemed to have left his brain. He squinted suspiciously. "Why are you asking about Zeidel? How do you know about him?"

Nati was still dangerous, even when he was drunk as Lot.

Felix took a risk. "You spoke about him five minutes ago," he lied.

Nati tried to recall whether he had mentioned Zeidel's name, but his mind was not clear enough. "I must have spoken about him without noticing." He let another glassful bathe his throat.

Felix took another risk. "You didn't like him."

A mighty struggle raged between the alcohol and Nati's keen senses. The level of alcohol won. The cobra had drowned in the bitter drop.

"I certainly didn't like Zeidel," said Nati. "But what do you care?" His hand shook, and the glass tipped at a dangerous angle. A thin shower of whiskey flowed onto his light trousers and spotted them. He tried to wipe it with a silk handkerchief but missed.

"I don't care at all," said Felix cautiously. "I didn't like him either."

"Did you know him?"

"What a question!"

"Nonsense!" Nati gave a wild, drunken laugh. "No one knew Zeidel better than me. I'll tell you who Zeidel was!"

❧❦❧

Moshiko's Renault sputtered and died. The ignition wasn't working. Someone had tampered with his car!

A story from Rebbetzin Simchoni–Freilich's lecture came to mind.

One rainy morning, Gail Ferguson was driving in the right lane behind a new van when she suddenly "saw" a message that said, "Pass to the left lane."

She obeyed her sixth sense and passed carefully through the middle lane to the left one. Suddenly the van went out of control. It swerved into the middle lane and rammed into the side of a small car. Then it was thrown back into the right lane, where it spun like a *dreidel* and crashed into the car behind it. Gail Ferguson's sixth sense had saved her from a serious accident.

Why am I being reminded of this? Moshiko asked himself. Perhaps it was because he was now "seeing" a message that said, "Riding in this car is dangerous."

Am I really beginning to believe in this nonsense? He laughed at himself and decided go for a ride in the car.

This time, the ignition worked. The car moved only a few feet, when suddenly a silhouette crossing the street caught his attention. Thinking it was Sheket, he immediately stopped, shut the motor, and got out of the car — so quickly that he forgot to pull the hand brake.

"Leonardo, wait a minute," he called as he hurried after the silhouette.

It wasn't Leonardo. A stranger turned around and regarded Moshiko with the dazed look of a drug addict. Moshiko mumbled a few words of apology as he quickly retreated. Then he turned back toward the street and gasped.

His car had started rolling down the street!

Moshiko blamed himself for forgetting to pull the hand brakes. But the car had other brakes. Why weren't they working?

As it rolled down the street, the Renault picked up speed. Moshiko stood by, helplessly watching the rolling car and praying with all this heart that no one would be run over.

The wheels had been turned slightly to the right. Now the car veered right, approached the curb at high speed, and then crashed into a lamppost. The front of the car, including the driver's seat, was demolished. It was clear that someone had tried to take Moshiko's life.

He was surveying the remains of his car when someone cried excitedly, "Moshiko! How did it happen?"

"Where have you been, Sheket? I've been waiting for you for hours, and I got tired of waiting. To answer your question, someone released the brakes on my car. I could have been killed."

"Whew!" Sheket slapped himself on the cheek. "Come Moshiko, let's go home." He extricated Moshiko from the growing circle of curious passersby that gathered around him. "I have a feeling that in five minutes the police will want to hear your testimony. Let's go home and have a drink before all the excitement starts."

Moshiko pushed Sheket's hand away. "No," he said sharply, glancing at his watch. "I'm going to Rue Alexander Dumas."

S heket grabbed Moshiko's arm and tried to pull him toward his house. "What are you talking about? What do you have on Rue Alexander Dumas?"

"Let go of me," snapped Moshiko. "If it interests you, come along and see for yourself."

He tried to go, but the growing crowd surrounding Moshiko blocked his escape. People on all sides called out to him and touched him. Wanting to believe that he had been saved by a miracle, they rejected his statement that he had not been in the car.

Two policemen made their way through the crowd. They questioned Moshiko, asked to see his driver's license, and made him sign a number of forms. Satisfied with his cooperation, they let him go. Then a tow truck removed the Renault, thereby ending the brief drama.

Moshiko began walking toward Rue Alexander Dumas. Sheket had difficulty keeping up with his broad strides. "What is on Rue Alexander Dumas?" Sheket asked.

"The Patriarch Abraham Synagogue."

"But Moshiko, you aren't religious!"

"Since when are only religious people allowed to go to synagogue? Wait another two minutes, and you'll see."

They reached the synagogue just as Flora completed her lengthy lecture. A throng of noisy admirers gathered around her to ask questions.

Moshiko and Sheket stood on the side and waited for the tumult to subside. When it did, Flora approached them. "Did you want something?" she asked in fluent French.

"I heard your lecture but left early," Moshiko replied in French. "You spoke about a woman whose sixth sense saved her from a deadly traffic accident. Ten minutes after I left your lecture, I was saved from an accident."

Flora was enthralled. "Tell me exactly what happened."

"I waited for my friend here," said Moshiko, pointing to Sheket. "Since he was late, I drove down the street looking for him. I thought I saw him and hurried out of the car without putting on the hand brakes. Suddenly the car rolled down the street and smashed into a lamppost. Had I been in the car, I wouldn't be here now to tell the tale."

Flora put her hands over her cheeks, and her eyes opened wide in astonishment.

"Aside from that," said Moshiko. "I have a sixth sense, and I wanted to hear more from you about it."

"Give me your phone number," said Flora. "I may want to bring you to one of my lectures."

Moshiko protested, but Flora would not let him go until he gave her his cell phone number.

"What's gotten into you, Moshiko?" asked Sheket as they walked back together. "A synagogue, a Rebbetzin, a sixth sense! Soon you'll put on a *shtreimel* and turn into a Chassidic rebbe!"

Moshiko smiled sadly. "That appeals to me more than staying in some hole in Paris and waiting for Nati and Asaf to decide how to dispose of me."

❧❦☙

The El Al flight from Tel Aviv landed in Charles de Gaulle Airport in the evening. Devorah and Chedvi felt lost until two enthusiastic fans of Flora greeted them. The women deemed it a great privilege to escort the Israeli guests from the airport to the Bloch home, where the Rebbetzin was staying.

Devorah covered up a tired yawn. "I thought the airport was close to the city," she said, as she looked out the car window.

"The Charles de Gaulle Airport is 35 kilometers from Paris, the same as the distance from the Ben Gurion Airport to Jerusalem," one of them answered.

"You are very fortunate to be guests of the Rebbetzin," said the other, who immediately launched into wondrous stories about Flora.

Chedvi could not believe her ears. The Mindelman sisters in Jerusalem considered Flora a charlatan in the worst case and a wierdo at best, but in Paris, intelligent, educated, middle-aged women held her in awe and quoted her with a sparkle in their eyes. Chedvi's opinion of Flora began to change.

Two hours after landing, the group entered Paris' Jewish quarter — the same Pletzel that seventy years earlier had been a ghetto for religious immigrants from Eastern Europe. They went down Rue des Rosiers, a narrow street filled with shops selling *sefarim,* kosher food, and even falafel, and came to the house of the Blochs, an older couple whose children were all married. Aryeh Bloch, a wealthy businessman, spent the day in the office and the evening at Torah classes in the local synagogue. His wife Sarah was usually out volunteering in a local charity organization that raised funds and planned events for sick children.

Sarah warmly welcomed the travelers. They sank wearily into the comfortable living room sofa, beside a marble coffee table laden with refreshments.

Flora came out of her room, and her eyes lit up at the sight of Devorah and Chedvi. She was all smiles. "Welcome!" she cried joyfully. "I'm so happy that you came. How good it is to see familiar faces! You have brought the fragrance of the Land of Israel to France."

She got directly to the point. "You have no idea what a wonderful *shidduch* I have for Chedvi!"

Chedvi blushed and lowered her head. Flora's way of speaking upset her, but the would-be *shadchan* did not take the hint. She went on to sing the prospective *chasan*'s praises.

When Flora said that he combined erudition in learning with practical knowledge of this world, a red light went on in Chedvi's mind. The fellow probably intended to leave *kollel* after a short time. Chedvi was determined to marry a budding *talmid chacham* who would learn in *kollel* for many years, and to accomplish this goal she was prepared to make do with little and work to support the family herself.

As if out of a dream, Chedvi heard Flora saying, "Right after my lecture, what I spoke about happened to him. He came to me with his friend, and I tell you, Devorah, I took his phone number because I wanted to tell him something very important. Good that I remembered. I'll call him immediately."

Flora's thin fingers dialed quickly. "Hello, are you Moshiko Sharabi, who was at my lecture and came to tell me about the accident? Tell me, is your friend still with you — the tall one with the flat nose and three earrings in his left ear, who was standing next to you? He's not with you? Good."

Devorah and Chedvi listened in astonishment as Flora continued, her eyes flashing. "Listen to me well, Moshiko. Your sixth sense protects you from danger but does not reveal your enemy's identity, correct? Let me tell you something that will surprise you. Your friend with the earrings is plotting against you! How do I know? Rely on Flora Simchoni–Freilich. I have experience. Your car did not roll down the street by accident. Someone played with the brakes. I warn you, stay away from that friend!"

After putting up a short argument, Moshiko promised to keep in touch since she was so concerned about his welfare.

When Chedvi heard the details of the incident, her opinion of Flora became much more favorable. She was even ready to go ahead with "the French suggestion" despite her prejudices against it.

⌘

Fearful of being drafted into the Turkish army, Elitzafan Poliakov acquired the passport of a young Jerusalemite, Shmuel Portman, who had died of typhus, changed his family name to Portman, and fled from Jerusalem to Egypt. When World War I ended, Elitzafan returned to Jerusalem and to his wife after a six-year absence. Their first two daughters were born prematurely and did not survive. Only Avraham Zeidel, born in 1925, entered the world strong enough to deal with it.

Elitzafan would often tell little Zeidel about the terrible Kishinev pogrom. As they sat together by the light of the Shabbos candles after the meal, Elitzafan would pat Zeidel's head and say, "Every night in my dreams, I see the house; I hear Poppa and Mamma's helpless screams. They had to fend off a barbaric mob with bare hands. Just imagine, Zeidel, had Poppa owned a gun on that seventh night of Pesach, he would have stood in the doorway and shot at those *goyim*. After he killed five or six, the rest would have run off like frightened mice. They would not have slaughtered Poppa and Mamma, Bubby Chedvah Freidel, Menashe, and Kreindel."

Little Zeidel's eyes reflected the small flames, and his tender heart longed for revenge.

The guns that were missing that Pesach night became Elitzafan's fixation. He forgot that "it is not the snake that kills, but the sin," and that conversely, if Heaven decrees that a person will live, he will evade a thousand murderers. Elitzafan himself, frustrated and bitter, died of a heart ailment in his forties, but not before he had taught his six-year-old son Zeidel to look at the world through a gun sight.

Zeidel matured and studied in a well-known Jerusalem yeshivah at a time when hatred of the oppressive British rulers was rampant and many youths were attracted to the underground. Youngsters dropped out of yeshivah, shaved their curled *peyos,* and threw away their *chalats* — using as an excuse the tough teachers of the *chadarim* who had hit them when their thoughts wandered, as was an accepted practice at the time. Often only two or three remained observant out of a class of twenty-five. Ironically, Zeidel, who had been inculcated as a small child with blind adoration for weapons, did not see a contradiction between fighting one's enemies and observing the Torah. He continued to adhere to his *charedi* way of life while participating in Etzel operations, such as blowing up the King David Hotel.

A few years later, though, when the fledgling State of Israel began to promote secularism and to fight the *charedi* way of life, Zeidel turned into a zealot. His previous enthusiasm gave way to deep disgust for the Zionist state, in which he now saw the Jewish people's true enemy. He awaited the day that the Holy Land would no longer be under their rule.

❧

"Imagine two cousins at opposite ends of the spectrum." Nati laughed tipsily. "Zeidel Portman is a *charedi* with opinions of a zealot. His cousin is a secularist kibbutznik from HaShomer haTza'ir, an honorably discharged army officer who did not want to return to the kibbutz and who found himself without bread to eat."

"Who is this cousin?" asked Felix curiously.

Nati roared with laughter. "The man who is drinking with you, that's who!"

Felix was pleased that Nati thought he, too, was drinking. "You and Zeidel were cousins?"

"Of course," hooted Nati, enjoying Felix's surprise. "Our fathers were brothers."

"But you're Morgan and he was Portman."

Nati looked at him with half-closed eyes. "People are fools. They ascribe too much importance to surnames, which are meaningless conventions.

"Our grandfather Avraham Poliakov lived in Kishinev with his wife, Sima, his old mother, Chedvah Freidel, and their four children, Menashe, Kreindel, Elitzafan, and Shaul. Only the last two survived the pogrom, and they went to Jerusalem. During World War I, Elitzafan changed his surname to Portman to evade the Turkish army. My father, who left Jerusalem and religion, went to Deganiah, where he was adopted by a nonreligious kibbutznik named Yosef Morgenstern. That's why my father was called Shaul Morgenstern, and yet he was Elitzafan Portman's brother. After his death, I shortened my surname to Morgan."

Felix's plan was working better than he could have hoped. His research before the trip revealed that Nati was cold and chronically suspicious but had a weakness for alcohol. Felix had decided to exploit this weakness in order to get Nati to talk.

Nati lit a new cigar and continued his story. "My cousin had a keen business sense," he said with grudging admiration. "In those days of rationing, he bought a failing pipe factory outside Jerusalem for pennies and converted it into a plant for manufacturing cannon nests and tanks. Here, too, his investment was minimal. He had good friends in the Ministry of Defense, and his plant was its unofficial producer."

"I'm surprised," said Felix. "How did a zealot like him cooperate with the Zionist State?"

"If you have patience, you will get an explanation," chuckled Nati.

☙✶❧

Moshiko was taken aback by Flora's warning that Sheket was plotting against him. What nonsense! Sheket, his heart-and-soul friend from the crack commando unit, would betray him? And if so, why? What could his motive possibly be?

Perhaps he was obeying orders. But surely Sheket would have confided in him and not obeyed like a robot.

Moshiko went out to the balcony and stared at the Eiffel Tower soaring in the distance, outlined in lights that emphasized its unique structure. Suddenly he recalled their discussion about taking a trip together. "My car is in repair," Sheket had said, "so I'll come to you soon by Metro, and we'll drive there in your Renault."

In repair?

Two hours earlier, Moshiko happened to have passed Maison Pierre. Sheket's Citroën had been parked in its usual spot, looking just fine.

Sheket had been late, and meanwhile someone had staged an attempt to steal the Renault so that Moshiko would not think of the possibility that the brakes had been sabotaged.

Was Sheket capable of doing such things to him?

Moshiko went inside with a heavy heart. From now on he would have to have eyes behind his head.

For the first time since coming to Paris, he was gripped by a paralyzing fear.

29

An hour before sunset, Devorah and Chedvi stood at the edge of a large group of tourists watching the breathtaking big-city panorama from the Eiffel Tower. The air was clear, and all of Paris was spread at their feet. The group listened eagerly to the tour guide.

"This tower in which you are standing," the tour guide enthusiastically said, "contains seven thousand tons of steel, eighteen thousand metal pieces, and two and a half million rivets. Its 320-meter height made it the world's tallest building for forty-one years, until New York's Chrysler building was built in 1930.

"The day the tower was opened, not one of its elevators worked. Its builder, Gustave Eiffel, and his crew of sixty men were forced to climb the 1,710 steps in order to raise the French flag on the top.

"At first there was a great deal of opposition to the tower. Local people were afraid it would sway and collapse, crushing their homes. Three hundred members of the intelligentsia signed a petition against its erection. After it was opened, the author Guy de Maupassant became a regular guest at its second-story restaurant because it was the only place in Paris from which one could not see the tower!

"The tower was meant to stand for only twenty years, but its height saved it. The metal structure proved to be an excellent antenna, and the first news program was broadcast from it in 1921."

Devorah and Chedvi stopped listening to hold a whispered conference. Only outside their hosts' house could they speak freely.

"What do you say about Yom Tov Feldman?" asked Devorah. "I was favorably impressed. He looks good-natured, he has intelligent, expressive eyes, and he's tall and handsome. I did some investigating in the community and heard good things about him."

Chedvi stared at the big buildings of the metropolis but saw nothing. Her thoughts wandered to the Blochs' study, where she had met Yom Tov.

"So what do you say?" asked Devorah.

In the background, the guide was still speaking. "...six million visitors a year. Whoever hasn't yet seen the filmstrip of the tower's history can do it now, when we go down to the first floor. Don't forget to have the post office there stamp your postcards." Devorah was not particularly interested. Chedvi's impression of Yom Tov Feldman was much more important to her than the Eiffel Tower.

Chedvi closed her eyes, trying to concentrate. "It is true that he is smart and impressive, refined and clever. By the way, his name is Yom Tov only for purposes of being called to the Torah and for *shidduchim*. All his friends and acquaintances call him François. Regarding his plans for the future, he told me explicitly that after five years in *kollel* he is planning to go out to work as his father did. He will devote fixed times to Torah study and participate in a *daf yomi shiur* every day. That is his maximal Torah ambition. A *charedi* French *baal habayis* with a fragrance of Torah. That's not what I want," she said, eyes flashing. "My dream is to marry a *talmid chacham*. Do you want me to give up my dream?"

Devorah took her daughter's hand. "Chedvi, life is Paradise for those who compromise and Gehinnom for those who are stubborn. You *must* compromise."

"What you are asking me to do goes way beyond compromising."

Devorah would not relent. "Chedvi, you're not firmly attached to reality. You can't take an excellent suggestion from Rebbetzin Flora and throw it in the garbage. Have we flown to Paris for nothing?"

Chedvi smiled bitterly. This *shidduch* was important to her mother only because of who had suggested it.

When they returned from the tour of the Eiffel Tower to the pleasant house in the Pletzel, Chedvi closeted herself in the room for a long time. When she came out, she informed Devorah that she was prepared to meet François Feldman a second time. Perhaps she would see a different, more spiritual side to his personality.

❧

When his military service ended, young Nati Morgenstern found himself with nothing. He did not want to return to the kibbutz because he despised the collective lifestyle; his capitalistic personality hankered to make money. He tried his luck in the private market a few times without success, but kept his failures a secret from his friends lest he damage his image.

When Nati was down to his last penny, he went to visit his father. With him, there was no need to keep up pretenses; Nati could speak openly.

They sat down together on a bench on one of the paths of Kibbutz Deganiah. Shaul Morgenstern's hand, calloused from years of manual labor, tenderly patted the cheek of his only son, who so often brought him bitterness. The smell of oats and alfalfa was in the air; not far from them, ten kibbutz members were gathering bundles of hay into a large silo. From time to time, a breeze carried the smell of manure from the huge cow shed. Nati's nose wrinkled in distaste.

Shaul was not surprised by his son's story. "I knew it! You can fool all your friends, but you can't fool your father. You think I don't know that you speculate in air?"

Nati ignored his father's insults. He knew his father was upset that Nati didn't want to follow in his footsteps and be faithful to the kibbutz. Well, what did the father expect? He, too, had left *his* father's ways and fled from a life of Torah to the fields of the kibbutz.

Shaul stared at a tractor making straight furrows in the loose earth as it rolled through the fields. "I toss in bed at night and think about what to do with you," he confided. "You know, you have a very successful cousin — the son of my older brother, Elitzafan. His name is Zeidel Portman."

A few days later, a thin, suntanned young man in jeans and T-shirt knocked on the door of Samson Steel Industries, Ltd. outside Jerusalem. Zeidel Portman was surprised when the nonreligious fellow introduced himself as his first cousin. But after Nati brought him warm greetings from his father, Zeidel recalled that an Uncle Shaul had left Torah observance and disappeared.

At first Zeidel suspected that Nati was lying, but Nati produced documents that verified his story. Zeidel was convinced, but did not understand what Nati wanted from him. Finally the young man admitted shamefacedly that his father had sent him to ask his only relative in the Land of Israel to give him work, since he had no money for food.

Nati's appeal hit the target. Compassion was one of the strongest aspects of Zeidel's personality; any beggar who held out a hand received a generous gift. Nati aroused Zeidel's compassion. "I need a clerk," he said after a moment's thought, "to organize my office and type letters. Do you know how to type?"

"No," Nati admitted, "but I can learn."

"So sit down right here. Put two sheets of white paper with a carbon paper between them into the typewriter, turn the knob on the side, and start hitting the keys."

Thus began Nati Morgenstern's career. Nati had no experience, but Zeidel was patient and took the trouble to personally train him on the job.

At that time, Samson Steel was in the business of manufacturing bullets. Zeidel felt comfortable keeping the company's vague old name from its previous lifetime. Beneath the facade of a pipe manufacturer, he was able to run his life undisturbed. He lived as a *charedi* Jerusalemite with zealous views while producing live ammunition for the small, expanding army of the Zionist State.

ও∮৯

"By the way, despite Zeidel's extreme anti-State views, he carried out very honest business with the Ministry of Defense."

Felix put the glass to his lips and again sipped two drops. "I understand that he manufactured cannon nests and tanks, but not live ammunition."

"Nonsense," said Nati excitedly. "Zeidel began with nests. One day a senior official of the Ministry of Defense suggested that he go into bullets and cannon balls. Zeidel checked the turf, saw that there was big money to be made, and entered a new market. From then on the company mushroomed.

"I watched my cousin raking in money while I remained a clerk earning pennies. My mind began to work feverishly. Instead of typing, I spent hours trying to figure out how to advance.

"Besides, I knew that before long he would fire me — and justly so. I was a failure as a clerk; I even sent Zeidel to important meetings with the wrong documents."

"So what did you do?" asked Felix curiously.

An evil gleam flashed in Nati's eyes. "I'll tell you what I did."

⌘

Zeidel's grasp of business and of weapons manufacture amazed his colleagues. They wondered how a Jew from Meah Shearim who studied only Torah could understand what university graduates did not. But he had a weak side: administration and order. The office of Samson Steel permanently looked as if it had just been ransacked by thieves. The business ran smoothly despite the chaos, thanks only to the boss's excellent memory. Zeidel knew the details of all the purchases and sales by heart.

Zeidel had hoped that his newly found cousin would put the files in order, but he was sorely disappointed. Nati was lazy and wanted to be paid for doing nothing. He began sorting the files but gave up after two hours.

Nati sensed that his layoff was imminent. With the survival instincts of a hunted animal, he searched for something that would keep him at his job. He found it — in the files.

Zeidel nearly fainted when Nati showed him a discrepancy between quantities of arms ordered and paid for by the army and quantities supplied to it. Samson Steel had been paid for 4,000 cannon shells but had supplied only 3,150. In bullets, the situation was much worse. Out of 85,000 gun bullets ordered, only 48,500 had been delivered, but payment had been received for the entire order. The stench of treason filled the room.

"To the best of my knowledge," said Zeidel, horrified, "we supplied the full amount."

"The best of your knowledge won't stand up in court," said Nati casually, as he waved the papers. "Especially not against written documents."

"What can we do?" asked Zeidel.

"First of all, we must make sure that no outsider ever hears about the chaos in your office," said Nati in a meaningful tone. "All Samson Steel employees must be kept silent. One word to a sensation-seeking journalist, and tomorrow you'll be in court using up all your savings on a lawyer."

Zeidel understood the veiled message. Nati was not fired.

⊘⊰✵⊱⊘

Sheket scanned his e-mails. One newly arrived message sent his pulse racing. "Triple Zero has not been carried out as of now. What is the meaning of the delay? Perhaps opposition to the plan?"

He typed back, "Triple Zero was implemented yesterday without success. The subject left the car suddenly."

Five minutes later, the reply came, sharp and cold. "It will be carried out today, without any excuses, please."

What's the rush? wondered Sheket, as he started shutting the store lights in preparation for closing. Questions notwithstanding, he would have to improvise something.

He knew the daily schedule of his "subject." Moshiko might complain that he was locked up in the house, but it simply was not true. Every evening he went to Saint Martin Boulevard, parked his car, and took a long stroll. Invariably, he stopped beside a large bookstore and scanned the headlines of the newspapers on the stand outside. The sidewalk was very narrow, and every car that passed had to honk the readers to take a step forward.

If so, the plan was simple. Tomorrow he would hire a jeep with front-wheel drive. He would ride down the boulevard quickly, and when he approached the bookstore, he would press down on the gas petal, then flee and leave the car in a dark alley.

Sheket had been taught a useful rule: Whenever you decide on a plan of action, consult someone. If you have no one else to consult, get a second opinion from yourself by imagining that you are consulting a person with great authority.

Sheket would imagine Yirmiyahu, his mentor at the Mossad, a fellow with brilliant analytical abilities. Now he "consulted" Yirmiyahu, and he could hear his voice saying decisively, "No! Even if the risk of getting caught is miniscule, don't take it. The result does not justify the scandal that will be created if you are caught. Find yourself a dark, quiet alley in some outlying neighborhood."

The Barbes quarter where Moshiko lived fit the bill. Violent gangs of blacks, Hispanics, and Arabs roved the streets, and the police were loathe to enter the neighborhood.

After locking the store, Sheket took the subway a few stops, got out near an Avis branch, rented a solidly constructed SUV, and headed toward Moshiko's house. To make sure nothing went wrong, he would follow Moshiko before carrying out the action.

Night had already fallen when he drove onto the street where Moshiko lived. He passed the building to which Moshiko had pointed when they strolled together during Moshiko's first week in Paris. "This is the headquarters of my boss, Asaf," he had said proudly. Nati's name was not to be mentioned.

Sheket glanced at the building and thought he saw Asaf's gleaming bald pate through the window of the stairwell. So Asaf was coming downstairs. The seasoned instincts of a Mossad agent told him to slow down and prepare to tail the arms dealer. He continued on another five meters, turned off the motor, and shut the lights. The car's panoramic mirror gave him a good rear view.

Asaf was not alone. A group of five, speaking in hushed tones, left the building. Sheket recognized Asaf, Dubik, and Malkiel from pictures Moshiko had shown him. The two others had a markedly Middle Eastern look. From his work in the Mossad, Sheket recognized them as agents of the Iranian secret service.

What were three Israeli arms dealers, whom the Mossad considered upright and honest, doing with enemy agents?

Sheket continued to watch the five as they entered two waiting limousines and took off down the dark street. When the limousines turned right, Sheket turned the key in the ignition. He had to know where the five were going and what they were up to.

The two limousines, followed at a safe distance by Sheket's rented Isuzu Trooper, drove for a long time — several times longer than necessary, perhaps to shake off any would-be followers.

Although Sheket knew Paris well from his long stay there, he lost his bearings as they turned right and left, crossed intersections and plazas, went around rows of buildings, and passed main streets. Fifty minutes later they arrived in the Luxembourg Gardens, a large park that had not changed much since the nineteenth century, when it was a private garden.

Two minutes after the limousines parked, Sheket turned off the motor of his SUV, so far away that he nearly lost track of them. The five crossed grassy lawns, rows of trees, and decorative flowerbeds before settling down on benches facing a Roman-style arcade. Behind them was a manicured hedge.

Sheket blessed them in his heart. Under cover of the hedge, he managed to get within a meter of them and hear every word.

Asaf began. "We all know why we are meeting," he said in English, "but until we get the okay from Nati, we can do nothing."

"How will he send you the okay?" asked one of the Iranians, a thin, moustached man with eyes like glowing coals. Sheket recognized Hassan Abu Dahari, known as The Cutter from his secret police days.

Asaf pointed to a small cell phone he was holding. "He'll call at any minute. We made up for ten."

As if to confirm his words, the shiny blue screen suddenly lit up and began to vibrate. Asaf pressed the button and said, "Hello."

❧❦☙

"While pretending to restore order," said Nati, downing another glass, "I searched for every discrepancy in the files and made a potential scandal of it. Zeidel continually promoted me to prevent my leaking information to the media. Before a year had passed, he put me in charge of the production department. The lazy kibbutznik who didn't know how to put a document into a looseleaf became responsible for a production line of bullets and cannon shells. I was drunk with success.

"And it didn't stop there. For religious and ethical reasons, Zeidel's life revolved around the plant, the synagogue, and the house. He appointed me as his representative to the world at large. I traveled abroad, rubbed shoulders with famous generals, participated in exclusive cocktail parties, was photographed with the big shots, and lived it up. My wildest dreams were fulfilled."

Felix nodded and pretended to take another sip. The information that flowed from drunken Nati's lips was important, yet they had not yet gotten down to the main part: the years of joint management and the dirty arms deals. It would be necessary to place new bait on the hook, but Nati was not the type to make the same mistake twice. It was doubtful that he would agree to another party like this one that would unmuzzle his mouth again.

"Now you see how I maneuvered my naive cousin?" An expression of amusement appeared on Nati's face. He reached into his cigar box, but suddenly stopped short. "No, I mustn't smoke any more. I've already overdone it." He closed the box and glanced at his watch. "It's almost ten. We've been sitting here for hours. Your company was very pleasant, Felix." He slapped the scientist's shoulder. "Will you forgive me if I leave you for two minutes?"

Without waiting for an answer, Nati got up, hurried downstairs, left the club, and crossed the street. At the corner of St. James Street, he whipped out a cell phone.

When Asaf's voice came over, Nati announced, "We hit the jackpot!"

"I don't believe it, Nati. Congratulations!" Asaf's voice dripped flattery and amazement. "How did you do it?"

"Don't ask. I pressured him as hard as I could, and even then it cost me plenty. But Malkiel was right. Felix is ready to sell his own mother for the right price."

"How much?"

"A lot."

Asaf moved away from the group. His voice turned angry. "You can talk like that to Malkiel and Dubik, but not to me."

"You're right." Nati sounded pressured by Asaf's anger. "We agreed on twenty."

"Are you out of your mind? How did you give in to such an outrageous price?"

"I had no choice." The lies glided out of Nati's mouth like marbles out of a hole in the bag. "He's tough. If I had pressed him any more, he would have dropped everything and walked out."

"Twenty is ridiculous," said Asaf coldly. "I hope our intake will cover it."

"Our intake will be fifty."

Expecting fifty million dollars from Iran for something that cost them twenty? Either Nati had lost his mind, or else he was deceiving him. Lately Asaf had suspected that Nati was giving him false reports about their profits. It was hard for him to put his finger on a specific point — Nati was wily, slippery, and evasive — but too many deals were yielding low profits. And when the pie was divided among all the partners (besides Nati, who held the cards close to his chest), even Asaf's share was measly. Asaf decided to teach Nati a bitter lesson.

Nati could not read Asaf's hostile thoughts. He continued pouring words into the phone. "He showed me a demo CD. We have the jackpot in hand."

Asaf was stunned. The business had succeeded beyond expectation. "Has he already given you the CDs?"

"Of course not. He agreed to supply the merchandise on condition that I transfer the money to him in advance. Meanwhile he has only a demo CD, which I need you to pass on to the people you're dealing with. Are they there?"

"Both of them."

"Excellent. I'll take the CD from him now, and in six hours it will be in Paris. Make up to meet them tomorrow morning at ten."

"Fine." Asaf put the phone down on a ledge, walked back to the benches, and whispered with the two Iranians. Then he returned to the phone. "They're excited. They ask you to e-mail them the contents of the CD so they can see it right now."

"It's blocked against copying," said Nati. "They'll have to wait patiently for a little while."

He hung up and returned to the club. Felix had just enough time to return to his place, settle comfortably in the armchair, and seem to be absorbed in cutting the tip of a new cigar.

Thanks to a remarkable ability to recover from alcohol, Nati was now completely sober. Felix handed him the demo disc with an expressionless face. The two agreed to meet again in the club the following evening at the same hour. Felix would bring the set of ten CDs, Nati would bring a blank check, and his bank manager in Mexico, Señor Miguel Churchas would confirm by phone that the sum was covered.

⊗⅜⊛

Asaf returned to the benches. He had a perfect plan. If Nati was misleading him and taking the lion's share of every deal for himself, Asaf could do the same.

"Any progress?" asked the second agent, Muhamad Ibn Darvish, with a wicked gleam in his black eyes. He, too, was a dangerous fellow whom you would not want to meet in an alley even during the daytime.

"Friends, we almost have the Bow in our hands." Asaf sounded excited. Behind the hedge, Sheket gnashed his teeth and hoped no one heard. "But there's a big problem."

"What's the problem?"

"The seller of the CDs suddenly changed his mind about the sum. He's demanding three times the amount."

"I understand it's a private party," said Hassan Abu Dahari. "How much could one person demand? At most, ten million."

"That's what you think." Asaf's eyes shone with a wily glint. "He wants four times that."

"Forty million dollars?" Muhamad Ibn Darvish was furious. "May his house be destroyed! How does one man get the audacity to demand so much? But I don't understand your Nati. Even after he gives the seller what he wants, he will still have 110 million in hand. Isn't that enough to distribute to the whole crew?"

Hassan Abu Dahari gave Muhamad Ibn Darvish a sharp look that made him cringe in fear. They were absolutely forbidden to let anyone under Nati know the true size of the deal. This was a serious slip of the tongue.

Asaf's blood boiled. So Nati was indeed deceiving him. Iran was prepared to pay $150 million to expose Israel to her new Shihav missiles. Nati was planning to keep the money for himself except for a few crumbs that he would share with his workers as if they were dogs to whom one threw bones. To make it worse, the "dogs" endangered themselves meeting enemies in deserted places and risked being caught by an intelligence agency or the police, while Nati sat safely in an office in Paris or Tel Aviv.

"We'll meet tomorrow night same time, same place," Asaf announced.

The five rose and left as silently as they had come. Behind the hedge, Sheket remained alone with his thoughts.

Sheket listened intently to the conversation between Asaf and Hassan Abu Dahari. They spoke only of the Bow, but to Sheket it was obvious they were using a code name for the Arrow missile.

How low could these arms dealers sink, selling their country's defense against nuclear missiles? Which corrupt scientist was about to betray his people by giving the Arrow plans to their enemies? And how had the traitor laid hands on one of Israel's most closely guarded secrets?

Moshiko had argued all along that Morgan Consolidated was preparing to sell secrets and weapons to Israel's worst enemies. So these had not been unfounded suspicions after all. Nati's corporation was about to strip Israel of its defenses and leave its five million Jews exposed to the whims of Moslem-extremist Iran, which was only a step away from an atom bomb.

❦

Asaf had been angry when he finished talking to Nati. It seemed Asaf had been told to present the CD to the Iranians at ten in the morning but had delayed the meeting by twelve hours. Apparently Nati was betraying not only his country, but also his partners in crime, and Asaf was not about to let him get away with it. A great drama was about to take place.

Sheket had a lot to tell his superiors in the Mossad. But first he would have to fill in many missing links, and for that, he needed a partner. Alone he had no chance of exposing the wily members of Morgan Consolidated.

The ideal partner was Moshiko. His sophisticated listening equipment could supply necessary information about the activities of Nati, Asaf, and their men. But by now Moshiko must have put two and two together and realized that it was Sheket who had sabotaged the brakes of his car.

Then there was another problem. What would he tell his immediate superior in the Mossad, who had given him the Triple Zero order?

As Sheket returned to the Isuzu Trooper, thousands of warning sirens went off in his ears. He would skip his immediate superior. Israel was about to be exposed to genocide — he had to warn the head of the Mossad before it was too late.

Asaf collected the cards and shuffled them. He was in a stormy frame of mind that night, after the meeting in the Luxembourg Gardens. He played poorly and lost the first game of poker.

Malkiel's mind was not at rest, either. He suspected that Asaf was about to push Nati out of the corporation just as Nati had once done to Zeidel, and he, Malkiel, wanted to come out on the winning side. He decided to ask the question. Asaf would surely get annoyed, but would probably soften up after a short display of anger.

"Tell me, Asaf, why did you get angry at Nati?"

"No special reason."

"Come on, tell me."

"Leave me alone, Malkiel!"

Asaf set the cards down on the table and studied his carefully trimmed fingernails for a long time.

Malkiel waited tensely for Asaf's anger to subside. Asaf poured himself a small glass of brandy and downed it in a single gulp. Then he rolled the crystal glass in the palm of his hand and pressed hard on it. The thin crystal submitted to the pressure. There was a sound of breaking glass, then of pieces falling to the table. Asaf jumped to his feet and examined his right hand. Red drops appeared in several places.

Malkiel quickly brought water to wash the cuts, but Asaf pushed it away and put a tissue on his bleeding hand. "Malkiel, are you a child who gets excited about a few drops of blood? By the way, what do you mean that I got angry?"

Malkiel recoiled from the powerful giant. "Look, you spoke with Nati at a distance of two meters from me. I'm not deaf. Something happened, right?"

"Certainly something happened." Asaf suddenly sat down, crossed his legs, and looked entirely at ease. He had already decided that Malkiel would be his partner in the next step.

His voice turned stern and sharp. "I'm going to tell you something, but it must stay strictly between us. Top secret."

Malkiel nodded. "You know my mouth is tightly sealed. You've already tested me a thousand times."

"True," Asaf agreed. "And I've seen that you're a good fellow. I can rely on you."

He brought his chair closer to Malkiel. "You know that Nati has used the method of Divide and Conquer to lord it over us. Since no one knows how much anyone else is getting, he manages to fool us all. He takes the whole kitty for himself and throws us a few crumbs."

Malkiel would not have called a salary of ten thousand dollars a month "crumbs," but he held his tongue.

"For instance," Asaf continued, "take the Arrow CDs. Felix Goldmark offers to sell them for $20 million. Nati told me that Iran was ready to pay us $50 million for them. But two hours ago, I trapped Muhamad Ibn Darvish by telling him that the scientist had demanded $40 million, and I got the true price out of him: $150 million. In other words, Nati hid more than $100 million from us!"

Malkiel's eyebrows arched. "Meaning what?"

Asaf stood up again and flexed his muscles. Even at fifty-nine, he looked like an Olympic athlete. He beat his massive chest like a tribal chieftain and his eyes flashed. "Meaning I'm going to turn the tables on Nati."

"How?"

"Have you heard of the Saudi billionaire Abdul Hasugi?"

"Who hasn't?"

"You know him through the media. I know him personally. I've made several deals with him and we get along famously.

"Lately a wave of extreme nationalism has been sweeping the Arab world. With Iran at her side, Saudi Arabia is becoming its patron. She funds Al-Qaeda, and many of the terrorists involved in the attack on the Twin Towers were Saudis."

He paused for a moment.

"Go on, I'm listening," said Malkiel, enthralled.

"Abdul Hasugi is very close to the Saudi rulers. For several weeks now, I've been quietly negotiating with them through him. Saudi Arabia will pay any sum I ask for the Arrow CDs, and then hire Korean scientists to develop a missile that the Arrow won't be able to knock down. The privilege of being the Arab nation that liquidates Israel is worth half a billion to them."

He slapped Malkiel's shoulder. "Let's go. Pack your toothbrush and your contact lens solution. We're off."

"Where to?"

"To London, in my private plane. We'll meet Felix Goldmark and get two steps ahead of Nati. I postponed the meeting with the Iranians by twelve hours to gain time."

"Meet Felix Goldmark?" Malkiel's face contorted in disgust. "That skunk? Never!"

"Why not?" laughed Asaf. "Doesn't half a billion suit you? When we split it in half, that makes a quarter of a billion for each of us — all in one shot. You can retire tomorrow and live to the end of your days like Abdul Hasugi, with a fleet of cars, a private yacht, and an army of servants. You'll buy a dream villa for two or three million on some Polynesian island and sway in a hammock between coconut and palm trees. When you get bored, you'll hop over to Israel for a visit."

"If there is an Israel, after it's left defenseless!"

Asaf winked. "Don't be naive. The whole thing is one big game, a power struggle among nations. In the end, neither Iran nor Saudi Arabia will dare to use nuclear weapons against Israel, and not only for fear of her reaction. Israel is safe — but we can make the most of the game."

"I can't look at Felix Goldmark's face." Malkiel spat out the words. "When I was working in Elta, I caught him trying to sell national secrets and I stopped him. In revenge, he slandered me and had me fired."

"A hairsbreadth separates the wise from the foolish," said Asaf, apprising Malkiel of his theory of life. "The ability to be flexible is that hairsbreadth. If you're flexible now and come with me to meet Goldmark, you'll gain a quarter of a billion dollars. But if you wallow in yesterday's hurts, you'll remain buried forever in small deals, an Uzi submachine gun here, a Strela missile there. Nothing serious. Do you want to manage a supermarket chain or be forever a small grocer, who checks his customers' hands to see whether they took an extra bag?"

Malkiel switched tactics. "We don't even know where Goldmark is."

Asaf laughed. "We're meeting him tomorrow for breakfast in the dining room of London's Victoria Park Plaza Hotel."

"Where do you get your information?" asked Malkiel, stunned.

"If I didn't know it, my name wouldn't be Asaf," laughed the giant. "Why do you think I regularly grease the palms of the Havana Club's bartender?"

"What's the connection?"

"A riddle of logic," announced Asaf dramatically. "Where did Nati and Felix meet? In the Havana Club. Fact. Every guest signs in upon registering. Fact. So the bartender gave me Felix's address: London, Victoria Park Plaza Hotel."

෴

The CD from London arrived in Paris at 3 a.m., and Malkiel picked it up because Asaf relied on no one else. Malkiel was tired the next morning, but despite the fact that his cheek had not touched a pillow in more than forty-eight hours, Asaf was energetic, fresh, and in top shape. After a short flight in Asaf's private plane, they entered a typical damp, gray, foggy London morning. They continued in a rented car that got stuck in traffic, and an hour later reached the reception desk of the Victoria Park Plaza Hotel.

"Mr. Goldmark? He is in suite 614."

Asaf began striding toward the elevator. Suddenly Malkiel grabbed his arm. "Hey, you said we were meeting in the dining room."

"I had forgotten that he's an Orthodox Jew who won't eat a thing in a nonkosher hotel. He probably bought a roll and butter in a kosher store in Golders Green or Stamford Hill, and right now he's in his suite, spreading the butter on the roll."

Asaf's assumption was close. Felix had just finished *bentching* after eating a kosher roll with butter when there was a knock on the door of his elegant suite.

He welcomed them with a smile and shook their hands. "We met a few days ago in the Havana Club, didn't we?"

"It was very pleasant," said Asaf. "You told some sharp jokes."

"I didn't know you liked cigars," said Malkiel. "When we worked together in Elta, you always strongly objected to smokers."

Asaf shot a fiery glance at Malkiel, but Felix was as cold as a fish in a frozen river. He regarded Malkiel with half-closed eyes and commented, "Only a donkey never changes its mind."

Asaf decided to extinguish the flame of dissension while it was still a mere flicker. "Gentlemen, we have come for a reason. Felix, you're a clever fellow. Guess why we came."

Felix slowly lit a fat Punch Double Corona cigar and inhaled strongly until the entire tip of the cigar turned red. Then he exhaled a cloudlet of heavy smoke and said quietly, "Perhaps to discuss the spread of Moslem fundamentalism in the world."

"You're very close." Asaf reached into Felix's cigar box and helped himself to one. "You have good taste. Did you know that the hedonistic Egyptian king Farouk, who was ousted by Gamal Abdul Nasser, used to buy five thousand cigars at a clip? At one point he ordered forty thousand Hoyo de Monterrey Double Corona from the Davidoff store in Geneva."

Felix chuckled quietly. "Speaking of Arab nations, when Winston Churchill hosted Saudi Arabia's Emir Faisal for lunch, he offered the king a cigar and whiskey, both of which the king politely declined. Churchill instructed the interpreter to tell the king, 'If his religion forbids his majesty to drink or smoke, I must point out that my religion includes the holy custom of smoking cigars and drinking alcohol before, after, and during each meal, as well as in between them.'"

Asaf winked at Malkiel. "Interesting that you mentioned Saudi Arabia," he told Felix. As if the suite belonged to him, he went to the small refrigerator, took out a can of cold beer, and gulped it down. "I know that you agreed to supply Nati Morgan with a set of highly classified CDs. How about canceling the deal with him and giving me the merchandise instead? How much did he offer you, twenty million dollars? I'll give you thirty. He plans to send the CDs to Iran, but I'll sell them to Saudi Arabia for a much higher price."

Felix listened without blinking an eyelid. Then he said quietly, "I asked Nati for fifteen million, and he bargained me down to eleven."

Asaf did not share Felix's amazing self-control. He slammed the empty beer can down on the glass top of the coffee table. "What?" he cried. "The swindler told me he promised you twenty. Another one of Nati's lies. Listen Felix, my good friend, I like truthful people. Even though you lost a good bargaining position by revealing your secret, I'll stick to my word and pay you thirty for the set of CDs. Just say yes to me, and you've netted yourself an extra nineteen million."

Felix got up and paced back and forth on the thick carpet while humming an off-tune version of Johann Strauss's *Blue Danube*. He paused at the window. The majestic drapes were opened to let in the maximum amount of light, which was not very much.

"I don't know what to say," he muttered at last, staring out at the Thames River, barely visible through the fog. "Your offer is tempting, but I'm already committed to Nati. It isn't right to back out now."

"It isn't right," said Malkiel mockingly. "Look who's talking!"

"Silence!" came Asaf's deep bass voice. He waved a clenched fist in front of Malkiel's eyes, as if he were about to smash his chin. In the end he grabbed the knot in Malkiel's tie. "Keep your wisecracks to yourself. Understand?"

Malkiel quietly adjusted his tie while riveting his eyes to the tips of his shoes.

"Okay, Felix," Asaf continued. "I understand that it's hard for you to go back on your word. I like a faithful man. But do you know who you're being faithful to? Give me an hour of your time, and I'll tell you the story of Samson Steel."

Felix was overjoyed, but he had to play the game. He pretended to consider for a minute, and then said in a lukewarm tone, "All right. Let's hear."

"In a minute. Now it's ten o'clock, time to call Nati and give him a report." He winked at them as he took out his cell phone. "Hello, Nati," he said happily. "Are you still in London? Yes, they're with me at home, the two nice Iranians. I just handed them the CD. Yes, Malkiel received it from the contact man this morning at four, as we made up."

He listened a few seconds longer and then said, "Don't worry, everything is under control."

Afterwards, Asaf sucked the shrinking cigar pensively for a minute and blew out a long breath of smoke. "That snake suspects something," he hissed. "He asked too many questions. We don't have much time." He turned to Felix. "Nevertheless, I promised to tell you what you need to know."

"Let's hear," said Felix, stretching out in his armchair.

"It was in the good old sixties," Asaf began. "Samson Steel was flooded with orders for weapons from all over the world."

❧

Flora walked around enveloped in joy. Her plan had succeeded beyond all expectations. In her rosiest dreams she had not imagined that François could be influenced so easily.

From François' point of view, the Israeli *shidduch* had introduced him to new images, none as colorful as the Rebbetzin whose tongue raced faster than a spaceship. Before his second date with Chedvi, she gave him a pep talk on the *talmid chacham*'s mission in the world.

"I, too, would like to dwell in the house of Hashem all the days of my life," he explained to her pleasantly. "But I cannot guarantee that ten years from now I will be able to sit in *kollel* all day. I might want to teach Torah or write mezuzos."

"Excellent! That is working for Heaven," the Rebbetzin enthused, her eyes closed in concentration. "In addition, you will of course set aside fixed times for Torah study, a minimum of three hours a day, correct?"

"Three hours? That's too little. Five!"

Flora thought she detected a note of mockery in his voice. She opened her eyes and glanced at the young man sitting on the other side of the heavy mahogany desk. François' face looked innocent and serious.

"Engaging in the work of Heaven while studying Torah five hours a day is called 'dwelling in the house of Hashem all the days of your life.' Why do you have to push away the girl by telling her you'll go out to work in five years? When you meet her this evening, undo the negative impression you made the first time and apologize for not having explained yourself well. Let her understand that you aspire to Torah and not to business, and you intend to occupy yourself with Torah and service of Heaven until a hundred and twenty."

"No problem," answered François. "If Hashem grants me two hundred forty years of life, half of them will surely be in the *beis midrash*."

Flora was unsure of the meaning behind those last words, but his face looked full of charming innocence, and he kissed the mezuzah reverently as he left. Her heart filled with ecstasy. She hoped that in France, she would give Devorah and Chedvi Mindelman the happiness for which they had waited so long.

32

Moshiko was exhausted from two days of flight and escape.

Who was behind the attempt on his life? Moshiko suspected that his old army buddy Sheket had done the work at the instigation of Nati and Asaf. Although they still occasionally sent him to meet a buyer's representative, it was clear that he had changed from a trusted employee to *persona non grata*. At the same time, as he knew from "listening," two gigantic deals were underway, one with pitchblende and the other with a set of CDs. Evidently the bosses also knew that he knew. One of them had connections everywhere, perhaps even in the Mossad. Apparently they had passed false information about him to their contact man there. They had slandered Moshiko as being an enemy and set his best friend against him.

He could not understand Sheket. Even if Sheket had received orders from the Mossad, wasn't his head working? Had he turned into a robot without a flicker of feeling, a death machine that would not stop until the picture of a lifeless Moshiko was displayed on its screen and its infrared sensors found no heat in his body?

Ever since Sheket had begun to pursue him, Moshiko had turned into a hunted animal. To his sorrow, he had been forced to leave his room with its sophisticated listening equipment and instead hang around public places, where he felt safer. One day he had visited the d'Orsay Museum of Art, blended in with a large group of tourists, and surveyed paintings, sculptures, and graphs and designs beneath the tall, arched glass ceiling of a former train station. From there he had gone to the Eiffel Tower, strolled down the Champs Elysées, and circled the Arc de Triomphe, as if he were eager to see the wonders of Paris.

Today he had spent hours walking through the Louvre Museum, where he gazed at masterpieces by Leonardo da Vinci and Michaelangelo. Then he had visited the Tuileries Gardens. Strolling along the bank of the Seine River until Place de la Concorde, he had chatted with local artists who were painting the view.

For a tourist these would have been pleasant excursions. Moshiko, however, was drained by the unremitting tension and the need to be permanently on the alert.

At night he came home exhausted and grabbed a bite to eat. Afterwards he went to open the window. That was when he noticed two limousines parked across the street, under Asaf's apartment. He immediately put on his infrared glasses.

The limousines were empty. His gaze roved restlessly over the area. An Isuzu Trooper was parked down the block. The SUV was silent but there was someone in the driver's seat. He looked carefully at the silhouette and trembled. It looked like Sheket. "My angel of death," he whispered fearfully.

At that moment, the light went on in the stairwell of the facing building. Soon after that, he saw a few figures slip into the limousines: Asaf, Dubik, Malkiel, and two men with Middle Eastern features. The limousines pulled out and a few seconds later the Isuzu Trooper glided after them with its lights off.

A minute later, Moshiko's rental car followed the limousines and the SUV. He, too, had followed the secret meeting in the Luxembourg Gardens from behind the bushes, but he left a few minutes before the conclusion.

◈◈◈

Question marks fluttered in his head when he finally went to bed. He did not sleep long. At 2:30 a.m., the cell phone rang.

With eyes closed, Moshiko put the phone to his ear. "Hello," he said groggily.

"Moshiko, it's me, Sheket."

"Who?" Moshiko was still half asleep.

"Leonardo Pantoloni, if you prefer." From the tone of voice, Sheket was grinning.

Moshiko was not at all inclined to smile. Suddenly he became alert. "You didn't succeed with the brakes, so you're trying to liquidate me with the cell phone?" he asked with hostility. "What did you put into it, 50 grams of plastic explosives like they did for Yichya Ayash, or do you have something more sophisticated for a good friend?"

"Moshiko, what are you saying?"

"Stop playing innocent, Sheket. How stupid do you think I am?"

"But you're my best friend." Sheket sounded upset.

"I was."

"Why, what happened?"

"You think I can't guess that you were ordered to liquidate me? You won't be satisfied until you do it. You monkeyed with my brakes, and then you rented an Isuzu Trooper to run me over. You think I didn't see you waiting down the block in an SUV, waiting for me to come out for an evening stroll?"

"It is true that I rented an SUV and sat in it. I tailed your nice friends. Something big is about to happen, and only you, with your sophisticated listening equipment, can help me."

Moshiko yawned. "You're welcome to visit. What gift will you bring me — cyanide pills, a poison injection, or a pistol with a silencer?"

Sheket was quiet for a moment. Then he said, "Moshiko, I swear that I have no such intentions. It's true that the Mossad gave me orders and that I disabled your brakes. Someone inside has been bought by Nati and Asaf. I was told you were a traitor who wanted to sell security secrets to the enemy. It took me a while to realize that they themselves are doing just that, and they wanted to use me to get rid of you. Moshiko, if we work together, we can foil their evil schemes!"

Moshiko did not bother answering. He hung up and turned the cell phone off. Sheket could shed crocodile tears and apologize a thousand times; Moshiko would no longer trust him. Sheket reminded Moshiko of the big bad wolf who pleaded with the pig to open the door, solemnly promising not to hurt him….

⚬❧⚬

The relations between the head of Samson Steel and its secretary were complex and rocky. Zeidel soon regretted having compassionately hired his penniless relative. He understood immediately that Nati was exploiting the disorder in the files to intimidate him. One day, after Nati showed him some discrepancies in the records, Zeidel became disgusted and began to search for an additional secretary. He placed ads in the papers, interviewed several candidates, and finally found one he liked. As soon as the dark, smiley, overweight Yemenite walked into the office and said, "My name is Yoel Tzadok," he found a warm spot in Zeidel's heart with his integrity and charm.

"You will assist my secretary, Mr. Nati Morgan," Zeidel told Yoel. "You will be in charge of keeping the paperwork in order."

This was a heavy blow to Nati, who was sitting at the next desk with a bored expression, diligently sharpening yellow pencils until their graphite points were thin and sharp as a pin.

As Nati watched openmouthed, Zeidel ordered a taxi for the secretary's new assistant — a privilege reserved for the wealthy in those years — and escorted him from the office. While they waited for the taxi, Zeidel explained to Yoel what his job really entailed. "My secretary is, how shall I put it, a bit slick. I suspect he is trying to cheat me. To keep him out of the office, I made him responsible for a production line. Next week he's going to Germany to buy tank parts. While he is gone, you will go over the files, checking these in particular." He handed Yoel a long list of problematic files, winked at him, and whispered, "You will get a hundred lirot for each file whose problems you solve."

At the time, a hundred lirot was a fortune.

The following week, Yoel placed two orderly files in Zeidel's personal mailbox during Nati's long lunch break.

Zeidel pored over each paper and document carefully. His face turned purple with rage. "That cheat!" he whispered. "The goods delivered correspond exactly with the goods ordered. Nati simply changed the numbers in order to frighten me."

"Keep up the good work," Zeidel told Yoel. On the spot, he raised Yoel's salary and gave him additional benefits.

Yoel became Zeidel's hidden eye, continually supervising Nati's actions on the sly.

Yoel was the exact antithesis of Nati — an efficient, diligent clerk. In two weeks, he whipped all the botched files into order and took all the air out of the balloon of scandal. Zeidel heaved a sign of relief. He knew he had never cheated anyone deliberately, but feared there might have been some mistakes along the way. Now it turned out that all the merchandise ordered and paid for had indeed been supplied, down to the last pistol.

Zeidel was considering how to phrase Nati's letter of dismissal when the phone rang.

"What's doing, Zeidel?" It was Nati, calling from Germany. He sounded very happy. "Managing with Yoel? You two fit together like a horse and buggy.

"I'll tell you what I'm calling about. Are you interested in buying seven tanks from a good firm?"

"Seven tanks?" asked Zeidel in astonishment. "What's that all about?"

"At a cocktail party yesterday I met Steve McMeilor, a big arms manufacturer. He has a surplus from a large order from the American army. You can have seven tanks for a very good price. I've already negotiated the deal, and all I need now is your consent," said Nati lightly, as if it were an everyday occurrence. "Maybe you'll sell them to the Israeli army."

Nati carefully avoided the term "Israeli Defense Forces" lest he kindle Zeidel's wrath. "The safety of Eretz Yisrael depends on Hashem," the zealous Jerusalemite would hiss sarcastically and launch into his staunch anti-State views. Nati had learned to sidestep the subject completely. Anyway, the bottom line was business, not political views.

"I'm not sure the Israeli army needs my tanks," said Zeidel with some reservation, as he looked at the latest files that Yoel had placed on his desk. How much of a middleman's fee was Nati planning to take for himself? He would surely report twice the actual price of the tanks and help himself to the difference.

"When they see this merchandise, I think they'll change their minds," said Nati with a smile you could hear over the phone.

"I'm flying to Germany," said Zeidel. "I want to see the merchandise with my own eyes and not buy a cat in a sack. If I see that it's a good deal, we'll buy the whole lot."

"Great!" said Nati. "Come today. You won't believe how many good deals can be made here, but I don't have the nerve to do them without you."

Zeidel traveled to Germany for a week. Nati had not misled him. The new-generation tanks were top-notch merchandise that dwarfed everything he had known before. In addition to them, he bought two used training planes in good condition, a large supply of new parachutes that an unnamed African nation had ordered two weeks before it crumbled, and two thousand illuminating bombs, all at rock-bottom prices.

The Israeli army chose not to buy, so Zeidel looked for markets abroad. Over the next two months, he sold the whole lot to various buyers around the world at several times what he had paid. Zeidel had become an international arms dealer.

Nati's letter of dismissal was shelved until further notice. Zeidel discovered that the lazy, troublesome clerk was a brilliant, capable salesman. At banquets and cocktail parties, Nati rubbed shoulders with the world's top brass and cooked up clever deals with the biggest weapons manufacturers of Europe and America. Thanks to him, Zeidel turned from a small manufacturer of bullets and cannon nests to one of the world's biggest arms dealers.

After the first deal in Germany came another one in France, and then one in Nicaragua. Nati diligently followed goings-on throughout the world. He shocked Zeidel with astronomical phone bills but covered them with a fraction of the profit from successful deals. He moved the corporation a whole generation forward.

Before long, Zeidel changed his mind about Nati entirely. The suppressed hatred and anger and the plans to get rid of him at the earliest opportunity gave way to warm enthusiasm about the successful buyer and salesman that he had become. Gradually Zeidel stopped suspecting Nati's every movement and even began to trust him somewhat.

Even in the happiest moments, though, Zeidel remained careful, like a sleepy cat with one eye open. He turned Yoel Tzadok into a permanent watchdog. Yoel sat in the office and carefully scrutinized each paper that Nati brought to make sure he would not cheat the boss.

But Nati deceived them both. He skimmed the cream off of every large deal for himself, while making sure to keep the official documents proper.

Little by little, Nati acquired the trust of his employer, who more than once found himself thinking that it was not he, Zeidel, who was helping his cousin, but the other way around. The brilliant weapon salesman catapulted Samson Steel to fame and success.

෬⊰✷⊱๑

On her way back from a lecture, Flora stopped at in a shop on Rue de Rosiers for baguettes and cheese. She found Chedvi alone in the house. After François left, Devorah had gone out as well.

Flora invited Chedvi to join her for a late supper in the kitchen. Chedvi watched admiringly as Flora expertly cut the baguettes with a sharp knife, filled them with cheese, olives, and various spices, and set them on plates. The Rebbetzin did everything with a flair.

Flora spoke excitedly about the great thirst for Judaism that she was discovering in France, in the halls and lectures and in the street. "The anti-Semitism here is causing the youth to come back to their forgotten heritage," Flora declared with an outburst of joy as she poured orange juice into two glasses.

"Now tell me, how did the date go?" she asked with a mischievous wink.

Chedvi glowed like a *kallah* at her wedding. "I don't understand how I made such a mistake on the first date," she said with a happy smile. "This evening he told me that he had not explained himself well the previous time, and that what he really wants is 'to dwell in the house of Hashem all the days of my life.' Exactly what I want."

"Wonderful," enthused Flora.

It never occurred to Chedvi that François' declaration was the contribution of Flora, who maneuvered people like marionettes on a string.

"So what do you say? Would you like a third date?"

Chedvi blushed. "I haven't spoken to my mother yet. In any case, I want to sleep on it."

Flora cleared the table. For her part, Chedvi could sleep on it for two nights and speak to her mother as much as she wished. Devorah would do whatever her Rebbetzin said.

33

Zeidel smelled the intoxicating fragrance of the international weapons market and liked it. In the past, his head had been in a production line of bullets, cannon shells, and cannon nests. After Nati made a few trips that brought in high returns, Zeidel began to think big. He bought German Leopard tanks, Fougah Magister training planes, and even Hawk missiles and recoilless cannons, which he sold a short while later for a handsome profit. The scope of the business broadened steadily. The simple office of Samson Steel Industries, Ltd. on the outskirts of Jerusalem was replaced by a posh office building in Tel Aviv.

Nati Morgan's standing in the corporation rose along with the profits. Five years after he first came to work for his cousin, the hungry kitten that had straggled into the house had grown into a tiger. Nati became almost an equal partner. He no longer handled the paperwork, but he detested Yoel Tzadok, who took care of the files, with all his heart. He felt that Yoel was tailing him. He would have fired Yoel, but Zeidel had protected the position of the devoted clerk with a notarized contract which made his severance pay great enough to bankrupt the corporation.

Nati knew that Yoel enjoyed special favor, but it was beneath the dignity of the man of the big world to pay attention to an office mouse in oversized glasses who gnawed at documents. The two employees were climbing the ladder of success, each in a different area. Yoel managed the office affairs of Samson Steel, while Nati managed its purchases and sales.

The original production line of the corporation, cannon shells and gun bullets, continued to run on the back burner in order to honor signed agreements with the Ministry of Defense. Nati made periodic excursions to various corners of the world, from which he never returned empty-handed. Samson Steel flourished. In the mid-sixties, the business branched out to encompass anything from shoe mines, commando knives, and tracer bullets to napalm bombs and light airplanes.

Zeidel would have made do with that; he had never been money hungry. But Nati was insatiable; he wanted to expand more and more. Zeidel did not stop him as long as everything was run legally and honestly. Every deal had to be glatt kosher. Zeidel bought weapons second hand or from approved manufacturers and sold to independent, known nations, and sometimes acted as a go-between between different parties for a high commission. As opposed as he was to the Zionist State, never did he supply weapons to Israel's enemies. Zealous opinions were one thing, but betraying his fellow Jews was another.

⸙

In the mid-sixties, Nati discovered that Africa, with its frequent military takeovers and revolutions, was a gold mine. The Congo and Angola, Kenya and Ethiopia, Nigeria and Uganda were only part of the list of nations in which tribal strife and rapid changes of rule created a need for weapons. Each side was willing to pay well to gain military superiority over the other. Along with his weapons purchasing trips to Europe, Nati began to fly also to Africa, to sniff out bloody conflicts with prime potential for arms sales.

He did not have to strain himself. The clashes and small wars in Africa were no secret. Nati contacted army commanders and presented the menu of Samson Steel to hungry consumers: guns and pistols, grenades, mines and mine detectors, jeeps, camouflage equipment, and detonators. They wanted everything, and he sold everything. Without excessive pangs of conscience, he negotiated with both sides of a conflict, sometimes even on the same day, and armed both of them in the evening with sophisticated weapons for killing each other the next morning.

So that Zeidel would not ask unpleasant questions, Nati did not tell him too much. The boss knew only that the monthly turnover was increasing steadily and the profits were rising rapidly. The bank account smiled, and in its wake, so did all of the corporation's employees. Zeidel understood that Nati was making deals that were not especially aesthetic, but money does not smell, and as long as the quiet was undisturbed, Nati operated a company within the corporation. Thus the first buds of Morgan Consolidated, Ltd. appeared within Samson Steel.

A beehive of faithful men surrounded Zeidel, of which the main ones were Yechezkel Shoshan, Zev Shachar, and Yoel Tzadok — Samson Steel's long-time employees. These quiet, modest people were cast in Zeidel's mold and were totally devoted to him.

Nati, weaving dreams of the future, began to crystallize a nucleus of his own followers. Zeidel gave Nati a free hand to hire assistants for his trips to Africa. Nati hired Yosef Berning and Dubik Cooperman, who would eventually become key figures in Morgan Consolidated.

೧೪೦

"And Malkiel Yahalom, of course," put in Felix. He looked out at the Thames River, still covered with thick gray fog. Asaf's story had enthralled him.

"Malkiel arrived many years later," laughed Asaf, and landed a friendly blow on Malkiel's shoulder. "Right? You were still in high school in those days, if I'm not mistaken."

"Making campfires and roasting potatoes." Malkiel's eyes shone. "What ever happened to the pure days of our youth?"

"Just a minute," said Felix. "Dubik I met. Malkiel wasn't around then. But who is Yosef Berning?"

"He died," Asaf deadpanned.

Felix thought quickly. "Didn't you say he turned into a key figure in the corporation?"

Asaf's mouth opened into a smile that stretched from ear to ear. "Yosef Berning died, and out of his corpse emerged Asaf Niv. Yours truly."

"What do you mean?" Felix, supporting his chin with his hand, looked pensive and curious at once.

Asaf glanced again at his 270,000-shekel Patek-Philippe watch to see whether he had time to tell the whole story. He hesitated before continuing, but it was merely a show. His first priority now was to win Felix over, even if it delayed his return to Paris.

"An official death certificate was issued for Yosef Berning and properly signed by a Brazilian doctor," he said coolly. "But I like to tell things in order. Meanwhile we will make do with the fact that Nati invited me to assist him on his trips to Africa."

⊗✸⊗

The lobby of Kenya's Hotel Africaine resembled an African tent. A local band played tribal folk songs on drums and ox bone flutes in the background. Oversized ceiling fans tried unsuccessfully to banish the warm noontime humidity and the swarms of flies buzzing in the crowded lobby. Dark-skinned servants dressed in light-colored suits stood near the guests, cooling them with fans made of broad coconut leaves and occasionally refilling their cups with cold water from glass pitchers.

The guests were attending the international weapons trade show of August 1966. Dressed in well-tailored jackets, crisply ironed shirts, colorful ties, and cuffed trousers, they exchanged information more precious than gold. Weapons catalogues, still printed at that time in black and white, were passed from hand to hand. The dialogue was conducted mostly through inference, such as "Two on the day," meaning two million dollars on the day of delivery, or "Five and a half — a half minus one," meaning five million to be paid half upon signing and the rest on the day preceeding delivery. Deals were closed with a handshake or a signature.

Off to the side sat a balding young giant, looking like a boxer who had wandered in by mistake. He crossed and uncrossed his long legs and kneaded a catalogue into a paper ball with his huge palms. Isaac was already an hour and a half late, and they had no way of contacting him. They did not know his phone number, his address, or even his real name. He would phone them, identify himself as Isaac, tell them where and when to wait for him, and hang up.

To the right of the giant sat a short, thin, young man whose casual Sabra clothing looked out of place. Every few minutes he glanced at his watch and tugged at the sleeve of the giant's leather jacket. "What will be, Yosef? What if he doesn't come?"

"Keep your hands off me, Zev!" said Yosef Berning, giving him a murderous look. "Do you think I don't know it's eleven-thirty already? He must be taking care of important business."

As if to disprove his words, just then a silhouette appeared in the lobby entrance. "Here he comes," said Zev Shachar excitedly.

Isaac was not perturbed about coming late. His clients would still be there even if he kept them waiting a whole day. They needed his merchandise.

Zev knew that the merchandise was eighteen Sikorsky helicopters. Other than that, Yosef told him very little about the new deal. He couldn't figure it out. The Israeli air force had its own buyers and did not need them as intermediaries. And what Third World guerrilla organization could pay for eighteen almost-new helicopters? When Zev asked questions, Yosef brushed him off as if he were an annoying mosquito. Yosef's evasive answers aroused Zev's suspicions.

This was the first deal of its kind that was not reported to the boss. Zeidel was in the hospital for a few days with a complication of ulcers, and in his absence Nati was running the corporation alone. While Yosef and Zev went to Africa, Nati surprised the Samson Steel employees, including Yoel Tzadok and Zeidel's other faithful men in the Tel Aviv office, by treating them to a paid four-day vacation in Eilat. The employees were too happy to ask unnecessary questions. They packed their suitcases and enthusiastically headed south.

Nati and Dubik had a heyday that week. They did as they pleased, making sure not to leave a single incriminating paper in their wake.

Zeidel was released from the hospital pale and weak. He showed up unexpectedly at the office and was stunned to discover that none of his employees were around.

"Where are they?" he asked, sinking weakly into his executive chair.

"They were exhausted," Nati answered with a saccharine smile, "so I sent them to air out in Eilat."

Zeidel lacked the strength to raise his voice. "Very nice," he said quietly. "Fourteen orders are lying here on the desk, and you send the staff on vacation." A dark cloud covered his pupils. "Tell me, why didn't you go to Eilat too, huh?"

"Someone has to do the dirty work," said Nati lightly, and went to the kitchen to make himself a glass of tea.

Zeidel followed him. Nati leaned over the kettle to check why it wasn't whistling yet. Zeidel's thin gray beard shook as he spoke, and his small eyes flashed through his thick glasses. "Since when are you so devoted to employees like Yoel and Yechezkel? And why didn't Dubik go down to Eilat?"

Zeidel felt dizzy. He clutched the edge of the counter.

Nati glanced behind him, then turned back while stroking his chin. "Would you like tea?"

"I don't want your tea," fumed Zeidel. "If you make it, it will reek of aftershave. Anyway, I have to drink a lot of milk. The doctors forbade everything: fried eggs, shnitzel, citrus fruit, pita with falafel. I can't have anything but milk and toast."

Nati was delighted at the turn the conversation had taken. "I'll make you rosemary tea; it's excellent for soothing a nervous ulcer. My father says it helps him a lot. Let me take care of you. You'll soon feel better."

"I'll feel better when I know why you sent my men away and what you've been doing in my absence," said Zeidel sternly. "Nati, I don't like what's going on here."

Nati stopped stirring the tea and gave Zeidel a penetrating glance. It was time to attack. "I've been working for you for seven years, and never have you sent a single employee of yours to even half a day's outing. What kind of boss doesn't understand that his workers have a right to a few days' vacation together? Besides, it's great for company morale and unity."

They walked back to the executive suite and sat down. Zeidel sipped the fragrant tea with appreciation. "You spout platitude, but the question is: What are you hiding behind your back?"

"A big knife," replied Nati angrily. "You're talking nonsense. I don't like to boast, but who took your lazy little firm that dealt in trifles and turned it into a giant corporation? I've made the name Samson Steel known throughout the world. I've entirely changed the balance of payments. Ask Yechezkel how much the company earned five years ago and how much it earns today!"

Zeidel sipped his tea slowly and blinked. No suitable retort came to mind, so he kept silent. Nati took advantage of the opportunity to attack further. "You don't always have to make me feel like a snake lurking under a rock, trying to undermine you at every opportunity."

"You said it, not me," said Zeidel, turning his attention to a stack of documents on his desk.

Nati stormed out of the room looking hurt and insulted. He slammed the door behind him in anger.

As soon as he was on the other side of the door, Nati burst into quiet laughter. He had put on a perfect act. Zeidel had recoiled from his crushing attack and fallen silent at the beginning of the investigation. Zeidel would never find out that eighteen helicopters had changed owners and that Nati, Yosef, and Dubik had amassed quite a nest egg. The incriminating documents had been carefully hidden away. Moreover, this was the first layer of a wall that would close in on Zeidel sometime in the future. Zeidel would yet regret every insulting word he had said to Nati.

Nati knew, though, that Zeidel was not finished with the matter. The watchdog that the boss had attached to Nati had smelled a fat bone in Eilat — but that was the last time. Yoel Tzadok would never again get off Nati's tail, even if Nati were to offer him a free flight to Honolulu. The next time Zeidel was away from the office, even a tow truck would not be able to move Yoel from his post.

⚜

Late at night, Asher Klein sat in his dormitory room and looked through the old notebooks. He hoped to find more of young Elitzafan Portman's Purim writings. A little humor would help him sleep better.

He was disappointed. There was not a trace of humor in the pile of notebooks he had taken to yeshivah. On the contrary, the writing went from serious to melancholy. Elitzafan had studied the subject of honoring one's father. The questions he asked himself shocked Asher.

Is a son required to honor a father who is reputed to have committed crimes? What should the son do if there is strong evidence of the father's guilt, yet the father claims that he is innocent and that his enemies deliberately ruined his name in order to make him an outcast, rejected even by his own family?

These questions had surely been accompanied by many tears and pangs of conscience. They were followed by a lengthy analysis based on sources in the Talmud and the Rambam.

Asher wondered how the situation in Zeidel's home had deteriorated so badly. What had the youth gone through to make him write such sharp words? Couldn't he have given his father the benefit of the doubt? Why hadn't he asked a Torah authority instead of trying to answer the questions himself? Asher did not condemn young Elitzafan; he sympathized with him. He knew that one must never judge another person until one steps into his shoes.

It would be interesting to see whether Mr. Mindelman would recognize these notebooks. Was it really his handwriting, or was Asher's father mistaken when he identified the two Elitzafans as one?

34

From the air, Tel Aviv's Central Bus Station looked like a giant urban monster sending out black asphalt limbs and spewing metal boxes on wheels. From the ground, it looked as it did on any ordinary day. Passengers rushed to catch a bus; calm shoppers hunted for bargains in the plethora of stores. Always on the alert for suicide terrorists, armed guards with metal detectors checked every traveler who passed through the gates.

A tall, broad-shouldered young man with three rings in his left ear approached from the side, went around the long line, and called, "Yaniv!"

The guard was too preoccupied to respond. He merely glanced in the caller's direction. That was enough to make a nebula of anger cover his eyes as he continued the security checks.

The man persisted. "I've brought you greetings from Moshiko."

The mention of Moshiko's name had its effect. The guard's angry look softened, and his face broke into a smile. He continued to check the travelers with his metal detector as he hissed quietly, "I heard you, Sheket, but don't disturb me now. Go have a bite to eat. I'll join you soon, during my break."

Sheket found a place, sat down at a table, debated between a frankfurter and a hamburger, and eventually decided to start with a bottle of diet cola and a portion of French fries. Before he was even halfway through eating, Yaniv was standing beside him.

Sheket jumped up. "Shalom, Yaniv. Are you free?"

"I have a half-hour break," said Yaniv, glancing at his watch. "I didn't know you were in Israel. I thought you were in Paris, busy on a manhunt."

So Moshiko had told him everything! That explained the sour expression on Yaniv's face when he saw Sheket.

Sheket took a sip of Cola. "I landed two hours ago. I came straight here from the airport."

"Why? Am I so important to you all of a sudden?"

"Yes, you're very important to me. I came to Israel especially to meet with you," Sheket said openly. The fact that he had also come to alert one of the heads of the Mossad was not Yaniv's business. "I had a falling out with your brother. He lost his trust in me."

Yaniv nodded. The angry look returned.

"Moshiko is right to be angry at me." Sheket sounded embarrassed. "I received orders to kill him. Do you think it was easy for me? But they claimed he was a traitor."

The blood rushed to Yaniv's face. "Moshiko is trying to plug up a breach in the dam with his finger, and you call him a traitor?"

Instinctively, Sheket grabbed Yaniv's arm so that he wouldn't run away. "Yaniv, you don't have to tell me who Moshiko is! We spent four years together, day and night, in the commando unit. Our friendship was forged in steel."

"You tried to run over him with steel," said Yaniv bitterly.

"Give me five minutes to explain," pleaded Sheket. "I'm a dedicated soldier who has no choice but to carry out commands. Now I know there was no foundation to the charge."

Yaniv looked at Sheket accusingly. "What would have happened if Moshiko hadn't gotten out of the car in time? Would you have visited his grave and placed a flower on it?"

Sheket fell silent and waited for Yaniv to calm down. "There's a rotten apple in the Mossad who tried to exploit me. But that's it, I've wised up. At this moment I'm violating orders, even though by doing so I have placed myself in danger."

Yaniv was silent. Sheket continued. "At night, when I tailed your brother, I suddenly saw Asaf leaving his house with a group. I followed them to the Luxembourg Gardens and heard everything they said there. Yaniv, unless they're stopped in time, they'll destroy this whole nation."

He pushed the food aside and studied Yaniv's uniform as if he were seeing it for the first time. "You're guarding the Central Bus Station against suicide terrorists, who might kill twenty or thirty people at most. I'm speaking about a mass explosion with thousands of human sacrifices. Asaf's group wants to help Iran fulfill its nuclear dream."

Yaniv ordered shish kebob and French fries. That was a good sign.

"I'll tell you something," Yaniv said in a softer tone. "Do you know what saved Moshiko? His sixth sense. It repeatedly warned him that he was in danger. It even compelled him to accept that you — his good friend — intended to kill him and it warned him to distance himself from you. I also am in possession of a sixth sense and I feel that at this point you're okay."

"Thanks," whispered Sheket.

Yaniv's order arrived at the table. He pulled the small cubes of meat off the skewers. "What exactly do you want from me?"

"Good you remembered to ask," laughed Sheket. "I can't possibly deal with this gang alone. I need Moshiko and his listening devices."

Yaniv got himself another cold bottle of soda. "Sometimes I wonder how naive people can be. You know that Moshiko is always listening. Didn't you ask yourself whether he knows everything you do? Why should he need you? And what can you do for him, aside from making him live in constant fear?"

Sheket's face clouded. "I know it's my fault. I see I have not convinced you, and if that's the case you surely will not convince your brother. Farewell, Israel; I return to Paris empty-handed. When history asks me, 'What did you do to save your people?' at least I will be able to answer, 'I tried.'"

He stood up and left, melting into the crowds of travelers running every which way. Yaniv's pensive glance followed him for a moment, and his lips turned up in a thin smile.

ও৯৶৳৩

Before the third date was to take place in the Bloch's study, Flora spoke quietly with the lady of the house. Mrs. Bloch looked confused and hesitant, but Flora insisted.

After the date, Chedvi and Devorah went for a stroll in the streets of Paris. Their real purpose, though, was to discuss the progress of the *shidduch*.

They passed a renowned Jewish restaurant. "I'm hungry," said Chedvi.

Devorah frowned. "Don't dream of going in there. Despite the Jewish name and menu and the Palestinian terror attack against it twenty years ago, the food isn't kosher."

"I wasn't thinking of eating there," said Chedvi. "It only reminded me that I was hungry." She didn't tell her mother how tired she was. She had spent the past few sleepless nights debating whether to continue with this *shidduch*.

As they walked on, the discussion returned to the date. The *shidduch* was definitely progressing. Despite differences in mind-set and lifestyle, François and Chedvi seemed to get along well, and that was what mattered most.

Meanwhile, Flora found herself home alone. Aryeh Bloch was attending Torah classes as usual, and Sarah was busy organizing an upcoming charity event.

Flora walked into the study. With a smile, she approached the table, bent down, and — thank you, Sarah Bloch. The mini-recorder was glued to the underside of the table. With a triumphant smile, she undid the instrument from the strip of glue. She hoped François and Chedvi hadn't heard the click at the end of the recording, but even if they had, neither of them would have thought to look under the table to check the source of the suspicious noise. The tape would provide an excellent indication as to where the two were headed.

Flora took the tape recorder to her bedroom, closed the door, and pressed Play. She heard the flowing conversation as well as the hesitations and difficulties. Obedient François spoke enthusiastically about "dwelling in the house of Hashem all the days of my life," and Chedvi sounded very pleased. They were of the same opinion.

A vort is in the offing, thought Flora ecstatically. She could not resist singing *Od yishama*.

The phone rang, and she went to answer it.

"This is Elitzafan Mindelman from Jerusalem. May I please speak with Devorah?"

"Shalom, Mr. Mindelman," cried Flora joyfully. "It is a great privilege to hear from the father of a happy Chedvi."

In the modest apartment in Beis Yisrael, the phone nearly fell from his hand. What was cooking in the French kitchen?

"What are you talking about?" asked Elitzafan in surprise.

Flora could not hide her delight. "Mr. Mindelman, apparently your daughter is about to become engaged to a wonderful boy — sweet, learned, tall, and strong, with good character and fear of Heaven. He is surely the answer to your prayers. You will have true *Yiddishe nachas* from your son-in-law. When are you coming?"

Elitzafan's heart pounded like a drum. "Only yesterday I spoke to Devorah and she gave me no clue that Chedvi is about to get engaged. Don't you think you might be proceeding too quickly?"

Flora did not let the reins slip from her hands. "No, no, Mr. Mindelman. You are not sufficiently up to date. Your daughter has just met Yom Tov Feldman for a third, decisive date, and apparently today or tomorrow we will break a plate. I invite you to pick up a ticket from the Quick Flight travel agency and fly at my expense to the *vort* of your eldest daughter."

Elitzafan was thunderstruck. Devorah and Chedvi had spoken nonchalantly about the trip. They had not expected anything to come of the French *shidduch*, but when you are given two free tickets, you say thank you and go see the Eiffel Tower. That clever Rebbetzin certainly knew how to manipulate people. But she could not bribe him with an airplane ticket!

"I'm not so sure that I'm coming to France," he said. "What's the hurry?"

"Mr. Mindelman," said Flora, "surely you know that a life partner was decreed for each person, together with the time the couple will get engaged and married. These things are determined in Heaven, not here. Evidently it was decreed that your daughter would find her life partner in France, and the joyous moment is about to arrive. You have prayed well for Chedvi, and your prayers have been accepted. I am a little surprised that you are not happy for her. She is overjoyed. It would be worthwhile for you to travel to Paris even if you had to walk all the way just to see her happy smile."

"I don't understand." The seeds of anger seeped into Elitzafan's normally moderate voice. "As Chedvi's father, do I have any say in the matter, or doesn't my opinion count at all? The boy is about to become my son-in-law. I want to meet him and see whether he fits into the family. And what is his lineage?"

It was on the tip of Flora's tongue to retort, "And what is your lineage?" Fortunately, the words remained stuck there, like a spaceship disabled on the launching pad. "Your son-in-law-to-be has quite a distinguished lineage. He is the offspring of the well known Feldman line of rabbis, beginning with the grandfather, Rabbi David Hirsch Feldman, author of the *Ma'adanei Sadeh*, who was martyred during the Chmielnicki massacres. The boy's mother, Mrs. Clara Feldman, is the granddaughter of the Rabbi of Bangkok, of blessed memory."

"I never heard of them," Elitzafan protested weakly. "Now I would like to speak to my wife please."

"She went out with Chedvi."

Elitzafan mustered the remnants of his strength. "Tell Devorah when she comes back that I want to speak with her urgently, okay?"

"Certainly," Flora assured him.

Afterward, Flora regretted how she had spoken. *I was too uppity. He thinks I'm a fool. Tomorrow I'll correct that impression.*

❧

Nati Morgan's cell phone rang, startling him. For two hours he had been sitting and waiting for Felix and the scientist in the Havana Club. But the scientist had not arrived. What audacity! Maybe now he was calling to explain his delay.

But he wasn't. "Hello, Dubik," said Nati without enthusiasm. "What's happening on the home front?"

"Everything is fine," said Dubik. "What's happening in London?"

"Our new friend has been keeping me waiting." He glanced again at his watch. "Today we have to tie up the loose ends. I'm about to part with hundreds of thousands of dollars for a piece of plastic that weighs fifty grams."

"But there's a lot in that round piece of plastic." Dubik tried to comfort his apprehensive boss, but evoked his fury instead.

"Tell me, are you sleeping there in Paris?" Nati attacked him. "Get cracking. When is the first group going out to take care of the pitchblende?"

If Asaf could be tough with Nati, Dubik could, too. "I'm not at all sure I feel comfortable to be dealing with pitchblende. Don't you think we're crossing a red line?"

"Dubik, do you really think that Iran needs favors from us? Do you really think she needs us to deliver a few dozen cylinders of enriched uranium? There are sites for uranium enrichment all over Iran!"

"If so, why is Iran paying us to make these deliveries?" asked Dubik.

"For one of two reasons," said Nati. "Either Iran failed in her own attempts to enrich uranium, or else she wants to hide from the West the fact that she is close to producing an atom bomb.

"Either way, Western intelligence organizations maintain that Iran will not hurry to press the nuclear trigger; all she wants is political superiority in the Arab world. So you need not feel any pangs of conscience, and you'll be handsomely rewarded for your trouble."

☙❦❧

A stone hurled at a street lamp in Kfar Shmaryahu plunged the area into darkness on that August night in 1966. Shortly thereafter, Yoel Tzadok ran through the grass toward Nati Morgan's spacious private home. The master of the house, a bachelor who lived alone, had flown to Capetown two days earlier.

Yoel quickly cut an opening in the plastic *tris* covering the bedroom window. The windowpane came out easily with the aid of a glazier's knife, and Yoel grabbed it before it could fall and shatter.

Aided by a small flashlight, he felt his way through the big house, trying to figure out where the documents were hidden.

Yoel opened drawers and closets and rummaged around everywhere. He had almost given up when he discovered a few sealed envelopes under a pile of old newspapers in a drawer. He opened the envelopes carefully, spread the documents on the kitchen table, and photographed each one. Now came the hardest part of all: returning the documents to their envelopes without leaving a sign that they had been touched. He arranged the documents in the envelopes and carefully smoothed them many times until he was satisfied.

Mission accomplished. As a finishing touch, he went into the living room and ransacked the china closet to make Nati think his house had been broken into by thieves. Then he quietly left.

Now he had only to develop the two rolls of film and decipher all the material, and hopefully he would answer the question that tortured Zeidel more than his ulcers — the question of what Nati had done during the week that his employees were vacationing in Eilat.

Yoel could be pleased with himself, but doubt gnawed at him. Throughout his "visit," he had sensed a pair of eyes watching him. Was it merely fear? Time would tell.

35

The eyes of Rafi Zamir, one of the Mossad's top operatives, were riveted to Sheket as he heard him out. Afterward, Rafi said, "Each of the details that you're presenting sounds logical. But the general picture that emerges is somewhat strange."

"Aren't my proofs strong enough?" Sheket felt personally insulted. His words were running into a stone wall of disbelief — and from the very person from whom he had expected support!

"You mean the e-mail ordering you to eliminate Moshiko Sharabi? True, the address of the sender is from the level above you, and the matter must be looked into. As for Nati Morgan and Asaf Niv, I find it hard to believe that they are collaborating with Iran. They may be greedy, but they have always been loyal Israeli patriots."

Sheket left without knowing whether or not he had succeeded in convincing Rafi that the Land of Israel was in imminent danger.

❧

"Elitzafan, when you see François you won't believe he's French. He looks like a yeshivah *bachur* from Bnei Brak. His Hebrew is flawless; he's clever and lively; he plays piano and guitar, which does not interfere with his diligent Torah study; and he is tall, slim, and handsome, with sparkling blue eyes. What's so terrible about being born in France?"

"Devorah," he said, his heart pounding, "aren't you letting yourself be blinded by externals? Are you sure that the scandalous Rebbetzin Simchoni–Freilich hasn't brainwashed you? Perhaps the foreign air has affected you.

"At any rate, you can't possibly announce an engagement before I've met the boy!"

"So come to Paris," said Devorah enthusiastically. "We're preparing a royal welcome."

"Who is 'we'?" muttered Elitzafan. "Rebbetzin Simchoni–Freilich? I can do without that. I am not prepared to come to Paris, no matter what happens. If it's a *shidduch* with her pulling the strings, I'm not participating. Break the plate without me."

Devorah was appalled. "Elitzafan, why are you speaking to me like that? The *chasan* of your dreams is waiting here in France. Now that a wonderful *shidduch* has finally come along after six years of waiting, must we turn it down just because you have something against the Rebbetzin?"

The argument continued for several minutes, with Devorah strongly defending the boy and Elitzafan stubbornly rejecting him. After the conversation ended with the issue unresolved, Elitzafan was overcome by tremendous weakness and a strong headache. He lay down in bed unable to move.

Perhaps I'm rejecting a Heavenly gift, he thought in confusion. *Perhaps François is really okay. Devorah is as selective as I am, and she seems to speak from deep inner conviction.* His eyes closed.

Just then, light steps were heard on the staircase, and then knocks at the door. Tirtzah went to open it. A tall young man in hat and jacket, with an alert, curious expression, asked to speak with Mr. Mindelman.

"Abba receives the public between eight and ten in the evening," Tirtzah said apologetically. "Now he is resting."

Asher tried diplomatically to prevent the door from being closed in his face. "Excuse me, I did not come to consult him. I just wanted to speak to him."

"Then you will certainly have to wait for another opportunity. Abba is very strained and tired. He needs his rest." Tirtzah began to close the door when she heard her father's voice from the bedroom. "Who is it?" he asked.

Tirtzah left the front door open and hurried to the bedroom. "A yeshivah *bachur* wants to speak to you," she said quietly.

"Ask him who he is and what it's about," he said.

Tirtzah returned a minute later. "Abba, his name is Asher Klein and he claims you know his father well."

"Tell him to come in."

"To your bedroom?" asked Tirtzah in confusion. Her father had always guarded his privacy zealously.

"Yes. What's wrong?" It did not embarrass him in the least that this unknown *bachur* should see him resting in bed.

A short distance from the bedroom door, Asher regretted this rash visit with all his heart. Mr. Mindelman's humility was beyond his comprehension. Red-faced and confused, Asher entered the bedroom.

Elitzafan raised himself to a sitting position and greeted his guest. Was he dreaming? He was sure that that François with all the superlatives from France had come over the phone straight into his room. Hadn't Devorah said, "tall, slim, and handsome"? That was him. This Asher had a very impressive appearance. He radiated rare nobility. All of Elitzafan's anger and ill feelings evaporated instantly.

"Sit down, make yourself comfortable," said Elitzafan. "I'm sorry I can't receive you properly in the living room. I'm not feeling well. Which Klein are you?"

"I think you know my father, Daniel Klein from Rechaviah."

Elitzafan blinked. How diligently Daniel Klein had worked on the *shidduch* with Shmuli Patankin, only to retreat at the last moment.

"What brings you to me?"

Asher's cheeks burned. He had prepared well for this moment, but now his hands and feet were trembling. The courage he had mustered before leaving yeshivah melted into a puddle of fear. "I came to consult you," he somehow managed to say, "about a question that troubles me deeply." He fumbled with the blue plastic bag he had brought along, and fell silent.

"I don't eat people," said Elitzafan with an encouraging smile. He liked this polite, refined boy.

Asher continued. "I happened to read the personal diary of a young yeshivah *bachur* from almost thirty years ago." His eyes wandered around the room and stopped at the window, where a carefree bird hopped and chirped merrily on the bars. *If only I could join that bird right now and fly into the blue sky!* thought Asher. *What foolishness to put myself into such an embarrassing situation!* He had been too curious about becoming acquainted with the diary's author.

A wave of sympathy and compassion inundated Elitzafan. "Would you like a glass of water?"

"No, it's not necessary, thank you." Asher took a deep breath. "The diary was written in a notebook, and I discovered a charming *bachur* who learned seriously but was lively and happy. He recorded the *shiurim* he heard from his rabbis and also wrote clever satires and parodies. Then, poof! Everything changed. He became melancholy. My heart went out to that *bachur,* and I felt that if I had lived in his time, I would have done everything in my power to help him. But I became acquainted with his enchanting inner world thirty years too late."

Elitzafan's eyes, which were somewhat out of focus at the beginning of the conversation, became clear and sharp. He surveyed Asher suspiciously.

"Who is the *bachur* who wrote those diaries?"

Asher hesitated and cleared his throat several times. Finally he opened the blue plastic bag he was holding. "The notebooks will speak for themselves."

He took out two notebooks that bore the title, "*Shiurim* in *Bava Kamma.* Recorded by Elitzafan Portman."

❧✴❧

"I don't use room service because of *kashrus,*" said Felix. "May I prepare a cup of coffee for you?"

Asaf looked again at his watch. "No thanks. Beer and coffee don't go together in my stomach."

Malkiel yawned. "I could sure use a cup of hot coffee. I didn't sleep last night."

Felix boiled water in his own electric kettle, opened a few small cans of different kinds of coffee, mixed them together, and stirred. A fragrant aroma filled the room. "I've changed my mind," said Asaf.

Felix set down three cups of coffee. Malkiel was the first to drink. The hot liquid burned his tongue slightly. "Ouch!" he exclaimed.

"Coffee is meant to be drunk carefully, in tiny sips, to check it out," Asaf enlightened him. "If all is in order, you continue to drink.

"And now, with your permission, Felix, I'll tell you the main story of Samson Steel and what took place between the boss and his assistant — a story that has direct consequences for us today."

Malkiel interrupted him. "Just a minute. Why give away your secrets before the other side gives *you* something? Perhaps the information about the Arrow missile can be obtained through the Internet? And what's the big deal about the Arrow anyway? It works on the same principle as the Patriot!"

The look on Felix's face told Malkiel that he had spoken nonsense. Asaf, mortified, seemed to shrink into himself despite his massive size. If not for Malkiel's popularity with the employees of Morgan Consolidated, which would be helpful in getting rid of Nati, Asaf would have dumped Malkiel long ago.

"First of all, you will not get the information I'm about to supply you on any Internet site in the world; it's top secret," said Felix. "Second, the Patriot and the Arrow are as different as heaven and earth. I'll tell you just one of the many differences between them. The Patriot, made to intercept planes, travels at relatively low speed. The Arrow, made to intercept missiles, travels at high speed."

The polite tone in Felix's voice restored the sunshine to Malkiel's face. Asaf did his part to appease Malkiel by asking Felix for more information.

"Very well." Felix rose and began pacing the room. "You remember that in the Gulf War of '91, Israel was hit by Scud missiles. To protect Israel against the Scuds, the United States sent us Patriot missiles, which failed in a big way. First of all, when a Patriot intercepts a flying missile, it splits the missile in two so that it causes twice as much damage. Second, the interception occurs in the skies over Israel — which is too late. Had the Scud been equipped with a nuclear warhead, you can imagine the consequences.

"We worked on developing a new missile that would give the perfect solution to missile attacks on Israel. The result is the Arrow. It has been tested with excellent results.

"In a recent experiment, Israel was 'attacked' by four missiles simultaneously. The radar discovered the missiles, the order to fire was given, and the Arrow system blew up all four before they ever reached Israel."

"Sounds good," muttered Malkiel.

"It is," said Felix as he toyed with his cigar box. "We're working together with the United States to improve it even further."

"And what happens if many enemy missiles are sent, including dummies?" asked Malkiel.

Felix answered obligingly, "The Arrow can tell the difference. It ignores the dummies and attacks only the real warheads."

"In short, a clever missile," said Asaf.

"Not clever," said Malkiel enthusiastically. "Brilliant!"

Felix smiled. "You don't know how right you both are. The Arrow's brilliance lies in its radar system, which obtains information from the Amos and Ofek satellites. They patrol the skies and inform the system in real time."

"That means the enemy will want to disrupt communication between the Arrow and the satellites," said Asaf.

Felix agreed. "That is precisely what we're talking about."

36

At midnight, eight men took to the skies in Nati's new corporate jet. Dubik, despite his protests, had been unable to disobey Nati's unequivocal orders.

Their destination was the black market for weapons on the Russia–Kazakhstan border. Until a decade ago, the market dealt in Chinese Scud missiles, American equipment for decoding global positioning data from satellites, Panther attack helicopters, Chilean mines, German explosives, and French chemicals. In recent years, the market has been selling a broad range of more sophisticated modern weapons. Rumor has it that several suitcases containing nuclear contents have even changed hands there.

Dubik's men had been instructed that upon arrival, they were to show their faces in the market but nothing would happen. Only in the evening would they go to the foot of a mountain, deep in the heart of mountain greenery, where contact people were waiting to give them dozens of unmarked steel containers. The men would then divide into four groups, each taking a different route, and transport these containers to the final destination.

Dubik stared pensively out the window into the black skies of France. He wondered how many of his men knew that the steel containers contained rods of enriched uranium. They certainly did not know the final destination of this trip. Nati liked to keep his employees in the dark.

Beside Dubik sat a chubby young redhead whom he trusted implicitly. Roni Nagler's appearance was deceptive. Even without stained overalls and a cap, he looked like a typical plumber; upon meeting him the first time, you automatically looked for the wrench in his hand. Roni made good use of the cover his appearance provided. In recent years, he stood behind Nati Morgan in both senses. This did not prevent him from carrying out minor assignments, such as keeping watch over the corporation's purchasing agents on their way to important meetings. It was he who had exchanged Moshiko's noisy shoes on the way to the Charles Aznavour Park. Roni was always a blurry figure in the background who knew how to disappear at the right moment.

To Dubik, though, Roni was not elusive at all. The two good friends often sat together, as they did now.

"What's going to happen?" asked Dubik, compulsively chewing gum so as to prevent his ears from popping during takeoff.

"Nothing special." Roni put his head back and tried to doze.

"Come on, tell me."

Roni agreed to offer a bit of information. "Transfer of steel containers from place to place, followed by counting piles of greenbacks, twenty million dollars cash."

"Iran has invested billions of dollars in its nuclear project," said Dubik casually, "and everything is about to collapse in the face of American threats. If the United Nations Security Council imposes economic sanctions — meaning that Iran won't be able to sell its oil — Iran won't survive financially for more than a month."

The provocation worked. Roni became fully alert. "I see you're up on things," he said in amazement.

"There's one thing I don't understand," Dubik pressed on. "The International Atomic Energy Agency suspects that Iran is manufacturing enriched uranium and perhaps even separating plutonium. Why, then, does Iran need us to smuggle more uranium rods into her territory?"

Roni laughed. The freckles on his face shook and seemed to get bigger. "We're part of a big diversionary deception. Intelligence agents of many countries will keep track of our every move. Dozens of espionage satellites will photograph us. And in another week, when they catch the uranium rods in a sensational, carefully orchestrated media scoop, world attention will focus on the miserable rods, and everyone will forget what Iran has been achieving in the depths of the earth.

"Don't worry, we won't be there when it happens," added Roni when he saw Dubik's white face.

He continued, "Iran is working now on all fronts to put everyone, especially the United States, to sleep. Iranian diplomats are traveling all over to convince the world that her reactors are solely for civilian purposes. Actually she is busy trying to produce enriched uranium for her atom bomb; without it, the billions she has already invested will go down the drain. Lately, unmarked Russian military carrier planes have brought her powerful excitation lasers for enriching uranium, together with Russian experts who assembled them and taught the Iranian technicians how to operate them."

"Are you sure?" Dubik blurted. He had been totally left out, while Roni was in on everything!

"One hundred fifty percent. I'll let you in on another secret. Excitation lasers are already operating in two of Iran's nuclear sites, Natanz and Mu'allim Kalayeh. The second location in the Elburz mountains, forty kilometers north of Teheran, is a village occupied by hundreds of scientists and technicians. Nuclear experiments are performed there in a network of very tall tunnels dug underneath mountains."

"What a happy situation," Dubik fumed. "Iran is striding quickly toward an atom bomb, and the world is asleep."

"But Iran isn't sleeping." Roni poured kerosene on the fire of Dubik's wrath. "In fact, she's also working on developing a new missile, Shihav 4, with a projected range of 5,000 kilometers and the ability to carry a nuclear warhead."

"And we have to be involved in this horror?" asked Dubik.

"You're starting to talk like Moshiko," Roni pointed out in a chilly tone. He chose a comfortable position and curled up in the soft upholstery. Dubik was considering how to reply, but Roni's rhythmic breathing informed him he might as well save his breath. He dimmed the overhead light and tried to doze.

☙❧

Elitzafan Mindelman thumbed through the notebook. "I recorded those *shiurim* while I was still in *mesivta*," he told Asher Klein. "I remember them till today."

Asher was as satisfied as a police investigator whose suspect finally admitted his guilt. For the first time, Mr. Mindelman had admitted any connection between himself and the name Portman.

"What happened along the way? How did the happy, bubbly youth turn so serious and melancholy?" Asher dared to inquire. One slip, and a tightrope walker falls; one slip of the tongue, and Asher would be thown out of the house. In fact, if Mr. Mindelman had not thrown him out yet, it was only because the man was a *tzaddik*.

"Patience," mumbled Elitzafan and opened the second notebook. He looked curiously at the first page. It was one of his humorous Purim notebooks. "What, it still exists? I thought this notebook had been lost."

"It's the funniest parody I've ever read," said Asher.

"Yes, I remember," said Elitzafan with a weary smile. "We were young boys, full of energy. We recorded our thoughts on paper late at night. I think we did a good job."

"The question arises…" said Asher, in the sing-song melody of Gemara study, and stopped.

Elitzafan continued with the same melody, "…how does such a boy suddenly make a complete turnabout?" His face turned serious. "I should have thrown you out. You are unbelievably impertinent, invading a stranger's house and his soul. On the other hand, your mischievousness is charming." He brandished his finger in Asher's face with a smile that was half angry, half amused. "It's a long story. Perhaps now I will tell it to you from the beginning."

The phone rang. A few seconds later, Tirtzah came to the bedroom door. "Abba, Ima wants to speak to you. It's urgent."

Asher left quickly, but not before Elitzafan had invited him to return whenever he wished.

෴

The passengers filed slowly toward the plane's front door, where the pilot said goodbye to each one. Elitzafan, carrying his flight bag, was among them.

"How did I sink so low?" Elitzafan berated himself. "How did I allow myself to fall into Rebbetzin Simchoni–Freilich's honey trap? Now I'm going to have a French son-in-law. I'll have to start saying *bonjour* and *merci beaucoup!*"

He recalled his conversation with Devorah after Asher Klein had left the house.

"We won't find such a boy for our Chedvi again," Devorah had declared solemnly. "You know how critical I am, Elitzafan, and I tell you François is wonderful. In Israel there's no one like him. When you meet him, you'll love him."

"For your information, just a minute ago I was visited by a wonderful yeshivah *bachur* who looks exactly as you describe François."

Devorah had snickered. "If the boy who visited you just now is as wonderful as you say, he's a mere semblance of François."

Elitzafan found himself at the head of the line, thanking the pilot. Ten minutes later he was reunited with his wife and daughter, who were waiting for him impatiently. He was caught up in their joy and excitement. At last, the Mindelmans were taking steps toward the long-awaited *simchah*.

37

The day he arrived in Paris, Elitzafan met François and conversed with him about Gemara topics as well as worldly matters. After he escorted François to the door and returned to the Blochs' living room, three sets of eyes studied Elitzafan's face, trying to decipher his reaction.

Chedvi expressed aloud what Devorah and Flora asked wordlessly. "So, Abba, what do you say about him?"

Elitzafan waited a moment, out of respect for the gravity of the question. Then he smiled happily. "A first-rate fellow, a wonderful boy, learned, a *mensch*, also clever. The *chasan* of my dreams."

"Right, he doesn't have a French accent?" said Chedvi with a smile.

Elitzafan, too, was drunk with happiness. "No, and he doesn't have a French mind-set either. He's like a natural-born Israeli."

"Even so, I'm still worth something," said Flora, with a pronounced French accent. Everyone burst into whole-hearted laughter.

Flora did not rest on her laurels. She immediately called the Feldmans and arranged for the two sets of parents to meet the following morning.

Elitzafan was pleasantly surprised to discover that his future *mechutan* was not only an agreeable person but also knowledgeable in many Talmudic tractates. The necessary negotiations went smoothly, and the financial arrangements were recorded in Elitzafan's beautiful handwriting. It was agreed that the young couple would live in France for two years and then move to Israel. The *vort* would take place that evening. The Feldmans wanted a lavish banquet but graciously acceded to the Mindelmans' request for a modest affair "according to Jerusalem custom."

The Mindelmans felt a bit lost making a *simchah* without any family, friends, or neighbors. Chedvi remembered the names of two French girls who had studied with her in seminary, Devorah called a second cousin, and Elitzafan rounded up a former colleague.

A festive air permeated the Bloch home in anticipation of the *vort*. The huge, gold-framed mirrors reflected the lights of the gleaming crystal chandeliers. The enticing aroma of freshly-baked cakes beckoned to the refreshment-laden tables that had been set up for men in the dining room and for women in the living room.

The Feldman family arrived wearing elegant clothing and happy smiles. Upstairs, Devorah helped Chedvi complete her preparations for the great evening. Devorah wanted every detail to be perfect, and she made sure Chedvi looked exactly as a *kallah* should on the evening of her engagement.

Everything was ready. The guests arrived, two rabbis from the *chasan's* yeshivah graced the table, and all that remained was to read the *tena'im* and break the plate.

⊱✦⊰

Moshiko stood on the bridge over a pond in the Luxembourg Gardens and gazed at the small ripples that the wind made in the water. Suddenly, he felt a pair of eyes cutting into him from his left side. His head rotated to the left like a door on its hinge.

Beside a bronze statue some distance away stood Sheket, looking at him with sad eyes that asked, "Is it o.k. to approach you?"

Moshiko nodded.

Sheket approached slowly, as if to demonstrate the innocence of his intentions. All that was lacking was a theatrical raising of hands to show they were weaponless. "Moshiko, how are you?" he asked heartily. The heartiness was a bit exaggerated, but the smile was natural.

"Fine," Moshiko answered in a flat voice.

"Are you still angry at me?"

"Let me put it this way. If Yaniv hadn't brainwashed me, there would have been no meeting, here or anywhere else," said Moshiko frankly. "You've destroyed my faith in people. If my best friend tried to do me in, what's left?"

Sheket sank onto one of the green metal chairs placed along the length of the promenande. He placed his hand over his heart. "I'm really sorry, Moshiko. Believe me, I've regretted my foolisness a million times over. Even if it means the Mossad will fire me, never will I obey such orders again."

Moshiko shivered as he recalled the Renault crashing loudly into the lamppost. If he had not gotten out of the car a minute earlier, he would have been killed. Even after Yaniv's intercession, Moshiko would never be able to truly trust Sheket again.

"I went to Rafi Zamir, one of the Mossad's top men," said Sheket. "I told him what was going on in Paris and how your bosses are collaborating with Iran. His response left me in a quandry."

"I happen to know Rafi," said Moshiko, crushing a dry leaf between his fingers. "He'll make a discreet, fundamental investigation and won't rest until he gets to the bottom of it. You can relax, even if he didn't seem sympathetic to you. That's how he is."

"Nevertheless, considering what's going on, don't you think we should keep on top of the developments too?"

"Did you think I abandoned my listening positions?"

"That's exactly why I'm here," said Sheket. "I need you."

Moshiko sat down on a chair near Sheket and looked around to all sides. Then he laughed bitterly at himself. Here he was, worrying about strangers, when the person he was speaking with was liable to liquidate him at any moment. "Even as we are talking, a group of Nati's men are on their way to the black market for weapons on the Russia–Kazakhstan border. There they will be given fifty steel containers containing rods of enriched uranium."

"What!" exclaimed Sheket, horrified.

"The rods will eventually get to Iran," declared Moshiko, staring into space. "What else would you like to know?"

"Who went? What route are they taking?"

Suddenly a red light lit up before Moshiko's eyes. He threw himself to the ground a second before a bullet whizzed through the air where he had just been sitting.

Moshiko waited for a few minutes before he got back on his feet, seeking cover behind a tree trunk. His accusing look burned Sheket's red face, and his voice was hoarse with emotion. "Perfect alibi. Invite me to the Luxembourg Gardens and stand me before a firing squad. How elegant."

"I have no part in this scene," said Sheket, trembling. "What was is over now. Understand?"

Moshiko departed hurriedly. Once again, intuition had saved him from certain death. But his intuition was useless when it came to Sheket. One moment Sheket seemed to be a good friend, the next moment a dangerous assailant. Where had he put the phone number of that Rebbetzin who had lectured about the sixth sense?

⌘

Amidst the tumult of the joyous gathering, the *chasan* was seen whispering with his father and smoothing his silk tie. The father looked uncomfortable. Elitzafan smiled at Mr. Feldman and asked whether there was any problem.

"The *chasan* hasn't *davened Ma'ariv* yet," Mr. Feldman stammered in embarrassment.

"No problem," said Elitzafan as he poured apple juice into a sparkling crystal glass. "Let him go *daven*. We'll wait ten minutes for him."

"That's exactly what we were discussing," said Mr. Feldman. "I told him to go into the study and *daven*. But Yom Tov rejects the idea. Since his bar mitzvah he has never *davened* without a minyan."

Elitzafan glanced at his watch. "In Jerusalem you can *daven* any time of day or night in the *shtiblach* of Zichron Moshe, but is there a *minyan* in Paris at nine p.m.?"

"There's a small shul with a late *minyan* not far away," said the *chasan*, standing up to his full height. "I'll hop over there for a quarter of an hour. Meantime the two *mechutanim* can get better acquainted." Flashing a charming smile that evoked waves of love for him in Elitzafan's heart, he quickly left the house.

The happy tumult continued. The guests nibbled on the cakes and pastries. The clinking of crystal glasses punctuated the chatting that filled the house. From time to time the door opened, and another guest arrived and was welcomed warmly. The two fathers, involved in a pleasant conversation, did not notice the time pass. No one seemed troubled by the *chasan's* half-hour absence.

At last Elitzafan remarked, with a warm smile, that the *chasan* was evidently praying with great devotion. But Mr. Feldman did not take the matter in the same good spirit. "I hope nothing has happened to him," he said worriedly.

"Try calling his cell phone," the *chasan's* younger brother suggested.

The cell phone was off. Evidently he had turned it off when he went to *daven*.

Gradually the atmosphere changed. The lively merriment subsided; the refreshments were no longer touched. Everyone was alarmed by the *chasan's* strange disappearance. With every passing moment, the confusion and concern mounted. Finally a younger brother went out to look for him in the small shul, and reported back that he had not been there for *Ma'ariv*.

The women's section of the party was thrown into quiet panic. The *chasan's* mother nervously called every place that her son might possibly be. The guests did their share, too. They got on their cell phones and called the police, fire department, first-aid stations, and hospitals. The answer was always the same. François was nowhere to be found.

Devorah would have fainted if not for Flora, who held her hand and whispered continuously, "Everything will come out all right in the end. Perhaps he dozed off somewhere. Maybe he became overexcited at the last moment."

But when two whole hours had passed and the *chasan* had not yet returned, Devorah lost control and began to sob softly. Her blackest nightmares were coming true. The situation was hopeless. Even in distant France there was no chance of getting Chedvi engaged. Chedvi's *chasan* was like quicksilver, escaping as you come close. "Chedvi Mindelman" and "engaged" were two parallel lines that would never converge.

At last it occurred to one of the guests that François might be at the home of an old friend who had not come to the *vort*. He called the friend's home, and then quietly told Mr. Feldman, "I found him."

"What?" cried Mr. Feldman. "Let me speak to him!"

With trembling hands he grabbed the cell phone. For a moment he spoke excitedly in rapid French. Suddenly he fell silent and listened tensely. The blood drained from his face. He looked aghast at Elitzafan, who was nervously fingering the edge of the lace tablecloth. Mr. Feldman returned the phone and let out a heart-rending groan.

"What did he say?" asked Elitzafan in a shaky voice. "Why didn't he come back?"

Mr. Feldman's shoulders shook. "I can't repeat what he told me."

The guests could not hear what the two fathers were saying. They could only look compassionately at Elitzafan's face, which matched the gray of his beard.

Elitzafan's whole body trembled. "Please," he pleaded, "you must tell me." He had to know whether his nightmare was about to end or whether it was just beginning.

Mr. Feldman cleared his throat and looked down. "He was warned not to enter the Mindelman family because of a skeleton in their closet."

Elitzafan's eyes bulged, his lips turned white, and beads of perspiration appeared suddenly on his brow.

Mr. Feldman continued quietly, "Because of the information he received, François wants to rescind on his promise to Chedvi. He cannot go through with the engagement."

Elitzafan went to the entrance of the living room and called Devorah and Chedvi aside. He broke the news to them as gently as he could.

Devorah turned white as plaster. The beautiful dress she was wearing in honor of the *vort* hung on her like a sack on a scarecrow. "I knew it! We spoke on the phone, and *he* listened. Our bad *mazal* pursues us everywhere."

Then she fainted.

⌘

In the office of Samson Steel, Zeidel Portman paced back and forth. "Where is that schemer, Nati Morgan!" he hollered into the silence. "If he were here, I would teach him a bitter lesson."

Fortunately for Nati, "that schemer" was in Chile on business. The boss could pour out his wrath only on the office shelves and the colorful landscape paintings.

The copies of documents that Yoel Tzadok had brought from Nati's house in Kfar Shmaryahu justified the daring nighttime action. They showed that while Zeidel was in the hospital, Nati had sold the Brazilian Freedom Fighters eighteen large transport helicopters. Zeidel did not mind the large profit that Nati had taken for himself; he was upset about the suspicious veil of secrecy covering the sale. Why did Nati need to send all the corporation's employees away to Eilat just then?

Zeidel had summoned his right-hand man, Yoel, and told him, "I need you to discretely investigate the identity of the Brazilian Freedom Fighters."

"You're turning me into a detective," said Yoel. "I must have proven myself in Kfar Shmaryahu."

Zeidel smiled. "You were a real Sherlock Holmes."

Yoel conducted a thorough investigation that began with a long series of phone calls and ended with a trip to Brazil. One month later he returned with an unequivocal answer. Brazilian Freedom Fighters was a fictitious cover for the purchasing agents of Egypt — Israel's number one enemy in 1966, the year before the Six-Day War. It was then that President Gamal Abdul Nasser spoke openly about pushing all the Jews of Israel into the sea.

Zeidel felt the earth trembling beneath his feet. He sat in the office, now supporting his wrinkled forehead with his hands. True, he himself was an ideological opponent of the State of Israel, but selling weapons to an enemy? No Torah-observant Jew, regardless of how extremely zealous his views, would betray his brothers. But Nati Morgan, the kibbutznik who displayed blue-and-white flags on Israel's Independence Day, had put a knife into the hands of Ishmael to slaughter Jews.

Zeidel's first impulse was to fire Nati as soon as he returned from Chile. On second thought, he chose to lay a trap for Nati and his henchman Yosef Berning.

Nati and Yosef were among Samson Steel's most effective employees, but Zeidel feared that under them, a daughter company of Samson Steel was shaping up — a daughter that would devour its mother. He had to fight the crocodile while it was still small, before it grew into a man-killer.

He summoned his right-hand man. "Yoel, I want you to plant a small, sophisticated tape recorder in Nati and Yosef's office to record all his conversations, especially the phone calls. I need to know what Nati is plotting with that bald giant."

Yoel took advantage of the absence of Nati and Yosef to make changes in their room. He had bought sensitive listening devices from the German intelligence service surplus. Now the original walls were knocked down, listening devices planted at several points, and new walls built. Henceforth, every word spoken in that room would go directly into Yoel's earphones.

He just needed to wait for Nati and Yosef's first slip, and then hand them over to the police.

The phone rang. Zeidel, who was alone in the big office that morning, picked it up.

"Is Nati there?"

Zeidel recognized the voice. It was Aaron Telem, a young fellow from Haifa who wanted to introduce Nati to his sister.

Nati did not appear to be interested in getting married and establishing a family. He was always in over his head in buying and selling, preparing for the next trip abroad, or traveling. But even if he himself was not thinking of fitting a wedding into his busy life, others were thinking for him.

Aaron was one of them. He even managed to convince Nati to consider postponing some of his visits abroad for the sake of the lofty purpose of marriage.

"Nati is not in the office," said Zeidel, switching over to a high-pitched voice that sounded like a woman's. "Can I give him a message?"

"With whom am I speaking?"

"With his secretary," chirped Zeidel, surprising himself with his own ability to change his voice.

"Can you please tell him that Aaron was looking for him?"

While Aaron was still on one phone, the second office phone rang. Zeidel himself had dialed from the third phone. In those days, when ordinary citizens of Israel had to wait months to obtain a phone line, only government offices, big companies, and people with pull had several lines. Zeidel met the last two criteria. He had three lines.

"Just a minute, please," he chirped, "I have to answer the other calls. I'll take your number soon."

He spoke into one of the phones. "Hello.... Yes, I'll call the boss right away."

He waited a minute, stood up, and walked through the room, imitating the sound of high heels. "Mr. Portman, you have a phone call," he chirped.

Then he immediately switched to his regular voice. "Hello, Nati. How are sales going in Uganda?"

He was silent a moment, as if listening. Then he said in an angry tone, "Nati, a thousand times no! I won't participate in such things." He lowered his voice and partially covered the mouthpiece of the first phone with the palm of his hand, as if to prevent Aaron from overhearing.

By now Zeidel was almost hollering. "Listen, Nati, selling weapons to straw agents who are covering for Egypt is collaboration with the enemy! The deal is off. No, Nati, I will never authorize such deals. There is a limit to greed!"

By the time the mock conversation between Zeidel and Nati ended, Aaron was no longer holding the line. The suggested *shidduch* had been nipped in the bud.

Zeidel smiled. Revenge was sweet.

At the time, Zeidel himself did not know what made him stoop so low. Looking back, he realized it was anger and frustration. The relative whom he had compassionately hired had turned into a Trojan horse and betrayed him.

Zeidel smelled foul play. He could have sworn that Nati was continuing to deal with straw agents of enemy countries, but he had no proof. That was not all. Zeidel suspected that Nati was plotting against him, but he did not manage to uncover the plot any more than he managed to incriminate Nati — despite the listening devices planted in the walls and despite the alert eye of his faithful watchdog Yoel. Had Zeidel known how malicious the plot actually was, he would have done much worse than sabotage Nati's *shidduchim*.

Zeidel did not stop after the phone call with Aaron Telem. Whenever Nati was moving in the direction of matrimony, Zeidel found out and let the girl know, through messengers or anonymous phone calls with a disguised voice, that Nati was a mean, treacherous character who would sell his mother for money.

Nati was a lone wolf, totally absorbed in his work. He had almost no desire to start a family. Yet even he occasionally entertained serious thoughts about his future, and whenever that happened, he would become involved with another potential marriage candidate. But every such attempt was nipped in the bud.

Nati had everything going for him; he was rich, energetic, personable, and tall. Yet he remained a bachelor. Many good souls tried to help him settle down in life. They could not understand what went wrong time after time. Some gave up and thought that Nati did not really want to get married.

Nati did want to get married, at least sometimes. He, too, asked himself who or what was sabotaging every attempt of his to fulfill that wish. How was it that every time things started to look promising, the bubble burst?

Nati was sure that it was Zeidel who was ruining his chances of getting married. He searched for evidence to prove his theory but could not find a single clue. He waited for Zeidel to slip up and incriminate himself while Zeidel waited for proof of Nati's evil deeds.

It was a duel in which two knights fought with invisible swords. Zeidel had a living shield: Yoel Tzadok. Nati Morgan had a living shield: Yosef Berning. The dueling knights held their shields close to their bodies, moved around one another like two wolves in the wilderness, and searched for an exposed spot in which to plunge their swords.

The atmosphere in the office was highly charged. Although the two heads of Samson Steel walked on tiptoe to maintain some semblance of harmony at work, the tension between Nati and Zeidel was palpable.

For a few years the seesaw of Samson Steel's top men remained balanced. But it was clear that one day, the balance would be disturbed, and one of the sides would triumph. The question was only who would slip up first.

"The answer to that question is history." Felix exhaled a cloud of smoke into the room. "The future of 1966 has already turned into the past. It is clear that Nati won the dual."

Felix was pleased. Unaware of what he had done, Asaf had given him the key to understanding Elitzafan's problem. Now everything was clear. Apparently, Nati was taking revenge. Decades after Zeidel had ruined Nati's *shidduchim*, Nati was doing the same to Zeidel's grandchildren.

"I'm not sure that Nati will have the last word," chuckled Asaf.

Felix gave him a cool, serene look. "How could that be? Zeidel has already gone to the next world, while Nati is still alive and kicking!"

"Where are you hurrying to?" asked Asaf, brushing away Felix's question with his hand. "You're indulging in premature speculation. Let me finish the story, and then you'll understand what happened between those two tycoons and why I'm not sure that Nati really had the last word."

"Let's have the whole story in full," said Felix casually. "The day is young. The sun has barely made half its course over London." He stretched out comfortably in the armchair.

"You aren't going anywhere?" asked Asaf.

"I already told you I wasn't."

Asaf glanced at his watch. It was already noon, and they were still stuck in the hotel suite with the annoying *charedi* scientist! But there was no chance of convincing Felix to sell him the Arrow CDs before telling him the whole story.

For his part, Felix had preferred to see the two gangsters on the other side of the door from the moment they came in. But if he had come this far, he would invest a bit more effort. In the end, he hoped to see concrete results. Perhaps he would end the nightmare of Chedvi's ruined *shidduchim*, and he might even succeed in his main mission: protecting Israel from Nati and Asaf's treachery.

"But first," said Asaf, "we would be pleased if you would call room service and order lunch for us. Steak for me, and pate liver for my partner. What do you think, Malkiel, about lunch at Felix's expense?"

"For reasons of *kashrus*, I eat nothing at the hotel," murmured Felix. "You don't have problems with it?"

"Okay, out of respect for you, I will disregard my hunger. Please make me another cup of strong coffee."

Felix ignored the jibe. Asaf could eat as he wished at home, but Felix would not help him sin. He refilled Asaf's cup.

Asaf took a careful first sip, sighing with pleasure as the steaming liquid slid down his throat. "The great rain forest, Brazil, 1975. Something happened there that remains a mystery to this day. But one thing is clear. It was the watershed that separated Nati and Zeidel, after which Samson Steel fell apart and was rebuilt as Morgan Consolidated."

"What happened there?" asked Felix curiously.

⌘

A few hours after the attempt on his life in the Luxembourg Gardens, Moshiko found the phone number of Rebbetzin Simchoni–Freilich in the memory of his cell phone. "I must have entered it without paying attention," he muttered in relief, and phoned her immediately.

It was hard to hear her. There was a tumult in the background, with people shouting, "Pour water over her" and "No, that's dangerous. Tilt her so that her head is down and the blood can flow into it."

"Rebbetzin Simchoni–Freilich? This is Moshiko Sharabi."

"Can you call back later?" Flora asked tensely. "A woman here has fainted."

"Where are you?"

"In a private house on Rue des Rosiers in the Pletzel."

"I'll be there within a few minutes; I have experience with artificial resucitation. What's the house number?"

By the time Moshiko arrived on the scene, his help was no longer needed. Devorah was sitting in an armchair, surrounded by concerned women. Chedvi, looking very fragile, was stroking her mother's hand. Devorah sighed deeply. Her face was white, and her whole appearance pitiful.

Flora recognized Moshiko and took him aside to a quiet corner. "They've already revived her. But whenever she thinks about what it was that made her faint, she wants to die. Poor thing."

"What's going on here?" asked Moshiko. "It looks like a party. Did she faint from excitement?"

The Rebbetzin sighed. "We were about to celebrate her daughter's engagement, when the *chasan* ran away."

"Why?"

Flora told him.

Moshiko empathized sincerely. Then his sixth sense went into action, and sparks lit up in his pupils. "I would like to hear more background information, if you have two minutes for me."

Flora told him briefly about the anonymous caller who had been systematically ruining every one of Chedvi's *shidduchim* for the past six years.

"Rebbetzin Simchoni-Freilich," said Moshiko, "two weeks ago you spoke to me in the Avraham Avinu Synagogue after a lecture about the sixth sense."

"I remember," said Flora alertly. "In all this tumult, it was hard for me to recall how I knew you, but now I do. You came with a friend after your traffic accident and asked me about your sixth sense. I called you later to warn you that your friend with the earrings was scheming against you."

"Correct," confirmed Moshiko. "He had been ordered to kill me, but now he claims he will no longer obey such orders." The Rebbetzin could not be told that Sheket was a Mossad agent. "I came here now to consult you as a spiritual authority."

"Yes," said Flora.

"My intuition is confusing me. I met the same friend a few hours ago in a public place. I felt he was sincere and honest when he expressed regret, yet two minutes later someone shot at me. What should I do?"

"Just a minute." Flora went over to the table and poured herself a cup of juice. Her hands were still shaking from the evening's experience. She waved off two curious admirers and returned to the corner. "One thing at a time," she told Moshiko. "I noticed before that you had an idea regarding the *shidduch* saboteur. Am I right?"

"Yes. In my mind's eye, I saw a sign that said, 'Go for it.' I intend to follow my instincts."

Under other circumstances, Flora would have pounced on the opportunity to find out how Moshiko's sixth sense operated. But now was not the time. Devorah needed her emotional support.

She glanced in Devorah's direction. Chedvi was sitting with her parents by the window. The three looked as if they were on the verge of collapse. They sat huddled together, trying to comfort each other.

Mr. Feldman went over, shook Elitzafan's hand, and whispered, "I'm sorry," with tears in his eyes. Then he and his wife, with heads bent, disappeared quietly. The guests, realizing that their presence was superfluous now, also left. The house gradually emptied.

Flora turned back to Moshiko, "If so, please try to find out who is behind what happened tonight," she pleaded.

"I'll do my best," he assured her.

39

As Moshiko was leaving the Blochs' home, he remembered something and turned back.

"The reason I came here," he told Flora, "was to ask you how to regard that friend whom you met. Sometimes I think he's a good friend; other times I'm afraid he's a deadly enemy."

The Rebbetzin looked up at one of the gleaming chandeliers. How much joy had been in their hearts just a short time ago, when the brilliant lights were turned on! Who would have imagined that all that joy would be slashed by the sword of slander!

"Put him to the test," Flora heard herself advising Moshiko. Suddenly the Rebbetzin who advised multitudes every evening could come up with nothing more than a standard formula. "Be extra careful, keep a safe distance, and don't turn your back on him."

❦

Nati's corporate jet soared above Germany, Poland, Czechoslovakia, and Ukraine. After refueling in Kiev, it flew through the skies of Russia, passed over the Caspian Sea, and approached the border of Kazakhstan.

They landed in the Kazakhi military airport not far from the city of Kustchagil. Although it was late morning, the eight passengers were exhausted. "Is everyone here?" asked Dubik sleepily. "Let's count ourselves to make sure no one jumped out of a window. Is the redhead here?"

"Together with his freckles," called Roni Nagler.

"Amit Mizrachi?"

"Trying," answered a young man with curly hair and a narrow face. His square chin expressed determination and strength.

"Ido? Professor Ido Bloom?"

A man with carefully combed black hair, high forehead, and small metal-rimmed glasses waved back without lifting his eyes from the science journal through which he was browsing.

"Muli? Where is Muli Pear?"

"I thought it was hard to miss me," complained a tall fellow with broad shoulders and muscular arms.

"Good. Phillip Maximov?"

A short, balding man gave an elegant bow. This newcomer to Israel had worked with one of Russia's nuclear reactors before immigrating.

"Our twins, Sagi and Kobi Bashan, where are you?" asked Dubik.

They were present. They did not look like brothers, let alone twins. It was hard to believe they had been born to the same mother, and only fifteen minutes apart. Sagi was twenty centimeters taller than Kobi and weighed seventy kilograms more.

"We're all here," noted Dubik. "You can all disembark now."

Asaf had good reason for giving Dubik command of the group. His fatherly attitude to his employees and his feeling of responsibility were irreplaceable assets in complex operations like this one.

They left the plane — and were immediately surrounded by a unit of Moslem fighters with mottled uniforms and drawn guns. All the men had long beards, except for one tall fellow with a trimmed beard who seemed to be the commander. The fighters had angry faces. They burst into a chilling roar, "*Allah akhbar!*"

Dubik and his men were frightened. Had they walked into a trap?

The tall fellow announced in excellent, American-accented English that the new arrivals were the guests of honor of Teheran's Guards of the Islamic Revolution.

"Don't be afraid. That's Regi Fahid," Roni Nagler whispered in Hebrew. "Formerly Roger Island, an American criminal from Massachusetts who turned into an Islamic fanatic after becoming convinced of the righteousness of Islam, Iran, and especially Iranian money."

"And what about us? Aren't we also convinced of the righteousness of Iranian money?" whispered Amit Mizrachi. "We've done everything but convert to Islam."

"Shh!" said Dubik. "Don't get the fellows angry. They look nervous."

Regi Fahid kept his finger on the trigger as he approached them. With a fanatic gleam in his clear green eyes, he proclaimed theatrically, "Our deep respects for having joined the Islamic Revolution. We shoot Zionist dogs, but you cleverly defected to the side of the victors when you smelled the collapse of your Zionist state. You saved yourselves in time. We will compensate you properly for aiding our cause."

Dubik's men exchanged glances. Was that the welcome for which they were waiting? Nati and Asaf had promised each of them a hundred thousand dollars upon completion of the assignment. No wonder the corporate management was offering so much. They would be lucky to come out alive.

Surprisingly, though, they were led from the airport to a Bedouin-style tent, where a feast awaited them: big stacks of warm pita breads, spiced chickpeas, tempting balls of cheese in olive oil, large olives, and hot red peppers that burned their tongues and innards like bonfires. For dessert, there were small mugs of boiling coffee straight from the *finjon* and sweeter-than-honey *baklava*. The hosts apologized, "Normally we serve guests mutton filled with rice and curry sauce. We didn't slaughter a sheep in your honor because you are Jews."

For the first time in his life, Dubik felt deeply ashamed that he did not keep kosher.

After they had eaten their fill, a military vehicle took them on a winding dirt path to the bottom of a mountain. It stopped beside a tall gate, which swung open after Regi exchanged a few Arabic words with the guard.

For several minutes they drove through a small forest. Then the military vehicle made one last turn and screeched to a halt, raising a cloud of brown dust.

Another barrier rose out of the earth to greet them: a heavy steel door.

"Everyone out," barked Regi and leaped nimbly out onto the loose earth. They followed him out with clumsy jumps.

"What technological innovations to have in such a primitive setting!" exclaimed Phillip Maximov, as Regi stood before the closed-circuit camera and waved a colorful document with a signature in flowing Arabic letters.

A delicate hum announced the opening of the steel door. From that moment on, three armed guards attached themselves to the group. They walked a few dozen meters and stopped beside a small house with an oversized motor on its roof.

"Here we are," announced Regi. "This is where the merchandise is."

"In such a simple little house?" wondered Dubik.

Regi chuckled. "Wait till you see what's happening inside."

The house with the motor on its roof contained an elevator large enough to hold twenty men. It took them down into the bowels of the earth and let them out in a tunnel hewn into the mountain. The tunnel was lined with fiberglass and brightly lit. Regi led them into a cool, small hall with a musty smell. In a corner of the hall stood five stacks of steel cylinders.

They shivered.

"There is no reason to be afraid," Professor Ido Bloom assured them. "The uranium is wrapped in lead envelopes to block the radiation. There is no danger."

Nevertheless, Philip Maximov took two giant steps backward. "There are tens of thousands of radiation units in these cylinders. To give you an idea of what this means, cancer patients are treated with about 180 radiation units. If a patient were given a double dose for a tumor in his foot, the radiation would destroy all the tissue in the foot, including the bone. And we have to rely on a lead envelope. Do we know if the manufacturer did the job right?"

"That explains why Nati and Asaf aren't here," muttered Amit Mizrachi. "Why should they absorb high levels of radiation, when they can sit in a safe place and count greenbacks?"

❦

After his men had calmed down from their first encounter with the cylinders, Dubik split them into three groups, each with its own load of cylinders and its own route.

The twins Sagi and Kobi Bashan would take a train that would pass the cities of Uralsk, Kandagash, Kuzhegil, and Shvaktachstan, cross the borders to Uzbekistan and Turkmenistan until the city of Mary, and finally stop at the city of Mashhad in Iran.

Roni Nagler and Phillip Maximov would travel by truck through a short land route in Kazakstan via the Ost Ort Mountains. From there they would cross the border to Turkmenistan via the city of Karsnobodsk, and then proceed to the city of Gorgan near the Elbruz Mountains, not far from Iran's secret new reactor.

The most difficult assignment was given to Amit Mizrachi and Muli Pear. They would take a very long, winding route through Astrachan to Georgia, Chechnya, across Turkey through the city of Tabriz, and on to Teheran.

Dubik Cooperman and Professor Ido Bloom would fly in the corporate jet, without any cargo, directly to a small airport on the Iranian border.

"It's always best to be on the management side," Muli commented sarcastically. "*Vive la difference!* A short flight in a comfortable armchair far from radiation-emitting bars, instead of dragging days and nights in trains and trucks, in the warm embrace of the angel of death."

"Silence!" hollered Dubik. "Whoever is dissatisfied can leave right now. Is that clear?"

"I'm ready to leave," Muli muttered to his shoes, "but I'm not familiar with the area."

"Apart from that," said Dubik, lowering his voice, "the passengers of the last route, the most difficult of all, get a special bonus." Asaf had instructed him to keep everyone quiet and satisfied. If necessary, money could be used as a balm to heal resentment.

The elevator took them back to ground level. The cylinders were covered with styrofoam and packed in the cartons of standard General Electric household refrigerators. To assist the camouflage, Dubik's men were handed delivery certificates for refrigerators.

"And now we will stand here under the open sky for half an hour until the trucks come to take the refrigerators," announced Regi Fahid gleefully, waving his submachine gun in every direction. He looked heavenward and shouted, "You, satellite up there, come take a picture of me. Are the refrigerators okay?"

After recovering from a wild burst of laughter, he continued. "There must be five or six hundred Western espionage satellites revolving about the earth, and at these very moments, all their cameras are focusing on us. In the coming hours, every single intelligence agency in the world will get a report about a load of 'refrigerators' being transported from the black market for weapons on the Russia–Kazakhstan border.

"Which is precisely what we want. From now on, many eyes will be on you. Don't worry, no one will touch you, because everyone wants to catch Iran in the act of importing uranium.

"Right now, Iran is conducting important experiments that will bring us a giant step closer to our goal. You are helping us to divert world attention from important things to nonsense. Bravo! It was worthwhile investing a fortune in you."

Regi waved his free fist and shouted, "And now, everyone to the road. Two groups taking four refrigerators each, one taking two, with two of our men attached to each group. Is everything clear?'

"And how." Sagi threw down his cigarette and crushed the tip with the sole of his shoe. "It is clear that someone will not come out of this trip alive. Either we or they."

Regi turned to him suspiciously. "What did you say?"

"Nothing special," said Sagi. "I explained to them that the refrigerators are actually heaters."

Regi laughed hoarsely and slapped Sagi's shoulder. "I like your humor. Too bad we're usually on opposite sides of the fence."

He means, "What a pity that I will liquidate you in the end," thought Dubik. *All I need is for this lunatic with the submachine gun to hear what someone said....*

◌⋎⋎◌

"Aren't you afraid something will go wrong down there?" Ido pointed toward the ground, moving further and further away from them. "The plan is bound to fail because we're too far away to maintain control. Never have I seen such poor management!"

Dubik laughed. "I hope everything goes wrong. I hope someone will catch the cargo and ask questions."

"Why?" asked Ido.

"Simple. If an international scandal is made of it, one of two things will happen: either Iran will achieve its purpose and its prank will succeed superbly, or — and this is what I am hoping for — this whole traitorous operation will fail, and an end will be put to Nati and Asaf's collaboration with our enemies."

"I understand," muttered Ido as he reached for a can of soda.

When the door opened, Moshiko needed only a single glance to take in the stylish draperies, the grand piano, the elegant sofas, the decorative lamps on small marble tables — and the gloomy atmosphere.

"How can I help you?" asked Mr. Feldman, forcing a smile.

"Rebbetzin Simchoni–Freilich asked me to speak to François."

The forced smile changed to an expression of genuine sorrow. "Only twenty-four hours have passed since yesterday's trauma. It's difficult for him to speak."

Moshiko was prepared to use persuasion or do battle, as necessary. "I know. It was no less a trauma for Chedvi. We need to know what made your son leave his engagement party."

Mr. Feldman's legs trembled. "My heart was broken yesterday. The *shidduch* looked wonderful, the parents as well as the girl."

"So let me speak to him," Moshiko insisted. "I want to hear the story in his own words."

Mr. Feldman's body language said, "Do me a favor and leave." Moshiko ignored the message. Mr. Feldman relented. He led Moshiko up the carpeted staircase to François' room.

François was sitting on his bed, trying to read but unable to concentrate. He looked as miserable as his father did.

"I brought you a visitor, a messenger of Rebbetzin Simchoni–Freilich. Please have a few words with him." After saying this, Mr. Feldman left the two alone.

Moshiko did not waste a moment. "I understand that something serious must have happened to keep you away from your engagement party. I would like to hear exactly what it was."

François sighed. For three long minutes, the only sound was his father's nervous pacing downstairs.

Suddenly François spoke. "I don't know whether a tragedy befell me or I was saved from one. I went out to *daven Ma'ariv*, when suddenly a car pulled up beside me. Someone peered out of the window and asked, 'Are you François Feldman?' When I said, 'Yes,' he handed me a gift-wrapped package and said, 'This is an engagement present for you.'

"I thought a friend had sent a present by messenger to surprise me," continued François. "I opened the package curiously and found dozens of photostatted documents. It took me five minutes to understand that this was not a prank. The first document, certified by the Israeli Ministry of the Interior, revealed that Mr. Elitzafan Mindelman had changed his name and was actually the son of Avraham Zeidel Portman. The next documents proved that Avraham Zeidel Portman sold weapons to Syria, Egypt, and Jordan."

François opened a large manila envelope and poured the contents out on the bed. Many of the documents bore the stamp of Samson Steel Industries, Ltd. and the signature of Avraham Zeidel Portman.

Moshiko went over the documents. One of them testified to a large arms sale to Syria with a third country serving as middleman.

"This is one big forgery," said Moshiko carefully.

"And what do you think of this?" François shoved a large sheet of paper into his hands.

It was a picture of a plaque given in gratitude to Mr. Portman by the United Catholic Churches "for his generous help in obtaining articles of worship for substantial reductions."

Moshiko's face contorted in disgust. "I don't believe it!"

"The proof is in front of your eyes," said François. "Chedvi's grandfather sold arms to the Moslems and crosses to the Christians."

"But why does Chedvi have to suffer for her grandfather's deeds?" Moshiko asked in frustration.

François pushed the documents aside. "I really wanted this *shidduch*. For her sake, I agreed to sit and learn Torah my whole life, even though that's not really for me. But to marry the granddaughter of a traitor? No way!"

"I suggest you read these letters." Moshiko handed François letters from decades ago that Elitzafan had given him as his last hope.

☙✿❧

Motza'ei Shabbos Toldos, the 5th of Kislev, 5737 (1977)

My dear, beloved son Elitzafan,

When you visited me at your stepfather's request, you asked how I got into this terrible situation. Seeing you after such a long separation, I was speechless with emotion. Now that the storm has subsided, and the winter Motza'ei Shabbos is long as the exile when I'm alone, I'll try to answer you in writing.

It has been clear to me for a while already that Nati Morgan wanted me out of Samson Steel Industries, Ltd. so that he could take over.

As early as 1966, I suspected him of conducting nonkosher business, but I never managed to implicate him. Yoel Tzadok and I did everything we could to gather evidence. We even planted sensitive listening devices in his room at the office. But we came up with nothing.

For years the office was in a state of tension, with Nati and me locked in a cold war. Then, in January of 1974 came a turning point. Nati walked into my room and told me he was tired of the quarrels and the ugly atmosphere in the office. He said, "I want to make up."

I couldn't believe my ears. I raised an eyebrow and asked, "What are you plotting this time?"

Nati looked hurt. "You never miss an opportunity to make me feel like a swindler. Let me put my cards on the table. I will never forget your kindness, giving me a job when I was hungry, even though in due time the clerk got the corporation off the ground and became assistant to its head. But there's one thing I can't stand, and that's the foul atmosphere in the office." His voice broke and his eyes filled with tears. It was the first time I saw any evidence of emotion in him. "I'm willing to sacrifice a lot for the sake of peace."

He continued, his voice trembling. "I'm forty-five and still a bachelor. Every time I thought I was about to get married, the bride-to-be fled."

Nati gave me a meaningful look, and I cringed in fear. He took a chair and sat down beside me. Suddenly he started to cry.

I was thunderstruck. He pressed my limp hand warmly. "You have it good," he whispered through his tears. "You have a son. One day he will get married and build a family. When you die, you will leave behind offspring who will perpetuate your memory. But the day after I am buried in the earth, no one will remember me. My name will be blotted out."

I was breathing heavily. Beads of sweat covered my forehead, which was burning despite the cold.

"Don't speak that way," I cried out. "A Jew should never despair. We must hope for good."

Nati again stabbed me with his pained look. "Is that so? And what are you prepared to do so that I should not despair? Will you stop making anonymous phone calls to scare people away from marrying me?"

I turned white. I confess, I had my failings. For seven years I had prevented him from building a home solely because of a desire for revenge.

Suddenly I felt as if a white-hot iron were cutting into my intestines. I was consumed with regret. I realized that I myself had become evil. But how can one confess such a crime? I couldn't very well say, "Nati, I ruined your marriage possibilities twenty times. On account of me you have remained a bachelor. But from today, we will start a clean slate."

I found myself arguing, denying, and lying brazenly. "I don't know what you're talking about," I said, pretending to be insulted. "Such a thing never happened."

Nati sighed deeply, wounding my heart. "Zeidel, I am no *tzaddik* myself," he said. "I have more than my share of shortcomings. At least I am a man of truth, though. I confess that I have done a few nonkosher things in the corporate framework for which I could be sent to jail. But, the sordid stuff is behind me now. From this day on, everything will be clean and pure as snow.

"But don't pretend you're innocent. Here, listen."

Nati whipped a small tape recorder out of his pocket and pushed Play. We heard someone inquiring about Nati, and my voice calling him a swindler and a traitor.

I was pale as a corpse.

"The walls have ears," whispered Nati. "Why do you hate me so much? Am I so evil? Is it forbidden for me to get married?"

He looked me straight in the eyes. I crumpled under his pained, agonized look. A wave of shame, pity, and regret washed over me. For five minutes I could not open my mouth. In the end I whispered in a trembling voice, "Do you forgive me?"

Nati likewise trembled all over, "Yes, Zeidel, I forgive you."

Suddenly we found ourselves embracing and sobbing on each other's necks. We apologized to each other for all the grief we had caused one another. He confessed all the injustices he had done me, and I confessed to the conversation he had recorded. I didn't openly admit to other things, but my silence spoke louder than words.

We felt clean and purified. The old wounds had been opened and the pus drained from them. We resolved that from that day on we would be open and honest with one another and never go behind each other's backs.

Nati was so delighted that on the spot he called his aged father, Shaul Morgenstern, and told him we had made up. Uncle Shaul almost danced from excitement, and his spontaneous reaction was to call me to the phone. He spoke with me briefly, and asked me in a voice trembling with emotion to see to it that his son would not die childless. A month later, Uncle Shaul died of a stroke.

From that day on, the poisoned atmosphere was gone. The office functioned in perfect harmony. Even Yosef Berning, whom I feared like the angel of death, began to smile at me and even flatter me occasionally. Samson Steel became a place in which it was pleasant to work.

But the financial side went from bad to worse. Between January of 1974 and the summer of 1975, Samson Steel sank very low. For eighteen months straight, the bank balance was negative. We got stuck with weapons for which there was no demand and explosives whose expiration date had passed. Our prestige declined, and our competitors made mincemeat of us. We considered laying off some of the workers or selling the corporation's real estate holdings so that we could stay afloat until the crisis passed.

One morning in July 1975, Nati was waiting for me when I came into the office. He wore the expression of someone who was hiding a secret. "Mr.

Portman," he said, "there is news." Such a formal address indicated high spirits. Normally he called me Zeidel.

"What kind of news? Have our stocks gone down another two points?" I asked as I hung up my jacket.

"Good news, very good." He looked as if he had won the lottery. "A giant deal is in the offing."

"Who is the deal with?" I asked.

"The Red Brigades. It's a dream come true." Nati looked all around as if he were afraid of being overheard. Ironically, at that precise moment, the listening devices that Yoel had planted in his room broke down. Anyway, they had not fulfilled their mission.

I winced. The Red Brigades were Italian terrorists.

"What's the matter?" complained Nati. "I'm telling you that Samson Steel is about to get a new lease on life, and you look at me as if it's a day of mourning. Why?"

"Why can't we make kosher deals?" I asked bitterly. "Why is it always necessary to look for criminals and terrorists to do business with? You know very well that your shady deals have given Samson Steel a bad reputation. Five years have passed since our last contract with the Israeli Army."

In former days, Nati would have retorted sharply, and we would have quickly gotten embroiled in a heated argument. Not this time. Nati had made an iron resolution to keep the peace no matter what. A quarrel required two sides, and he was not about to be one of them.

"Look, Zeidel. I have no problem doing business only with pure, upright people. Bring me an honest buyer, and I'll sign a fat contract with him this very minute. Why, really, don't you sit with representatives of the Ministry of Defense?"

"They're not interested," I said darkly. "After what the Americans send Israel, do they need our junk?"

"Listen to what you're saying," said Nati. "We have no clientele. In hard times like these, we can't afford to check the piety of our clients. Hold your nose and sign the contract."

"I have no desire to get into trouble with the Vatican," I muttered.

Nati argued that the Vatican itself secretly supported the Red Brigades against the Italian government. That sounded unlikely to me, but we really were in a very bad decline and I had to consider all options.

"All right, I agree," I said, spreading my hands helplessly.

"He agreed!" Spontaneous shouts of joy burst out at once from all sides. All the employees came running into my room, hugged me warmly, and slapped me on the back.

Two facts became clear. One, I was still the big boss whose word was final. Two, our financial situation was much worse than I had thought.

With an enormous smile, Nati handed me the purchase order.

I didn't believe my eyes. After the long drought, a flood had come. The list included thousands of tank shells and cannons; millions of bullets; thousands of hand grenades, illuminating bombs, shoe mines, guns and submachine guns; and even a hundred-fifty Strela shoulder missiles.

My suspicion was immediately aroused. "The Red Brigades do nothing more than shoot from an ambush and hide a few bombs in parked cars. What will they do with all these weapons?"

Nati and Yossi exchanged nervous glances. That look took only a split second — but I've always had a sharp eye.

Nati signaled the celebrating employees to leave the room. After they had gone, he whispered to me, "Why do you have to spoil the party? What do you care what the Red Brigades do with the weapons? For my part, they can use them to fry eggs for breakfast. What counts is that they pay cold, hard cash. In my opinion, they sell the weapons to other terrorist organizations. But why is that my problem?"

"And where will the deal be made, in Italy?" I asked. "The whole Interpol will be at our necks. Why don't you just take a lock and put it on our front door?"

"Zeidel, what's gotten into you? If you want to go touring, we'll take you there one afternoon." He laughed until the tears streamed down his face. When he finally calmed down, he apologized. "The deal will be carried out in a country where the law exists only in books — in Brazil, at the edge of the giant rain forest near the Amazon River. Aside from a few snakes, no creature in the world will testify about what happens there. We'll buy off some government officials, and the entire delivery will change hands without anyone checking. They'll take the weapons, we'll count the money, and the story will end."

I was overwhelmed by Nati's torrent of words. When he wanted something, his power of persuasion was phenomenal. Truth be told, the idea intrigued me. I wanted to travel myself to Brazil, to peek into the closed, primeval world of the rain forest. I can't understand how I could have been so foolish.

Enough for today. In the next letter I will tell you exactly what happened in the rain forest and how it affected me and you.

Love,

Your father who seeks your well-being,

Avraham Zeidel Portman

Sunday, the 6th of Kislev, 5737 (1977)

To my dear, beloved son Elitzafan,

I continue where I closed my previous letter.

Although I myself was carried away by Nati's slippery tongue and his descriptions of the profits expected from the Red Brigades deal, my right-hand man and good friend, Yoel Tzadok, was not. He had not changed over the years. From the moment I first saw Yoel — a quiet, humble Yemenite who keeps Jewish tradition — I knew I could rely on him. Indeed, he remained faithful to the rule I had taught him the first day he came to work in the office: "Don't trust Nati Morgan!"

Yoel did not trust him.

Whatever Nati schemed to do, Yoel was two steps ahead of him. My guardian worked slyly, cleverly, and independently. Of course there is One Supreme Guardian, but He had a human representative on earth, and his name was Yoel Tzadok.

From time to time Yoel would send me a note to remind me that someone was protecting me continuously. For instance, "Remember that I felt two eyes following me in Nati's house in Kfar Shmaryahu? I saw them yesterday during a courtesy visit there. It was Freddy, his Siamese cat." Or "I bought a small movie camera. I'm planning to check its operation in the coming days."

What happened was this: Yoel accompanied Nati to Germany, and while Nati was buying tanks from the German army surplus, Yoel bought two movie cameras from the German intelligence service for a bargain price. These genuine spy cameras can be camouflaged in a thousand and one ways, and you won't see their lens even if you stand right in front of it.

When they returned to Israel, Yoel concealed the cameras in a decorative plant, which he placed in Nati's room as a birthday surprise. Nati was so touched by the gesture that he hugged Yoel — as I saw in black and white two days later, after the film was developed.

At any rate, I foolishly agreed to the Red Brigades deal, and here is what happened.

⊙◦✦◦⊙

Three giant unmarked Hercules carrier planes, loaded to bursting with weapons, took off at night from a military airport in Montevideo, Uruguay. We had bought the planes from the American Army — second-hand but in good condition, like 90% of our purchases.

The weapons were accompanied by Yosef Berning and two of my faithful men, Zev Shachar and Yechezkel Shoshan. They flew toward the Amazon Valley in northern Brazil. The planes were to land in a military airfield in Aitituba where we had paid good money to keep curious eyes away. But from this point, we lost contact with our men. I can report to you only what I found out later in court.

Nati left Israel at the same time as the others, but then suddenly disappeared. The lack of a commander is a sure recipe for disaster, especially in such a complex operation. The vacuum had to be filled, so Yosef Berning took command.

The contact person between us and the buyer was Robert Brown, who I knew slightly from his visits to our office. This Vietnam veteran, an officer of unknown rank in the United States Marines whose background was shrouded in fog, was a hero of the weapons business in the sixties and seventies. He was short and thin, with straw-colored hair, watery blue eyes, and a wide red nose. He presented himself as a clerk, but no one knew in what office. Actually, he was a courier for terrorist organizations and a middleman in major weapons deals. He had a finger in every pie and seemed to be the main hinge without which no deal could go through.

Robert Brown was deeply involved in our deal with the Red Brigades. According to Nati (whom I don't necessarily believe), it was Robert Brown who came up with the idea and advised that the transfer of weapons take place at the edge of the rain forest, near the village of Dilo de la Pedra.

The transport planes landed and the merchandise was unloaded. Cranes worked for hours unloading the crates of weapons into twenty giant trucks. Yosef, Zev, and Yechezkel drove a Mrecedes to the village, ahead of the slow caravan of trucks. Our caravan was supposed to arrive near the village toward sundown and meet the buyer's caravan. The Red Brigades informed us that they had not managed to obtain big trucks, so for every truck of ours they were bringing two. Everything was proceeding smoothly.

Then Nati gave Yosef the following message over the walkie-talkie: "I'll arrive in a Cessna plane toward sunset. I was warned that someone mentioned my name to the Brazilian police force. Despite all the bribes we gave to officials in the Defense Department, I'm worried. To be on the safe side, keep far away from the weapons. My code name for the operation is Eagle. No one should dare to mention my real name. The three of you, too, should use your code names."

Yosef, Zev, and Yechezkel were worried. Two years before, in the summer of 1973, a similar arms transfer was to take place in Cambodia. At the last moment, army forces appeared, arrested our men, and confiscated the weapons. Our lawyers had to work zealously to extricate our men from the Cambodian prison. Apparently, someone had squealed; I have no idea who it might have been.

We were afraid of someone squealing here, too. Robert Brown might have tried to make some extra money on the side.

Yosef, Zev, and Yechezkel sat in a yard in Dilo de la Pedra and waited for the caravan of trucks and for Nati. They had some contact with him. He said he had been delayed but would arrive soon. They heard the roar of engines as the trucks climbed the mountain and heaved a sigh of relief when they saw the silhouette of a Cessna plane gliding toward them.

From that point, everything went wrong.

The light plane landed in a small clearing in the forest, near the place where the trucks were to meet. Yosef and Zev came running to meet Nati, who was expected to arrive with Robert Brown.

The door of the plane opened. But instead of Nati and Robert Brown, out jumped three men wearing ski masks that completely covered their faces. They sprayed Yosef and Zev with dozens of bullets.

Yechezkel had followed the drama from afar. Cool and level-headed, he dropped to the ground, crawled from there to the house that our men had been using in the village, and contacted me on the walkie-talkie.

Foolishly, I had not adhered to the rules of caution. Instead of waiting in the office in Tel Aviv for everything to be arranged, I had followed Nati's advice and come to Brazil. I wanted to see the rain forest. I was in my magnificent hotel room in Rio de Janeiro awaiting developments when the walkie-talkie buzzed. I recognized Yechezkel's voice.

"Kodkod, do you hear me? It's Barak."

I pressed the button. "Kodkod to Barak, did all go well?"

"Negative. All was destroyed." He was sobbing. "Eagle didn't arrive. Someone on the inside betrayed us. They liquidated Yosef and Zev."

I was dumbstruck. I was prepared for a colossal failure like the one in Cambodia, but not for such a death blow. For a minute I was at a complete loss. When I recovered I hollered into the walkie-talkie, "Barak, go over to emergency procedures. Wait for us to get you; meanwhile, make yourself inconspicuous."

"Roger," said Yechezkel. "Kodkod, I know who betrayed us."

I very much wanted to know who it was, but I was afraid of losing Yechezkel, too, so I tried to stop the conversation. I called, "Barak! Don't talk over the walkie-talkie. We'll speak face to face. Barak? Barak? Barak?"

But Yechezkel did not answer. The walkie-talkie suddenly went dead. Later I learned that he had been shot in the head while I spoke to him.

My blood froze. Suddenly I understood everything. Why had I been so stupid?

Nati had drawn me into a trap.

I tossed the walkie-talkie out the window. I didn't know that the police had already surrounded my room and that the walkie-talkie fell into their net, to be used as evidence against me.

Ten minutes later, there were loud knocks at my door. I opened it. Two uniformed policemen shoved me roughly inside and handcuffed me. They announced that I was under arrest for illegal arms-trading and that anything I said could, and would, be used against me in court.

I declared that I was indeed an arms dealer but I had done nothing illegal.

With sadistic glee, the policemen showed me a document proving that I had sold arms to the Red Brigades terrorist organization. They also had documents proving that I had purchased arms illegally from local criminal organizations, which was totally false.

Later, I found myself in a foul-smelling prison cell, sharing a thin, narrow mattress with hundreds of hungry fleas. I was sustained by only water for two weeks. They kept me in isolation. My requests to see a lawyer fell upon deaf ears.

Then a government official visited me in jail. Although I did not expect good news, I was happy to see a human face.

My happiness quickly evaporated. He informed me in broken English that I could expect a difficult trial, and almost certainly a death sentence because — Elitzafan, pay careful attention to this part! — because I spread black plague, which claimed the lives of two hundred fifty villagers in Dilo de la Pedra.

"I also sank the Titanic," I said with parched lips. "What is this nonsense?"

The government official informed me that the trucks carrying the weapons had been totally destroyed, but apparently the trucks had also carried biological weapons, which caused an epidemic in the village. Dilo de la Pedra was quarantined, and they were even considering evacuating all the villagers.

I was in shock. Never had I dealt in nonconventional weapons.

The government official enjoyed seeing the last spark of hope in my eyes extinguished. He indicated how the noose would be tightened around my neck and he looked very pleased.

After he left I asked myself a few questions. (1) Where had Nati disappeared to? (2) What exactly happened in Dilo de la Pedra? (3) What happened to Yosef and Zev? (4) What happened to Yechezkel? (5) Where would all this lead?

The answers came sooner than I expected. But more about that next time.

Your father, who misses you,

Avraham Zeidel Portman

The train wound through a valley between green mountains. It passed small Kazakh villages with straw-roofed houses and old wells surrounded by herds of cows and flocks of sheep grazing tranquilly in broad pastures. A thick layer of clouds hung in the dark skies, occasionally releasing heavy drops of rain mixed with snowflakes.

The three passenger cars, with their hard benches and strong odor, seemed to have come out of a previous century. Directly behind them were four closed freight cars containing electrical appliances, including refrigerators, followed by twenty open freight cars containing coal, bauxite, and iron.

One of the windows in the first passenger car was open despite the fierce cold. A curly head peeked out, and a round face looked right and left.

"Sagi, close the window!" hollered Kobi Bashan. "You have a thick layer of fat to protect you, but I don't."

"This trip will never end," sighed Sagi as he closed the window. "What's the matter, my brother, the stick? Are you cold?"

"Freezing," said Kobi, shivering in his green sweatshirt.

Sagi glanced at his watch. "According to the conductor, in six hours we'll cross the border to Uzbekistan."

"And in Uzbekistan, how long will we have to ride in this horrible train?"

"Two days," said Sagi. "Why take it so hard? Keep your mind on the bonus. Think of buying your own private house with a garden and a swimming pool. Think of the dreams that are about to come true for you. It's worth a few days of suffering."

"Easy for you to say." Kobi wiped his running nose. "I'm on the verge of pneumonia."

Without warning, the train slowed down. Then, with a sharp screech of the brakes, it lurched to a halt, almost throwing Kobi and Sagi out of their seats.

Sagi again opened the window and stuck his head out.

Twenty meters in front of the train was a barricade. Beside it were two large cars, a dark blue one bearing the initials IAEA, and a white one with the letters UN large enough to be seen a kilometer away. Sagi quickly ducked inside and closed the window.

"That's it, Kobi," said Sagi gravely. "We've been caught. We're about to be inspected by the International Atomic Energy Agency and the United Nations."

Now the twins shivered from fear more than from cold. As they waited in dread, they reviewed the instructions they had been given for such an eventuality.

Within minutes, three men with suits and ties came into the car and formally introduced themselves. Two big, husky Europeans were UN inspectors. The third, who had a Middle Eastern look, was from the IAEA.

"What freight are you transporting here?" asked one of the UN inspectors.

They recited the first answer, according to instructions: "Electrical appliances."

The inspectors laughed. They slashed the innocent-looking refrigerator cartons open and easily found the steel containers.

It was time for the second answer. "This is our job," they recited. "We were instructed to accompany packed refrigerators and know nothing beyond that."

This answer, too, was rejected instantly. Under pressure, the two gave in and recited the third answer. "The destination is Iran. Speak to the Iranian Foreign Ministry."

The twins waited tensely while the inspectors consulted the office of the UN General Secretary in New York. Sagi cracked his knuckles; Kobi's right eye twitched nervously. This was the moment of truth. Was an international scandal about to unfold? Would the headlines, "Israeli Arms Dealers Caught Transporting Uranium to Iran," capture the front pages of all the world's newspapers? Would the brothers suffer public disgrace and sit in jail for decades? Or would a miracle save them?

It was a long, nerve-wracking half hour. Kobi found himself praying. He resolved that if he came out of this safely, he would lay *tefillin,* refrain from eating non-kosher meat, and keep Shabbos. Anything to get out of the mire in peace.

The answer that came back astounded even pessimistic Kobi. "The United Nations has discussed the matter with the Iranian Foreign Ministry and accepts its explanation that the uranium is meant for peaceful purposes. It will fuel a civilian nuclear reactor to produce cheap electricity.

"You may continue on your way," the inspectors told the astounded brothers and left the train.

Kobi's resolutions left with them. The brothers laughed in relief. "We're free!" they sang, as they broke into a wild dance in the middle of the car.

There was no doubt about it. One of the higher-ups was interested in having the uranium reach Iran safely.

⌘

"It began after the Yom Kippur War," Asaf told Felix. "Business declined, and Samson Steel was sinking fast. Nati made every effort to keep the corporation afloat, but Zeidel Portman sat back and did nothing but organize an office *minyan* and make sure the food was kosher. Nati and I hated him and wanted to get rid of him. In the summer of 1975, Nati came up with a plan.

"Nati wove the web around Zeidel patiently and diligently. He convinced Zeidel to let Samson Steel buy an enormous quantity of weapons legally and sell them to the Red Brigades. Zeidel never dreamed that the weapons were to continue directly to Syria and Egypt, or that his own signature would appear on the contract beside the enemy's signature. For this purpose we used a blank piece of stationery that bore his signature. How did we get it? Although Zeidel was always suspicious and cautious, occasionally he slipped up.

"Nati counted on public opinion condemning Zeidel because of his extreme anti-State views. They would assume that a zealot like him would want to help Israel's enemies. Nati knew that Zeidel would never betray his people, but to him, the means justified the end — which was to oust Zeidel and take revenge on him. Nati did not let me in fully on his schemes, and I was totally shocked by what actually happened.

"At first, all went as planned. The weapons left the military airport in Montevideo in three giant Hercules transport planes. I accompanied the weapons, along with Zeidel's lackeys, Zev Shachar and Yechezkel Shoshan. We flew to the Amazon Valley in Brazil and landed in a military base in Aitituba."

"Nati was with you, of course," said Felix. He sucked his cigar.

"You'll be surprised to hear that he was not." Asaf drew a cigar fom Felix's box and joined the party. "Nati knew what was going to happen, and he made sure not to be there when it did. After he and Zeidel personally supervised the loading of the weapons onto the Hercules planes in Montivideo, Zeidel flew to Rio de Janeiro, and Nati disappeared. Only afterwards did I learn that he had rushed back to Israel so that he could cluck in sorrow as the media ripped Zeidel to shreds.

"At the edge of Dilo de la Pedra, late in the afternoon, we sat back in easy chairs outside the house as we waited for the purchaser's and seller's trucks and for Nati's plane. As time passed, we grew nervous. We listened intently, but heard nothing but the screeching of birds. I told Yechezkel that apparently we had been tricked. He said we should wait half an hour longer. The pastoral silence continued.

"I jumped to my feet. My patience had run out. I told them we should not have relied on Robert Brown. He was a traitor; I had thought so from the first minute I saw him. He wanted to earn double — from us and from the Brazilian authorities. Zev argued that Robert Brown was merely a courier. But I was nervous.

"Yechezkel tried to contact Nati. He took out a walkie-talkie and hollered into the mouthpiece. 'Eagle, Barak here. Do you hear me?'

"At first the instrument was silent. Then it became filled with static. Suddenly the jarring sounds turned into significant sentences. I heard Nati's voice clearly. 'Eagle here. I hear you, Barak. We had a delay. We'll be arriving in five minutes.'

'Eagle, are you sure?' asked Yechezkel.

"'You're coming over garbled,' stammered the instrument, and again went silent.

"Something was strange, but we didn't know exactly what. The delay was frightening.

"Just before we gave up in despair, a silhouette suddenly glided into the edge of the horizon. A minute afterwards, we saw the plane dropping and heard the noise of its light motor. It slid steadily toward the small clearing in the forest just outside of Dilo de la Pedra. At the same time, we heard the welcome roar of approaching trucks. The tension gave way to satisfaction and relief."

"And then what happened?" asked Felix, his eyes focused on Asaf's face.

Asaf sighed. "To this very day, I shudder when I recall those moments.

"The plane landed. Zev and I ran to greet Nati. The door of the plane opened. But instead of Nati, out came three masked men with submachine guns. They sprayed us with bullets. I fell down unconscious.

"Fifteen minutes later I regained consciousness thinking I had died and arrived in Hell. The entire valley was one big fire. The trucks were ablaze, and the air was filled with suffocating smoke. In the background I heard explosions. Zev lay dead beside me.

"Ten minutes passed before I realized that I was still in this world. I looked around and was glad to see that Yechezkel seemed to have escaped.

"I crawled back into the house we had been using. I almost fainted when I found Yechezkel dead, shot in the head."

Felix was bitterly disappointed. The tiny tape recorder in his jacket pocket was capturing Asaf's words, but Asaf was careful not to incriminate himself. "I thought you knew who had liquidated Yechezkel Shoshan," Felix said casually.

Asaf slapped his knee. "I told you that a few riddles remain unsolved. To this day, I don't know why I wasn't killed when they sprayed us with bullets, or who liquidated Yechezkel.

"Getting back to the business at hand, now that you've heard who Nati Morgan is, you surely understand that it is not in your best interests to deal with him. Nati will connect you with Señor Miguel Churchas, manager of a Mexican bank, who will confirm that the entire sum has been deposited in an account under your name, ready for you to come and withdraw it in cash.

But when you get there, you will discover that Señor Miguel Churchas is not a bank manager, but a drunk who works for Nati for a handful of pesos."

"I'll think about it," said Felix.

Asaf stood up and approached Felix threateningly. "Stop wasting time. You will fly to Israel to bring the Arrow CDs, and two days from now at seven p.m. we will meet here in the room. I don't play games. The money will be deposited in whatever bank you wish, in any country you choose. And just to show my good faith, I'll give you an advance right now."

Asaf opened his attaché case and theatrically drew out a checkbook. Before Felix could mutter a weak protest, he filled out the details and signed it.

Felix froze. Half a million dollars, dated yesterday.

"You can cash the check in my Tel Aviv bank as soon as you land. My bank manager will give you the cash. How's that?"

"I feel happy and sad at the same time," said Felix sincerely.

"Don't be sad." Asaf's big hand landed on Felix's shoulder, almost crushing him. "If you did business with Nati, you'd have good reason to be sad. See you the day after tomorrow at seven p.m."

Malkiel and Asaf left the suite. Felix did not have to look at his watch to know that the meeting had taken all day; his hungry stomach told him so. His first priority now was to *daven Minchah* before the sun set. He put the thoughts of the interesting, dangerous days to come out of his mind for the moment in order to concentrate on his prayer.

⸙

François folded up the old letters that Chedvi's grandfather had sent her father. He returned them to Moshiko.

"What do you say?" Moshiko asked enthusiastically. "Convincing, no?"

François stretched out on the bed wearily and put the pillow under his head. "Terribly convincing." He rubbed his eyes, which were red from lack of sleep. "They taught me once that you don't stick a healthy head into a sickbed. The Feldman family is a healthy head; the Mindelman family is a sickbed. I don't know whether the man who shoved the documents into my hand is an enemy of the Mindelmans or a friend of mine, but it doesn't matter. The zealousness of friends ruins life no less that the hatred of enemies. I cannot get engaged to Chedvi Mindelman."

"Are you sure?" persisted Moshiko.

"Enough," said François with eyes closed. "Leave me alone."

"Just one more question before I go," pleaded Moshiko. "Would you recognize the man who handed you the envelope?"

François' forehead wrinkled in thought. "Yes, I think I would. He had a very distinctive look."

"I'm sure it's one of Nati's group," mused Moshiko. Suddenly he jumped up. "Did his eyebrows meet, and did he have a long, eagle-like nose?"

"I think so," said François, suddenly wide awake.

"And was his speech slow and awkward?"

François tried hard to remember. "He didn't say much, but there was definitely something strange in his speech."

"I'm going to reconstruct your meeting with the man in the car. Listen to me and tell me if this is how he sounded."

Moshiko grabbed the book that François had been reading. He sat on a chair next to the bed, leaned toward François with the book in his hand, as if extending it through the car window, and asked, "Are you François Feldman?"

"Yes."

Moshiko handed François the book. "This is an engagement gift."

François jumped up. "Unbelievable! That's exactly how he sounded. How can you imitate someone you didn't see?"

Moshiko laughed. "He's someone I see quite a lot of — Adam Dushman, Nati's courier in all sorts of situations. Thank you very much, François. You've been a great help."

When Moshiko came downstairs, Mr. and Mrs. Feldman looked at him with sad, questioning eyes. Moshiko gestured that there was nothing to talk about.

"Just a minute, please," called François from the top of the staircase. "You didn't tell me how you know him."

"What's the difference?" laughed Moshiko. "The important thing is that the *shidduch* saboteur has been exposed."

43

Twenty-four hours after the fiasco of the *vort*, the Mindelmans were still far from recovery. Elitzafan looked like someone who had just undergone a difficult dental treatment. Devorah's eyes had difficulty focusing, and her fingers nervously rubbed the edge of her sleeve.

Chedvi accepted Heaven's decree with love. Her serenity reflected her complete trust in Hashem. The normal color had returned to her cheeks. But Elitzafan was worried. Her bravery was exceptional, but what was going on inside? Emotions are not so easily overcome. He was afraid the suppressed anguish might erupt in a sudden breakdown.

Moshiko reported to them and Flora in the Blochs' living room. They were relieved to hear that the *shidduch* saboteur had been exposed. A human being is less frightening than a mysterious threat that imagination blows up out of all proportion. On the other hand, the human being in question was not one to be taken lightly.

"It's exactly what I was afraid of," said Elitzafan. "Adam Dushman is a courier for Nati Morgan — and Nati can be a deadly enemy."

"Has Nati been listening in on the Mindelmans' calls for the past six years?" asked Flora.

"No, not Nati himself," said Moshiko, helping himself to a pastry left from the previous evening. "He's too big for such things. He would have hired others to do the job."

"Who said it's only the phone?" asked Elitzafan. "Maybe he planted listening devices in the walls of our apartment. How can we return home, if every word we say there is intercepted by an enemy?"

"Go home and conduct your business as usual," Moshiko advised. "Just take the subject of *shidduchim* entirely out of the house."

"Good idea," said Elitzafan, stroking his graying beard. Many black hairs had turned white recently. "Let me ask you something else. What did François have to say for himself?"

Moshiko thought for a moment about how to answer the question so as to cause the least pain. Then he said, "François returned the letters that I gave him. But just before I left, I gave him a photocopy of your father's last letter. Maybe that will change his mind."

Elitzafan rose heavily from the armchair, went over to the window, and looked out into the night. Paris sparkled with millions of lights and drew tourists from all over the world. His own memories of Paris, though, would always be ugly.

"My feeling," he told Moshiko, with his face toward the window, "is that nothing will come of this *shidduch*. I didn't pin high hopes on it to begin with, and had Rebbetzin Simchoni–Freilich not pushed it so hard, we would all have stayed in Israel and been spared much heartache. Apparently Heaven had decreed another portion of affliction for us, and we will accept it with love. But we have nothing more to look for in France. We return to Israel tomorrow."

Moshiko went over to the window and stood beside Elitzafan. "Aren't you being hasty? I have a feeling that after François reads your father's last letter and sleeps on it, he may have second thoughts. You're liable to return to Israel in the afternoon and hear in the evening that François wants to go ahead with the engagement after all."

"Nothing doing," said Elitzafan bitterly. "He broke our hearts. My daughter's emotions are not to be toyed with."

Moshiko had to stop Elitzafan from speaking that way; the boy might yet become his son-in-law! He quickly changed the subject. "Do you remember what was in the letter?"

"Could I ever forget?" He let out a short, joyless laugh. "Actually, it was a mistake to give it to you. It may convince François of my father's innocence, but it will also reduce my worth in his eyes to zero. It contains a stinging rebuke, which drove me even further away from my father."

෧✺ᔭ

Elitzafan, my beloved son,

After the Brazilian government official left my prison cell, I began to prepare seriously for leaving this world.

Two and a half weeks more dragged on in that miserable jail cell. Then suddenly I was told to get ready.

For what? I was not told. But if they had me shower and dress in clean clothes I figured they were not leading me to my execution.

I was taken away in a closed police van. I could not see out, but after an hour I heard the sound of airplanes. It was music to my ears. Brazil was returning me to the Israeli authorities! Freedom was minutes away!

I was wrong.

I returned to Israel in handcuffs. Two policemen escorted me off the plane and delivered me to the Shabak for interrogation.

My two interrogators played the roles of good cop/bad cop. Peter, tall and broad, with a shaved head and swollen face, was the frightening one. George, of medium height and slight build, with neatly combed blond hair, was the good one. Playing their carefully rehearsed roles well, they tried to extract a confession saying that I had negotiated with enemy agents and supplied weapons to hostile states.

I mustered the remnants of my strength not to succumb. "I never negotiated with agents of hostile states," I repeated stubbornly. "I signed no arms deal with representatives of Egypt or Syria. We were about to supply weapons to the Red Brigades, nothing more."

During the trial, which took place behind closed doors, I learned that there was a piece of evidence against me: a detailed sales agreement that stated explicitly, "The weapons will be transferred to the hands of agents of the defense ministries of Egypt and Syria through the Red Brigades." My signature was on that document.

I told the truth. "I signed a few blank papers. Someone used one of them to frame me."

I thought the deception would be exposed and I would be vindicated. Then the district attorney summoned the main witness, Nati Morgan.

When I saw the judge smile at him, my heart sank. I knew the game was over. Even if a hundred eyewitnesses were to testify that Nati spied for Syria, the accusation would be dismissed at the outset. But for Zeidel the zealot, an outrageous slander based on a single document was gratefully accepted.

For two whole minutes, Nati, dressed to the nines in an off-white suit and enveloped in the scent of aftershave, pretended it was hard for him to testify against his partner and friend. He was still in shock over the discovery of the crimes that had been committed secretly. But he recovered quickly, with the prosecutor's help, and spewed forth blatant lies in a confident voice. He said he had suspected I was negotiating with the enemy behind his back, and even tried to prevent the deal from going through, but without success.

The district attorney treated Nati with silk gloves; he didn't cross-examine him over and over again as he had done to me. My lawyer was unsuccessful; he didn't ask the right questions. And I, broken by my troubles, lost my head and forgot that I actually had crucial evidence. The photographs that Yoel Tzadok had taken in Kfar Shmaryahu of Nati's documents proved that Nati had sold Egypt eighteen Sikorsky helicopters through the fictitious Freedom Fighters of Brazil. A little help from Yoel would have sufficed to indict the true criminal. So would a bit of thinking on my part.

But the wheels in my brain had stopped turning. I sat on the defendant's bench like a defeated scarecrow and allowed my enemy to devour big chunks of my flesh. Why? Because of you, my precious son! Without your support, I was as weak and helpless as Shimshon after his hair was cut.

Why didn't you believe me, your own father, when I protested my innocence? I forgive your mother. She had never understood my views as a zealot and never had faith in me. Our relationship had always been rocky, so it's not surprising that when it was put to the test, she demanded a divorce. But what happened to you?

Now I had answers to my questions in the Brazilian jail: (1) Nati Morgan returned to Israel on the way to Brazil in order to be here when the scandal broke. (2) Dilo de la Pedra was a trap. The weapons deal was meant to fail in order to cause my arrest. (3) Yosef Berning disappeared. I was told he had *been killed in the rain jungle forest with Zev Shachar. (4) Yechezkel Shoshan was killed while speaking to me on the walkie-talkie. I don't know who killed him or why. (5) All this led to a four-year prison sentence and terrible disgrace for me, which caused my family and friends to treat me like a pariah, while Nati took over the corporation that I had founded and built.*

What hurts the most, though, is that when I needed a shoulder to lean on, you ran away from me in shame.

Your father who loves you despite everything,
Avraham Zeidel Portman

Chedvi and her parents took off from France in the late afternoon and landed in Israel at night. The ride home was slowed by the pouring rain. They arrived in Beis Yisrael at midnight, bent in body and spirit.

Tirtzah, Leah'le, and Kreindy welcomed the sad group home. How the three had looked forward to rejoicing with their eldest sister when she returned!

As if nothing were wrong, Chedvi put her suitcase down on a chair and unpacked the gifts and souvenirs she had brought from Paris. Models of the Eiffel Tower, decorative key rings, colorful, fragrant soaps, dolls for friends' little sisters, and a new camera quickly covered the dining-room table.

"Did you bring back pictures of Paris?" asked Tirtzah, trying unsuccessfully to sound enthusiastic. Acting had never been her strong point. Chedvi looked drained, and Tirtzah would have preferred to weep together with her.

Chedvi was, in fact, in better shape than her sisters thought. True, the French *shidduch*, from the first meeting to the *vort* fiasco, had left her drained and exhausted. True, the discovery that a powerful enemy named Nati Morgan was bent on making their lives unbearable added to her emotional burden. But she was not broken.

"Of course I brought pictures, Tirtzah. Come see Ima and me at the Eiffel Tower, or you won't believe we were in Paris. This is the Pletzel, and here is the home of our hosts in Rue des Rosiers. This lady is our hostess, Mrs. Bloch, a charming and righteous woman. Here is Rebbetzin Flora Simchoni–Freilich delivering a lecture, here is Ima in the Metro, and this is me in the Place de la Concorde." There were smiles and even giggles as the four sisters leafed through the photos together, while Devorah unpacked the new clothes she had bought for every member of the family.

Everyone tried their best to act as if nothing painful had happened — everyone, that is, except Kreindy. Outspoken and emotional, Kreindy could not participate in the reunion as if all were well.

Kreindy left the party and went over to the window. Tirtzah and Leah'le were engrossed in the photographs of the Arc de Triomphe. Ima and Chedvi looked like tiny ants beside it.

Chedvi was the first to notice Kreindy standing with her back to them, her shoulders trembling. She hurried to her side. "Kreindy, what's the matter? Didn't I bring you a nice enough souvenir? I did my best, but it's not always easy to find just the right thing."

Kreindy turned around and looked at her with damp eyes. "Chedvi, you're so wonderful. Even now you're not thinking of yourself at all, but only of us."

"So why are you crying?" asked Chedvi, ignoring the compliment. "What are you missing?"

"Pictures of Chedvi's *vort*, that's what I'm missing. Who needs pictures of Paris?" Two streams of tears flowed continuously from the corners of Kreindy's eyes to her chin. "I so much wanted to rejoice with you. We were sitting at home counting the hours for the phone to ring and Ima to say excitedly, '*Mazal tov*, Chedvi is engaged.' Instead, what do we get? 'There's no *vort*; the *chasan* ran away.' So how am I supposed to react? To wear a mask and delve into the beauty of the Eiffel Tower? What will be? When will the Mindelman family get out of the mud? Why do we, of all families, have a terrible enemy?"

Chedvi brought Kreindy a glass of water. "Kreindy, you're doing the easy thing — thinking how hard it is for us and crying bitterly in despair. You let out your pain, and I'm glad you feel better. But just between us, is that the training we received from Abba and Ima?

"Did you take advantage of your grief to ask Hashem, in Whose hands our fate is, to sweeten the bitter pill? And have you thought that Hashem is arousing us a little to feel just once what He has felt since the *Beis HaMikdash* was destroyed? Have you thought that the pain should bring us closer to Him?

"So next time your heart is sad, dear Kreindy, take your pain up a level and direct it to Heaven. Cry because Hashem is in pain. Cry because Hashem is sad that we remember Him only in distress and forget Him when things go well. Crying the right way will help Tirtzah and me get engaged soon."

"Really?" Kreindy's eyes sparkled.

"For sure," said Chedvi warmly. "You'll see."

The room was totally silent. Five sets of eyes followed Chedvi in admiration as she quickly finished unpacking while humming a quiet tune to herself.

Little did they know that a plan of action was shaping up in her head. There was no time to lose. Tomorrow she would go!

44

"I'm going to Meiron," Chedvi announced as they breakfasted together the morning after their return from Paris.

"Wonderful," said Devorah. "*Daven* well."

But Elitzafan tensed. "How long will you be gone?"

Devorah answered for her. "One day. She'll leave soon and come home tonight, as usual."

"Today? Aren't you tired?" Elitzafan asked Chedvi.

"Yes, but I want to *daven* there," she replied.

"How long?" he repeated.

"A few days." This time Chedvi answered for herself.

"Please don't go," he said quietly.

"But Abba, what's the problem with going to Meiron?"

"There's no problem, but I still don't want you to go. The security situation is tense. The *intifada,* terrorist attacks…."

Chedvi looked up in surprise. What had gotten into her father?

Elitzafan's real concern was not the *intifada,* but his daughter. Yes, she was tough and brave — but that was exactly the problem. Who knew when the emotional stress she suppressed might push her over the edge? Praying at the grave of Rabbi Shimon bar Yochai was harmless enough, but who knows what rash things Chedvi might do if she stayed in the Galil for a few days. She might try to visit the grave of Yonasan ben Uziel in Amukah, a popular site for praying for a *shidduch,* at two in the morning.

His secret fear was that Chedvi would go to the Galil to pray and then disappear. For days they would search frantically for her from Meiron to the Negev. In the end, police officers accompanied by a doctor would knock on the door to bring the dreaded news....

"I don't think you should go," he repeated. "Either stay home, or else I'll go with you."

Chedvi left the table looking hurt. Devorah rebuked her husband in a whisper. "She's all grown up. What's wrong with letting her go to pray and pour out her grief? It will make her feel better."

"I'm afraid she might do something foolish," said Elitzafan.

Devorah looked at her husband sideways. Why was he consumed by fears and worries? "Let her go," she pleaded.

Was Chedvi really on the verge of despair, or was he just worrying too much? "Okay, but I hope I'm wrong," he whispered.

He sipped the coffee he had made for himself. It was bitter; he had forgotten to put in sugar. He hoped the future would not be like the coffee.

༄༅

Humming one of his favorite Beethoven sonatas, Felix entered the courtyard of the house in Beis Yisrael with a flight bag slung over his shoulder. His spirits were high. Events were proceeding exactly as he had planned. What remained was a few hours of removing material out of Elta, and everything would fly like an arrow shot from a bow.

Just then Chedvi, escorted by her parents, came downstairs with her tote bag. Elitzafan smiled weakly at the sight of his neighbor and hurried to shake his hand. "*Shalom aleichem,* Felix," he said. "How are you?"

"Wonderful, *baruch Hashem,*" Felix smiled. "What's new?"

Elitzafan sighed from the depths of his heart. "A lot." He looked ahead. Devorah and Chedvi had continued on without him. They were walking toward the street, navigating around the giant puddles left by the heavy rain. "We returned from Paris yesterday. Chedvi was about to get engaged, and again they ruined it at the last minute. Evidently Nati Morgan, my father's former partner, is behind it."

"Nati Morgan! I sat with him a few days ago in a London cigar-smoker's club," said Felix. "He has longer hands than Pharaoh's daughter; they reach till Paris. Don't worry, Elitzafan, Nati's day of judgment is approaching. I built him a trap that he couldn't imagine. He's about to walk into it like a blind fox; you'll see."

"If only it will work," said Elitzafan, raising his eyes to the cloudy sky. "But don't be so sure of yourself. You're wonderful, Felix, but you're an innocent schoolboy compared to Nati."

Felix thrust the key into his door. "Even an innocent schoolboy like me can drive an elephant crazy."

"Elitzafan," called Devorah, "come say goodbye to Chedvi. The taxi is waiting."

Elitzafan left Felix and ran out to the sidewalk. "Take care of yourself," he told Chedvi, who was waiting in the back seat of the taxi. "And please don't be a daredevil. I forbid you to go alone to Amukah at night."

Chedvi laughed. "Amukah? I hadn't thought of going there even during the day. I want to sit in the cave in Meiron and say *Tehillim*."

"If so, fine. Travel safely and may Hashem watch over you and accept all your prayers."

"Amen, Abba," she answered fervently.

The taxi pulled away from the curb. Devorah sobbed a little. Elitzafan followed the taxi with tears in his eyes and whispered the words of the priestly blessing, "May Hashem bless you and protect you ..." until it was out of sight. A black sack seemed to envelop his heart.

🙥🙦

At four that afternoon, Felix went through the gates of the Elta plant in Ashdod. His friends welcomed him back from his brief absence with warm smiles. Pleasant and amicable, Felix was one of Elta's best-liked employees. His high-level position in ballistics and aeronautics had not made him arrogant, and his impeccable reliability had gained him access to closely guarded secrets.

Today, beneath the pleasant, smiling exterior, his nerves were on edge.

"I tell you, Evri, the more we give in to terror, the bolder the Arabs become. We have to be tough with them."

"Nothing can be done, Mordy. Even the United States can't operate against terror as it used to. Hey, here's our good friend Felix. When did *you* return?"

Felix hoped that his white-coated colleagues who brushed past him in the corridor would not hold him up. He exchanged friendly hellos with them, and then hurried away, muttering something about work that had piled up while he was away.

The magnetic card shook in his hand when he tried to pass it through the optical reader, but at last the door to his room eased open.

The room looked exactly as he had left it five days ago except for a few specks of dust on the desk and bookshelves; at his express request, the cleaning crew had not come in during his absence. Dozens of phone messages had been left on his answering machine. He listened to some.

Then he picked up the receiver and dialed. "Yes?"

"Yasha, this is Felix. I wanted to let you know that I've returned from abroad. I'm here at the plant. You can include me in the work schedule."

"Terrific!" exclaimed Yasha. "When did you get back?"

"Today."

"And you're here already? What a dedicated worker!"

Yasha Stashevsky was responsible for scheduling extra assignments in missiles and space systems.

"Wait a minute, I'm checking," said Yasha. Felix heard Yasha's radio playing in the background. "Nothing special today. Call me tomorrow morning and I'll fit you into the new schedule."

Felix hung up and turned on his computer. Because of his senior position in the plant, he had access to top-secret computer files. Months earlier, when the Arrow missile guidance software was completely updated, Felix had copied the old program onto his own computer. Now the time had come to reap the fruits. In the next few hours, Felix copied parts of the program directly to CDs, added other files, wrote, erased, changed, and edited.

At nine that evening, he put three identical sets of ten CDs into his attaché case and left his office. He was in high spirits when he said goodbye to the guard on the way out.

When Asher Klein studied Torah, the world ceased to exist for him. His parents had the unusual pleasure of arguing with him not to harm his health by spending overly long hours learning too much. He was capable of immersing himself in a sugyah for hours on end, ignoring basic needs like food and sleep, and certainly luxuries like chatting, reading, or listening to music. For Asher, the melody of Gemara study was the sweetest music, and the Gemara the most enthralling of books. A contented smile hovered permanently on his rosy lips, reflecting the inner joy of someone who loves what he does and does what he loves.

"Asher, you're twenty-four already," Peninah would remind him occasionally. "How long are you planning to wait?"

"Twenty-four is young," Asher would say nonchalantly. "What's the hurry?"

"That was true once. Societal conventions have changed. On the *shidduch* market, your rating goes down the older you get."

Asher would not argue. Instead, he would go to the bookcase, take out *Gemara Sotah,* and read aloud, "Forty days before the embryo is formed, a Heavenly voice rings out and says, 'The daughter of So-and-so is for So-and-so.'"

"An emendation must be made in the margin of the Gemara," Asher would declare with a smile. "'Today society's conventions have changed, and the Heavenly voice no longer rings out. Therefore if you don't hurry, you will never be able to get married.'"

Peninah would laugh, and the discussion would end until the next time.

When Asher became interested in an undertaking, he would not let it go until he had gotten to the bottom of it. Now he was involved in the riddle of Mr. Elitzafan Mindelman, who decades earlier had abruptly changed from merry to melancholy. Asher felt warm empathy for this devoted communal worker, who had evidently suffered greatly. The anguish in the man's eyes touched Asher's heart. Suddenly, without any rational explanation, Asher decided to drop in on him again. He hoped that this time, at nine in the evening, he would not be disturbing his host.

Asher was surprised to find a long line of people on the staircase waiting to consult Mr. Mindelman on a variety of issues. He took the last place in line.

At ten-thirty, the visitor ahead of him left. Asher entered the study and Elitzafan gave him a warm smile and said, "How are you, my young friend Asher Klein?"

Elitzafan was tired. Only yesterday he had returned from Paris and from the heartache of the *vort*. But the sight of his young visitor breathed new life into him. "It seems to me that we were in the middle of an interesting conversation when you came that afternoon." He spoke with a smile and a mischievous twinkle in his eyes.

"I'll continue from where we left off." Again Elitzafan smiled. A sudden joy came over him; he did not know why. "My father was a fascinating person...."

Elitzafan described his life as the pampered only child of a wealthy *charedi* arms dealer who divided his time between his office and the synagogue, where he prayed and studied Torah. His father held the views of a zealous extremist, at which his mother looked askance.

Now Elitzafan was no longer smiling. "I walked a tightrope between my parents until the disaster in Brazil's rain forest, following which my father was put on trial and sentenced to four years in prison. Although the trial took place behind closed doors, rumors spread through the street — and I was the victim. My friends began to keep their distance from me. From being one of the stars of the yeshivah, loved and respected by all, I turned into the miserable son of an outcast."

For a moment, Elitzafan was silent, and his Adam's apple bobbed up and down. A storm of emotion attacked him as suppressed memories rose to the surface. His voice broke.

"Everyone was talking about how my father betrayed his people and sold arms to their enemies. Can you imagine what it felt like?"

Unaware, Asher shed a tear. Elitzafan continued in a choked voice. "It snowballed from day to day. One said he was a drug dealer, another that he sold crosses to churches. A third claimed to have seen him eating in a *treif* restaurant. They turned him into a villain suspected of committing every sin in the Torah.

"I didn't know whom to believe. I knew my father as a fine, upstanding person, but three factors combined to weaken my trust in him. First, we never had a close relationship. He was an authoritative, demanding father who expected his son to excel in his studies. Second, my mother transmitted her negative opinion about him to me. She claimed his extreme views had caused him to sin. She was at hand, and I heard her words over and over, especially while he was away in jail. Third, I heard so many accusations against him that I began to believe some of them.

"The result was that I tried to distance myself from him. When my mother married Mr. Shimon Mindelman, I adopted his name. The name Portman had been disgraced. I wanted no part of it. My stepfather made this possible for me."

Elitzafan's eyes were closed, and his face was wet with tears. Asher felt very close to him at that moment.

Suddenly Devorah came into the study. Her face was pale. "Elitzafan, I've been trying to contact Chedvi all evening to find out how her trip was."

"And?" asked Elitzafan with a look of fear.

"There's no answer. Her cell phone is not on. Her hosts in the Meiron *moshav* don't answer either!"

Elitzafan grimaced and clutched his chest. "What I feared is coming true!"

"What happened?" asked Asher. "Can I help?"

For a moment Elitzafan and Devorah were silent. In their fright, they forgot they had a visitor. Elitzafan was the first to recover.

"Our daughter went to Meiron alone, and we've lost contact with her."

"How old is she?" asked Asher innocently.

"Twenty-five," said Elitzafan.

Devorah was aghast. How could he reveal her true age? He should have taken off two years at least!

Asher raised his eyebrows. How could they worry about an adult as if she were a small child?

"Excuse me," said Devorah. "We're entitled to worry when our daughter can't be reached." She turned around and left the study.

Asher tactfully rose to leave.

"Asher, wait a minute," said Elitzafan. He clasped his visitor's hand warmly. "We are simply worried for various reasons. My wife is a bit upset; don't hold it against her. Be in touch."

"When should I be in touch?" Asher stammered with an embarrassed smile, and straightened out his hat.

"Whenever you want," said Elitzafan emotionally. "My house is open to you day or night."

Asher felt Elitzafan's pain cutting into his own heart. Suddenly he longed to bind his fate to this tormented man. He blushed as he said, "Thank you."

☙❧

Elitzafan shuffled toward the bedroom. He found Devorah speaking on the phone.

"Rebbetzin Flora, my husband was right. She shouldn't have gone. I'm afraid she may have done something rash. Shall I bring a small bottle of oil and some wicks? But we were in France over Shabbos! Oh, new wicks?"

Devorah looked up and was startled by her husband's angry look. He grabbed the receiver.

"It's a pity you didn't remain in Paris forever. Charlatans like you, who take advantage of people's troubles to make money, should get their just desserts.

"Our daughter has disappeared, and you're convincing my wife to come to you with wicks at one o'clock in the morning? Whom are you trying to fool? You read wicks like I read chocolate.

"I knew this moment would come. Chedvi swallows more and more, but her soul is not a toy. You dragged us to Paris for nothing, gave her false hopes, and your bubble of lies burst." He groaned. "Now it seems she's had a breakdown. Who knows what she has done to herself!"

He was about to hang up, but the sounds issuing from the receiver caused him to put it back to his ear.

"Mr. Mindelman, do you hear me?" Flora spoke so quickly that he had to listen very carefully to understand what she was saying. "Our Sages said that a person is not blamed for what he says when he is suffering, so I forgive you completely for all the harsh words you've unjustly hurled against me. I operate only according to the Torah and Halachah and I fool no one. I gave you three airline tickets to Paris at my expense. I believed that François would become engaged to Chedvi, and the fact that your enemy ruined the *shidduch* at the last minute is not my fault. For several years I have served as your wife's life preserver. If not for the steady doses of encouragement that I give her once or twice a week, she would have been in a mental asylum long ago. Your daughter went to pray in Meiron, and for half a day her cell phone is off, and you lose your head."

The whole speech took seconds. Afterwards, as if nothing had happened, Flora asked to speak to Devorah again. Twenty minutes later, the two women had met and Devorah was watching her trying to read Chedvi's fate in the tiny flames of the burning wicks.

"Go to Meiron tomorrow morning," Flora said at last.

Devorah grabbed Flora's hand fearfully. "What do you see? Tell me only good things!"

"There are definitely no tragedies," said Flora. "But I would advise that your husband and you go there. Take all the girls." Flora did not react to Devorah's startled eyes. "The Holy One, blessed be He, longs for the prayers of the righteous. Your husband is a good man; he helps many people." Flora's voice was soft, without a trace of hard feelings or hurt.

When Devorah rose to leave, Flora told her warmly, "Take the Jordan Valley road. It will get you there faster."

❧

Elitzafan and Devorah had another sleepless night. Devorah said *Tehillim* in the kitchen; Elitzafan sat with an open Gemara. From time to time, they tried Chedvi's phone, but it was off. Imagination painted frightening pictures before Elitzafan's eyes.

With the first light of day, Elitzafan and Devorah *davened vasikin,* he in the *shtiebel* of Beis Yisrael, she at home. When they finished, Chedvi's phone was still not on, and she could not be reached in the *moshav* guest house either.

Elitzafan gave in to Rebbetzin Simchoni–Freilich's advice and hired a mini-van with a driver to take the family to Meiron. It was expensive, but at such a time, money was no object. Tirtzah, Leah'le, and Kreindy came along, and so did fifteen-year-old Nachum'ke.

The morning air was fresh, the skies clear blue as the van set out through the Judean hills. "There's nothing like a change from daily routine," said Elitzafan. The youngsters believed that they were all going to Meiron to pray that Hashem send Chedvi her life partner quickly. Elitzafan did not want to frighten them by revealing the real purpose of the trip.

There were few cars on the calm, smooth Jordan Valley road. The driver put on a quiet tape with Chassidic songs. All the Mindelmans dozed as the van rolled toward the Judean desert.

Elitzafan woke up suddenly in a cold sweat. He scanned his surroundings. They still had a long way to go. He wanted to close his eyes again, but something that he could not put his finger on disturbed him.

He turned around. A banged up Nissan pickup truck was tailing them. Remnants of paint testified that when it had come off the assembly line it had been white. Why was it tailing them? And weren't the driver and the two passengers Arabs?

A lone van on a quiet road could easily fall victim to a staged accident. *Weren't there warnings not to travel via the Jordan Valley road?* he asked himself with growing fear.

"Devorah, wake up," he whispered, careful not to spread panic in the van.

"What's the matter?" she whispered back with closed eyes.

"I suspect the car behind us has evil intentions."

Devorah opened her eyes briefly and cast a glance toward the Nissan. "Elitzafan, I think you need a tranquilizer. Lately you've been in a perpetual state of panic."

Elitzafan let her go back to sleep while he continued to keep an eye on the Nissan.

Suddenly Devorah sat bolt upright. Elitzafan's words had seeped into her consciousness. "Maybe you're right. Tell the driver."

"Hello," said Elitzafan.

"My name is Yitzchak," complained the driver. "I'm not Hello, understand?"

"Nice to meet you, Yitzchak. I'm Elitzafan. Listen, there seems to be a problem behind us. The car there is too close to us."

"I've been on the road for almost forty years," said Yitzchak. "You don't drive, right?"

"Correct."

"So let me tell you something. No one gets a license until he learns to notice what's happening on all sides of the car, not just the front. I saw this Nissan ten minutes ago. You're right that it's too close, but aside from that everything is in order."

Elitzafan was not relieved. Yitzchak would get high marks as a driver, but zero as a detective. The evil intentions of the men in the Nissan were obvious. Elitzafan opened his safety belt so that he could keep turning around to look back.

The distance between the two vehicles narrowed. Yitzchak, too, became suspicious. He slowed down. Although the opposite lane was empty, the Nissan did not try to pass. It, too, slowed down to a crawl, like the van in front of it.

The minivan reached a narrow part of the road. The Nissan let them move a little further ahead. Then, suddenly, it zoomed forward. In a desperate attempt to get out of the way, Yitzchak turned the wheel sharply to the right. Elitzafan was thrown to the left, and banged his shoulder painfully. The van screeched to a halt at the edge of the road. The Nissan slammed into it, bashing in the trunk.

Tirtzah, Leah'le, and Kreindy awoke in fright and screamed. Nachum'ke turned white as snow and said *Shema Yisrael*. Yitzchak's face, too, lost its color. "Elitzafan," he said in fright, "I apologize. You were right. They want to kill us."

As if to prove the truth of his words, the men in the Nissan looked at the Mindelmans with hostile eyes. They looked not like Arabs, Elitzafan decided, but like criminals. One was holding a pistol in his right hand and a picture in his left. He kept glancing from the picture to Elitzafan.

"Let's say *vidui*," said Yitzchak. "We're about to get a visa to *Gan Eden*." Then he wailed, "*Ribbono shel olam*, help us! I have a wife, children, and grandchildren. I promise that if I get out of here alive, I'll give a lot of money to charity!"

The Mindelmans, too, were sure this was the end.

The man with the pistol aimed it at Elitzafan, obviously relishing the fright he was giving the family.

Elitzafan, white as snow, said *vidui*. The driver was right. He was about to get a visa to *Gan Eden*.

The man with the pistol played cat and mouse with Elitzafan. Three times, he aimed at him. Each time, he compared the picture to the face of Elitzafan to make sure he had the right victim. The third time, he stuck the pistol as far out of the Nissan's window as his arm could reach, and his finger slowly closed around the trigger.

There was absolute silence. Desperately, Devorah looked around for help. There were no other cars on the road.

Suddenly the man with the pistol shouted to the driver, and the Nissan raced ahead. It disappeared from sight, leaving the Mindelmans and Yitzchak shivering from fear. The brush with death had lasted a minute or two but would remain with them for many years.

They got out of the van and walked to the side of the road. Elitzafan groaned in pain.

"*Baruch Hashem,* we escaped with our lives," muttered Yitzchak. He surveyed the van. "The insurance company will pay for the damage. But your husband," he said to Devorah, "seems to have a dislocated shoulder. We'll have to take him to the hospital."

"No," said Elitzafan, breathing heavily. "It's nothing. I can move my hand. We're continuing on to Meiron."

"As you wish," said Yitzchak. "We have experienced a major miracle. If I hadn't had the situation under control, some of us wouldn't be here now. We must inform the police before those terrorists try to kill someone else on the road."

"Terrorists? I don't think so," said Elitzafan. He turned to Devorah. "Who was it that advised you to go early in the morning to Meiron, and to use the Jordan Valley road?"

Devorah was speechless as she absorbed the implications.

"How did she put it — 'It will get you there faster.' The righteous Flora evidently meant that we would get to Heaven faster."

<hr>

Asaf and Malkiel were sitting in their room in the Sherlock Holmes Hotel, drinking tequila and playing cards. They were tied in knots from the tension. Would Felix manage to obtain the Arrow CDs? Would he bring them?

At midnight, the sounds of the Turkish March issued from Asaf's phone. He answered quickly, and a broad smile spread over his face. "It's him," he whispered to Malkiel. "What's happening, my friend?" he said into the phone.

"I have the CDs," said Felix simply.

"Are you out of your mind? Why do you mention the word?" cried Asaf. "Don't you have a code?"

"No one knows what we're talking about," said Felix calmly. "What's the problem with CDs? The whole world is full of them."

Asaf waved his hands in despair. Felix was brilliant in advanced science but stupid in ordinary prudence. "When will you be here?"

"At the moment I'm still home. Tomorrow morning I'll get on the plane. Meet me at the same place we met last time."

"Bravo, I see you've got some sense in you," said Asaf, in praise of Felix's newfound caution in speaking. "No problem. What time?"

"Seven in the evening, as you requested."

"Have you been to the bank in Tel Aviv?"

"How could I? I sat for hours with the CDs."

"Stop mentioning that word!" shrieked Asaf, his face purple. "Idiot! You're ruining everything!" He inhaled and waited a minute for his fury to subside. "In ten minutes, my branch manager will call and request the number of your bank account. Immediately afterwards, he will deposit $100,000 as an advance. The remaining $400,000 you will receive when you return to Israel, and the entire amount, as we made up, in two weeks, in whatever currency you wish — Sterling, Euro, dollars, yen, just choose."

"You know what?" Felix sounded very wary. "Never mind the advance. Give me the full amount when I return."

"Are you sure?" asked Asaf in surprise.

"One million percent. Tomorrow at seven p.m. the CDs will be in your hands."

Felix hung up quickly before Asaf unleashed a string of curses. Asaf was nervous and tense as a spring, and it was no wonder. Many millions depended on this deal.

Felix's next phone call was to Nati Morgan.

"Shalom, Nati," said Felix amicably when Nati's sleepy voice came over the phone. "I'm a good friend who met you in the Havana Club. Remember?"

Instantly Nati was fully alert and clear as a bell. "Of course I remember. What's new? Do you have the material?"

"Yes, all ten CDs, as we arranged."

"Evidently you haven't smoked a good cigar in a few days, so you've lost the remnant of your intelligence," Nati attacked him wrathfully. "Why do you have to mention that word?"

"Why is the word suddenly forbidden?" asked Felix calmly. "The whole world is full of CDs. You can't take a step without bumping into a pile of them."

"Are you trying to get me angry?" hollered Nati. "When are you delivering the goods?"

"Tomorrow night at ten I'll be in the club, with a box of Primo del Rey for a change. How does that sound?"

"I, too, like some variety once in a while. I'll bring along Henry Clay, from Havana, of course. Henry Clay Breva a la Conserva, to be more precise. Agreed?"

"Agreed."

"Just a minute. Doesn't the subject of money interest you? I closed on a price with you and I haven't changed my mind. Let me give you the phone number of my bank manager in Mexico, Señor Miguel Churchas. Make up with him when you want to fly to Mexico and get the money."

"Very good," said Felix laconically, as if he hadn't been tipped off about Señor Miguel Churchas.

ை෴

Felix's calls about the Arrow CDs touched off two celebrations.

In the Sherlock Holmes Hotel, Asaf and Malkiel threw pillows at each other. When they calmed down somewhat, they made plans for a rosy future. Asaf would shove Nati aside and take over Morgan Consolidated himself. Malkiel would be appointed Asaf's second-in-command. Their lives would turn into one big party.

In the Le Meridien, Nati uncorked a bottle of champagne. The scientist was opening new gates to tomorrow before him. Even the sky was not the limit.

"It's time to give Nati the daily report," Asaf told Malkiel.

"I hope I didn't wake you up, Nati."

"Not at all, I'm reading *The London Times* with a glass of champagne."

"And I have to stay in Paris and work like a dog," complained Asaf, hoping he sounded convincing. "I wanted to report in."

"I'm listening."

"All the groups are fine; our men are progressing toward their destinations without hindrance. But there are many complaints. The routes we chose are very rough.

"The redhead complains that he and Phillip went through hundreds of kilometers of muddy roads and nonstop rain instead of the short overland route in Kazakhstan by way of the Ost Ort Mountains, as they were promised. On the way to Turkmenistan, they passed through several forests that we didn't know about. They claim that, surrounded as they were by thick, damp vegetation, with the lofty treetops blocking the sun, they suffered from claustrophobia.

"Amit complained bitterly about going ten days without a shower. The twins nearly suffered frostbite on the train, and they were detained for a short while by inspectors of the UN and the IAEA in Kazakhstan. But as you foresaw, everything continued smoothly. Some higher-up in the UN accepted Iran's official explanation that she needs the uranium to produce cheap electricity."

"Didn't I tell you?" said Nati. Asaf could almost hear him smiling. "Looks like now no one will stop Iran from completing her first atom bomb."

"In short," Asaf summed up, "everything is going at the right pace, to my full satisfaction. Have a good night in London. How is the weather there?"

"Very cold and foggy."

"In Paris it's a little warmer, and now it's raining," said Asaf, relaying what Adam Dushman had told him half an hour earlier. "Good night and pleasant dreams, Nati."

"Good night to you, too, Asaf."

Nati finished the glass of champagne and fell asleep with a happy smile.

Four kilometers away, Asaf put down the phone and laughed. "Nati isn't what he used to be. Age has affected even that wily fox. He really believes that I'm in Paris. If he knew that tomorrow the CDs will be in my hands instead of his, he wouldn't be smiling."

"I'm still afraid of him," said Malkiel as he filled two big beer mugs. "You've forgotten whom we're dealing with."

"Don't spoil my mood." Asaf emptied the mug with a few gulps. "This time we have the advantage over him. He has no reason to know that we're not in Paris. All the boys are dancing to Teheran with uranium cylinders, and Adam Dushman is completely devoted to me."

"Let's hope. Maybe Adam Dushman, like us, has a dual allegiance."

❦

The big, high-ceilinged cave in Meiron was almost empty. The heaters suspended on the walls did little to relieve the bone-penetrating cold. Beside the iron gate around the grave of Rabbi Shimon bar Yochai, a middle-aged woman with a smile, reading glasses, and two head coverings was chanting *Tehillim* softly. Chedvi liked Brachah immediately. She brought over a chair and sat down beside her.

Elitzafan had decided that his daughter was at the point of no return, but his interpretation had been wrong. Chedvi was not depressed or embittered.

Each person has his own life schedule determined by the Creator, and she would tread, unpressured, in her own route.

Recently, though, she had felt spasms in her soul. Perhaps it was jealousy of her married friends, several of whom had celebrated the *chalakah* of their firstborn sons in Meiron. Of her whole seminary class, only three were still single. One of them was suffering from a chronic illness, and she, Chedvi, was suffering from a skeleton in the family closet. Why did she have to pay for what her grandfather had done? But that was the way of the world. Once a label was stuck to you, there was no getting rid of it.

"Where's your *bitachon*, Chedvi?" she chided herself. "Heaven has assigned you a portion of suffering. When it's filled to the brim, your salvation will come in a twinkling."

Now Chedvi had decided to take action. She entered the cave firmly resolved to stay until the gates of mercy opened. Whether it took two days, a week, or even longer, she was going to nullify the evil decree.

She considered whether to shut her cell phone and decided not to. Her parents would worry if she didn't answer. But the phone didn't have to be conspicuous; it could be in her pocketbook.

There, unseen, the words "no service" appeared on the screen because the cave's thick walls blocked reception. But Chedvi never so much as glanced at the phone.

She set down her flight bag, which held three packs of crackers and two bottles of mineral water, took out her *Tehillim*, and began saying chapter after chapter, slowly, with concentration. Two sweaters and a winter coat, spread over her like a blanket, protected her from the cold; but the main warmth came from the *Tehillim*. Chedvi focused on King David's immortal words and forgot the rest of the world.

Even on an ordinary winter day, Meiron is not deserted. Women old and young, singly and in groups, came to pray and left. Only three figures did not move: the old woman, the woman with two head coverings, and Chedvi.

She finished the entire *Tehillim* without a break after almost three hours. Now was the right time to make her own requests. She began to pray and to entreat, but her heart was heavy. She felt that her prayer was not yet ripe; she still had a long road ahead. She took a short break, ate a few crackers, and drank two cups of water.

Someone who seemed to be in charge approached Chedvi and gently touched her arm. "*Shalom,* I'm Miriam," she said. "There's free food downstairs for people who come to pray here. Go have some salad, kugel, or fruit. Why eat only dry crackers?"

"Thank you, but I'm fine."

"Are you sure?" Miriam eyed her with a worried look. "It's very cold here at night. Why not drink some hot tea?"

"I want to finish all of *Tehillim* three times," said Chedvi.

"But by the time you finish, everything will be closed. Meiron in the winter is not like on Lag B'Omer, *mamma'le.* You'll be hungry and thirsty until morning."

Chedvi shrugged.

Miriam looked at her curiously. She saw a lovely girl in her mid-twenties whose soul radiated outward and lit up her face. Her eyes betrayed an inner anguish. Sometimes you have to let such a person afflict himself in order to ease the pain.

"Okay, my *tzaddekes,* say your *Tehillim.*"

Chedvi started the second time. After sixty chapters, she was overcome by exhaustion. Only thirty-six hours earlier she was still in Paris, and since then she had slept very little. Now her eyes closed and her head drooped — but her fingers refused to let the *Tehillim* go. From time to time her grasp weakened. Then she would immediately clutch the book in her sleep, like a drowning person clutching a life preserver.

Two hours later she awoke to hear Brachah chanting *Tehillim.* For a moment she was confused. *Where am I?* she wondered. *Why am I sleeping in a chair?*

She quickly remembered and wanted to resume her own *Tehillim,* but fatigue weighed her down like a lead blanket. She tried to fall asleep, but the melody enchanted her. She listened carefully.

Suddenly she recalled the righteous elderly widow who had joined them for Shabbos meals when Chedvi was little. She, too, had chanted *Tehillim* in the same captivating melody.

A wave of nostalgia washed over her. Memories came to life, clear as if they had happened yesterday. The pictures ran through her mind like a film on high speed.

Her first shoes, her first day in school…. Third grade… sixth grade. Always accompanied by her best friend, Betty, who had come from America barely able to speak a word of Hebrew. How they had played, laughed, quarreled, and shared secrets together! Today Betty lives in the Negev with her husband and three children.

She continued to remember and to bleed.

In her mind's eye, Chedvi saw the Mindelman family walking to Rechaviah for their one and only visit to Saba Portman. Why had her warm, loving father acted like a stranger toward *his* father?

Her whole life ran before her: the beautiful moments, the disappointments, the crises.

With a shiver of expectation, she had entered the world of *shidduchim*. Everyone had been sure that she would soon be engaged to a wonderful boy. Then the blows began to land one after another. If the *shidduch* saboteur did not nip the *shidduch* in the inquiry stage, he ruined it before the *vort*, as with Shmuli Patankin and François Feldman.

Someone once said that David did not compose *Tehillim,* nor did he say it. He ached it, he screamed it. Chedvi opened her *Tehillim* and wept with the words. The sobs burst out with irrepressible force, like water from a broken dam.

To Chedvi's embarrassment, the weeping intensified. She tried to hide it, but wellsprings of sorrow and pain gushed from her broken heart. She recalled what she had told Kreindy just the previous evening: "So next time your heart is sad, dear Kreindy, take your pain up a level and direct it to Heaven. Cry because Hashem is in pain. Cry because Hashem is sad that we remember Him only in distress and forget Him when things go well." But Chedvi's pain was so great that she could not carry out her own instructions.

She wept bitterly, casting off a sea of sorrow, disappointments, frustrations, aches, and rejections. How many times had hope begun to sprout, only to be destroyed? Her emotions erupted from the depths of her soul like millions of tons of boiling lava erupting from a volcano.

Suddenly a compassionate hand caressed her wet cheek. Brachah removed her glasses, looked at Chedvi with clear, kind eyes, and waited quietly for her to calm down. When Brachah saw that the weeping was only intensifying, she intervened. "Enough, Chedvah, calm down," she whispered. "It's forbidden to cry that much."

With concerted effort, Chedvi stopped herself. "Do you know how much I ache?"

"I can just imagine," whispered Brachah, handing her a pack of tissues. "I, too, once wept very much in Meiron. I didn't have children. I came, prayed, and wept."

Chedvi silently absorbed Brachah's words. Then she asked, "And what happened?"

"I never had children," Brachah replied with calm resignation. "That is my lot. I've accepted the will of my Creator. I understand a little about tears and prayers, and I am absolutely confident that these prayers of yours have not gone to waste. Soon you will find your partner in life."

"First you knew my name, now you also know what I'm praying for," said Chedvi with an embarrassed smile. Shudders of weeping still shook her body every few seconds.

Brachah smiled gently and poured a cup of hot tea from a thermos into a disposable cup. "In the eight hours I've been sitting beside you, I've heard you ask dozens of times for a *shidduch* for Chedvah bas Devorah. You have a beautiful soul; it shows. Give me a hand and let's take a little stroll together through your life. I think you won't regret it."

There was a captivating simplicity and innocence about this humble woman, who was so different from the fast-speaking know-it-all Rebbetzin Simchoni–Freilich.

Chedvi opened up and spoke. She finished shortly before dawn.

Brachah was deeply moved. "Listen to me. With Hashem's help, you will get engaged very soon. I didn't see it in Heaven, but I felt that tonight you shook worlds."

"There was already a Rebbetzin who promised me such things," said Chedvi bitterly, and she told her about Flora.

"I don't want to judge someone I don't know," said Brachah pleasantly. "I am a simple woman. But I know that prayer from the depths of the heart is accepted, and I, too, can bless you from the depths of my heart…"

Her voice grew stronger, and her eyes closed tightly, making a web of delicate wrinkles in the corners.

"…that your prayers will be accepted and you will soon find your partner in life — a good, Heaven-fearing boy — and you will build a faithful house in Israel."

"Amen," answered Chedvi fervently, as warm tears streamed from her eyes.

Chedvi felt that this blessing, uttered in this holy place before dawn, a time of grace, dislodged her destined *chasan* from his hiding place. She had received her salvation.

Now she was free to return to her hosts in the Meiron *moshav* and sleep normally in a bed. Or was she? No, it was out of the question. She mustn't wake people up at such an hour. She would stay here until after *Shacharis*.

Chedvi went out to the courtyard to stretch her legs. She walked under the slowly lightening skies. She heard the chirp of the early-rising birds, and imagined she could hear them singing, "*Avinu Malkeinu*, our Father our King, open the gates of Heaven to our prayers."

Tonight, the gates of Heaven had opened for her.

47

The loudspeaker had already announced his flight, but Felix, calm and relaxed, continued to read on a bench in Ben Gurion Airport. Beside him rested his flight bag, with its two plastic boxes of ten CDs, a gift of computer games for his young nephews in London. His demeanor was completely calm and reserved, as if the whole State of Israel would not have turned upside down had anyone discovered one of its top scientists taking top-secret information out of its borders.

He remained calm even after the four-hour flight, when Asaf and Malkiel arrived at his suite in the Victoria Park Plaza at seven that evening. Unlike him, they were excited and happy about the event that would open the gates of wealth to them.

"And now, the demo," announced Asaf, when Felix presented them with the set of CDs. "Forgive me for being suspicious, but how do we know this is not a trick? I don't believe anyone, not even the nicest, most honest person in the world."

"I think your request is entirely legitimate," agreed Felix. "I never dreamt of giving you the CDs without presenting their contents to you one by one."

He took his laptop computer out of the safe, plugged it into the socket, and turned it on. Two minutes later, the flat crystal screen filled with bluish lights.

He inserted the first CD of the series into the drive. A line of letters appeared on the screen: "The program is checking whether the computer is approved."

Two seconds later, the computer beeped to indicate an error, and a new line appeared: "The computer is not approved." Then the screen went dark.

"What?" hollered Asaf. "You flew here without checking what you were bringing along?"

"Patience," murmured Felix calmly. "Do you think Israel's most classified program can be viewed by just anyone? Obviously there must be a series of passwords to keep undersirables out. I removed all but two, in case the program fell into the wrong hands. Now you will learn how to neutralize them."

He shut down the computer and then turned it on again. When it started to reboot, he pressed a key to enter the BIOS, which specifies the computer's hardware. After changing a number of parameters, he announced solemnly, "Now I have neutralized the first line of defense. With your permission, I will shut down and boot up again."

A small red light flickered in the computer when he booted up again. Felix put the CD back in. He was right. This time the line, "The program is checking whether the computer is approved," did not appear.

"The program must recognize the computer," said Felix coolly. "If it doesn't, the CDs won't work."

Asaf's thick thumb dug into his chin as he digested this important piece of information. "That means that if we take the CDs as they are, we might as well throw them into the garbage."

"Of course," said Felix as enthusiastically as a proud father. "But if I give you the parameters that I just typed into the BIOS screen, you, too, will be able to adapt these discs to any computer."

He handed them pages of instructions that he had typed before leaving Israel.

"What are these?" asked Asaf.

"Forty-seven procedures," replied Felix, "that must be carried out in order to neutralize the defenses."

"Are you making fun of me?" Asaf fumed. "I don't know anything about computers."

Malkiel browsed through the papers. "Easy as pie," he said enthusiastically. "Even I can do it."

"You're deluding yourself," said Asaf angrily. He grabbed the papers from Malkiel and kneaded them into a ball. "I'm about to pay you an astronomical fee, and you can't even give me a finished product?"

For the first time, Felix no longer looked calm and indifferent. He was obviously frightened. His hands shook as he tried to straighten out the papers.

"Leave them alone!" hollered Asaf. "I want something without any defenses and passwords. My friend, you will give me your computer!"

"I have many programs on it without backups," whispered Felix, white-lipped.

"You should have thought of that before." Asaf's thick lips opened wickedly. "Your portable computer goes with me. But first neutralize the second password."

Felix did not reply. He was shaking all over. He attacked the small computer with open arms as if he were about to choke it. For three minutes, his fingers danced expertly over the keys. His eyes did not leave the screen for a second. When he finished, he noted with satisfaction, "Okay, the computer and its programs are at your disposal. There are no defenses, no passwords, everything is exposed like a bank safe after a visit from Houdini."

Asaf and Malkiel were thrilled. They expressed their satisfaction with hearty slaps that made Felix's shoulder ache.

"And now," Asaf demanded, "let's see how the Arrow works."

Felix applied himself to the computer like a violinist merging with his violin.

Suddenly a voice issued from the computer, "The Arrow program is preparing the demonstration."

Short filmstrips of the most recent experiments with the Arrow appeared on screen, showing how the Arrow hones in on the attacking missile and destroys it. Next came a simple, understandable explanation of how all the Arrow systems operate: warning radar and fire control developed by Elta, Tadiran's fire control system, Israeli Aircraft Industries' launch control center as well as its operating launcher and missiles.

"We've seen all that already," said Malkiel scornfully as he peeled the plastic wrapper from a pack of chewing gum, which he generously offered to Asaf and Felix.

Felix declined politely as he changed the CDs in the drive. "Now the real thing is starting," he said with satisfaction.

Without taking his eyes off the screen, Asaf scooped up a handful of gum sticks and thrust them all into his mouth.

"Now you will get everything you want." Felix exuded satisfaction. "The Arrow is entirely before you, from the first sketch down to the last screw. All the secrets, codes, and weak points, how it hones in on attacking missiles and locates mock missiles, and how to fool it or make it deviate from its path."

Felix put in one CD after another. Asaf and Malkiel watched, enthralled, for two hours straight as the entire Arrow program was demonstrated before them. They saw sketches and photographs of all its parts, from the nose to the end of the tail. All its secrets were exposed.

After the tenth CD was viewed to the end, Asaf hooted triumphantly, "The Arrow is in our hands! You're worth every penny I invested in you!" He whipped out a signed check. "You didn't want an advance, but I decided to surprise you. Here is a check for $500,000. Do with it as you please."

"I don't believe it." Felix took the check and read the amount in amazement. "Unbelievable," he muttered again and again.

"When we return, you'll get the rest!" Asaf almost broke into a dance with the pack of CDs. The two of them had done the unbelievable: They had managed to lay hands on one of Israel's most closely guarded secrets. "Malkiel, we're setting out tonight for Dubai."

When they stood near the door, Felix looked at them over his glasses with a typical academic expression. "You forgot something," he noted dryly, pointing toward the portable computer on the table.

Asaf hurried back. "Oops, how did I forget the main thing? Nonsense, I would have remembered in the elevator." He turned the computer off and packed it into his case. "The operating instructions are in the case," said Felix. "Easy enough for a three-year-old."

Asaf shook a finger at Felix and said, "This time I'll forgive you."

The door slammed closed behind them. They took the elevator down to the lobby carrying an innocent-looking attaché case. Asaf's private jet was waiting for them, fueled and ready to go. The pilot needed only the name of the destination.

Dubai in the United Arab Emirates.

Felix had no time to even smile mockingly toward the closed door. The CEO of Morgan Consolidated was waiting impatiently for his call.

❦

The Mindelmans returned from Meiron tired, hungry, and thirsty. Devorah fried eggs for everyone, Tirtzah quickly prepared a salad, Leah'le sliced some bread, and Kreindy set the table.

"Why didn't you call?" asked Devorah when they sat down to eat.

"To tell the truth, I forgot the whole world," Chedvi confessed. "Only this morning I realized that the cell phone hadn't rung at all. At that point I wanted to call you, but I didn't want to disturb the family at six in the morning."

"Exactly when we left Jerusalem," said Elitzafan.

"At seven-thirty in the morning, I went to my hosts in the Meiron *moshav*. I stretched out on the bed and slept like the dead for four hours," said Chedvi. "When I woke up, I went back to the cave, and there you all were, looking as if you had just come out of the Holocaust. Your eyes were full of fear and worry, and Abba was rubbing his shoulder in pain."

"That's because of what happened to us on the Jordan Valley road," said Tirtzah bitterly.

After the meal, Elitzafan put up a sign on the door saying, "We are not receiving people this evening. Please do not disturb," and they all got ready for bed.

Despite the sign, there were firm knocks at the door. Nachum'ke opened it. "Abba, they've brought you registered mail and want you to sign."

A ponytailed mailman handed Elitzafan the letter in return for his signature. Instinctively, Elitzafan looked for the return address. There was none.

Something about the letter sent chills up his spine. He took it into the bedroom. Devorah followed him in and closed the door.

Hands trembling, he tore opened the envelope. A folded piece of paper covered with handwritten block letters fell out.

Dear Mr. Elitzafan Mindelman,

On the Jordan Valley road today, I gave you a small demonstration of what I can do. How does it feel to look into the barrel of a pistol? Have you recovered?

Do you want to know who has been sabotaging Chedvi's shidduchim for the past six years? It is I!

You are in my hands for better or worse. I know every step that you take. I hear you speak; I almost hear you think.

How is Menashe? Have you spoken to him in yeshivah lately? He should stop chatting so much during second seder.

I can restore the shidduchim that went awry. If you do what I tell you, soon Chedvi will marry a young man whom you very much want; you can guess whom I mean. Two days from now I will send you a document. Sign it, and you will soon dance at Chedvi's wedding. If you don't sign, I will make sure that none of your seven children will ever be able to get married. Think it over.

Yours truly.

"Devorah, are you okay?"

Her cheeks were drawn, her eyes were rolled back, and her breathing was rapid and shallow. A ghastly voice said, "Elitzafan, this is the end. Let's write a will."

"Why do you talk like that?"

The blush of life returned to her face. "We thought our situation was tough, but this letter proves that it can be much worse."

"What if it is your Rebbetzin Simchoni–Freilich?"

Devorah got angry. "Don't suspect the innocent, Elitzafan! Flora is perhaps not your idea of a Rebbetzin, but she is no criminal. The author of this letter is undoubtedly Nati Morgan, or one of his colleagues, like Asaf Niv. Only they could make such low threats and gloat over other people's suffering!"

Elitzafan sighed. "A pity he didn't send the document. I could have signed tonight and been finished with this nightmare."

"Why do you think signing will help?" said Devorah. "Nothing stops him from continuing to torment us for his own sadistic pleasure. I feel the angel of death standing behind the door, waiting for us."

"Stop," said Elitzafan. "Remember how hard we prayed and how many tears we shed in Meiron? Nothing is more powerful than prayer, and the gates of tears were never locked."

Devorah brightened up a bit. "Oh," she said suddenly, "I forgot that I left the kitchen a mess."

She hurried out of the bedroom to find the table spotless, the dishes washed, and the floor swept. The girls had cleaned up. But in the living room, the scene was heart-rending. The girls and Nachum'ke were sitting around the table tearfully saying *Tehillim*. Tirtzah had listened at the bedroom door and reported back to the rest.

The Mindelman home was filled with fear of the unknown enemy who knew everything about them.

☙❦❧

At noon, Yasha Stashevsky checked the work schedule. An urgent task had come up. All the CDs and documents that were past the expiration date, including some top secret ones, had to be fed to the shredder. For such work, he needed someone as trustworthy as Felix. Perfect! Only yesterday Felix had told him he was available.

He dialed Felix's office, and when there was no answer, he left a message on his answering machine: "Felix, this is Yasha. At four this afternoon, before you return to Jerusalem, you have a two-hour shredding project. Please confirm."

Felix did not get back to him.

At three, Yasha was nervous and angry. An urgent task had to be carried out, and he still had no one to do it. He called Felix's office again. Again there was no answer.

Yasha immediately contacted the director of the shift and asked him where Felix was.

The director of the shift looked into the matter and learned that Felix had not appeared at the plant that day — despite the fact that he had just returned to work after a five-day absence. Strange. Felix was anything but flighty. A worker as meticulous and dedicated as he was hard to find. They called his house and his cell phone, but there was no answer on either.

The director of the shift informed the assistant manager. That same evening, an urgent meeting was held in the management office. In a security-sensitive place, any hint of suspicious behavior is enough to erode trust in even the most reliable employee. Felix had done something foolish, and the result was quick in coming. He was marked "suspicious."

They searched for him everywhere without success. He had cut off all contact. As a last-ditch effort, they checked the lists of people who had left the country in the past twenty-four hours. The name Felix Goldmark appeared beside his destination: London.

he Havana Club is not the ideal place for exchanging discreet information tonight, thought Felix as he strode toward Nati's table. The place was packed, and the only vacant seat was the armchair that Nati was holding for his guest. Even Nati had unexpected company. A broad shouldered fellow with a pockmarked face leaned backwards and puffed gray jets of smoke into Felix's face.

Nati smiled apologetically. "How are you, Felix? We have a distinguished guest, Mr. Harry Falls, one of the senior weapons authorities of the United States. Harry, meet Professor Felix Goldmark, one of Israel's most distinguished scientists and a world expert in the field of ballistics."

"Pleased to meet you." Harry extended a rough hand and gave a firm handshake. "I expected to do business here tonight, but I understand that you've come to see Nati, so I won't disturb you. I'll be leaving soon."

Nati smiled sweetly. "When Harry says, 'I'll be leaving soon,' he means in half an hour. Right, Harry?"

Harry burst into laughter. "Quite true. Would you care for one of my cigars?"

"No thanks," said Felix, "I brought my own." He set a box down on the table.

"Primo del Rey. I see you have class," Harry said admiringly. He turned the box over and looked at the bottom. "Yes, you know what to buy. Ordinary smokers fall for the seal *hecho a mano*, which means that the cigar is hand-finished. You get *totalmente a mano*, which means that the cigar is hand-made from beginning to end. Where did you buy them? Surely at Davidoff, from Edward Shakian."

"You will be surprised to hear not. I decided to try the cigar department at Harrod's."

"Nati, you really know who to make friends with. Tell me, Professor Goldmark, which American president was an avid cigar smoker?"

"Five of them were," Felix shot back immediately: "The fourth president, James Madison; the sixth, John Quincy Adams; the seventh, Andrew Jackson; the twelfth, General Zachary Taylor; and especially the eighteenth, Ulysses S. Grant, who almost never appeared without a cigar in his mouth or his hand.

"And while we're discussing history, let me point out that the Prince of Wales smoked cigars, to the chagrin of his mother, Queen Victoria. In 1901, at a state dinner after his coronation as King Edward the Seventh of England, he made an announcement that changed the face of his country: 'Gentlemen, you may smoke!'

"So what mark do you give me in history?"

"One hundred," answered Harry bemused. "Nati, I like your friend."

"I see that," replied Nati with a sour face. He whispered to Felix in Hebrew, "He's a real nuisance. I'll give him another two minutes, and then if he doesn't leave by himself, I'll send him out with a powerful kick."

Nati turned to Harry, "Now I'll tell you something, and with that we'll conclude our meeting. Mark Twain normally smoked three hundred cigars a month, but he got to double that amount while writing *The Adventures of Tom Sawyer*. And now, my friend, be gone post haste."

Felix was shocked by Nati's way of speaking, but the two old chums were accustomed to each other. Harry left on a friendly note, promising that he would gladly return should Nati feel bored.

"Where's the merchandise?" Nati asked impatiently as soon as he and Felix were alone at the table.

"Right here in the black case," said Felix, pointing toward the floor. "Don't tell me you want a demo here and now."

Nati chuckled. "No, I didn't think you would expose the material right here. In any case, I don't need any demo. I have my own ways of checking the material even without your help."

"Excellent, sir. If so, I can leave." Felix began to get up.

"In principle, yes, although a certain matter is still open between us." Nati winked. "Are you releasing the material without payment? Take the business card of my bank manager, Señor Miguel Churchas. But I don't want you to leave empty-handed now. Here, take this box with you."

Smiling, he handed Felix an expensive, ornately carved wooden cigar box with a small lock, beside which dangled a tiny gold-plated key on an antique chain. "This box was sold in its time at a public auction of Christie's, but the cigars that were in it were smoked long ago. Open it."

Felix complied. Instead of twenty-five long, fat cigars, the box now contained a plastic bag through which dozens of large, polished diamonds sparkled.

"This package is worth half a million dollars," said Nati, his cigar resting in a corner of his mouth. "You have no reason to regret having met me."

A pack of cards suddenly appeared in his hands. "Harry, you can come back," he called out to his friend, who was standing and chatting with a group of smokers.

Holding the box firmly in his hand, Felix left the club, hailed a taxi, and returned to his hotel. In his pocket was Asaf's check, and in his hand Nati's diamonds. Everything had been well planned, but leaving London with a million dollars was a surprise development.

Had Felix looked behind him, he would have noticed a blue Pontiac following his taxi. When he got out of the taxi, the name Victoria Park Plaza on the elegant façade reminded him of cigar-hating Queen Victoria. He chuckled at the irony of it all: precisely in the hotel bearing her name, he had made deals with the help of cigars. His thoughts distracted his attention from two slim young fellows with bleached hair who were following him.

When he entered his suite, one of them said into the sleeve of his blazer, "He went into his hotel room. When should we act?"

After receiving the answer from a tiny earphone stuck into his ear, he gave his friend a barely perceptible hand signal, and the two disappeared — for now.

⊱✿⊰

Elitzafan and Devorah went through another difficult night. They jumped at every sound. The discovery that someone knew every detail of their lives banished any peace of mind left.

In the morning, Elitzafan called Yeshivah Kol B'ramah and asked to speak with Menashe Mindelman.

Elitzafan waited tensely. More than ten minutes passed before Menashe came to the phone.

"*Shalom*," said Menashe at last.

"What happened to you, Menashe?" asked Elitzafan worriedly. "Where were you? Are you all right?"

"Healthy and well, *baruch Hashem*. I was sleeping, that's all. They looked for me everywhere except in my room."

"Still sleeping — at eight-thirty?"

"I went to sleep at three o'clock in the morning."

"And what's doing in second *seder*?"

"Everything is as usual."

"Is it true that you chat with your *chavrusah* during *seder* instead of learning?"

Menashe started stammering.

"I expect you to pull yourself together on all fronts," Elitzafan concluded with a heavy heart.

He turned to Devorah, who was late leaving for work. "Menashe is not doing as well as he should be. But what bothers me even more is the fact that whoever wrote that anonymous letter knows everything about us. How did he know that Menashe chats with his *chavrusah*? How do we know that a sniper's gun is not aimed at his head at this very moment?"

"Let's not become paranoid," laughed Devorah, slinging her pocketbook over her shoulder. "There are many ways of finding out what Menashe does in yeshivah. It's not a well-kept secret. The letter writer is trying to frighten us with cheap tactics.

"I've been thinking about his tactics," she continued. "Registered mail is not delivered at night. The man who brought the letter was a mailman like I'm a mailman. Next time he comes, we have to follow him and find out who sent him."

Then, with head up and a smile on her face, she left for work.

During the next two days, the level of fearful tension in the Mindelman home rose and fell. Then, close to midnight, the ponytailed "mailman" returned. He silently presented them with a sealed envelope and requested a signature.

Elitzafan tried to follow him, but his shoes made noise on the stairs. The "mailman" quickened his pace and disappeared from sight.

Defeated, Elitzafan returned to his apartment. "I'm not much of a detective," he told Devorah.

He opened the envelope and found the following note:

Please sign the attached document, put it in the envelope, and return it to the messenger when he comes back in half an hour.

The attached document said:

I, Elitzafan Mindelman, formerly Portman, relinquish my entire share in the estate that my father, Mr. Avraham Zeidel Portman, bequeathed me in his will. I have no claims or arguments against the heir, whose name at this time is not revealed.

Elitzafan gasped. With one signature, he would forfeit a fortune. His father had been very wealthy. In addition to the apartments in Rechaviah and Tiberias, he had real estate holdings, stocks, and bonds. On the other hand, with this one signature maybe Elitzafan would acquire peace of mind. Perhaps Chedvi would finally be able to get engaged.

A flash of lightning suddenly exploded in his mind, turning into myriads of white lights that pricked his brain and tickled every sleepy cell. Why hadn't he thought of it before? "I know who he is!" he roared like a wounded lion. "I know who's behind it all!"

⌘

In contrast to cold, rainy Europe, the Persian Gulf principality of Dubai was hot and dry from the fierce sun.

Two figures in sunglasses emerged from their rented Rolls-Royce and disappeared into an arched entrance that bore the flowing Arabic letters of the name Emir Abd al-Aziz ibn Muhammad in colorful mosaic tiles. The two walked through a huge courtyard filled with spacious lawns, beautiful flower gardens, water fountains, and small ponds in which exquisite tropical fish swam. They could not see behind the palace to the garage with its fleet of Rolls-Royces, the Olympic-size swimming pool that reflected the sun's blinding rays, or, even further away, the clean stable where well-groomed purebred Arabian stallions awaited the riding pleasure of the hedonistic Emir.

The door opened. A white-uniformed servant led them inside the opulent palace. Here the cultures of past and present, East and West, blended. Persian carpets, wall niches, arabesques, arched windows, smoking corners with nargilehs and backgammon sets coexisted with the Italian marble floor, crystal-and-gold chandeliers, armchairs covered in leopard fur, and ivory telephones.

"We were not mistaken when we put all our eggs into the Saudi basket," Asaf whispered to Malkiel.

The servant led them through a cream-colored corridor scented by roses in clear flasks hanging from the ceiling in a gold holder. Then he unlocked a steel door and brought them into the Emir's office.

A short man with many chins, wearing an expensive three-piece Western suit, was sitting beside two large computer screens. Emir ibn Muhammad lived in Dubai, where he had oil wells, but that was a convenient cover for his top-level position in Saudi Arabia's secret service.

He greeted them with a smile and gestured toward a pair of deep armchairs. "Please be seated." They sank into the soft upholstery with pleasure, leaned back, and inhaled the cool air scented with refreshing mint.

"You have brought the merchandise," said Emir ibn Muhammad, half asking, half stating.

Asaf waved the small case. "This case contains the personal computer of the scientist who developed the Arrow missile. The first of the ten CDs is already in the drive, ready for a demonstration. Would you like to see it?"

The Emir gave them an icy look. "No, I understand nothing about missiles and ballistics. For that I have two top-notch scientists, Nikolai Zubakin of the Leningrad University and Jacques Nidam of the Sorbonne, who was one of the builders of Iran's Shihav missiles."

"I await them eagerly," said Asaf, rubbing his huge palms together in anticipation.

The Emir typed something on the keyboard. The second screen, which until then had merely displayed the colorful screensaver, came to life. Two pictures appeared on it.

"This is a live conference call," announced the Emir. He pointed to a small video camera hanging on the opposite wall. "Professor Zubakin and Professor Nidam, good morning to each of you."

The professors nodded. Professor Nidam spoke English with a pronounced French accent. "*Bonjour.* Are these the two Israelis?"

"Correct," said the Emir with satisfaction. "They have brought the CDs, which I will present on the portable computer of the Israeli scientist who sold them. I will use my camera for a closeup picture. You will be able to see everything."

Asaf started the computer as Felix had taught him. The CDs worked flawlessly.

While Asaf was showing the second one, Professor Zubakin suddenly stopped him. He asked to see the sketches of the missile again and again.

When Asaf showed the third CD, Professor Nidam was very vocal and asked to see the motors five times.

Asaf was about to load the fourth CD when a shout from Professor Zubakin stopped him. "Enough! This is nothing more than a conglomeration of nonsense."

"What?!" gasped Asaf.

Professor Nidam entered the picture. "I heartily concur with my Russian colleague."

The blood drained out of Asaf's round face. "What are you talking about? It's the most up-to-date version of the Arrow!"

"Nonsense!" thundered Professor Zubakin. "It's a combination of several scenarios that were rejected. I recognized a few characteristics of the Patriot missiles. In addition, the diameter of the motor is out of proportion to the tail wings. Someone has tricked you."

"I agree with every word of my honorable colleague," the French scientist confirmed with a serious face. "It is indeed a brilliant creation, a cross-breeding of the Arrow and the Patriot, but it is all deception. The wool has been pulled over your eyes."

The blood that had previously drained from Asaf's face now returned to flood it with bright red. "I don't believe it, Malkiel. Felix tricked us!"

The scientists disappeared from the computer screen, and the screensaver took their place. The Emir spread his arms out theatrically and said, "Sorry, I do not pay for garbage."

At the press of a button, a white-uniformed servant appeared to escort Asaf and Malkiel out of the palace.

Asaf gnashed his teeth as he started the rented Rolls Royce. "Felix will pay for this with his life."

Malkiel agreed. "His behavior is totally dishonorable! There isn't a shred of decency in him."

Asaf pressed down on the gas pedal with all his might. The car leaped to the road like a launched missile.

"Our revenge will be sweet as honey," said Asaf. He kept his foot on the gas pedal. The speedometer recorded 160 kilometers per hour, and the scenery flew past them at high speed.

"Hey, what's that?"

A few meters ahead, a police car blocked the road. Asaf eased off the gas pedal and transferred the full force of his weight to the brakes, which emitted a frightening screech. The Rolls-Royce stopped short just before the roadblock.

Two dark-skinned policemen approached Asaf. "Sir, may I see your pilot's license?" one of them asked serenely.

Asaf writhed in his seat and clutched his neck. "I'm in terrible pain," he groaned. "I'm rushing to the emergency room."

The policeman spoke politely but firmly. "First you will come with us to the police station. Your license is hereby revoked."

"What is this?" hollered Asaf. "I'm a diplomat. I'll lodge a complaint with the Foreign Minister, and you'll be fired."

Asaf's threats failed to move the policemen. Steel handcuffs were placed on the wrists of the two arms dealers, and they were unceremoniously thrown into an armored vehicle with bars on the windows.

The two were frightened. In liberal Dubai, speeders were not punished so severely. Something strange was afoot.

Out of earshot of Asaf and Malkiel, the "policeman" spoke on the phone. "Emir ibn Muhammad, they are in my hands! I had an excuse for arresting them: excessive speed, as I predicted."

"Excellent. But what would you have done if he had driven slowly?"

"I would have found an excuse. You can count on Hassan Nuzhir."

The Emir gloated like a cat that has caught a pigeon. "Good. Sweep them away, but quietly."

49

Age had not dulled Nati Morgan's sharp senses. Less conceited than Asaf and Malkiel, he knew the limitations of his knowledge. Moreover, he had a set of tough principles that always guided him. One of his principles was that before paying a high price for an item, he had it checked thoroughly. Before he flew to Iran with the CDs, they would be reviewed by an expert.

Nati invited Dr. Helmut Schroeder, a young German missile expert staying in London, to his hotel room. Before Dr. Schroeder arrived, Nati neutralized the password protection with relative ease by following the instructions Felix had provided.

The German scientist viewed the CDs on Nati's computer. "It looks very professional," he said. "But I would like to consult my mentor, Professor Sigmund Ziegler of the University of Berlin. Would you permit me to take the material to him?"

"No," said Nati, "but he can view it on his own computer screen. Just give me his phone number, and within an hour I can set up a video conference in which he will be able to see everything."

Three hours later, Professor Ziegler had finished viewing all the CDs. "Mr. Morgan," he said, "this presentation is on a very high level. But it is difficult for me to decide in one viewing. Something does not smell right, but it is hard for me to pinpoint the problem. I think the diameter of the motor is out of proportion with the size of the tail. Can I view it again?"

"*Danke schön,* but that won't be necessary. I already have my answer." If, after a quick view, a scientist of medium stature found a flaw in Israel's most closely guarded security project, something was very wrong.

So Felix tricked me, thought Nati. *What a low-down crook! I'm certainly not going to Iran; I won't leave there alive if anything goes wrong with this deal. Felix will pay dearly for his crime.*

Nati decided to go to Israel. He knew where Felix lived and where he worked, and he had many ways of taking care of him.

The armored vehicle traveled for an hour in the blazing sun. The two hot, thirsty prisoners felt faint in the backseat. A thick plate glass window separated them from their captors. In the front seat, the policemen were enjoying air-conditioning and cold drinks.

Asaf banged on the glass window with his powerful fists.

The policemen turned around. "What do you want?" one of them asked.

"Where are you taking us?" shouted Asaf.

"You'll soon see."

The armored vehicle drove on in the heat for two more hours. The prisoners were on the verge of losing consciousness.

At last the vehicle turned onto a side road, where it continued a few more kilometers between golden desert dunes. Finally it stopped before an abandoned two-story building of gray concrete in the heart of the wilderness. Asaf and Malkiel got out slowly.

"What are you going to do to us?" Asaf's eyes were riveted to the building, which reminded him of a prison facility.

"You will stand trial and may expect a death sentence," said the policeman calmly.

"What! You must be kidding."

"No, I am quite serious."

"For what, speeding? No country in the world gives the death penalty for speeding," groaned Asaf.

"Silence!" Hassan Nuzhir kicked him. "When you drive at 180 kilometers per hour, you are inviting the angel of death. If you yourself give away your life, why should I have mercy on you? It may be said that I pulled your shattered body out of a smashed vehicle and now I am doing with it as I please. By the way, that is what will be written on your death certificate when we return your bodies to your bereaved families."

"I didn't drive at 180," Asaf protested, rubbing his eyes. Any minute he would wake up in his bed in the London hotel and see that this was all a dream. But even after he closed his eyes and opened them again, the two policemen were still standing there with pistols aimed at him.

"The radar on our patrol car showed 180. Machines are more truthful than people."

"What have we done? What do you want from us?" Asaf pleaded. "Listen, I can transfer a million dollars to a bank account for you in exchange for our lives. Let us go, and no one will ever know about it."

"Thanks, but we cannot accept your generous offer," said Nazhir firmly. "Our lives are worth more to us than a million dollars. If Emir ibn Muhammad doesn't see pictures of your corpses, he will slaughter us."

"What does the Emir want from us?"

"You tried to deceive him. Whoever deceives the Emir pays with his life."

"But it wasn't my fault," croaked Asaf. "Someone deceived me."

"Tell that to the judges at your trial. But don't expect mercy. Our judges grew up on the *Koran*. A robber's hand is cut off, a swindler's tongue is cut out, and the soul of the heretical Zionist enemy is removed slowly and painfully."

As the two policemen pushed them along, Asaf and Malkiel hoped that at least in the dark building they would find relief from the heat. They were mistaken. Emir ibn Muhammad knew how to make the most of this facility for imprisonment and torture, which served Saudi intelligence with the silent consent of the Dubai principality. Asaf and Malkiel were isolated in separate cells, given only water but no food, and interrogated under torture. The Emir, convinced that two Mossad agents had fallen into his hands, was determined to extract information from them.

After the first week in prison, Asaf and Malkiel were mere remnants of their former selves. Asaf suffered splitting headaches as a result of clubbings, and Malkiel was on the brink of insanity.

"I'll tell you the truth," said the Emir's chief interrogator. "You will not leave this place alive. But you can choose how much torture you will undergo until you give up your sinful souls. If you cooperate with us and reveal everything you know, we will end your suffering with a single shot. If not, you will die slowly, with terrible agony, over the course of months."

"I'm prepared to cooperate," panted Asaf. "I will reveal whatever I know about the Israeli army, and that's a lot."

"We know that, and we will write down everything you say. After that we will decide whether you have cooperated," explained the interrogator. "Actually, it is not we who will decide but Emir ibn Muhammad. Just pray that he is in a good mood that day, so you can meet your Father in Paradise quickly."

❧❦❧

"Elitzafan, why are you screaming?" said Devorah. "You'll wake up the neighbors!"

"I've solved the mystery," he said, clutching his chest. "I know who sent us the letter."

"Who?" Devorah was afraid he would get a heart attack from the tension.

"Daniel Klein."

"What?"

"Daniel Klein was my father's neighbor." Anger burned in Elitzafan's eyes. "He hoped to inherit the double apartment in Rechaviah. Besides, it was he who suggested the *shidduch* with Patankin and he can easily restore it, if he wishes — as he wrote in the first letter."

"Elitzafan, what's happened to you?" Devorah's voice was soft and quiet, but her eyes were piercing. "Daniel Klein is an honest, trustworthy, heaven-fearing man. How can you suspect him of doing such things? The anonymous letter writer is surely the same villain who sent Adam Dushman to stop François the evening of the *vort* — namely, Nati Morgan."

"Nati is a business magnate. He doesn't need my father's estate."

"You have a point," said Devorah thoughtfully. "But that's no reason to suspect Daniel Klein."

"Look, I'm not planning to act as if I suspect him," said Elitzafan. "I'll be circumspect. I'll call him and speak in a natural way. If he *is* the guilty party, he'll realize that I suspect him of sending the letters and he'll start stuttering."

Elitzafan grabbed the phone before Devorah could stop him.

Although it was after midnight, the Kleins were still awake. Daniel picked up the receiver.

"Hello, this is Elitzafan Mindelman. How are you?"

Daniel was very surprised. The memory of the Patankin *shidduch* floated to the surface, and he gave a light, embarrassed laugh. "I am well, *baruch Hashem,* and how are you?"

"Surviving, thanks to Hashem's kindness," said Elitzafan. *I must be losing my mind,* he thought, *if I suspected a worthy Jew like Daniel Klein of committing such criminal acts.*

"What brings you to call me?" asked Daniel pleasantly, without adding, "at such a late hour."

"My troubles," confessed Elitzafan, almost bursting into tears. "Remember the *shidduch* with Patankin?"

"Only too well," sighed Daniel. "Unfortunately, an anonymous caller phoned Simchah Patankin in the middle of the night and told him terrible things about your father."

"It's all lies!" said Elitzafan heatedly. "He was an arms dealer, but he never sold to Arabs. And he certainly never dealt in drugs or crosses."

"I believe you," said Daniel. "I knew your father well. He was an honest, upright man."

"So can't you convince Simchah Patankin?"

"I'm afraid not. He's very sensitive with regard to the subject of *yichus.*"

"Do you know why he's so sensitive to the subject of *yichus*?" Elitzafan said excitedly. "Because his own *yichus* leaves something to be desired!"

"If that's true, maybe we can put the *shidduch* back together again," said Daniel with growing interest. "What do you know about his *yichus*?"

"I spoke to a few old friends who knew Simchah as a teenager, when he first came to study in Jerusalem. They still remember him as Eddy. His father, Norman Patankin, was a New York taxi driver who wore a yarmulke only on Shabbos."

Daniel's eyes lit up. "Maybe there's hope for this *shidduch* after all. I'll go speak to him."

It took Daniel a few days to muster his courage. On Motza'ei Shabbos, right after he made *Havdalah*, Daniel knocked on the Patankins' door.

The Patankins' married daughter let him in. Daniel took a few steps and stopped, spellbound by the surrealistic sight.

The dining room table still bore the remnants of *seudah shelishis*. With backs bent in pious humility and hands folded behind them, Simchah and Zelda were circling the table in opposite directions. Both were fervently reciting the Yiddish prayer *G-t fune Avraham*, composed by Rabbi Levi Yitzchak of Berditchev.

Simchah's movements were full of *deveikus*. He stamped his feet and let out choked groans as he chanted the prayer, line by line, in Yiddish. Zelda said each line after him in Hebrew.

Simchah sighed and turned to his wife. "Zelda, how many times have we said it?"

"Twice, my dear husband. *Oy*, holy Rabbi Levi Yitzchak, thank you for composing this sweet prayer! If only every day were Motza'ei Shabbos. Ah, what a sweet supplication. *Ribbono shel olam*, send Shmuel ben Zelda the right match quickly."

From moment to moment, the pleas and groans grew longer and stronger. The couple, oblivious to the visitor, continued to read the prayer loudly until they had finished it the third time. Then Simchah filled the silver cup with wine and made *Havdalah*.

Daniel waited patiently while Simchah poured out the remnants of the wine, wet his eyes with his fingertips, and said the after-blessing with a great deal of swaying.

At last Simchah looked up and took note of his visitor. "*Gute voch*, my dear neighbor. What brings you here immediately after Shabbos? Is anything new?"

Daniel mounted a frontal attack. "I wanted to start the new week with good *mazal*. I would like to suggest a wonderful *shidduch* for your Shmuli."

"Excellent," said Simchah pleased. "Who is she?"

"A very special girl." For dramatic effect, he paused momentarily. "Chedvah Mindelman."

Simchah smiled bitterly. "Mindelman? I asked if anything was new."

"Is anything new with you?" Daniel retorted. "Has Shmuli gotten engaged yet?"

"No."

"So the news is that there is no news."

"I already told you that an anonymous caller phoned in the middle of the night and said that the girl's grandfather dealt in drugs and in crosses and sold arms to the Arabs. Tell me, do I need such *yichus* for my son?"

"In my opinion, it's all lies. They may have a neighbor who hates them," replied Daniel. "Anyway, since when does one check a grandfather's *tzitzis*? Check who Elitzafan Mindelman himself is."

"I've heard wonderful things about him. He helps many people in the community; he's a person to my liking. But I heard that he, too, is not entirely clean. He cut off contact with his father in a most shameful way."

"Let's analyze it logically," said Daniel. "If the grandfather was a criminal, you can't blame the son for keeping away from him. And if the grandfather was not a criminal, the granddaughter is kosher and permitted to marry a Jewish boy."

Daniel took a deep breath. "And besides, if we're speaking about *yichus,* what is the *yichus* of Eddy *ben* Norman?"

Simchah opened his eyes wide. "I see that a *shadchan* can also be a detective."

Daniel laughed genially. "Simchah, your friends from yeshivah still remember Eddy Patankin, the American boy who played basketball on Friday afternoons."

The pride was gone from Simchah's face. "You're right," he said. "I came from the United States as a teenager.

"In his youth, my father owned a butcher shop that sold *treif* meat. Gradually he began going to shul on Shabbos. At some point he gave up the store and became a taxi driver.

"A rabbi who used his services advised him to send me to a yeshivah in Israel. I'm an only child; you can imagine how hard it was for him to see me go. Only in the merit of his self-sacrifice was I fortunate enough to raise a family of *bnei Torah.*"

"So what do you have against Elitzafan?" said Daniel. "His father possibly sold weapons to Arabs and crosses to Christians; your father definitely sold *treif* meat to Jews. The two of you are perfectly matched as *mechutanim.*

Not to mention that Chedvi herself is a rare diamond, as you and Shmuli already know.

"By the way, what is the source of the custom to circle the table before *Havdalah*? I've never seen anything like it."

Zelda blushed. "My parents, of blessed memory, used to do it. It's a private family custom. But we have seen great salvation after this prayer. It's a terrific *segulah*."

"The salvation you want is right in front of your noses," said Daniel gravely. "The *segulah* is in your hands. A wonderful *shidduch* for Shmuel ben Zelda only awaits your consent."

Felix had just enough time left to take a taxi to the airport. He quickly packed his few belongings, stuffed Nati's bag of diamonds into his jacket pocket beside Asaf's check, and ordered a taxi. In the lobby, he returned the magnetic card to the reception desk; his bill was already paid. So far, everything was proceeding like clockwork.

He stepped out to the curb to wait for the taxi. As the winter wind blew against his face, he collected his thoughts.

The plan was working smoothly. Five hours from now he would land in Israel, having accomplished his mission of saving Israel from treachery; and he had come away with a million-dollar profit to boot. He had succeeded in tricking those two villains, Nati and Asaf. His feigned fear of parting with his portable computer had convinced Asaf that Felix had really given him the Arrow secrets. Nati was too clever to fall for that, but he would surely follow Felix to Israel to take revenge — and walk straight into the trap.

Felix had made one foolish mistake, though. Out of habit, he had called Yasha Stashevsky to volunteer for extra duty. If Yasha looked for him, Felix would be in trouble.

The taxi came toward him on the left side of the street. The driver sat on the right, as usual in London, where the rules of driving are opposite of Israel and the rest of Europe.

"Did you order a taxi to Heathrow Airport?" asked the driver in crisp English.

"Yes."

"Get in."

Felix sat down beside the driver. Distress welled up inside him like a blister. Something was wrong, but what was it?

The driver's English! The accent didn't sound real. It was an imitation!

Felix braced himself to jump out of the taxi while it drove.

Suddenly a cold piece of metal was pushed at his skull. Two slim young fellows with bleached hair sprang up behind him and aimed a drawn pistol at his head. "Don't think of it," said one of them in Hebrew. "Welcome home, Professor Felix Goldmark. You are under arrest by the Shabak. From now on anything you say may be used against you. You may consult an attorney."

"What are you accusing me of, if I may ask?" he inquired calmly.

His captors looked at one another, smiling. "As they told us, the glaciers in Finland are less frozen than you.

"To answer your question, you are accused of spying, transmitting classified information to enemy agents, and high treason."

"What are you going to do with me?"

"We are flying you to Israel for trial."

"Very well."

Here is a wrench thrown into my plans, thought Felix grimly. *Never mind. If they want a battle, they will have one. Good, let them put me on trial!*

⸲⸱⸳

The conversation with Daniel Klein left Elitzafan feeling empty. His brilliant theory that Daniel was the author of the anonymous letters had burst like a soap bubble. Elitzafan now saw Daniel in a different light: After years of devotedly caring for the aging Zeidel Portman, whose family had abandoned him, Daniel secretly hoped to receive some earthly reward in addition to the heavenly one. Curiosity had gotten him to check whether there was any connection between the Mindelman of Beis Yisrael and the Portmans of Rechaviah. When he realized he had stepped on sore toes, he tried to appease Elitzafan by suggesting the *shidduch* with Shmuli Patankin. There ended Daniel's connection with the matter.

Or did it? Ah, yes, there was something else. Asher! Elitzafan very much liked Asher Klein. *Why, then, did I rashly ask him to speak again with Simchah Patankin?* Elitzafan asked himself. Well, it was better to have two suggestions, one of which might work, than to have none.

"So should I sign?" he asked Devorah.

"We agreed that you would."

"But I'll lose the entire inheritance!"

"Why go over it again?" said Devorah nervously, "We've already spoken about everything. We've decided it's worthwhile to give up the inheritance in order to get a *shidduch* for Chedvi."

He picked up the pen with a steady hand and signed. One signature, a scrawl on a piece of paper, and a million dollars or more would be gone. Anything for a bit of joy, a little *nachas* from the children.

The messenger arrived. This time it was not the ponytailed fellow, but someone else. He came, took the envelope, and disappeared in a flash.

Elitzafan had hoped that now he would finally achieve the longed-for serenity. Instead, he began to torture himself with vexing doubts. What would be with Chedvi? Would something finally work? And what about Tirtzah and Leah'le? Would the Mindelman family know comfort after years of sorrow and distress?

"Trust in Hashem," he whispered to himself when he finally went to bed. "Trust in Hashem."

ভা᷒ক্টর

Daniel Klein's words caused Simchah Patankin a great emotional upheaval. The clever *shadchan* had put a mirror before his face and pointed out that his own *yichus* wasn't any better than Elitzafan Mindelman's.

About this, Daniel Klein was right. But what about the girl herself? Was she really as wonderful as they had thought? Yes, they had been ready for a *vort*. But if they were about to open the matter again, they should look at it with fresh eyes.

There was one person he wanted to consult: the *shadchan* who had the whole *shidduch* market at his fingertips — legendary, redheaded Emanuel Klopstein, whose notebooks listed all the boys and girls of Israel of marriageable age, each entry accompanied by a pithy comment.

Klopstein was standing in line at the bank when the cell phone in his pocket rang.

"Hello. This is Simchah Patankin."

"Excuse me, I was ahead of you in line; I just had to see the other clerk for a minute," someone told Emanuel. Simchah had to repeat himself.

"I wanted information about Chedvah Mindelman."

"Aha," said Klopstein enthusiastically. "She's the cream of the crop, the tip of the top. Why is she twenty-five? Because she was born twenty-five years ago. No, I'm not joking. You want to know why she wasn't snapped up? There are many answers. The first will hurt you a bit, Simchah. Your Shmuli is no baby either; why wasn't he snatched up? *Nu,* so they're both picky. If you want my advice, grab her before someone else does."

Simchah was satisfied. It was good to hear a glowing rating from Emanuel who, for a change, stood to gain no financial remuneration for his praises.

Without further ado, Simchah phoned Daniel and gave his consent to renew the *shidduch* with the Mindelmans.

A day earlier, Daniel would have been overjoyed. But just yesterday, Asher had told him how much he liked Elitzafan, and a brainstorm had flashed through Daniel's mind: Why not suggest Asher for Chedvi?

For two days, Daniel was assailed by doubts that gave him no rest day or night. Then he decided on a course of action. First he would pursue the Patankin–Mindelman *shidduch*. If that worked, it was destined from Heaven. If not, he would suggest his son Asher.

⁂

Emanuel Klopstein left the bank and sank into deep thought. Simchah Patankin had reminded him of the Mindelmans. How long would they continue to suffer? He recalled suggesting Matti Langer, an excellent fellow. Rabbi Langer had been enthusiastic at first, and then suddenly cooled off and made silly excuses. It was clear that the *shidduch* saboteur had called.

Experience had taught Emanuel that, in many cases, after a cooling off period there are second thoughts. He was not one to lose time. From the bustling street, he dialed the Langers.

To his delight, Rabbi Langer himself picked up the phone. Emanuel, in his usual direct manner, asked whether Matti was seeing anyone at the moment.

Rabbi Langer hesitated for a moment, and then answered frankly, "No."

"Then perhaps I can suggest a *shidduch* that we spoke about in the past?"

"Namely?"

"Chedvi Mindelman."

Rabbi Langer explained that the girl had a wonderful reputation, but an anonymous caller had warned him about her grandfather. Emanuel convinced Rabbi Langer to talk it over with his wife.

The Langers discussed the matter at length, analyzed it in depth, examined it from all angles, and at last came to a decision: One should consider only the girl and her parents, not the grandfather. They would go ahead with the Mindelman *shidduch*.

❦

Devorah Mindelman was floating in a pink cloud. Half an hour earlier, Daniel Klein had phoned to say that the Patankins would like to renew the *shidduch*. Devorah had played the calm mother to whom marrying off her twenty-five-year-old daughter was not urgent. She even pretended to have forgotten who Shmuli was. After she hung up, though, she shouted for joy.

She had barely digested the news when the phone rang again. This time it was Emanuel Klopstein. "Mrs. Mindelman?" His bass voice was a delight to her ears. "May I suggest an excellent *shidduch* for your daughter?"

Without waiting for an answer, Emanuel continued: "Mattisyahu Langer — or Matti, for short. When I first spoke to them they were evidently busy with something else. Now they are interested. So when can we make a date?"

"Patience." Devorah tired to cool the blaze named Emanuel Klopstein. "We have to inquire about them."

"By all means inquire. You will hear only good things. The boy is head and shoulders above the crowd. He's a rare flower. He has blue blood in his veins. The Langer family is among the elite of Lithuanian Jewry…."

Emanuel left her no choice. He extracted a commitment to give an answer (positive, of course) within five days at most.

Devorah walked around the house half drunk, utterly incapable of attacking her long list of tasks.

And what about Elitzafan? He had told her his heart was drawn to Asher Klein. "If only he would be our *chasan*," he had said, turning red. Perhaps they could drop a hint to Daniel Klein that he should think about his own son before the neighbor's.

The phone rang again.

"Devorah?"

"Oh, how are you, Rebbetzin Flora?"

"You sound happy," said Flora. "Any news?"

"We have several new suggestions," Devorah replied with satisfaction. "*Baruch Hashem*, since we returned from Meiron, they've been pouring in."

"Wonderful!" cried Flora. "I'm also calling for just that purpose."

"My head is starting to spin," laughed Devorah. "Either there's nothing, or there's a flood."

"Take my suggestion," said Flora decisively. "It's the best."

"Who's the boy?" Devorah asked curiously.

"Yom Tov Feldman of Paris. François."

"What?"

"Yes," said Flora. "You thought I forgot you, but I didn't rest for a moment. I spoke with François and his parents at length. They've reconsidered and realize that they made a mistake."

Devorah thought of the *chasan* who had abandoned the *kallah* on the evening of the *vort*, leaving her with a scar in her soul that might never heal. She wanted to protest, but Flora had such a powerful personality that her wishes were always hard for Devorah to resist. "How kind of you," Devorah stammered, "but now we have three suggestions from Jerusalem, whereas he would have to come from Paris."

"So what? Today people travel between continents more easily than they once traveled between neighborhoods."

"Nevertheless, I have three suggestions."

"Tell me the names."

Devorah's lips moved weakly. Flora always managed to suck the secrets out of her.

"You've already told me about them all," said Flora. "With all due respect, they don't come up to François' ankles. Shmuli Patankin is the grandson of a New York taxi driver who once sold bacon in a butcher shop. Langer is truly a distinguished Litvish family, but Matti himself is mediocre compared to Yom Tov Feldman. Asher Klein is nothing special either. Don't forget that François looks like an angel and his soul is close to Chedvi's.

"Devorah, you don't know how sorry he is about the evening of the *vort*. Ever since then he has had no rest. He wants to apologize to Chedvi in person for the shame and pain he caused her."

"To be absolutely sure, I lit candles for you, and in the flame I saw the words 'Mazal tov, Chedvah and Yom Tov.' If I am not speaking the truth, may my right hand dry up and my tongue cleave to my palate."

Devorah moved the receiver away from her ear. Her imagination was playing tricks on her. A bridal gown, a white veil, and a wedding ring were slipping out of the round holes of the phone. Of the four suggestions for Chedvi, one would surely work. The question was which.

"I have to consult my husband."

"Of course," said Flora melodiously. "Your husband is your crowning glory. But François has first rights. If not for that villain who intercepted him, he would long since have been engaged to Chedvi. He supersedes all the rest according to both Halachah and international law."

"I have no words to thank you."

"Thank me with deeds, not with words. I've invested my heart and soul in you, and a great deal of money besides. Plane tickets, phone calls, traveling, and secret expenses that I am not at liberty to reveal. I almost went bankrupt, and I still have to pay for a ticket for François. I could get the *shidduch* going in two days. All I lack is some cash to cover expenses."

That meant she wanted money.

"I will give you a nice donation."

"Thank you; may you merit many mitzvos. But I will determine the sum, and only if there is justification for collecting a fee from you."

"Many thanks."

"Remember, don't keep me waiting. Consult your husband and get back to me."

ജ഻ൟ

The Tel Aviv courtroom was closed to the media that morning at ten. Nevertheless, a few senior journalists were present — those to whom word had leaked out that the most serious espionage trial in the history of the State of Israel was about to take place.

Prosecutors Shalom Argaman and Michael Donag, busily examined their papers.

The defendant, who looked completely at ease, smiled from time to time when he met curious glances. To everyone's surprise, he insisted on defending himself and refused a lawyer's services. Donag was sure they would rip him apart, considering the solid evidence against him. Argaman, who was more seasoned, was worried by the defendant's self-confidence.

The six armed policemen guarding the entrance to the courthouse respectfully saluted a tall, solidly built man with carefully trimmed gray hair as he strode down the corridor. Judge Oren Tzur looked past them as if they were invisible.

Those present — twenty-nine people in all, including two stenotypists — rose to their feet when the judge took his seat on an elevated platform.

Oren Tzur banged his gavel on the table and proclaimed, "Order in the court!" He looked sternly over his reading glasses at the assembled and turned to Prosecutor Shalom Argaman. "Please begin."

Argaman glanced briefly at the defendant and then riveted his gaze on his files. He had been sure that when the moment of truth came, the defendant would show signs of tension. Instead, what he saw in the defendant's eyes was a calm, cool blue sea. Worse yet was the proud, intellectual gleam. Felix's serenity was maddening.

"The State of Israel against Felix Goldmark," he began.

P rosecutor/district attorney Shalom Argaman read the accusation in a chilly voice, making a supreme effort to ignore the defendant's piercing look.

Mr. Felix Goldmark, hereafter the defendant, is herewith accused of meeting with enemy agents on the 2nd and 3rd of February, 2003, and, in return for a very large payment, giving them top-secret material, knowing full well that this endangered all the residents of the State of Israel. Abusing the faith placed in him as a trusted employee of Elta, the defendant delivered all the details of the Arrow missile's structure and function to the enemy, as the prosecution will prove.

On account of this, Mr. Felix Goldmark is accused of high treason against the State of Israel. The prosecution requests that the court sentence him to the severest punishment possible under the law.

A murmur rippled through the courtroom. Shocked, accusing glances from all sides were cast at the errant scientist.

Judge Oren Tzur turned to the defendant. "I understand that you have refused the services of a lawyer. Nevertheless, the court is considering appointing a lawyer to represent you, and I suggest you consider this favorably."

"I have already considered the matter from every possible angle, Your Honor," said Felix. "I still prefer to represent myself."

"We respect your request." The judge turned to the prosecutor. "The court would like to hear on what basis you accuse Mr. Goldmark."

Argaman exchanged glances with his colleague, Michael Donag, and announced in a dramatic tone, "I invite the prosecution's first witness: Mr. Natan Morgan, CEO of the weapons company Morgan Consolidated, Ltd., who flew to Israel in order to testify. Mr. Morgan, please take the witness stand."

All eyes focused on Nati Morgan as he stood up and strode quickly to the witness stand. He exuded authority and a strong smell of aftershave. His expensive suit was carefully pressed, his head held high. He sat down, glanced around the courtroom, and turned to the prosecutor.

"Mr. Morgan," said Argaman, "do you recognize the defendant, Felix Goldmark?"

Nati cleared his throat and smiled. "Of course. His picture has appeared in the media, and recently I met him in person."

Argaman: Under what circumstances did you meet him?

Morgan: Felix Goldmark approached me with a shocking suggestion. He offered to sell me the secrets of the Arrow missile, which he developed.

Argaman: I understand that the defendant turned to you as an arms dealer.

Morgan (chuckling): Certainly not in my other capacity, of which he is unaware....

Argaman: Can you tell us about your other capacity?

Morgan (grinning): Yes. My superiors gave me permission to reveal that I am a Mossad agent.

Goldmark: What?!

Argaman: I request confirmation from Mr. Rafi Zamir, one of the heads of the Mossad.

All eyes turned to the benches. A short man, with bold, light green eyes that matched his suit, rose. The judge and the lawyers regarded him with awe.

Zamir: I hereby confirm that Mr. Natan Morgan is a Mossad agent who has been operating for close to fifty years under the cover of assistant manager of Samson Steel and then CEO of Morgan Consolidated.

Argaman: Thank you, Mr. Zamir. Mr. Morgan, please tell the court your whole story, in brief, from your entry into the Mossad until the contacts between you and Mr. Goldmark.

Morgan: Fifty years ago, the government of the newborn State of Israel was extremely concerned about national security and suspicious of anyone unusual. Arms manufacturer Avraham Zeidel Portman, a *charedi* with extremist views, was certainly unusual. One of the higher-ups saw him as a threat to the State and decided to attach an intelligence agent to him to make sure he would not sell weapons to the enemy.

I had just finished my army duty, where I had served in the intelligence corps. I was asked to continue to serve the State of Israel in the Mossad.

My superiors in the Mossad investigated Zeidel, and they discovered that he and I were first cousins and that he had a soft, sensitive heart. They assigned me to shadow him. I was to present myself as his hungry, unemployed cousin so that he would hire me to work in his corporation, Samson Steel, Ltd. He did.

Zeidel was shrewd and cautious. Nevertheless, I always felt that he was in contact with dubious weapons companies and that he sold arms to enemies of Israel. It was hard to prove, though.

Goldmark: Objection. Mr. Portman never did those things!

Judge: Objection overruled. The defense will be able to cross-examine the witness later on. For now, the witness will continue. Mr. Morgan, feelings are not facts. Do you have proof of what you just said?

Morgan: Yes. In 1966, Zeidel conducted secret negotiations with some straw companies in Africa. I managed to get my hand on a few secret documents showing that Egypt, which at the time was Israel's bitter enemy, was behind the straw companies.

Goldmark: Objection. Mr. Morgan is accusing Mr. Portman of things that he himself did.

Judge: Mr. Goldmark, if there is one more outburst, you will be held in contempt of court. The witness may continue.

Morgan: My superiors in the Mossad decided to keep me permanently tailing Zeidel. Thus I grew up together with Samson Steel.

In 1975, Zeidel made an arms deal of giant proportions with Egypt and Syria. The merchandise was to change hands at the edge of the Brazilian rain forest. Zeidel was tried, convicted, and imprisoned. I took over the corporation, which I renamed Morgan Consolidated, and my role as CEO served as a cover for my role as a Mossad agent. Now that I am about to retire, I do not mind exposing myself in this courtroom behind closed doors.

Argaman: Let's return now to your meeting with the defendant. What happened there?

Morgan: Goldmark offered to sell me the entire Arrow operating system on a set of ten CDs. I feigned enthusiasm and offered him an astronomical price. Goldmark returned to Israel, got the CDs, brought them to London, and walked right into the trap I had planted for him.

Argaman: I would like to present as evidence a set of ten CDs that Mr. Goldmark sold to Mr. Morgan. Assistant to the prosecution, Mr. Gadi Shiller, please.

Argaman's elderly assistant shuffled to the witness stand and presented a clear plastic box containing the incriminating CDs.

Judge: Have the CDs been checked?

Michael Donag rose. "Your Honor," he said, "the CDs were checked by authorized representatives of the Ministry of Defense. They verified that the CDs contain the original operating system of the Arrow missile from A to Z."

After the first witness came Yasha Stashevsky, who had noticed Felix's absence from work and alerted the management, and Mossad agents who had tailed Felix in London and photographed his meetings with Nati with telescopic cameras. The prosecution wove a tight net about Felix. After hours of testimony, Felix's conviction looked certain.

☙❧❧☚

Rebbetzin Simchoni–Freilich summoned Moshiko Sharabi to the Blochs' home for "an important and urgent mission." When he came, she gave him his assignment.

Moshiko carried it out obediently. His gratitude to the Rebbetzin for enlightening him about his sixth sense and how to use it knew no bounds. He was ready to go through fire and water for her.

After three days of professional-level investigations, Moshiko presented his findings. Flora's eyes shone with joy. Now she could easily sweep all other suggestions off the table.

She waited impatiently for Moshiko, her new lackey, to leave. Then she dialed.

"Devorah?"

"No, this is her daughter, Chedvi."

"Great. I'm actually calling about you. Isn't it wonderful, Chedvi, that your luck has turned around and everyone is chasing after you? I did not rest for a minute; I turned the whole world over for you. Now you are sure to get engaged. Don't forget whom you have to thank.

"Start preparing for your real *vort*, the ceremony that no force in the world will be able to ruin. It will take place in a few days, *b'ezras Hashem*. Now let me speak to your mother please."

Devorah came to the phone. "Listen," said Flora. "I checked all your suggestions very well. Here's the inside information.

"First of all, stay away from Matti Langer. The boy suffers from depression. I can even tell you what pills he takes."

Devorah felt her shoulders contracting. "It can't be. He's an excellent boy. We checked up on him very carefully in the yeshivah."

"My dear, you make me laugh. Your checking is worthless. You asked his neighbors, rabbis, and friends. You can only pray that they won't deceive you. I sent a professional detective with listening equipment and a telescopic camera. He has all the medical files.

"Let's move forward. Shmuli Patankin's grandfather was almost a *goy*. Asher Klein is really a handsome fellow, but that is precisely the problem. Do you want a *chasan* who primps in front of the mirror?

"Who is left? François Feldman. He has *yichus* — he's a descendant of the *Tosfos Yom Tov*, for whom he was named. Besides being learned, he has wonderful *middos* and a good heart. Between you and me, when your daughter needs help, whom will she ask if not a husband who knows when to close the Gemara and help his wife?"

Elitzafan, who had been listening in on the other phone, now spoke up. "Do your investigations stand up to all the criteria of Halachah? Or have you just transgressed the Torah's prohibition again *lashon hara* by slandering three young men and their families?"

"Mr. Mindelman, with all due respect, I disagree. Where does *lashon hara* come into *shidduchim?* Would you want your daughter to marry a sick boy? Do you prefer to hide your head in the sand? Isn't it better to know the whole truth and to be safe?

"I suggested a young man who is learned, Heaven-fearing, and also a fine human being. With such a husband, your daughter will be happy all her life."

"And what is your fee for making this *shidduch?*" asked Elitzafan.

"I worked on myself for years until I uprooted any desire for money," said Flora. "But I did invest all my energy in Chedvi. For her sake I stayed in France for many weeks. My followers left me and went elsewhere, and I've been left without a livelihood. I have huge expenses; my debts are in the hundreds of thousands of dollars."

"So how much do you want?" Elitzafan asked with a cynical smile.

"I would be satisfied," said Flora, "if you would sign over the apartment your father left you in Rechaviah."

"A very modest payment," chuckled Elitzafan. "It's worth at least half a million dollars."

"Believe me, I'm worth it," said the Rebbetzin. "I invested my whole soul in your family. There are people who pay me more, and they're not wealthy heirs like you are."

After they hung up, Elitzafan began to wonder how Rebbetzin Simchoni–Freilich knew about the apartment in Rechaviah. The conversation set a red light flashing in his head. It reminded him about the anonymous letter and how he had signed away his inheritance a few days earlier. Besides, his shoulder still hurt, a souvenir of the incident in the Jordan Valley road. It was she who had encouraged them to take that route.

52

The second hearing took place one week later. It was the end of the Jerusalem winter, when the seasons struggle for supremacy, often resulting in extremes. This particular day was hot. The dusty wings of the old fan stood still, but the air in the courtroom was cool and pleasant, thanks to four powerful new air conditioners.

The ranks of the original twenty-nine spectators had swelled. The newcomers included several army officers. Two senior journalists, who had promised to help Judge Oren Tzur advance in his career, had also been admitted to the closed-door session — on condition that not a word surfaced in the media until the government's judicial advisor permitted it.

Despite prison conditions, Felix did not look subdued or depressed. He sat straight, head held high. He had prepared well for the second round, where he would be stage manager.

"The State of Israel against Felix Goldmark. The second day of hearings is hereby convened," proclaimed Judge Oren Tzur, pounding his gavel. He looked sternly at the lawyers, who were holding a whispered conference on account of a newcomer who had just entered the courtroom.

The newcomer — a tall, fat man with round, dark cheeks, a black yarmulke clipped to his curly black hair, a blue and purple tie, and a brown jacket — smiled to everyone, waved to Nati and Felix, and quickly took a seat.

Judge: The representative of the defense may cross-examine the first witness.

Goldmark: Mr. Natan Morgan, please take the witness stand.

Nati strode through the narrow passage and smiled condescendingly at the scientist who had pretentiously taken on the role of lawyer.

Morgan (sarcastically): At your service, Mr. Attorney.

Laughter from the spectators.

Judge (banging his gavel): Silence in the court. A courtroom is not a circus.

Felix asked, "When did we first meet?"

Nati replied, "The day you visited the Havana Cigar Club in London. You wanted to make contact with me through my interest in cigar smoking. You made supreme efforts to pose as a cigar lover, but the involuntary expressions of disgust that flitted across your face when you sucked the cigar gave you away."

The spectators were amused. Nati held the reins firmly in his hand and answered Felix's questions arrogantly. Felix, unruffled, patiently continued the cross-examination. Nati described in detail the meetings in which Felix had sold him the ten CDs containing the secrets of the Arrow missile.

Goldmark: Did you study ballistics? Do you know aerodynamics?

Morgan: I did not study it, but I am quite familiar with it.

Goldmark: That is not what you told me at the club in London. What do you know about a missile's angle of falling? Let me phrase the question more clearly. If a missile has risen to a height of thirty kilometers, at what angle will it begin to fall?

Morgan: We're not in university now!

Goldmark: I ask the witness to answer the question.

Morgan (scratching his cheek): I don't know.

Goldmark: If the diameter of the rocket motor is 170 centimeters, what should the length of the tail protrusions be?

Morgan (shrugging): I'm not familiar with this foolishness.

Goldmark: What is the ratio between the weight of the missile and the weight of the warhead that it can carry?

Morgan: I don't know.

Goldmark: You just contradicted yourself. You said you were familiar with ballistics and aerodynamics. But we'll let that go. If you know nothing about missile science, how did you know that the CDs I brought you contained authentic material?

Argaman (jumping to his feet): Objection, Your Honor. The accused is diverging from the subject.

Judge: Objection overruled. The defense attorney has the right to ask any question that he deems relevant in building his line of defense. Furthermore, the defendant is now acting as defense attorney. The prosecutor is requested to treat the defense attorney with all due respect.

Argaman (with an embarrassed smile): I apologize, Your Honor.

Goldmark: Thank you, Your Honor. Mr. Morgan, with whom did you consult in order to determine what the CDs contain?

Morgan: With the heads of the Israeli Army, most of whom I know personally.

Goldmark: Allow me to refresh your memory. Weren't the CDs presented to the German missile expert Professor Helmut Schroeder? After that, were the contents not sent from your computer directly to that of Professor Sigmund Ziegler of the University of Berlin?

Morgan (turning pale): How did you know?

Goldmark: When I came to you in the club the last time, American arms dealer Harry Falls was sitting with you. During the last few days, I've spoken to him extensively by phone. Falls said that you told him about your consultation with Professors Schroeder and Ziegler. Ziegler smelled that something in the CDs was not right. True or false?

Morgan (shouting): False! You have a wild imagination!

Felix said, "I ask the court to present Exhibit #1, and to project a short video film before the judge and all those present."

Like a magician whipping a rabbit out of a hat, Felix drew a tape and a video out of his attaché case. "My colleague, Professor Ziegler from the University of Berlin," explained Felix, "relates what he found on the CDs that Mr. Morgan had him check."

A narrow face with sunken eyes filled the screen as the camera lens focused on Professor Ziegler for a close-up. He spoke in German. The Hebrew translation appeared on the bottom of the screen:

"I saw the material on the Arrow missile, which my colleague Professor Goldmark of Israel developed. The system described in the CDs belongs in a junk pile. There were a few gross mistakes, such as the length of the missile and the volume of the motor in relation to the size of the tail, that I did not catch in the first viewing. I caught them only upon analyzing the material later."

Argaman: I request that Exhibit #1 of the defense be rejected. This interview is fictitious, staged, and irrelevant to Goldmark's crime of treachery.

Judge: The acceptability of evidence presented by the defense will be decided by the court, not by the prosecution. The defense may continue.

Goldmark: Thank you, Your Honor. Mr. Morgan, do you know to whom I sold an identical set of ten CDs?

Morgan (pale): No.

Goldmark: Do you know where your employees Asaf Niv and Malkiel Yahalom disappeared to?

Morgan (nervously biting his lower lip): They have not disappeared. They are in Paris. I'm in constant contact with them.

Goldmark: You're lying.

Argaman (jumping to his feet): The defense has exceeded all bounds.

Judge: I request the defense speak more respectfully.

Goldmark: I apologize, Your Honor. Mr. Morgan knows, as I do, that Asaf Niv and Malkiel Yahalom traveled to Dubai with my personal computer and ten CDs that I sold them, supposedly containing the Arrow secrets. They tried to sell the material to Emir ibn Muhammad of Saudi Arabian Intelligence agency. Upon learning that it was a fake, he had the two imprisoned and tortured; their suffering will end soon with execution.

Mr. Morgan learned these facts from the same source I did: one of his men in Morgan Consolidated. Mr. Morgan is pleased that his work was done by others. Asaf Niv wanted to oust Mr. Morgan and take over the corporation himself, but Mr. Morgan managed to get rid of Asaf Niv instead.

Morgan: The accused made all this up. Not a single word is true!

Goldmark: It is all true, as I will prove in the coming days.

There was stunned silence in the courtroom. The lawyers huddled together and spoke in hushed tones. The ricocheting bullets of the accused wounded many as he conquered one stronghold after another. At this rate, Goldmark would turn from accused into accuser. He had to be stopped!

Argaman handed Judge Oren Tzur a note. The judge looked at it for a minute, then pounded the gavel and announced a half-hour recess.

୧୬୬୬

Once Moshiko Sharabi discovered that the man who had intercepted François on the evening of the *vort* was Adam Dushman, he did not stop there. He personally convinced the Feldmans that their son had fallen victim to a villain's wicked pranks. After a great deal of soul-searching, deep thinking, hesitating, and discussing, they did a turnabout. François decided that no girl could possibly compare with Chedvi. He was determined that this time, not even an earthquake would make him leave the *vort*.

Mr. and Mrs. Feldman decided to surprise Flora. Only after flying to Israel with François and settling down in a small *charedi* hotel in the center of Jerusalem did they call her to announce their arrival.

Flora nearly fainted — not just from surprise. Only the previous night, the Mindelmans had disappointed her with their lack of enthusiasm about renewing the *shidduch*. What a mess she had gotten herself into!

"I understand that the *vort* cannot be tonight," said Mr. Feldman innocently. "The young couple must meet first and warm up a pot that has cooled off. Please tell the Mindelmans that we've come to Jerusalem to complete the *shidduch*."

"I'll call them immediately," she said weakly.

For ten minutes Flora sat trembling. The phone conversation last night had been unpleasant. How was she going to get out of this one?

There was only one thing to do. She would use her magnetic influence to soften Devorah, and then give her an order.

Devorah answered the phone.

"How are you, my dear Devorah?" said Flora in her sweetest voice. "Yesterday I spoke to you harshly. Devorah, I love you with all my heart and I want you to forgive me."

Devorah was silent. What was Flora plotting?

"Don't you want to forgive me?" sobbed Flora. "After so many years of a wonderful friendship, you're angry at me? I was terribly tired, so I spoke nonsense. Really, Devorah. Tell me that you forgive me."

"I forgive you," Devorah heard herself saying.

"Wonderful." Flora tried to sound enthusiastic as always, but she was frightened. Devorah had not softened at all. "Devorah, day and night I think about what can be done for you. Now I've managed to do something you wouldn't believe."

"What?" asked Devorah curiously.

"I brought the Feldman family in from Paris. The father, the mother, and Yom Tov. Now everything depends only on you. If you wish, the *vort* can even be this evening. Just say the word, and Chedvi is a *kallah*!"

Devorah had to admit that Flora had amazing powers of persuasion.

"The Feldmans are in Israel?!" she exclaimed.

"Yes. They're here in Jerusalem, just a ten-minute walk from your house. If you like, I can arrange a meeting this very minute. It depends only on you — and on Chedvi, of course."

"And on me," came Elitzafan's voice over the extension. "I still have the last word in my house, and I say no. It shall not be. I understand that it is very unpleasant for you, but you will have to inform the Feldmans that they can return to Paris."

"How can you speak so harshly?" demanded Flora angrily.

"I am only saying the truth. No one can force me into a *shidduch* that I don't want. I did not ask the Feldmans to come to Israel, and therefore I owe them nothing. But I came to Paris at their express invitation, and they humiliated us. Chedvi's blood is not water, nor is that of her parents. It's a miracle that we survived that terrible evening."

"But it wasn't their fault," cried Flora. "They're wonderful people. Could they help it that some villain ambushed François? Okay, François didn't have to run away. I, too, think he should have returned and told his father what happened, but the Torah requires us to give people the benefit of the doubt. Panic overpowered his reason. You, however, are transgressing the Torah's prohibition not to take revenge or to harbor a grudge."

"In any case," said Elitzafan, ignoring the insult, "I was never overly enthusiastic about François. You brainwashed my wife and daughter. At the time there was a dearth of good suggestions, so they allowed themselves to be convinced. Now we are inundated with excellent offers to the point where we can't decide between them. François is not even in the running."

Flora flew into a rage. "Mr. Mindelman, now you're speaking like your father, who sold weapons to the Arabs so they could murder Jews." She continued with a series of insults, abuses, and juicy curses.

Elitzafan listened patiently without reacting.

"Now you are in the driver's seat with everyone running after you," Flora continued, "and you are sure that one of these suggestions is the right one. But Flora saw in the fire that François Feldman is Chedvi's *chasan*. Heaven has decreed that he is Chedvi's *zivug*, and she will have to return to him. Any other *shidduch* you make will be canceled. If she marries someone else, she won't have children, and all the curses in the Torah will come upon her head and yours. And may you have many more hard years like the last six." With that, she threw down the phone so hard that it broke.

"Such curses!" said Devorah fearfully. "I thought she was a Rebbetzin, but now I see the true Flora. I'm afraid of her."

"You have nothing to fear," said Elitzafan soothingly. "Let met tell you a legend from Jerusalem of a century ago.

"Rabbi Shmuel Zvil Shpitzer, who was in charge of various Jerusalem institutions, had many enemies. Once a bitter woman stopped him and cursed him. His escorts were terrified; they were sure he would die a strange death that very day.

"Rabbi Shpitzer, however, heard her out patiently. When she finished, he took off his hat, turned it over, and shook it out as if he were shaking off her curses. He went home serenely and lived for many more years."

"So turn your hat over," laughed Devorah.

Smiling, Elitzafan turned his yarmulke over and shook it out.

ஒ⸙ஓ

During the recess, Judge Oren Tzur informed the prosecution that he found nothing wrong with Felix's defense, and he would hear him out to the end.

"It was a mistake to choose Oren Tzur as the judge," Rafi Zamir of the Mossad whispered to Prosecuting Attorney Argaman. "We thought he was on our side, but we made a mistake. He's completely independent. We must take the case out of his hands. Why, the very honor of the Mossad is at stake. We cannot have one rotten apple named Nati Morgan ruin the Mossad's name!"

They returned to their places. Surprisingly, the courtroom was fuller than it had been before the recess. Judge Oren Tzur pounded his gavel to resume the hearing.

Felix called Yoel Tzadok up as his second witness.

Nati's eyes met Argaman's.

The tall, fat man with curly black hair moved toward the witness stand. He appeared at ease.

Goldmark: Mr. Tzadok, do we know each other?

Tzadok: Yes. We worked together many years ago at Elta, and recently we met again.

Goldmark: Where?

Tzadok: In Mr. Portman's apartment in Tiberias.

Goldmark: Please tell the court how you knew Mr. Portman.

Tzadok: Zeidel employed me at Samson Steel.

Goldmark: In what capacity?

Tzadok: As a clerk. I did all sorts of office jobs.

Goldmark: Is it correct to say that part of your work, if not most of it, was to shadow Mr. Morgan?

Tzadok: Yes.

Goldmark: Could you explain, please?

Tzadok: The files in the office were a mess, and Zeidel hired me to put them in order. But he also assigned me the task of keeping an eye on Nati Morgan. Zeidel distrusted Nati and suspected him of selling arms to our enemies behind Zeidel's back.

Goldmark: How long did you keep an eye on Mr. Morgan?

Tzadok: About twenty years.

Goldmark: And what did you find?

Argaman: Objection. The accused is trying to turn into an accuser. He has no authority to do so.

Judge (impatiently): Objection overruled. Mr. Tzadok, please answer the question.

Tzadok: I found nothing. Nati worked hard for the corporation. If he did anything improper, he did it so cleverly that there was no evidence against him.

Nati smiled, and the color returned to his cheeks.

Goldmark: You say you found no evidence that Mr. Morgan was involved in any illegal arms deals or in any transfer of weapons to enemy hands?

Tzadok: Correct.

Goldmark: Let's see what you have to say about Exhibit #2 of the defense. It's a film in which we will see Mr. Morgan…. But let the film speak for itself.

At Felix's request, a projector had been set up in the courtroom and hidden behind a gray divider. When Felix approached the divider, the battery of lawyers held a hasty conference, after which attorney Michael Donag rose.

Donag: Your Honor, we have reason to suspect that the defendant is presenting evidence that was obtained illegally. The prosecution would like to know where the accused obtained the film.

Judge: The prosecution surely meant to say "the defense."

Donag: Pardon me. From where did the defense obtain the film?

Judge: The question is addressed to the defense.

Goldmark: Mr. Tzadok testified that we met in Mr. Portman's apartment in Tiberias. He did not mention that I had let myself in with a key, which I was given by Mr. Daniel Klein, a neighbor who takes care of Mr. Portman's Jerusalem apartment.

Tzadok: Who took control of it, you mean.

Goldmark: I understand that various parties are fighting over Mr. Portman's estate, but that is not our subject now. I visited Mr. Portman's apartment in Tiberias several times, without Mr. Tzadok's knowledge. There, hidden in the depths of a closet, I found a few rolls of film. I understand they were taken with a hidden camera. Is that correct, Mr. Tzadok?

Tzadok (ignoring the question): I worked for Zeidel for many years and was extremely loyal to him. I came into an office that was financially successful but on the verge of collapse because of disorder. I worked hard and set it to rights.

(Tzadok takes an album out of his attaché case.) Zeidel very much appreciated my work, and we were very attached to each other. As you can see from these pictures, Zeidel attended my Yoezer's *bris* and my Shimshon's bar mitzvah. He even participated in the bas mitzvah of my Esther. When she died a year later, he came twice to comfort my wife and me, and he sat with us for many hours. (Sobs.) Zeidel was like his name — a grandfather to all his employees. I loved him fiercely.

Yoel's shoulders shook, and he wept uncontrollably.

Silence filled the courtroom. Everyone identified deeply with the pain of the bereft father. Only Felix was unmoved.

Goldmark: And now, with the court's permission, I would like to show the film.

Argaman: We request that the court deny permission on two grounds. First, the film might embarrass Mr. Morgan. Second, we suspect that the film has been tampered with and additional elements have been introduced.

Judge: Let us see the film and discuss it afterwards. Mr. Goldmark, the court is waiting to see the film.

The black and white film showed a younger, thinner version of Nati Morgan. He was sitting on an old-fashioned office chair, legs up on a desk, talking on a big, old-fashioned phone. A large one-day-at-a-time business calendar labeled "Meir and Meir, notaries" hung on the wall behind him. The date was May 30, 1975.

"The business is progressing wonderfully. No, Yosef, there is nothing to worry about. Zeidel left the office already. How are the purchases coming along? Go slowly and don't do anything rash! Negotiate until you get the price down to where you want it."

He listened a moment and spoke again. "Yosef, Zeidel doesn't have eyes in the back of his head. Don't be so scared. I take full responsibility for this project. This is going to be the deal of the decade. Huge quantities of arms are destined to all outward appearances for the Red Brigades.

"In Montivideo, we'll load the weapons onto Hercules transport planes, and from there we'll fly them to Brazil for delivery to the buyer. Why Brazil? Because control is lax over there, and I was able to bribe the necessary government officials to look the other way."

He listened again, shifted his position, and chewed the end of a piece of paper. "Yosef, I tell you there is nothing to fear. I've been building this operation for two years. It's a sure plan. This time Zeidel will fall to the sharks, unlike in '66 when he managed to escape. The deal will bear his signature. How? I managed to get a blank piece of stationery with his signature out of him, and on it I typed the agreement I made with buyers for the Egyptian and Syrian armies."

He slapped the armrest of his chair in pleasure. "Any judge will send him to jail for eighty years. You can be calm, Yosef; this time we're on solid ground. In two months at most, Zeidel will be behind bars and the corporation will be in my hands. I've already chosen a name for it. Instead of Samson Steel, I'll call it Morgan Consolidated. The name conveys power and progress."

He laughed with satisfaction. "Nonsense, Yosef. Zeidel will never know how it happened to him. I have it all worked out down to the last detail. I've built the plan layer upon layer like the Great Wall of China."

Again there was silence. "Yosef, no one would believe that behind the giant with iron fists hides a scared rabbit. Zeidel's time is up. In a few more weeks, I'll be sitting in his chair, and you will be my assistant."

⇢⇦

The courtroom looked like a street scene in ancient Pompeii after Mount Vesuvius erupted. The spectators, enthralled by the film, froze, each in his own position. Judge Oren Tzur's hand was wrapped around his gavel; Attorney Argaman's mouth hung open; his colleague Michael Donag looked like a parrot that had lost its tongue; Yoel Tzadok's eyes protruded with shock. Nati Morgan himself looked like a mummified crocodile from the graves of the Pharaohs. The message was so sharp, so crushing, that there was nothing left to say.

Attorney Donag tried anyway.

Donag: The prosecution maintains its opinion. The film has been tampered with, that is, a fake.

Goldmark: Allow me to read the expert opinion of the Coronation Camera Studio: "We have checked the film that Mr. Felix Goldmark gave us and which, according to its contents, was made on 5/30/75. The roll of film is whole and uniform, the proportions match, and all the details photographed are appropriate to the period in which the movie was made. Thus we are sure that the film is authentic."

Judge: The prosecution's objection is overruled. The defense may continue.

Goldmark: Mr. Tzadok, what do you say about this movie?

Tzadok: Why are you asking me?

Goldmark: You testified that Mr. Portman had hired you to keep an eye on Mr. Morgan. Aren't you the one who made this movie?

Tzadok: No!

Goldmark: The box of film contained a receipt from the laboratory that developed it. Here it is (waving it before the court). It says here, "A check for 150 lirah was received from Yoel Tzadok." It appears you did this work for Mr. Portman.

Argaman: Objection. The defense is using irrelevant material in order to divert the trial from the issue at hand.

Judge: There is something to what you say. If the defense does not prove the connection between Exhibit #2 and the case, I will order Mr. Tzadok to step down from the witness stand. It is not Mr. Morgan who is on trial but Mr. Goldmark.

Goldmark: Your Honor, with a few additional questions the connection will become clear. Mr. Tzadok, in the film, was Mr. Morgan speaking to Yosef Berning, who later evolved into Asaf Niv? And was the deal they were speaking about the so-called rain forest deal of 1975, as a result of which Mr. Portman was imprisoned and Mr. Morgan took over the corporation?

Yoel Tzadok was silent.

Judge: The witness is requested to answer the question.

Tzadok (with a grave face): The answer to both is positive.

Goldmark: It follows that Mr. Portman was innocent and that it was not he, but Mr. Morgan, who had signed an agreement to sell weapons to Egypt and Syria. Is this correct?

Donag: I object, Your Honor. The defense is putting words into the witness's mouth!

Judge: Objection overruled.

Goldmark: Mr. Tzadok, you testified that an important part of your job was keeping an eye on Mr. Morgan. Where were you when Mr. Portman was on trial? Why didn't you come to court and testify on his behalf? Why didn't you present this film to prove his innocence?

Tzadok: I was out of the country at the time.

Goldmark: Your name, sir, does not appear on the lists of those leaving the country by plane or boat in that period. During the trial, you were vacationing with your family in Tel Aviv's Palm Beach Hotel. You allowed your employer to be convicted of crimes he did not commit, when with a little effort you could have saved him.

Tzadok: I think a grave injustice has been done to me. I was more devoted to Zeidel than a son is to his father. I don't recall exactly why I did not show up to testify during his trial. More than thirty years have passed since then.

Goldmark (smiling): Thank you, Mr. Tzadok. That will be all for now. I would like to call on the next witness, Mr. Moshe Moshiko Sharabi, an employee of Morgan Consolidated.

❧

A burning desire for revenge possessed Rebbetzin Flora Simchoni-Freilich.

Over the years, Devorah Mindelman had been a regular, faithful client who had never argued about price. She had been emotionally depressed to the point where she gladly adopted any method of treatment Flora advised. Elitzafan had passively allowed Devorah to become addicted to the treatments without presenting obstacles. Suddenly something had gone wrong, and Elitzafan had sabotaged their wonderful relationship.

All along, Flora had been willing to do anything for Devorah and Chedvi. When she met the Feldmans in Paris, intuition had told her that François and Chedvi were a match made in heaven, and she had turned the world over to see the *shidduch* through. Now she would have to face the Feldmans and tell them that they had flown to Israel for nothing. By refusing the French *shidduch*, Elitzafan had made a fool of her.

She would punish him!

With a trembling hand, she took her cell phone and dialed.

"Hello," said an authoritative voice.

"Hello," she said. "Is this the Patankin family?"

"Yes."

"I would like to tell you something about a sensitive subject."

Simchah tensed. Another anonymous phone call? He had already had one. "Who is speaking?"

"It doesn't matter. The main thing is what I have to say."

"It *does* matter," said Simchah angrily. "I'm not prepared to speak to an anonymous caller."

"Okay, my name is Bluma Solomon. I'm a neighbor of the Mindelman family in Beis Yisrael. I understand that Chedvi has been suggested for your son."

"And if so, what is it your business?"

"It will certainly be *your* business soon, because you are about to get involved with the daughter of a woman who has been hospitalized several times for depression. Do you know, sir, that depression is hereditary?"

Simchah took the bull by the horns. "Do you know me? Do you know my son? Why are you so concerned about us? What do you care whether my son gets engaged to the daughter of a lunatic?"

"Every pot has its cover," Flora replied. "If your son is also problematic, I understand. But if your son is problem-free, let him get engaged to a girl who is also."

Flora put down the receiver without waiting for an answer and then attacked the phone book. "Klein. Where is it? Ah, here it is! Daniel and Peninah Klein…."

⁓

The arrogance and high spirits that Nati had displayed at the beginning of the hearing melted. He looked at his watch often and drummed nervously on the armrest of the bench. Every few seconds he cast an accusing look at attorneys Argaman and Donag, who were losing the case to a defendant who did not even have a lawyer.

In desperation, he sent a text message to Rafi Zamir's cell phone: "Do something!"

Two minutes later, the image of an envelope flickered on his screen. He read the answer: "We'll try to take the rest of the trial out of Oren Tzur's hands."

His fingers danced on the keys: "Too late. Arrange an accident."

Zamir did not reply.

Nati tried to look indifferent when Moshiko Sharabi took the witness stand. *This is the end!* he thought. *Felix will smash me to smithereens by setting my own men against me.*

At the management meeting of Morgan Consolidated in Paris a month ago, the matter of Moshiko and his eavesdropping had been raised again. Moshiko, with his technical sense, had been considered an invaluable asset to the corporation. Then he was caught planting listening devices anywhere and everywhere. The corporation's big brass wondered whether a button had even been planted in Nati's very body.

Malkiel thought that Moshiko still suffered from teenage complexes, which would soon pass. He proposed keeping him out of the action until he learned his lesson and stopped sniffing behind their backs. Asaf argued that Moshiko was an agent planted in their midst who posed a threat to Morgan Consolidated and should be eliminated in a clean, concise way. Nati had sided with Malkiel.

Now Nati saw that Asaf had been right. Moshiko was just waiting for the opportunity to tell his story. Felix asked a few leading questions, and Moshiko confidently sketched the story of Morgan Consolidated from the inside. He described a corrupt arms corporation that sold weapons to Israel's enemies and even transported enriched uranium to Iran.

The prosecuting attorneys interrupted him repeatedly, arguing that he had concocted the story to avenge himself against the boss, whom he disliked. Judge Oren Tzur rejected their arguments and allowed Felix to question Moshiko on condition that he prove Moshiko's claims.

Goldmark: I hereby present the court with Exhibit #3 of the defense: tapes of Morgan Consolidated management meetings.

Judge: How did you obtain these tapes?

Sharabi: I planted a few buttons in the conference rooms.

Judge: Buttons?

Sharabi: Miniature electronic listening devices.

In the next few minutes, those present shuddered in horror as they heard Nati himself give instructions to sell hundreds of shoulder missiles to two Hezbullah agents, Basm al Zarzur and Hilad abu Kishak.

Nati did not lose his head. He asked for permission to speak, and presented an argument clever in its simplicity.

Morgan: Today, a fictitious recording can easily be synthesized in a studio from a recording of a few sentences. Moshiko hates me, perhaps because I was too tough as a boss, and is taking revenge. I ask the court to see Moshiko Sharabi as a hostile witness and reject his testimony.

54

Rafi Zamir was at his wits' end. Someone hadn't done his homework properly. They had been sure that Judge Oren Tzur was on their side — and look what happened. Felix Goldmark was extricating himself from the spider's web, and Nati Morgan was being trapped in it. Nati certainly deserved to be punished for his treachery, but that was an internal matter for the Mossad to take care of. No outsiders needed to know that a Mossad agent had turned traitor.

While Rafi Zamir was considering various ways of taking the continuation of the trial out of Judge Oren Tzur's hands, the judge evicted a careless journalist whom he caught with a Palm Pilot activated. The other journalists who had been admitted to the closed-door trial scribbled quickly in small notebooks, occasionally raising nervous eyes toward the judge like students copying during a test.

Suddenly Rafi Zamir heard Felix saying, "The credibility of Mr. Moshe Moshiko Sharabi will be established by the testimony of the next witness."

Judge: Who is that?

Goldmark: Because of the sensitivity of the matter, I request permission to announce the witness's name only after he enters. He is waiting outside.

A policeman admitted a tall young man with a head of brown curls and three earrings in his left ear who was wearing a jacket and tie for the occasion.

Goldmark: The defense calls on Mr. Sheket Lapid to testify.

Sheket walked over to the witness stand with a lithe, springy step.

Goldmark: I understand that you have an additional name.

Lapid: Correct. My other name is Leonardo Pantoloni.

Goldmark: Is that your name from birth?

Lapid: No. In my work as a Mossad agent, I received the cover name Leonardo Pantoloni along with my Italian passport.

Goldmark: What is your connection with Mr. Moshe Moshiko Sharabi?

Lapid: We are close friends. We served in a commando unit together, and afterwards we both worked in Paris. I used the cover of a salesman in a clothing store; he worked at Morgan Consolidated.

Goldmark: Why do you speak about your work in past tense?

Lapid: I resigned from the Mossad because of something that happened and because I wanted to come testify.

Goldmark: Please tell the court what happened.

To Rafi Zamir, this was the last straw. No one outside the Mossad needed to know that Nati had abused his position as a Mossad agent to order Moshiko killed. The Mossad's dirty laundry did not have to be aired out in public. Rafi frantically sent a text message to Argaman: "Stop him!" But during the few seconds that the message was delayed on its way to the prosecutor's cell phone, Sheket galloped ahead at dizzying speed.

Lapid: My superior in the Mossad ordered me to do a Triple Zero on Moshiko, that is, to liquidate him in a traffic accident. The reason given was that he was about to sell the secrets of the State of Israel to the enemy.

Goldmark: How did you receive the order?

Lapid: It came by e-mail to my personal computer.

Goldmark: Do you have proof?

Lapid: Yes. It's right here, in the hard disk of my computer.

"He's a traitor!" hollered Zamir. Then he addressed Sheket sternly, "Your resignation does not release you from the requirements of secrecy. You will stand trial for treason and for damaging national security."

Judge: Sir, with all due respect, you are an observer at this trial and have no right to interfere in the proceedings. If you wish, you may ask the prosecution to cross-examine the witness.

Zamir fell silent. Argaman quickly received the message: "Don't let him present the contents of his hard disk under any circumstances!" He immediately rose.

Argaman: Your Honor, I request that for reasons of national security, the witness be barred from presenting the contents of his hard disk.

Judge (after consideration): Objection sustained. The defense may continue to examine the witness without using the hard disk.

Zamir, Nati, and a few others heaved a sigh of relief.

Goldmark: You testified that you received an order to kill Mr. Sharabi. Why didn't you carry it out?

Lapid: I confess shamefacedly that I tried, but Moshiko was saved by a miracle. Heaven saved him from death and me from killing an innocent person.

Goldmark: Why did they really want you to kill him?

The prosecutors, who were conferring in whispers, missed the defense's question. No one jumped up and cried, "Objection!"

Lapid: Moshiko told me that he had caught his employers, Nati and Asaf, actually the whole Morgan Consolidated management, negotiating weapons sales with enemies of the State of Israel. Nati knew that Moshiko knew too much. As a member of the Mossad, Nati sent an order to liquidate Moshiko that reached me.

"That's a lie!" hollered Nati.

Goldmark (ignoring Nati): I thank the witness. I would like to recall Mr. Yoel Tzadok to the witness stand.

☙❧

Peninah Klein tossed and turned in bed. Three times an anonymous woman had called and warned them that Chedvi Mindelman took pills for depression. The caller claimed that she had the medical records in her hand. How could Peninah let her Asher enter into such a *shidduch*?

"It's all lies," Daniel insisted. "For the past six years, someone has been trying to sabotage every *shidduch* with the Mindelmans. It's easy to strike an opponent in the dark. The anonymous slanderer doesn't need to prove the victim's guilt, while the victim doesn't know that he has to prove his innocence."

"But where there's smoke, there's fire!"

"That is not Torah law. Besides, in this case, there is no smoke. Someone claims there is, but I didn't see or smell any," Daniel added with a smile. "Someone once asked, 'How did Noah manage to build the Ark when he was blind?' He was told, 'Don't assume that Noah was blind, and you won't have the question.' Someone decided to slander Chedvi Mindelman, that all. It's simply malicious libel."

"And what if it isn't?" asked Peninah nervously.

Daniel jumped to his feet. "This has gone too far," he declared. "The time has come to take action."

He called the police and complained of anonymous nuisance calls in the middle of the night. "The next time it happens," Sergeant Reuven Shimoni told him, "get someone to call us from a different phone while you delay the caller as long as possible."

The phone rang after midnight. Daniel prepared himself emotionally for the encounter and then picked up the receiver. He asked the caller to identify herself. When she refused, he signaled Peninah, who called the police on the cell phone. He listened as the caller described Chedvi's illness. Then he argued with her. Finally he asked to see the girl's medical records and to speak with her psychiatrists....

The caller, thinking she had managed to crack a tough nut, was drunk with success. "Tomorrow I will send you the medical documents," she announced solemnly. "Mr. Klein, what is your fax number?"

"What's our fax number?" Daniel hollered into the space of the house, as he winked at Peninah, sitting beside him. "Here, I'll give it to you right away."

His cell phone vibrated. Apologizing for the inconvenience, he asked the anonymous caller to wait a minute while he brought her the fax number. Then he went into another room and answered his cell phone.

"Mr. Daniel Klein?"

"Yes."

"Sergeant Reuven Shimoni of the police. The name of your anonymous caller is Flora Simchoni-Freilich. Do you know her?"

"Not personally, but I've heard of her."

"The best thing is for you to deal with her yourself."

Daniel returned to the phone and said calmly, "Here is our fax number, Rebbetzin Flora Simchoni-Freilich."

There was shocked silence on the other side. Only a weak cough indicated that Flora was still on the line.

Daniel struck while the iron was hot. "Did you think you would stay anonymous forever? Today it's easy to find out whom a blocked number belongs to."

Flora recovered with amazing speed. "Fine, so you found out my name. I did nothing wrong. I merely wanted to protect your son."

"If Chedvi Mindelman takes pills for depression, why did you introduce her to a nice boy like François?" asked Daniel, who had spoken at length to Elitzafan Mindelman in the past few days.

He hung up and told Peninah calmly, "Now we can go into the *shidduch* with a calm heart."

"Never in my life," Nati hissed to the prestigious lawyer for the prosecution, "have I seen a pair of misfits like you. Tell me, what do you know how to do besides buy expensive suits? I sent you here to finish the trial in two hours and put that swindler of a scientist behind bars, and what do I get? Two idiots who let him stage his own show. At this rate, they'll hang me in Rabin Square!"

Argaman's lip quivered. People waited a year for the privilege of receiving his legal services, and Nati insulted him as if he were a bellhop. Well, Nati could eat the cereal he had cooked for himself. Argaman had a brilliant emergency plan for extricating Nati from Goldmark's jaws, but Nati didn't deserve it. Argaman returned to his seat.

"What did Nati tell you?" asked Donag.

There was a strange gleam in Argaman's eye when he whispered back, "From now on, we are not going to interrupt Goldmark even once."

Donag nodded.

Goldmark: Mr. Tzadok, you testified that although Mr. Portman hired you to keep tabs on Mr. Morgan, you found no evidence of any wrongdoing. Yet with a hidden camera, you filmed him discussing deals he was cooking up with Arab agents in order to do Mr. Portman in. How do the two statements fit together?

Tzadok: I was totally devoted to Zeidel. Had I known about the existence of this film, I would have hurried to his defense. I had nothing to do with the film.

Goldmark: How, then, did the film get into the Tiberias apartment?

Tzadok: I was not Zeidel's only employee. Someone else did this work for him — perhaps Arik Hadad, who worked in the office and did a variety of jobs. The poor fellow died a year ago.

Goldmark: Why was the receipt made out to your name?

Tzadok: Zeidel was a mysterious person. He probably did it to confuse his enemies.

Goldmark: I ask the court permission to present another film, the defense's Exhibit #4.

Judge: Permission granted.

Like the previous one, this film, too, was black and white. It showed a figure that looked like Yoel Tzadok but thirty years younger, with a submachine gun slung over his shoulder, walking amidst an inferno. Several corpses were strewn on the ground and vehicles were going up in flames.

Yoel's eyes bulged out of their sockets. He looked as if he were drunk with fear and anger, and his head wagged from side to side. All eyes were riveted on him, waiting to see what he would do.

Suddenly he made a decision. He turned to the microphone.

Tzadok: All right, I confess. I sinned greatly against Zeidel.

Already in my first week at Samson Steel, I had proof that Nati was working behind Zeidel's back. But the climax came in '66, when I broke into Nati's house in Kfar Shmaryahu at Zeidel's order and found documents proving that Nati had sold eighteen military transport helicopters to Egypt, Israel's number-one enemy at the time.

After that, we planted listening devices in the walls of Nati's room in the office, but Zeidel never managed to catch him selling even a single shoelace that was not kosher.

Goldmark: Why?

Tzadok (bursting): Because I sold my soul to Nati for money! I had a dual allegiance, which began even before I came to work at Samson Steel.

Nati knew Zeidel was about to fire him. He found me waiting in line to collect unemployment and he offered me work. "My boss," he said, "is looking for an efficient, organized clerk who will also keep an eye on me.

You look the part of an honest clerk. Come apply to Samson Steel. The boss will be calm, and I'll be able to do my own work quietly."

"But I really am an honest man," I objected. "Why should I start doing shady things?"

Nati shoved two hundred-lirah bills into my hands. In those days, that was a lot of money.

The next day I came to the office for an interview. As Nati had figured, Zeidel liked me — to put it mildly. He didn't know that I was the bait to trap him. Nati, of course, pretended to be upset that Zeidel had hired me.

From that day, I pretended to be shadowing Nati for Zeidel. From time to time, I threw Zeidel a small bone so he wouldn't suspect me. But in fact I helped Nati fool Zeidel down the line.

Goldmark: That explains why you didn't come to court to testify on behalf of Mr. Portman. But why did you film Mr. Morgan cooking up the rain forest deal, when you weren't planning to use the pictures?

Tzadok: As I told you, I had a dual allegiance. I really was very attached to Zeidel, who was a righteous, upright, kind man. I loved him with all my heart and loathed myself for betraying his trust. I felt that I was the most despicable creature on earth. But I couldn't give up the enormous salary that Nati was paying me.

From time to time I thought of handing Nati over to Zeidel. I even filmed Nati with a hidden camera. Nati knew about the camera but was confident that I would not betray him. And he was right.

Nati also knew about the sophisticated listening devices that I planted in the walls of his room. Obviously, I never managed to incriminate him.

May Zeidel, he should rest in peace, forgive me for all the injustices I did to him. I know I was wrong. I had a hand in making his life unbearable, and perhaps even in shortening it.

Morgan (boiling mad): You betrayed Zeidel, and now you're betraying me as well! Tell me, if you loved Zeidel so much, why have you been torturing his only son for the past six years?

Goldmark: The witness may step down. I ask the court's permission to call Mr. Natan Morgan to the witness stand.

Judge: Permission granted.

Goldmark: Mr. Morgan, are you prepared to testify?

Morgan: Gladly.

Dozens of heads turned like sunflowers at noon as Nati Morgan strode furiously to the witness stand. A volcano on the verge of eruption was an innocent sandbox compared to him. Nati stood beside the microphone, ready and waiting tensely. You could see that nothing mattered to him anymore. Come what may, he would settle the score with his worst enemy.

Rafi Zamir sent a message to Nati: "Go outside!" Then he said a few words quietly to the judge. Oren Tzur nodded. Zamir left the courtroom followed a minute later by Nati.

"Have you taken leave of your senses?" demanded Zamir. "Are you going to open your mouth?"

"I will do whatever I must to protect my good name and my own interests," said Nati.

"If you sling mud at the Mossad, you won't come out of it clean."

Nati suddenly looked old. "I'm no longer a young man, Rafi. It's impossible to threaten me. I've already lived my life. Decades ago I made peace with my fate of being childless. When I die, I will leave no trace behind in the world. All I have is my good name — and Yoel Tzadok is ruining it. I have to fight back and settle the score."

"Not at the expense of the Mossad," said Zamir, shaking Nati's arm excitedly.

"The Mossad!" Nati spat out scornfuly, pulling his arm away. "First restore its lost prestige, and then we'll discuss the damage that I'm causing it."

Rafi Zamir watched thoughtfully as Nati turned his back and walked into the courtroom. The damage would have to be minimized at all costs.

55

Tension mounted in the courtroom as Nati took the witness stand for his second round of testimony. Everyone felt was that this time, something was going to happen. Although the duel that Yoel and Nati fought was verbal, it was deadly.

Goldmark: Mr. Morgan, can you tell us what happened in the Brazilian rain forest in 1975?

Morgan: With pleasure. Yoel Tzadok filmed me moving the deal along. The film has not been tampered with; it is authentic to the last detail. We did indeed want to get rid of that weed called Zeidel Portman.

Judge: I request that you speak with proper respect of the deceased, who is unable to defend his good name.

Morgan: The judge is right. He was not a weed. A weed damages only vegetation, whereas Zeidel threatened the young State of Israel. I was sent into the arena by a higher-up of the government, as a Mossad agent, to ruin Zeidel's reputation. The rain forest deal was the only possibility I saw of accomplishing this goal.

Goldmark: Do you have a film of what happened in the rain forest?

Morgan: Yes, I do. I suspected something might go wrong in my absence and I wanted to know everything. I never dreamed that Yoel himself would do what he did....

Goldmark: Is the film here?

Morgan: I placed it in a vault in a bank down the street in case we needed it. With your permission, I will bring it immediately.

Judge: Mr. Morgan, you need not trouble yourself. A messenger will be sent to bring it. The court is hereby adjourned for twenty minutes.

⌘

Rafi Zamir seethed at the intolerable disgrace. Felix had turned the trial upside down. It was not a scientist at Elta who had betrayed the State of Israel, but a Mossad agent. Worse still, that Mossad agent had opened his mouth and forgotten to close it.

Zamir sent a warning to Nati's cell phone: "Stop immediately, or you'll pay dearly!"

After reading the message, Nati raised his head and speared Zamir with the proud glance of someone who is accustomed to giving orders, not taking them.

The messenger returned from the bank with a black attaché case. Nati unlocked it and took out a thin tin box, the standard packaging for a roll of film thirty years ago.

A tremor of excitement rippled through the courtroom.

Judge: Please show the film.

Argaman: Your Honor, allow me to express my surprise. This case was supposed to be tried behind closed doors. How is it then, that from session to session I see more people here, including several journalists?

Laughter was heard from the benches.

Judge: The policemen allow in only holders of special permits. I have nothing to do with it. If I hear one more disrespectful comment, I will have you removed from the trial!

After this rebuke, Argaman did not dare open his mouth.

Again the courtroom was darkened. Rays of white light emerged from of the projector, and turned into a series of pictures.

⌘

Nati's film was similar to the one Felix had shown, but sharper and fuller. At first they saw the inside of a small corporate jet, where young Yoel Tzadok sat behind three tense fellows with American faces. The camera had evidently been well hidden in the luggage compartment above the upholstered seats. From the uninhibited behavior and the eyes that passed indifferently over the face of the lens, it was evident that no one was aware of the camera.

Yoel looked out of the window and announced, "We're landing."

There was a jolt. Then the three Americans rose with guns drawn and checked their magazine of bullets. Yoel shouted in English, "Shoot all of them dead, but don't touch the giant!"

Nati interrupted. "I had instructed Yoel to protect the giant, Yosef Berning. The order to kill the rest was Yoel's own personal addition."

Tzadok: Nonsense. The whole order came from you!

Judge: I request that both of you keep silent until the film has been shown. Afterwards each may present his comments.

The movie continued. The Americans put on ski masks and walked quickly out of the range of the lens. Then the sound of the door of the plane opening was heard, followed by a burst of submachine gun fire. The camera continued photographing for a few minutes. Suddenly a voice hollered, "Yoel, come quickly. They're mowing down everything that moves. If you don't run out to them, they'll kill Yosef too."

Yoel was seen grabbing a Kalachnikov submachine gun and running down the aisle with it. For a moment he went out of view.

There was a pause of a few seconds, evidently to move the camera outside the plane.

"The photographer was the co-pilot," said Nati. "At my orders, he shadowed Yoel every step of the way."

The next pictures were of a huge conflagration coming from a row of flaming trucks. It lit up the sloped roofs of the one-story houses in the distance to the right, and the silhouettes of thousands of trees on the left, rising toward the darkening sky. On the ground lay two corpses. A giant sprawled motionless on his face beside a short, thin man lying on his back. In the distance, a figure escaped into one of the houses. Yoel followed it, a malicious smile on his face. The photographer followed from a distance as Yoel cautiously approached the house and entered it.

A minute later, a metallic voice, characteristic of old walkie-talkies, was heard from inside the house. "Barak, go over to emergency procedures. Wait for us to come get you; meanwhile, make yourself inconspicuous."

"Roger. Kodkod, I know who betrayed us," came the voice of someone inside the house.

"Barak! Don't talk over the walkie-talkie. We'll speak face to face."

Yoel went in with stealthy steps. Suddenly two shots rang out.

The walkie-talkie continued to croak. "Barak, Barak, Barak?"

The screen went dark.

"The photographer had to stop before Yoel came out of the house and caught him," explained Nati. He spoke quietly, but the audience did not miss a word he said. "Yechezkel Shoshan was hiding in the house. He ran to the walkie-talkie to tell Zeidel about the failure of the arms delivery. Yoel, why did you shoot him? I don't understand it to this day. He was one of your best friends."

Yoel's dull voice sounded in the darkness. "What could I have done? I was afraid of him. Yechezkel, who was one of Zeidel's faithful men, had followed you and me and heard us talking together. He realized that I had dual allegiance. It was only a matter of time until he delivered me into Zeidel's hands."

The lights went back on. Nati returned to the witness stand.

Goldmark: Why did Yosef Berning change his name to Asaf Niv after the rain forest deal?

Morgan: Yosef, the strong giant, is a scaredy cat. The Americans had instructions not to kill him; they only shot around him. He lost consciousness from fear. Afterwards he did not dare to get up. He lay there like a corpse for two hours. When all was silent, he rose and fled for his life.

He assumed that Yechezkel had told Zeidel about his part in the great betrayal, so he changed his identity and fled until things quieted down.

Goldmark: Why was Yosef Berning left alive while Zev Shachar was shot to death?

Morgan: Yosef was my faithful assistant. Zev was one of Zeidel's men, sniffing around like a hunting dog. Sooner or later he would have messed up our plans, so we had a decided interest in getting rid of him quickly. Yechezkel could have stayed alive for my part, but Yoel had different interests.

Tzadok (shouting): Villain! The entire village of Dilo de la Pedra was wiped off the map on account of you! Hundreds of peaceful, innocent Brazilian citizens died of an epidemic of black plague that broke out a few days later from the powder you put on the trucks. You wanted proof against Zeidel — so you offered hundreds of sacrifices on the altar of your self-interest. And then you talk about a single man that I killed!

Morgan: I deny it vehemently. Never did I use biological weapons.

Tzadok (sarcastically): Of course not! The boxes grew legs and climbed into the trucks by themselves.

Morgan (turning to the judge): Your Honor, I did not betray my country. Even if I negotiated with enemy countries, I did so upon the instructions of certain government leaders, as my good friend Rafi Zamir can confirm.

It is true that I brought a phenomenal amount of weapons to Brazil — but not one gun ever reached the enemy! We sprayed all the trucks. Everything went up in flames. All the weapons and explosives were destroyed, down to the last piece.

As for the plague, even if containers of powder *had* been put on the trucks, the heat of the fire would have killed all the deadly germs. The epidemic had nothing whatsoever to do with the arms deal. The village was too close to the rain forest, and an infected yellow monkey spread the epidemic among the villagers.

In short, my hands are clean. (Turns to Yoel.) But yours are soiled with the blood of an innocent man — Yechezkel Shoshan!

Tzadok: And what flowed through the veins of Zev Shachar, ketchup?

Morgan (calmly): Zev was executed by order of government leaders. But why are we dealing with the past? Tell the judge, please, how you planted listening devices in the Mindelman family's phone lines, and how you've been hounding Elitzafan Mindelman, the only son of Avraham Zeidel Portman, for the past six years!

Tzadok: Aren't you ashamed to lie? You instructed me to eavesdrop on all the Mindelmans' conversations to prevent Zeidel's grandchildren from ever marrying. Your motive was revenge. "He ruined all my marriage prospects," you said. "Because of him I will die childless. Therefore Zeidel will ultimately have no descendants either." In contrast to you, I began only after Zeidel died, and only because I desired to inherit his estate.

Morgan: Zeidel destroyed my life; why shouldn't I take revenge? You did it only for money.

Goldmark: Mr. Morgan, you stated earlier that you are still in touch with Asaf Niv and Malkiel Yahalom. Do you still maintain your claim?

Morgan: For the sake of truth, I will say that only after the fact did I learn that the two of them had been negotiating behind my back for the Arrow CDs. But whereas I, operating as a Mossad agent, was trying to draw you into a trap, Asaf and Malkiel actually planned to betray the homeland. I am not sorry that they fell into the hands of the Saudi intelligence agency.

Goldmark: I am grateful to the witness for his openness. I would like to call Mr. Yoel Tzadok back to the witness stand.

Judge: Mr. Tzadok, please take the stand.

On the front garden of the stately mansion, Mrs. Tzur was playing with her two black-and-white Dalmation dogs. Suddenly a passing car slowed down in front of the Tzur residence. From its window, a fragmentation grenade was hurled into the garden. The fragments scattered over a broad radius, killing the two beautiful dogs and lightly wounding Mrs. Tzur, who was taken by ambulance to the hospital.

A few minutes after the police investigators and a criminal identification unit left the area, fire broke out in the basement. Within minutes it reached the living room.

Fire fighters who rushed to the scene doused the flames with enormous water hoses and foam jets. Between the fire and the water, all the furniture and appliances were ruined, not to mention the extensive library and Judge Oren Tzur's pride and joy — his priceless art collection. The house and its contents were insured, but the original paintings by great artists were irreplaceable.

Mrs. Tzur tried calling her husband from the emergency room, but his cell phone was off. She dialed the court and spoke to the secretary. "Tell my husband everything," she concluded hysterically. She needed her husband at her side, even if it meant interrupting an important hearing.

The secretary entered the courtroom precisely when Judge Oren Tzur summoned Yoel Tzadok to the witness stand. She quietly informed the judge that his wife had been wounded lightly by a fragmentation grenade, the two dogs had been killed, and Mrs. Tzur wanted him at her side in the emergency room.

Oren Tzur recognized an attempt to derail the trial when he saw one. His sharp eyes focused on the face of Rafi Zamir. Neither the stony face of the Mossad man nor his clear eyes betrayed any emotion. But Oren Tzur was sure beyond doubt that Zamir was responsible for the grave incident — an obvious attempt to frighten him off the case.

No one could frighten Oren Tzur!

He left the courtroom for a moment, called his sobbing wife, and asked her to be strong for another hour until he could join her in the hospital. She was upset but agreed to wait. The trial would go on!

A moment later, the secretary again came to speak quietly to the judge.

"My house was burned down?" His eyes turned into two empty windows, open and screaming to the heavens.

"That's what I was told," whispered the secretary sadly. "Would you like to leave the trial and let it be conducted by Judge Eli Giora?"

This time he stopped to think. Did continuing the trial justify every sacrifice?

He made the difficult decision. "No," he said laconically. "But please bring me a cup of water."

Judge Oren Tzur was more determined than he had ever been in his life. It was clear as the noontime sun that some powerful party was trying to force him off this trial, but they would not succeed. He would continue to conduct the trial until his last drop of blood!

56

oel Tzadok was shaking so badly that a policeman had to support him on either side as he walked to the witness stand.

Goldmark: Mr. Tzadok, is it true that you have been harassing the Mindelman family?

Tzadok: Let me explain myself. For twenty years, I was Zeidel's right hand, and he promised to requite me. I was entitled to a good part of his inheritance!

Do you want to know how attached he was to me? He gave me a contract guaranteeing my position; it specified a severance pay which would bankrupt the corporation. Today I go where I wish and do as I please; no one can fire me.

Obviously, Zeidel would have remembered me in his will also. But he left half his estate to whoever would clear his name and prove that he had not betrayed his people. The second half he of course bequeathed to his only son, Elitzafan Mindelman.

There was no way I could go for the first half of the estate. Clearing Zeidel's name would have meant besmirching Nati's, and besmirching Nati's would have put a noose around my neck.

I decided to go for the second half. Nati had taught me how easy it was to enter someone else's life, and I took it further. I continued to harass the Mindelmans by ruining every possibility of marriage for their daughter. But in contrast to Nati, who wanted revenge, I wanted money. After I sent some thugs after them on the Jordan Valley road to rough up his car and frighten Elitzafan by displaying a pistol, he signed a document giving up his share in the inheritance.

Goldmark: But how did you tap the Mindelmans' phone lines for six years without their finding out?

Tzadok: Those *chareidim* are naive. They were never suspicious of the noise and rustles on the phone line. They never found the hidden camera that I planted in Zeidel's apartment in Rechaviah after his death either, not to mention the one in his Tiberias apartment, which stopped working recently.

Goldmark: Why did you plant a camera in an empty apartment?

Tzadok: I suspected that Zeidel had written an additional will that canceled the previous ones, and I wanted to find it. I manipulated Zeidel's neighbor, Daniel Klein, into doing the work for me. I even frightened him in various ways. He was actually convinced that if someone wanted him to stop searching, he must be on the right track.

I manipulated Daniel Klein into going to Zeidel's Tiberias apartment as well, and I planted a camera there, too. It suited my purposes to have Daniel Klein search for the will and meanwhile find the notebooks documenting how Zeidel sold weapons to Arabs and crosses to Christians.

But my main project was tormenting the Mindelmans. I even sent Adam Dushman to frighten away François on the evening he was to become engaged to Chedvi Mindelman in Paris.

In short, my plan was successful. I achieved my goal. Elitzafan relinquished his portion of the inheritance.

Judge: Mr. Mindelman's signature is invalid since it was extorted from him under threat.

Tzadok: It's not fair. I deserved a portion of Zeidel's inheritance. There is no justice in the world!

Judge: Mr. Tzadok, you will need to undergo a psychiatric evaluation. And now, the prosecution is invited to cross-examine the defendant.

౸

A victorious smile hovered over Shlomo Argaman's lips. He would manage to send the errant scientist to jail yet.

Argaman: Mr. Goldmark. What was in the CDs that you sold to Mr. Natan Morgan and Mr. Asaf Niv?

Goldmark (smiling): Garbage.

A gasp rippled through the courtroom.

Argaman: Are you calling the most closely guarded secrets of the State of Israel garbage?

Goldmark: Allow me to explain. When I cleared the worthless files out of my computer, I saved a few to make a simulation computer game for children. For the purpose of tricking Mr. Morgan and Mr. Asaf Niv, I made a composite of those files, mixed in a few outdated sketches of the Patriot missile, and called the final product the Arrow. I kept an identical set of the CDs for myself, and if the prosecution wishes, I will gladly present it.

Argaman: So you went to London, pretended to be a cigar smoker in order to meet Mr. Morgan in the Havana Club, and risked your career and status with Elta, in order to trick Mr. Natan Morgan and Mr. Asaf Niv. Why did you want to trick them?

Goldmark: To stop them from helping Iran construct an atom bomb.

Morgan: He's out of his mind!

Goldmark (turning to Nati): How much were you paid for sending your employees to transport cylinders of enriched uranium from the Russia–Kazakhstan border to Iran? Twenty million dollars, or even more? If you are here now in an Israeli courtroom, then I have accomplished my first purpose.

Argaman: And your second purpose?

Goldmark: Simple humane motives.

Morgan: You mean money, lots of it.

Goldmark (ignoring the comment): For six years, my neighbor Elitzafan Mindelman has been crying on my shoulder. He bears the scars of a childhood trauma: His father, Mr. Zeidel Portman, was framed and sent to jail for betraying the country. On top of that, someone has been ruining every marriage possibility for Elitzafan Mindelman's children.

I decided to enter the thick of it. I contacted Mr. Portman's former neighbor, Mr. Daniel Klein, who gave me the key to Mr. Portman's apartment in Tiberias. The first time I went, I encountered Mr. Tzadok there. Knowing him from the days we worked together at Elta, I had my suspicions about him. After that, I returned at night several times when Mr. Tzadok was not there, covered his camera with black fabric, and searched the apartment. That is how I found the film I showed you of Mr. Morgan speaking with Yossi Berning.

Argaman: What about the second film? The one of Yoel Tzadok in the rain forest?

Goldmark (laughing): That one has been tampered with.

The courtroom flew into in an uproar. Judge Oren Tzur banged his gavel.

Judge: Order in the court! Mr. Goldmark, please continue.

Goldmark: I understood that Yoel Tzadok had been in the rain forest and had done something wrong there. I obtained pictures of him from that period and had a studio produce the film according to the data I had gathered. But I was not far off. There is only a minor difference between my film and Mr. Morgan's.

I suspected Mr. Portman's former partner, Mr. Morgan. From hearing the recordings of the Morgan Consolidated management discussions, I guessed that Mr. Morgan is a heavy cigar smoker. I found out that Mr. Morgan frequented London's Havana Club, so I went there to get friendly with him. I figured that a corrupt arms dealer who supplied weapons to Israel's enemies would take the bait I offered him. He did.

I counted on one of two scenarios. If he took my CDs to Iran, he would be punished there when they discovered the deception. And if he discovered the deception himself, he would have to come out of his hideout to take revenge against me.

Judge (impatiently): We have heard enough, thank you. The trial is recessed.

⊷✽⊷

In the corridor of the courthouse, Sheket confided to Moshiko that he was afraid to walk in the street with the hard disk. Moshiko offered to watch it for him. Quickly and quietly, the small leather case changed hands.

Outside the building, Moshiko began walking down the steps when a feeling of imminent danger overtook him. Before he had a chance to react, someone rammed into him from behind and grabbed the leather case from his hand. Moshiko flew through the air and landed flat on his face on the sidewalk. Through the fog of pain that enveloped him, a comforting thought buzzed in his head. *I'm alive. The disk was taken and I got banged up, but at least I'm still alive.*

Then he lost consciousness.

⟨✦⟩

Representatives of the judiciary and the Mossad held a clandestine meeting far from the courthouse. After exhaustive discussion, they decided that since Nati Morgan was "one of us," his reputation was to be defended and the foul-smelling arms deals explained somehow. The testimony of Morgan Consolidated employee Moshiko Sharabi would be discounted because he was a hostile witness. Felix Goldmark had managed to prove his own innocence, but since he knew too much, he would have to leave Israel and remain under wraps until the unfortunate episode was forgotten. Yoel Tzadok would stand trial for violation of individual privacy, harassment, and threats, and would be sent to jail.

Nati was pleased. "So, Rafi, all's well that ends well," he said when they parted. "The Mossad stayed alive, and so did I."

Rafi gave him a friendly slap on the back. "That's right, Nati. Nothing terrible happened. Are you retuning to Paris?"

"Of course. I like to sit on the banks of the Seine toward evening and watch the French children frolic near the river. Believe me, Rafi, it's the only joy I get out of life anymore."

Twenty-four hours later, Nati got into his private plane in the airport. The trial had not ended entirely well, as far as he was concerned. Felix may have been banished from the country, but he was still alive —and in possession of half a million dollars in diamonds that he had cheated Nati out of. The matter had not come up in court; the wily scientist had elegantly avoided the subject. Nati would have to settle the score with him.

The plane lifted up off the ground, and the rhythmic noise of the motor put Nati to sleep. He awoke a few hours later, looked at his watch, and gasped. Seven hours had passed since takeoff. Why hadn't they landed yet in Paris?

He hurried to the cockpit. "Why haven't we gotten there yet?" he demanded angrily.

"What's your rush, Mr. Morgan?" asked the pilot. He turned his head around.

Nati was stunned. This was not his regular pilot, but a stranger who opened his mouth with an evil grin. All he lacked was sharp teeth in his jaws to look like a wolf.

A week later, the headlines of newspapers on various continents announced: "Arms Tycoon's Private Plane Disappears over Atlantic Ocean."

⸎

Elitzafan and Devorah could not decide between the two candidates. Both young men were wonderful, both were excellent learners, but each had his own flavor. Shmuli Patankin was serious and refined. No, Grandfather Patankin did not present a problem, and neither did Grandfather Portman. Asher Klein's lively personality and easy laughter had captured Elitzafan's heart from their first meeting. Devorah favored Shmuli Patankin; Elitzafan favored Asher Klein.

They were in a bind over which one to choose, when Elitzafan exclaimed, "I've got it! We can have our cake and eat it too. Rebbetzin Simchoni–Freilich was right after all. Do you remember what she told you about Chedvi's *chasan* by the light of the burning wicks? 'A terrific learner who is righteous, handsome, considerate, serious, and refined is approaching your house with giant strides.' Do you understand, Devorah?"

Devorah looked at him in astonishment, and suddenly she understood. She burst into a peal of happy laughter that turned into weeping. Covering her face with a handkerchief, she released all her pent-up feelings of the last six years.

Elitzafan ran out of the room for fear of breaking down like she had. He raised his head heavenward and whispered in a cracked voice, "Thank you, Hashem, for purifying us through six years of affliction. And thank you, Hashem, that it has finally ended!"

hedvi and Tirtzah ran around the kitchen in a frenzy, sifting flour, cracking eggs, adding flour and flavorings, whipping, and beating. Suddenly Chedvi felt panic spreading through her. She dropped everything, ran to her room, and grabbed a *Tehillim*. Tirtzah, looking worried, hurried to tell her mother.

A loving hand patted Chedvi's shoulder.

"What happened?" asked Devorah.

Chedvi raised her red eyes. The words that she tried to say stuck in her throat.

"Chedvi, I understand you. We're all very excited."

The lost words suddenly returned to Chedvi's dry throat. "Ima, I'm so scared!"

"Scared? You should be the happiest person on earth."

"I know. But I'm so afraid that everything will fall apart at the fateful moment. At night I dream that a happy crowd fills our apartment. You and the other mother are holding a plate in your hands, and together you drop it on the floor. But the plate doesn't break! And I say to myself, 'This is your fate, Chedvi. You lack *mazal*. The plate will always stay whole, and you, Chedvi, will stay broken forever.'

"Isn't it true, Ima?" she asked, the tears coursing down her cheeks. "Don't I lack *mazal*?"

Devorah mustered all her emotional strength. "Absolutely not, Chedvi. Why is it that a person's *shidduch* is compared to the splitting of the sea? The sea was split into twelve pieces, one for each of the Tribes of Israel. The routes were curved, so they had different lengths; some tribes had longer routes than others. Similarly, each of us has an individual route that he must go through until he finds his *bashert*; some have longer routes than others. It's not a matter of luck, Heaven forbid. It was determined by the Creator, Who knows the secret of our soul and its rectification. He assigned each of us our route, our measure of suffering, and our cup of sorrow, but also the happy moment that comes in the end.

"Do you remember Brachah, who sat beside you in Meiron?"

Chedvi nodded.

"Never take the blessing of a simple person lightly. I think that her blessing, together with all the prayers, had an impact and is about to be fulfilled."

Devorah smiled and gently patted Chedvi's wet cheek. "The nightmare is behind us now. We can talk on the phone, laugh, or speak with a *shadchan* without fearing that someone is listening to our every word.

"But remember that even in the worst bad, there is always some good. All of us have learned to guard our tongues. We have felt on our own flesh that every spoken word carries weight.

"And we have learned that there is a Hand that measures out joy and pain. The time of pain is over. The time for joy has come."

⌘

Before leaving for Florida with his family, Felix went upstairs to bid a warm farewell to Elitzafan.

He was overjoyed to see the Mindelmans as he hadn't seen them in years. They looked born anew. Gone were the tension, fear, and gloom that had hung over the modest home.

"Someone has been baking," said Felix appreciatively, inhaling the aroma wafting from the kitchen.

Devorah immediately appeared with a plate of samples.

"I don't know how to thank you for everything you've done for us," said Elitzafan. "You saved us from a six-year nightmare, and you cleared my father's name."

"Don't thank me," said Felix. "Thank Hashem. Without Him, my plans would never have worked."

"There's one more matter that remains to be resolved," said Elitzafan.

"What is that?" asked Felix calmly.

"My father left behind a huge estate, but no one knows where the will is. Any idea as to how I can find it?"

With a slight smile, Felix whipped an old brown envelope out of his pocket. On it was written, "The will of Avraham Zeidel Portman."

Elitzafan was speechless. It took him a minute to recover. Then he finally managed to stammer, "W…where did you find it?"

Felix again smiled. "In the film, Nati Morgan was sitting in front of a huge wall calendar that said 'Meir and Meir, Notaries.' I figured that if your father worked with Meir and Meir, he probably left the will in their care. I went to them, and sure enough, they have it.

"It isn't in this envelope. When you go to the office of Meir and Meir, notaries, you will receive the will legally. Actually, Mr. Meir is waiting for you to come at this very moment."

"And what was written in the will that Yoel Tzadok had, which I signed that I give up my rights to?"

Felix's face contorted in displeasure at the mention of Yoel's name. "The court declared that signature invalid because it was extorted from you. Your father thought that Yoel was on his side, and he divided the inheritance into two, one for you and the other for Yoel or anyone else who would succeed in clearing his name. That did not happen, so the whole estate goes to you."

"It did happen." Elitzafan's eyes twinkled. "You, Felix, cleared my father's name. Half of his estate belongs to you."

Felix smiled again and brushed away the thought with his hand. "The two other managers of the corporation left me well endowed. Nati gave me half a million dollars in diamonds, and Asaf gave me a check for the same amount."

Elitzafan looked at Felix with deep gratitude. He opened his mouth and tried to say something, but instead of words a sob burst out of his throat. Suddenly he fell upon Felix's neck and embraced him. His whole body shook with weeping. "Felix, Felix, how can I repay you for all that you have done for me?"

"Elitzafan, calm down. Why weep when one can laugh?" Felix hugged Elitzafan and his eyes, too, became suspiciously moist. The sharpest scientific reason could not sever the strong feelings as he shared in Elitzafan's joy while grieving over his own forced exile.

A few minutes passed before Felix managed to speak again, albeit with difficulty. "So, Elitzafan, the main thing is that it is all behind you."

"No, the good part is before me," whispered Elitzafan. "Just a second."

He stepped out of the living room and immediately returned with Chedvi.

Chedvi, radiant with joy, looked very much like a *kallah*. "I have no words to thank you, Mr. Goldmark," she said. "Hashem knows what you have done for us. May He pay you for your kindness."

"May I wish you *mazal tov* already?" joked Felix.

Her smile lit up the house. "Until nine this evening, it's still supposed to be a secret. You never know what can happen…."

"This time with Hashem's help there will be no last-minute surprises. At nine this evening I'll be on the plane to Florida. So I will bless you now. *Mazal tov*, Chedvi, may Hashem help you build a wonderful Jewish home!"

He turned back to Elitzafan. "Order a taxi right now, and go get your inheritance!"

❦

Elitzafan signed the documents at Meir and Meir, Notaries, and received the will that left him his father's entire estate. Afterwards, old Morris Meir called him over and gave him another envelope.

"What is this?" asked Elitzafan in surprise.

Morris Meir surveyed him with the wise, weary look of a man who has gone through much in life. "I was a good friend of your father decades ago. After he left his first will with us, I wondered whether he would write several other versions, as many people do. I was not surprised when he came up to our office two years ago and left the envelope. He asked me to give it to you together with the will, with instructions to read it at his grave on the day you received the inheritance."

"Must I go to my father's grave?" asked Elitzafan tensely.

"Certainly. It is a mitzvah to fulfill the wishes of the deceased," Morris Meir reminded him. "The same power by which he bequeathed you all his wealth is the power by which he requested that you visit his grave."

ভ৵৶ত

The yellow late-afternoon sun lit up the white gravestones. Elitzafan led Devorah and their seven children along the path until they reached the gravestone they sought.

The gravestone was simple, like all the rest. The inscription was short and plain.

Here lies Reb Avraham Zeidel
the son of Reb Elitzafan Portman
an upright, honest man,
who did not gossip or hurt any man,
and who honored those who honored Hashem.
Departed this world on Shivah Asar b'Tammuz, 5761.

"Is this Saba Portman's grave?" asked Kreindy.

"Yes," said Elitzafan.

Elitzafan gave out small books of *Tehillim* to them all. They recited the passages customarily said at graveyards. Then Elitzafan opened the envelope and took out a large piece of paper in the familiar writing of his deceased father. He began to read.

Baruch Hashem, Kislev 5760, the holy city of Jerusalem.

I am writing this letter to you, my dear son Elitzafan, to read at my grave. I write from the depths of my wounded heart, with my blood for ink.

Mazal tov, my dear son. Today you have turned into a wealthy man with extensive assets. I hope that my estate is passing to you intact and has not fallen into the hands of swindlers. Originally I had thought to leave half of it to Yoel Tzadok, but then I realized I was mistaken about him; he was faithful not to me but to another.

I still love you, my dear son, with the same pure love as when you first came into this world. A father's compassion for a son does not change even if the son behaves improperly.

I had expected your support in those years when only Hashem and I knew that I was innocent of any crime and that I never hurt any Jew (except for Nati Morgan). I never dreamt that you would flee from me and even change your family name. I never dreamt that you would leave your father alone in his old age, dependent on the chesed of neighbors, knowing that a mere half-hour's walk away he had a son, daughter-in-law, grandsons, and granddaughters whom he had no right to see because they were ashamed of him.

I give you the benefit of the doubt, my dear son. You became frightened and fled. But you are a good person, and you are surely sorry today for the break between us. I am sure that if you could turn back the clock, you would act differently. I have forgiven you completely for all that was.

Be comforted and cheered, my precious descendants. I am in a place that is completely good. I await the time of the resurrection, when we will all be reunited, and together we will visit the Holy Temple.

Please learn and pray for my sinful soul. I hope that the terrible afflictions I suffered in this world cleansed me a little and prepared me to take my inheritance in the world of souls, to be close to Hashem and to delight in the radiance of the Shechinah.

Peace be with you, my precious son Elitzafan, I loved you greatly, and I send you all the love in my heart.

Your father, who seeks your welfare,

Avraham Zeidel Portman

Elitzafan's voice broke. Two wet lines trickled from the corners of his eyes to the hairs of his beard. He handed the paper to Chedvi. "Read this part to everyone."

Chedvi held the paper. A strange feeling enveloped her heart, but she pulled herself together and began to read aloud, with expression:

To my dear daughter-in-law Devorah and to my precious, beloved grandchildren: Chedvah, Tirtzah, Leah, Kreindel, Menashe, Yehoshua, and Nachum.

Mazal tov! I participate in your joy.

There is a strong temptation in situations like mine to succumb to anger and vengeance and to leave one's money to strangers. I am happy that I have withstood the test. I hope you will use the money in good health to build good Jewish homes.

Many sons and daughters come to the place where you are now standing, to visit their parents' graves. Some of them are tortured day and night by guilt. They think, "If only we had done more!" Whether or not this thought is justified, one thing is clear: It always comes too late.

Why should you suffer these pangs of conscience? I beg you, my precious grandchildren: Honor your father and mother during their lifetime. Do what they ask, even if it is difficult. Above all, do not abandon them in their time of need.

Chedvi burst into tears. Choking on the words, she finished reading.

I will be with you always, in times of sorrow and in times of joy.

Your loving grandfather who hardly ever merited to see you,

Avraham Zeidel Portman

"He wished us *mazal tov*," sobbed Nachum'ke, "on the very day that we finally get a *mazal tov!*"

As the sun set in a blaze of pink, orange, and red on the horizon, nine bent figures stood weeping bitterly over a white gravestone.

The change of atmosphere was sharp and poignant. A short time after the Mindelmans returned home and dressed up in their best clothes, guests began to fill the apartment in Beis Yisrael. *Savta* Shoshana Mindelman was brought from the nursing home, and neighbors, relatives, and friends came to celebrate the engagement of Chedvi Mindelman to Shmuli Patankin. Daniel Klein, the *shadchan* who had worked long and hard to make this *shidduch*, glowed with pleasure.

Two weeks later, Daniel Klein returned for another *vort* in the modest apartment in Beis Yisrael. This time, he came as the father of the *chasan*. Elitzafan was delighted to welcome Asher Klein into the family.

Daniel Klein received his earthly reward for helping Zeidel all those years. Zeidel's granddaughter Tirtzah was a wonderful daughter-in-law; and the wedding, apartment, and furniture were all provided for from Zeidel's estate.

Felix Goldmark, forcibly exiled to Florida, was unable to attend the two weddings. But the man who had cleared Zeidel's name was allowed back to Israel in time to attend the *bris* and *pidyon haben* of Avraham Zeidel Klein. His cousin Avraham Zeidel Patankin was born one year later. The naming of both babies evoked profuse weeping as well as fervent hopes that Zeidel had *nachas* from the perpetuation of his name.